ELECTRIC DRIVES
AN INTEGRATIVE APPROACH

NED MOHAN

Department of Electrical and Computer Engineering
University of Minnesota, Minneapolis, Minnesota
USA

MNPERE
Minneapolis

PSpice is a registered trademark of the OrCAD Corporation.
SIMULINK is a registerd trademark of The Mathworks, Inc.

Published by:
  MNPERE
  P. O. Box 14503
  Minneapolis, MN 55414
  USA
  E-mail: MNPERE@AOL.COM
  http://www.MNPERE.com

ISBN 0-9715292-5-6

Printed in the United States of America.

To my
mother, father,
brother, and sister

ACKNOWLEDGEMENTS

Since the publication of this book in 2001, I have received positive feedback from a large number of professors. In addition to these colleagues, I once again gratefully acknowledge the contributions of my colleagues, friends, graduate students, and my family who made the year 2001 edition possible in the first place.

Ned Mohan
Twin Cities, Minnesota
October 2002

PREFACE

"Thanks – This was the best course that I have ever taken!" This is the type of reaction we can get out of students who have come to expect electric machines courses to be staid, boring, and old-fashioned.

In today's world of computers, wireless communication, and the Internet, is there a place for a course on electric drives in the EE curriculum? That's a rhetorical question; the answer is obviously Yes! However, the courses on electric machines and drives have not changed in decades. Therefore, we must carefully design a new course in order to prepare students for using and developing motion control systems in today's industry. This course must be based on fundamentals which are also essential to advanced courses in this field and to more R&D oriented careers.

OPPORTUNITIES. Electric drives offer enormous potential for energy conservation. A recent study by the United States Department of Energy points out that conservation methods using electric drives could annually save energy equal to the yearly electricity use in the entire state of New York! Transportation is another important application of electric drives. Hybrid-electric vehicles using internal combustion engines assisted by electric drives have been commercialized. Intense research in fuel cells may eventually make pure electric vehicles viable. Almost all hydraulic drives, from conventional automobiles to ships to airplanes, are under scrutiny for replacement by electric drives. Also, electric drives for motion control are essential to the automation of factories for higher productivity.

We should seize this opportunity and train students to meet the real needs of industry, based on solid theoretical foundations. Experience has shown that a properly designed course benefits a broad range of students not only from electrical engineering but also from other disciplines such as mechanical engineering.

THE INTEGRATIVE APPROACH. This book follows an integrative approach, which requires the minimum prerequisites of junior-level course(s) in circuits and systems and a course in electromagnetic field theory (which students may have taken in physics). This integrative approach allows us to examine in a single semester all of the subsystems that make up electric drives: electric machines, power-electronics-based converters, mechanical system requirements, feedback controller design, and the interaction of drives with the utility grid.

The hallmark of the approach used in this book is as follows:

- Stick to the basic principles in their simplest form.
- Cover the topics in a sequence (and depth) that maintains a high level of interest.
- Never underestimate students' capabilities – they have passed much harder courses in getting here.

ABOUT THIS BOOK. First, what this book is not: it is *not* intended to provide a superficial overview of topics in power systems, electric drives, and power electronics in a single course. Rather, it provides a very fundamental treatment of a broad range of topics, always keeping an eye towards applications. Out-dated techniques are omitted to save time and avoid confusion. This book is based on years of research *in* (yes, *in*) education, with the help of many colleagues.

This research has led to 1) the building-block approach for describing switch-mode power electronics used in modern-day drives and 2) making the space-vector theory approachable to undergraduates – as easy as using phasors (in fact easier, by providing a physical meaning to space-vector representations). The use of space vectors reveals the physical basis on which ac machines operate, thus allowing a clear understanding of how they ought to be controlled for optimum performance. An important benefit of this approach is the continuity between this introductory course and more advanced (mathematically-based) courses.

HOMEWORK PROBLEMS. A broad range of in-text examples and the homework problems at the end of each chapter are designed to reinforce the fundamentals in the context of applications. At the end of each chapter, a summary is presented in the form of a large number of conceptual review questions.

SOLUTIONS MANUAL. A solutions manual with complete solutions to numerical problems (excluding those which require computer simulations) is provided, as a matter of policy, only to instructors.

SUGGESTED TOPICS AND THE NUMBER OF LECTURE HOURS. This book is intended to be a textbook for a one-semester course. However, to cover the entire material in detail will require approximately 60 lecture hours (55 minutes each), more than are available in a semester. An instructor, based on his/her preference and the students' background, can select the topics and the extent of their coverage. Just as a suggestion, I have indicated the range of the number of lectures for each chapter (zero implies that this topic can be skipped or taught out-of-sequence, without impeding the flow). Of course, an instructor may decide to augment any topic with additional course notes.

Chapter	Number of Lectures
1. Introduction to Electric Drive Systems	1-2
2. Understanding Mechanical System Requirements	1-4
3. Review of Electric Circuits	0-2
4. Basic Understanding of Switch-Mode Power Electronics	3-5
5. Magnetic Circuits	4-6
6. Basic Principles of Electro-Mechanical Energy Conversion	3-4
7. DC-Motor and ECM Drives	0-7
8. Feedback Controller Design	0-3
9. Introduction to AC Machines and Space Vectors	4-6
10. Sinusoidal PMAC Drives and Synchronous Machines	2-4
11. Induction Machines: Steady State Analysis	5-7
12. Adjustable-Speed Induction-Motor Drives	2-4
13. Vector Control of Induction-Motor Drives	0-2
14. Reluctance Drives	0-3
15. Energy Efficiency and the Economics of Drives	0-2
16. Power Quality Issues	0-5
17. Sensors, ASICs, and Micro-Controllers	0-1

FEEDBACK NEEDED. Any new approach needs nurturing. One thing I am sure of is that this book can be vastly improved, and that is what I intend to do on a periodic basis. I would be very glad to receive your comments and constructive criticism in this regard.

Ned Mohan
Email: mnpere@aol.com

CONTENTS

Chapter 1   Introduction to Electric Drive Systems

1-1   History   1-2

1-2   What is an Electric-Motor Drive?   1-3

1-3   Factors Responsible for the Growth of Electric Drives   1-4

1-4   Typical Applications of Electric Drives   1-5

1-5   The Multi-Disciplinary Nature of Drive Systems   1-10

1-6   Structure of the Textbook   1-14

Summary/Review Questions 1-15

References   1-15

Problems   1-16

**Chapter 2   Understanding Mechanical System Requirements
for Electric Drives**

2-1   Introduction   2-1

2-2   Systems with Linear Motion 2-2

2-3   Rotating Systems   2-4

2-4   Friction   2-12

2-5   Torsional Resonances 2-14

2-6   Electrical Analogy   2-15

2-7   Coupling Mechanisms   2-17

2-8   Types of Loads   2-22

2-9   Four-Quadrant Operation   2-24

2-10   Steady State and Dynamic Operations   2-25

Summary/Review Questions 2-25

References   2-26

Problems   2-26

Chapter 3   Review of Basic Electric Circuits

3-1   Introduction   3-1

3-2   Phasor Representation in Sinusoidal Steady State   3-2

3-3   Three-Phase Circuits 3-11

        Summary/Review Questions 3-17

        References   3-18

        Problems   3-18

Chapter 4   Basic Understanding of Switch-Mode Power Electronic Converters in Electric Drives

4-1   Introduction   4-1

4-2   Overview of Power Processing Units (PPUs)   4-1

4-3   Analysis of Switch-Mode Converters   4-3

4-4   Converter Pole as a Two-Quadrant Converter   4-11

4-5   Implementation of Bi-Positional Switches   4-15

4-6   Switch-Mode Converters for DC- and AC-Motor Drives   4-17

4-7   Power Semiconductor Devices   4-22

        Summary/Review Questions 4-26

        References   4-27

        Problems   4-27

Chapter 5   Magnetic Circuits

5-1   Introduction   5-1

5-2   Magnetic Field Produced by Current-Carrying Conductors 5-1

5-3   Flux Density B and the Flux ϕ 5-3

5-4   Magnetic Structures with Air Gaps   5-8

5-5   Inductances   5-11

5-6   Faraday's Law: Induced Voltage in a Coil Due to Time-Rate of Change of Flux Linkage 5-14

5-7   Leakage and Magnetizing Inductances   5-17

5-8   Transformers 5-20

5-9   Permanent Magnets   5-29

        Summary/Review Questions 5-30

        References   5-31

        Problems   5-31

Chapter 6   Basic Principles of Electro-mechanical Energy Conversion

6-1   Introduction   6-1

6-2   Basic Structure   6-1

6-3   Production of Magnetic Field   6-3

6-4   Basic Principles of Operation   6-6

6-5   Application of the Basic Principles   6-9

6-6   Energy Conversion   6-11

6-7   Power Losses and Energy Efficiency   6-13

6-8   Machine Ratings   6-14

Summary/Review Questions   6-15

References   6-16

Problems   6-16

Chapter 7   DC-Motor Drives and Electronically-Commutated Motor Drives

7-1   Introduction   7-1

7-2   The Structure of DC Machines   7-3

7-3   Operating Principles of DC Machines   7-4

7-4   DC-Machine Equivalent Circuit   7-13

7-5   Various Operating Modes in DC-Motor Drives   7-15

7-6   Flux Weakening in Wound-Field Machines   7-19

7-7   Power-Processing Units in DC Drives   7-20

7-8   Electronically-Commutated (Trapezoidal Waveform, Brush-Less DC) Motor Drives   7-21

Summary/Review Questions   7-28

References   7-28

Problems   7-29

Chapter 8   Designing Feedback Controllers for Motor Drives

8-1   Introduction   8-1

8-2   Control Objectives   8-2

8-3   Cascade Control Structure   8-5

8-4   Steps in Designing the Feedback Controller   8-6

8-5   System Representation for Small-Signal Analysis   8-6

8-6   Controller Design   8-10

8-7   Example of a Controller Design   8-11

8-8   The Role of Feed-Forward   8-18

8-9   The Effects of Limits 8-19

8-10   Anti-Windup (Non-Windup) Integration   8-20

       Summary/Review Questions 8-20

       References   8-21

       Problems   8-21

Chapter 9   Introduction to AC Machines and Space Vectors   9-1

9-1   Introduction   9-1

9-2   Sinusoidally-Distributed Stator Windings   9-2

9-3   The Use of Space Vectors to Represent Sinusoidal Field Distributions in the Air Gap   9-12

9-4   Space-Vector Representation of Combined Terminal Currents and Voltages 9-16

9-5   Balanced Sinusoidal Steady-State Excitation (Rotor Open-Circuited) 9-22

       Summary/Review Questions 9-33

       References   9-35

       Problems   9-35

Chapter 10   Sinusoidal Permanent Magnet AC (Brushless DC) Drives, LCI-Synchronous Motor Drives, and Synchronous Generators

10-1   Introduction   10-1

10-2   The Basic Structure of Permanent-Magnet AC Syn. Machines   10-2

10-3   Principle of Operation   10-3

10-4   The Controller and the Power-Processing Unit (PPU)   10-18

10-5   Load-Commutated-Inverter (LCI) Supplied Syn. Motor Drives   10-20

10-6   Synchronous Generators   10-21

       Summary/Review Questions 10-25

       References   10-27

       Problems   10-27

Chapter 11 Induction-Motors: Balanced, Sinusoidal Steady State Operation

11-1   Introduction   11-1

11-2   The Structure of Three-Phase, Squirrel-Cage Induction Motors   11-2

11-3   The Principles of Induction Motor Operation   11-3

11-4   Tests to Obtain the Parameters of the Per-Phase Equivalent Circuit 11-33

11-5   Induction Motor Characteristics at Rated Voltages in Magnitude and Frequency   11-36

11-6   Induction Motors of NEMA Design A, B, C, and D   11-39

11-7   Line Start   11-40

11-8   Reduced Voltage Starting ("Soft Start") of Induction Motors   11-40

11-9   Energy-Savings in Lightly-Loaded Machines   11-41

Summary/Review Questions 11-42

References   11-44

Problems   11-44

Chapter 12   Induction-Motor Drives: Speed Control

12-1   Introduction   12-1

12-2   Conditions for Efficient Speed Control over a Wide Range 12-2

12-3   Applied Voltage Amplitudes to Keep $\hat{B}_{ms} = \hat{B}_{ms,rated}$ 12-6

12-4   Starting Considerations in Drives   12-12

12-5   Capability to Operate Below and Above the Rated Speed   12-14

12-6   Regenerative Braking in Induction-Motor Drives   12-16

12-7   Speed Control of Induction-Motor Drives   12-18

12-8   Pulse-Width-Modulated Power-Processing Units   12-20

12-9   Reduction of $\hat{B}_{ms}$ at Light Loads   12-24

Summary/Review Questions 12-25

References   12-26

Problems   12-26

Chapter 13   Vector Control of Induction-Motor Drives:
A Qualitative Examination

13-1   Introduction   13-1

13-2   Emulation of DC- and Brushless-DC Drive Performance   13-2

13-3   Analogy to a Current-Excited Transformer with Shorted Secondary13-4

13-4 D- and Q-Axis Winding Representation   13-6

13-5   Initial Flux Buildup Prior to $t = 0^-$ 13-7

13-6   Step-Change in Torque at $t = 0^+$ 13-8

13-7   Torque, Speed, and Position Control 13-13

13-8   Sensor-Less Drives   13-16

        Summary/Review Questions 13-17

        References   13-18

        Problems   13-18

Chapter 14   Reluctance Drives:

                Stepper-Motor and Switched-Reluctance Drives

14-1   Introduction   14-1

14-2   The Operating Principles of Reluctance Motors   14-2

14-3   Stepper-Motor Drives 14-5

14-4   Switched-Reluctance Motor Drives   14-13

        Summary/Review Questions 14-15

        References   14-16

        Problems   14-16

Chapter 15   Energy Efficiency of Electric Drives

                and Inverter-Motor Interactions

15-1   Introduction   15-1

15-2   The Definition of Energy Efficiency in Electric Drives   15-2

15-3   Energy Efficiency of Induction Motors: Sinusoidal Excitation 15-2

15-4   The Effect of Switching-Frequency Harmonics on Motor Losses
        15-7

15-5   The Energy Efficiencies of Power-Processing Units   15-8

15-6   The Energy Efficiencies of Electric Drives   15-8

15-7   The Economics of Energy Savings by Premium-Efficiency Electric
        Motors and Electric Drives   15-9

15-8   The Deleterious Effects of the PWM-Inverter Voltage Waveform
        on Motor Life 15-11

        Summary/Review Questions 15-11

        References   15-12

        Problems   15-12

Chapter 16   Powering Electric Drives: Power Quality Issues

16-1   Introduction   16-1

16-2   Distortion and Power Factor   16-1

16-3   Classifying the "Front-End" of Electric Drives   16-12

16-4   Diode-Rectifier Bridge "Front-Ends" 16-12

16-5   Power-Factor-Corrected (*PFC*) Interface   16-19

16-6   Front-Ends with Bi-Directional Power Flow 16-22

16-7   Phase-Controlled Thyristor Converters for DC-Motor Drives
         16-24

16-8   The Effects of Power System Disturbances on Electric Drives
         16-33

         Summary/Review Questions 16-35

         References   16-37

         Problems   16-37

Chapter 17   Ancillary Issues in Drives:
Sensors, ASICs, and Micro-Controllers

17-1   Introduction   17-1

17-2   Sensors   17-1

17-3   Application-Specific ICs (ASICs)   17-5

17-4   Micro-Controllers and FPGAs   17-5

17-5   Rapid-Prototyping Tools   17-5

         Summary/Review Questions 17-6

         References   17-6

CONVENTION OF SYMBOLS

1. Variables that are functions of time v, i or $v(t)$, $i(t)$
2. Peak values (of time-varying variables) $\hat{v}$, $\hat{i}$
3. RMS values (of item 1); also average values in dc steady state V, I
4. Phasors $\bar{V} = \hat{V} \angle \theta_v$, $\bar{I} = \hat{I} \angle \theta_i$
5. Space vectors* $\vec{H}(t)$, $\vec{B}(t)$, $\vec{F}(t)$, $\vec{v}(t) = \hat{V} \angle \theta_v$, $\vec{i}(t) = \hat{I} \angle \theta_i$
6. Average values (used for average modeling) $\bar{v}(t)$, $\bar{i}(t)$

* Note that both phasors and space vectors, two distinct quantities, have their peak values indicated by "^".

Subscripts:

Phases	a, b, c or A, B
Stator	s
Rotor	r
Armature	a
Magnetizing	m
Mechanical	m (as in θ_m or ω_m)
Leakage	ℓ
Field	f
Harmonic	h
dc-side	d
Control	c

Symbols:

p	Number of poles ($p \geq 2$, even number)
N_s	Total number of turns in each phase of the stator winding

(Continues to next page.)

Ideal Transformer:

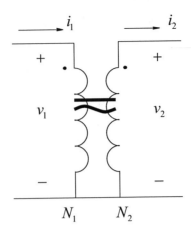

It is a hypothetical device that represents transformation of instantaneous quantities (ac or dc) from one side to the other in the following manner, based on the turns-ratio (N_2 / N_1):

$$\frac{v_2}{v_1} = \frac{N_2}{N_1}$$

and

$$\frac{i_1}{i_2} = \frac{N_2}{N_1}.$$

Therefore,

$$v_1 i_1 = v_2 i_2.$$

The above relationships also apply to dc voltages and currents represented by uppercase letters V and I, and to slowly varying average voltages and currents represented by $\bar{v}(t)$ and $\bar{i}(t)$.

CHAPTER 1

INTRODUCTION TO ELECTRIC DRIVE SYSTEMS

Spurred by advances in power electronics, adjustable-speed electric drives now offer great opportunities in a plethora of applications: pumps and compressors to save energy, precision motion control in automated factories, and wind-electric systems to generate electricity, to name a few. A recent example is the commercialization of hybrid-electric vehicles [1]. Figure 1-1 shows the photograph of a hybrid arrangement in which the outputs of the internal-combustion (IC) engine and the electric drive are mechanically added in parallel to drive the wheels. Compared to vehicles powered solely by gasoline, these hybrids reduce fuel consumption by more than fifty percent and emit far fewer pollutants.

Figure 1-1 Photograph of a hybrid-electric vehicle.

1-1 HISTORY

Electric machines have now been in existence for over a century. All of us are familiar with the basic function of electric motors: to drive mechanical loads by converting electrical energy. In the absence of any control, electric motors operate at essentially a constant speed. For example, when the compressor-motor in a refrigerator turns on, it runs at a constant speed.

Traditionally, motors were operated uncontrolled, running at constant speeds, even in applications where efficient control over their speed could be very advantageous. For example, consider the process industry (like oil refineries and chemical factories) where the flow rates of gases and fluids often need to be controlled. As Fig. 1-2a illustrates, in a pump driven at a constant speed, a throttling valve controls the flow rate. Mechanisms such as throttling valves are generally more complicated to implement in automated processes and waste large amounts of energy. In the process industry today, electronically controlled adjustable-speed drives (ASDs), shown in Fig. 1-2b, control the pump speed to match the flow requirement. Systems with adjustable-speed drives are much easier to automate, and offer much higher energy efficiency and lower maintenance than the traditional systems with throttling valves.

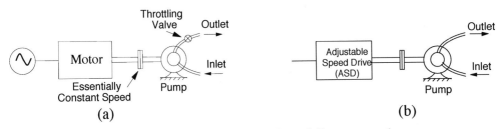

Figure 1-2 Traditional and ASD based flow control systems.

These improvements are not limited to the process industry. Electric drives for speed and position control are increasingly being used in a variety of manufacturing, heating, ventilating and air conditioning (HVAC), and transportation systems.

1-2 WHAT IS AN ELECTRIC-MOTOR DRIVE?

Figure 1-3 shows the block diagram of an electric-motor drive, or for short, an electric drive. In response to an input command, electric drives efficiently control the speed and/or the position of the mechanical load, thus eliminating the need for a throttling valve like the one shown in Fig. 1-2a. The controller, by comparing the input command for speed and/or position with the actual values measured through sensors, provides appropriate control signals to the power-processing unit (PPU) consisting of power semiconductor devices.

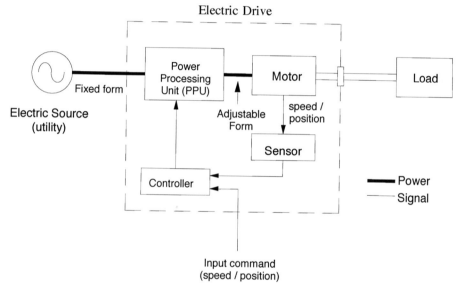

Figure 1-3 Block diagram of an electric drive system.

As Fig. 1-3 shows, the power-processing unit gets its power from the utility source with single-phase or three-phase sinusoidal voltages of a fixed frequency and constant amplitude. The power-processing unit, in response to the control inputs, efficiently converts these fixed-form input voltages into an output of the appropriate form (in frequency, amplitude, and the number of phases) that is optimally suited for operating the motor.

The input command to the electric drive in Fig. 1-3 may come from a process computer, which considers the objectives of the overall process and issues a command to control the mechanical load. However, in general-purpose applications, electric drives operate in an open-loop manner without any feedback.

Throughout this text, we will use the term *electric-motor drive* (*motor drive* or *drive* for short) to imply the combination of blocks in the box drawn by dotted lines in Fig. 1-3. We will examine all of these blocks in subsequent chapters.

1-3 FACTORS RESPONSIBLE FOR THE GROWTH OF ELECTRIC DRIVES

<u>Technical Advancements</u>. Controllers used in electric drives (see Fig. 1-3) have benefited from revolutionary advances in microelectronic methods, which have resulted in powerful linear integrated circuits and digital signal processors [2]. These advances in semiconductor fabrication technology have also made it possible to significantly improve voltage and current handling capabilities, as well as the switching speeds of power semiconductor devices, which make up the power-processing unit of Fig. 1-3.

<u>Market Needs</u>. Figure 1-4 shows the estimated world market of adjustable-speed drives, a 20 billion dollar industry in 1997. This market is growing at a healthy rate [3] as users discover the benefits of operating motors at variable speeds. These benefits include improved process control, reduction in energy usage, and less maintenance.

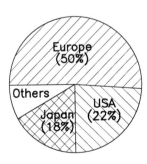

Figure 1-4 Estimated world market of adjustable speed drives.

The world market for electric drives would be significantly impacted by large-scale opportunities for harnessing wind energy. There is also a large potential for applications in the developing world, where the growth rates are the highest.

Applications of electric drives in the United States are of particular importance. The per-capita energy consumption in the United States is almost twice that in Europe, but the electric drive market in 1997, as shown in Fig. 1-4, was less than one-half. This deficit, due to a relatively low cost of energy in the United States, represents a tremendous opportunity for application of electric drives.

1-4   TYPICAL APPLICATIONS OF ELECTRIC DRIVES

Electric drives are increasingly being used in most sectors of the economy. Figure 1-5 shows that electric drives cover an extremely large range of power and speed - up to 100 MW in power and up to 80,000 rpm in speed.

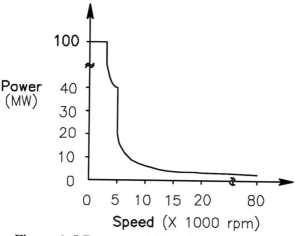

Figure 1-5 Power and Speed range of electric drives.

Due to the power-processing unit, drives are not limited in speeds, unlike line-fed motors that are limited to 3,600 rpm with a 60-Hz supply (3,000 rpm with a 50-Hz supply). A large majority of applications of drives are in a low to medium power range, from a fractional kW to several hundred kW. Some of these application areas are listed below:

- Process Industry: agitators, pumps, fans, and compressors
- Machining: planers, winches, calendars, chippers, drill presses, sanders, saws, extruders, feeders, grinders, mills, and presses

- Heating, Ventilating and Air Conditioning: blowers, fans, and compressors
- Paper and Steel Industry: hoists, and rollers
- Transportation: elevators, trains, and automobiles
- Textile: looms
- Packaging: shears
- Food: conveyors, and fans
- Agriculture: dryer fans, blowers, and conveyors
- Oil, Gas, and Mining: compressors, pumps, cranes, and shovels
- Residential: heat pumps, air conditioners, freezers, appliances, and washing machines

In the following sections, we will look at a few important applications of electric drives in energy conservation, wind-electric generation, and electric transportation.

1-4-1 Role of Drives in Energy Conservation [4]

It is perhaps not obvious how electric drives can reduce energy consumption in many applications. Electric costs are expected to continue their upward trend, which makes it possible to justify the initial investment in replacing constant-speed motors with adjustable speed electric drives, solely on the basis of reducing energy expenditure (see Chapter 15). The environmental impact of energy conservation, in reducing global warming and acid rain, is also of vital importance [5].

To arrive at an estimate of the potential role of electric drives in energy conservation, consider that the motor-driven systems in the United States are responsible for over 57% of all electric power generated and 20% of all the energy consumed. The United States Department of Energy estimates that if constant speed, line-fed motors in pump and compressor systems were to be replaced by adjustable-speed drives, the energy efficiency would improve by as much as 20%. This improved energy efficiency amounts to huge potential savings (see homework problem 1-1). In fact, the potential yearly energy savings would be approximately equal to the annual electricity use in the state of New York. Some energy-conservation applications are described as follows.

1-4-1-1 Heat Pumps and Air Conditioners [6]

Conventional air conditioners cool buildings by extracting energy from inside the building and transferring it to the atmosphere outside. Heat pumps, in addition to the air-conditioning mode, can also heat buildings in winter by extracting energy from outside and transferring it inside. The use of heat pumps for heating and cooling is on the rise; they are now employed in roughly one out of every three new homes constructed in the United States.

In conventional systems, the building temperature is controlled by on/off cycling of the compressor motor by comparing the building temperature with the thermostat setting. After being off, when the compressor motor turns on, the compressor output builds up slowly (due to refrigerant migration during the off period) while the motor immediately begins to draw full power. This cyclic loss (every time the motor turns on) between the ideal and the actual values of the compressor output, as shown in Fig. 1-6, can be eliminated by running the compressor continuously at a speed at which its output matches the thermal load of the building. Compared to conventional systems, compressors driven by adjustable speed drives reduce power consumption by as much as 30 percent.

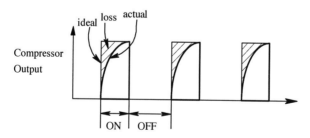

Figure 1-6 Heat pump operation with line-fed motors.

1-4-1-2 Pumps, Blowers, and Fans

To understand the savings in energy consumption, let us compare the two systems shown in Fig. 1-2. In Fig. 1-7, curve A shows the full-speed pump characteristic, that is, the pressure (or head) generated by a pump, driven at its full speed, as a

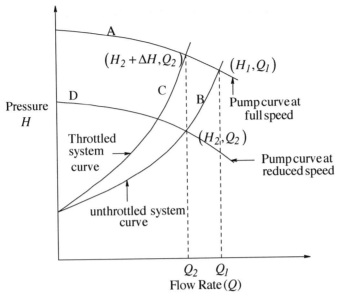

Figure 1-7 Typical pump and system curves.

function of flow rate. With the throttling valve fully open, curve B shows the unthrottled system characteristic, that is, the pressure required as a function of flow rate, to circulate fluid or gas by overcoming the static potential (if any) and friction. The full flow rate Q_1 is given by the intersection of the unthrottled system curve B with the pump curve A. Now consider that a reduced flow rate Q_2 is desired, which requires a pressure H_2 as seen from the unthrottled system curve B. Below, we will consider two ways of achieving this reduced flow rate.

With a constant-speed motor as in Fig. 1-2a, the throttling valve is partially closed, which requires additional pressure to be overcome by the pump, such that the throttled system curve C intersects with the full-speed pump curve A at the flow rate Q_2. The power loss in the throttling valve is proportional to Q_2 times ΔH. Due to this power loss, the reduction in the energy efficiency will depend on the reduced flow-rate intervals, compared to the duration of unthrottled operation.

The power loss across the throttling valve can be eliminated by means of an adjustable-speed drive. The pump speed is reduced such that the reduced-speed pump curve D in Fig. 1-7 intersects with the unthrottled system curve B at the desired flow rate Q_2.

Similarly, in blower applications, the power consumption can be substantially lowered, as plotted in Fig. 1-8, by reducing the blower speed by means of an adjustable speed drive to decrease flow rates, rather than using outlet dampers or inlet vanes. The percentage reduction in power consumption depends on the flow-rate profile (see homework problem 1-5).

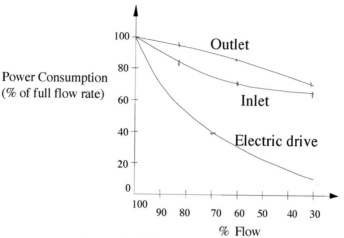

Figure 1-8 Power consumption in a blower.

Electric drives can be beneficially used in almost all pumps, compressors, and blowers employed in air handling systems, process industry, and the generating plants of electric utilities. There are many documented examples where energy savings alone have paid for the cost of conversion (from line-fed motors to electric-drive systems) within six months of operation. Of course, this advantage of electric drives is made possible by the ability to control motor speeds in an energy efficient manner, as discussed in the subsequent chapters.

1-4-2 Harnessing Wind Energy

Electric drives also play a significant role in power generation from renewable energy sources, such as wind and small hydro. The block diagram for a wind-electric system is shown in Fig. 1-9, where the variable-frequency ac produced by the wind-turbine driven generator is interfaced with the utility system through a power-processing unit. By letting the turbine speed vary with the wind speed, it is possible to recover a higher amount of energy compared to systems where the turbine essentially rotates at a constant speed due to the generator output being directly connected to the utility grid [7].

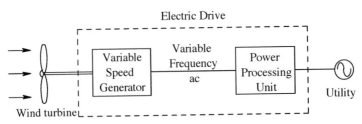

Figure 1-9 Electric drive for wind generator.

1-4-3   Electric Transportation

Electric transportation is widely used in many countries. Magnetically-levitated trains are being experimented with in Japan and Germany. High-speed electric trains are also presently being evaluated in the United States for mass transportation in northeastern and southwestern corridors.

Another important application of electric drives is in electric vehicles and hybrid-electric vehicles. The main virtue of electric vehicles (especially to large metropolitan areas) is that they emit no pollutants. However, electric vehicles must wait for suitable batteries, fuel cells, or flywheels to be developed before the average motorist accepts them. On the other hand, hybrid-electric vehicles are already commercialized [1].

There are so many new applications of electric drives in conventional automobiles that there are serious proposals to raise the battery voltage from its present value of 12 V in order to keep current levels manageable [8]. Also, there is an ongoing attempt to replace hydraulic drives with electric drives in airplanes and ships.

1-5   THE MULTI-DISCIPLINARY NATURE OF DRIVE SYSTEMS

The block diagram of Fig. 1-3 points to various fields, as shown in Fig. 1-10, which are essential to electric drives: electric machine theory, power electronics, analog and digital control theory, real-time application of digital controllers, mechanical system modeling, and interaction with electric power systems. A brief description of each of the fields shown in Fig. 1-10 is provided in the following subsections.

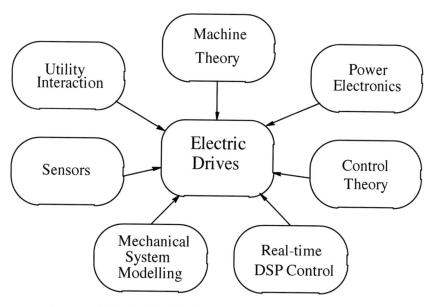

Figure 1-10 Multi-disciplinary nature of electric drives.

1-5-1 Theory of Electric Machines

For achieving the desired motion, it is necessary to control electric motors appropriately. This requires a thorough understanding of the operating principles of various commonly used motors such as dc, synchronous, induction and stepper motors. The emphasis in an electric drives course needs to be different than that in traditional electric machines courses, which are oriented towards design and application of line-fed machines.

1-5-2 Power Electronics

The discipline related to the power-processing unit in Fig. 1-3 is often referred to as power electronics. Voltages and currents from a fixed form (in frequency and magnitude) must be converted to the adjustable form best suited to the motor. It is important that the conversion take place at a high energy efficiency, which is realized by operating power semiconductor devices as switches.

Today, power processing is being simplified by means of "Smart Power" devices, where power semiconductor switches are integrated with their protection and gate-drive circuits into a single module. Thus, the logic-level signals (such as those supplied by a digital signal processor) can directly control high power switches in the PPU. Such power-integrated modules are available with voltage handling capability approaching 4 kilovolts and current handling capability in excess of 1,000 amperes. Paralleling such modules allows even higher current handling capabilities.

The progress in this field has made a dramatic impact on power-processing units. Figure 1-11a shows the reduction in size and weight, while Fig. 1-11b shows a substantial increase in the number of functions that can be performed [3].

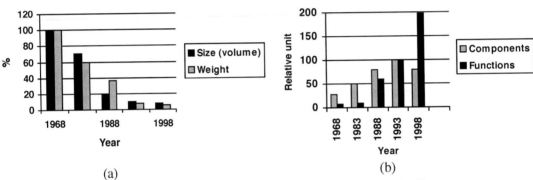

          (a)   (b)

Figure 1-11 Evolution of a 4kW Danfoss VLTR power processing unit [3].

1-5-3 Control Theory

In the majority of applications, the speed and position of drives need not be controlled precisely. However, there are an increasing number of applications, for example in robotics for automated factories, where accurate control of torque, speed, and position are crucial. Such control is accomplished by feeding back the measured quantities, and by comparing them with their desired values, in order to achieve a fast and accurate control.

In most motion control applications, it is sufficient to use a simple proportional-integral (PI) control as discussed in Chapter 8. The task of designing and

1-12

analyzing PI-type controllers is made easy due to the availability of powerful simulation tools such as PSpice™.

1-5-4 Real-Time Control Using DSPs

All modern electric drives use microprocessors and digital signal processors (DSPs) for flexibility of control, fault diagnosis and communication with the host computer and with other process computers. Use of 8-bit microprocessors is being replaced by 16-bit and even 32-bit microprocessors. Digital signal processors are used for real-time control in applications which demand high performance or where a slight gain in the system efficiency more than pays for the additional cost of a sophisticated control.

1-5-5 Mechanical System Modeling

Specifications of electric drives depend on the torque and speed requirements of the mechanical loads. Therefore, it is often necessary to model mechanical loads. Rather than considering the mechanical load and the electric drive as two separate sub-systems, it is preferable to consider them together in the design process. This design philosophy is at the heart of Mechatronics [9].

1-5-6 Sensors

As shown in the block diagram of electric drives in Fig. 1-3, voltage, current, speed and position measurements may be required. For thermal protection, the temperature needs to be sensed.

1-5-7 Interactions of Drives with the Utility Grid

Unlike line-fed electric motors, electric motors in drives are supplied through a power electronic interface (see Fig. 1-3). Therefore, unless corrective action is taken, electric drives draw currents from the utility that are distorted (non-sinusoidal) in wave shape. This distortion in line currents interferes with the utility system, degrading its power quality by distorting the voltages. Available technical solutions make the drive interaction with the utility harmonious, even more so than line-fed motors. The sensitivity of drives to power system disturbances such as sags, swells, and transient over-voltages should also be considered. Again, solutions are available to reduce or eliminate the effects of these disturbances. These power-quality related issues are discussed in Chapter 16.

1-6   STRUCTURE OF THE TEXTBOOK

Chapter 1 has introduced the roles and applications of electric drives. Chapter 2 deals with the modeling of mechanical systems coupled to electric drives, as well as how to determine drive specifications for various types of loads. Chapter 3 reviews linear electric circuits. An introduction to power-processing units is presented in Chapter 4.

Magnetic circuits, including transformers, are discussed in Chapter 5. Chapter 6 explains the basic principles of electromagnetic energy conversion.

Chapter 7 describes dc-motor drives. Although the share of dc-motor drives in new applications is declining, their use is still widespread. Another reason for studying dc-motor drives is that ac-motor drives are controlled to emulate their performance. The feedback controller design for drives (using dc drives as an example) is presented in Chapter 8.

As a background to the discussion of ac motor drives, the rotating fields in ac machines are described in Chapter 9 by means of space vectors. Using the space vector theory, the sinusoidal waveform PMAC motor drives are discussed in Chapter 10. Chapter 11 introduces induction motors and focuses on their basic principles of operation in steady state. A concise but comprehensive discussion of controlling speed with induction-motor drives is provided in Chapter 12. Position control using induction motors requires field-oriented control, whose physical understanding is provided in Chapter 13.

The reluctance drives, including stepper-motors and switched-reluctance drives, are explained in Chapter 14.

Loss considerations and various techniques to improve energy efficiency in drives are discussed in Chapter 15. The interactions between the drives and the utility, in terms of power quality, are the subject of Chapter 16. Finally, ancillary issues such as sensors and motor-control ICs are briefly described in Chapter 17.

SUMMARY/REVIEW QUESTIONS

1. What is an electric drive? Draw the block diagram and explain the roles of its various components.
2. What has been the traditional approach to controlling flow rate in the process industry? What are the major disadvantages which can be overcome by using adjustable speed drives?
3. What are the factors responsible for the growth of the adjustable-speed drive market?
4. How does an air conditioner work? (Consult a handbook such as [10].)
5. How does a heat pump work?
6. How do ASDs save energy in air conditioning and heat pump systems?
7. What is the role of ASDs in industrial systems?
8. There are proposals to store energy in flywheels for load leveling in utility systems. During the off-peak period for energy demand at night, these flywheels are charged to high speeds. At peak periods during the day, this energy is supplied back to the utility. How would ASDs play a role in this scheme?
9. What is the role of electric drives in electric transportation systems of various types?
10. List a few specific examples from the applications mentioned in section 1-4 that you are personally familiar with.
11. What are the different disciplines that make up the study and design of electric-drive systems?

REFERENCES

1. V. Wouk, et al, EV Watch, *IEEE Spectrum*, pp. 22-23, March 1998.

2. N. Mohan, T. Undeland, and W. Robbins, *Power Electronics: Converters, Applications, and Design*, 2nd edition, 1995, John Wiley & Sons, New York, NY.

3. P. Thogersen and F. Blaabjerg, "Adjustable-Speed Drives in the Next Decade: The Next Steps in Industry and Academia," Proceedings of the PCIM Conference, Nuremberg, Germany, June 6-8, 2000.

4. N. Mohan, *Techniques for Energy Conservation in AC Motor Driven Systems*, Electric Power Research Institute Final Report EM-2037, Project 1201-1213, September 1981.

5. Y. Kaya, "Response Strategies for Global Warming and the Role of Power Technologies," Proceedings of the IPEC - Tokyo, Japan, April 3-5, 2000, pp 1-3.

6. N. Mohan and J. Ramsey, *Comparative Study of Adjustable-Speed Drives for Heat Pumps*, Electric Power Research Institute Final Report EM-4704, Project 2033-4, August 1986.

7. F. Blaabjerg and N. Mohan, *Wind Power*, Encyclopedia of Electrical and Electronics Engineering, edited by John G. Webster, John Wiley & Sons, New York, 1998.

8. J. Kassakian, et al, "Automotive Electrical Systems Circa 2005," IEEE Spectrum, pp.22-27, August, 1996.

9. IEEE/ASME *Transactions on Mechatronics*, published regularly.

10. Bosch, *Automotive Handbook*, Robert Bosch GMbH, 3rd edition, 1993, pages 701-702.

PROBLEMS

1-1 A U.S. Department of Energy report estimates that over 100 billion kWh/year can be saved in the United States by various energy conservation techniques applied to the pump-driven systems. Calculate (a) how many 1000-MW generating plants running constantly supply this wasted energy and (b) the annual savings in dollars if the cost of electricity is 0.10 $/kWh.

1-2 Visit your local machine-tool shop and make a list of various electric drive types, applications, and speed/torque ranges.

1-3 Repeat problem 1-2 for an automobile.

1-4 Repeat problem 1-2 for household appliances.

1-5 In a process, a blower is used with the flow-rate profile shown in Fig. P1-5. Using the information in Fig 1-8, estimate the percentage reduction in power consumption resulting from using an adjustable-speed drive rather than a system with (a) an outlet damper and (b) an inlet vane.

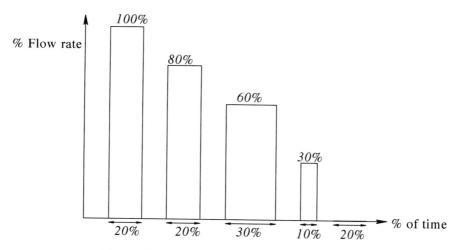

Figure P1-5 Flow rate profile of the blower.

CHAPTER 2

UNDERSTANDING MECHANICAL SYSTEM REQUIREMENTS FOR ELECTRIC DRIVES

2-1   INTRODUCTION

Electric drives must satisfy the requirements of torque and speed imposed by mechanical loads connected to them. The load in Fig. 2-1, for example, may require a trapezoidal profile for the angular speed, as a function of time. In this chapter, we will briefly review the basic principles of mechanics for understanding the requirements imposed by mechanical systems on electric drives. This understanding is necessary for selecting an appropriate electric drive for a given application.

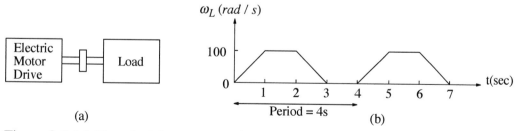

Figure 2-1 (a) Electric drive system; (b) example of load-speed profile requirement.

2-2   SYSTEMS WITH LINEAR MOTION

In Fig. 2-2a, a load of a constant mass M is acted upon by an external force f_e that causes it to move in the linear direction x at a speed $u = dx/dt$. This movement is opposed by the load, represented by a force f_L. The linear momentum associated with the mass is defined as M times u. As shown in Fig. 2-2b, in accordance with the Newton's Law of Motion, the net force $f_M (= f_e - f_L)$ equals the rate of change of momentum, which causes the mass to accelerate:

$$f_M = \frac{d}{dt}(Mu) = M\frac{du}{dt} = Ma \tag{2-1}$$

where a is the acceleration in m/s^2, which from Eq. 2-1 is

$$a = \frac{du}{dt} = \frac{f_M}{M} \tag{2-2}$$

In MKS units, a net force of 1 Newton (or 1 N), acting on a constant mass of 1 kg results in an acceleration of 1 m/s^2. Integrating the acceleration with respect to time, we can calculate the speed as

$$u(t) = u(0) + \int_0^t a(\tau) \cdot d\tau \tag{2-3}$$

and, integrating the speed with respect to time, we can calculate the position as

(a)   (b)

Figure 2-2 Motion of a mass M due to action of forces.

$$x(t) = x(0) + \int_0^t u(\tau) \cdot d\tau \qquad (2\text{-}4)$$

where τ is a variable of integration.

The differential work dW done by the mechanism supplying the force f_e is

$$dW_e = f_e \, dx \qquad (2\text{-}5)$$

Power is the time-rate at which the work is done. Therefore, differentiating both sides of Eq. 2-5 with respect to time t, and assuming that the force f_e remains constant, the power supplied by the mechanism exerting the force f_e is

$$p_e(t) = \frac{dW_e}{dt} = f_e \frac{dx}{dt} = f_e u \qquad (2\text{-}6)$$

It takes a finite amount of energy to bring a mass to a speed from rest. Therefore, a moving mass has stored kinetic energy that can be recovered. Note that in the system of Fig. 2-2, the net force $f_M (= f_e - f_L)$ is responsible for accelerating the mass. Therefore, assuming that f_M remains constant, the net power $p_M(t)$ going into accelerating the mass can be calculated by replacing f_e in Eq. 2-6 with f_M:

$$p_M(t) = \frac{dW_M}{dt} = f_M \frac{dx}{dt} = f_M u \qquad (2\text{-}7)$$

From Eq. 2-1, substituting f_M as $M \dfrac{du}{dt}$,

$$p_M(t) = Mu \frac{du}{dt} \qquad (2\text{-}8)$$

The energy input, which is stored as kinetic energy in the moving mass, can be calculated by integrating both sides of Eq. 2-8 with respect to time. Assuming the initial speed u to be zero at time t=0, the stored kinetic energy in the mass M can be calculated as

$$W_M = \int_0^t P_M(\tau)d\tau = M\int_0^t u\frac{du}{d\tau}d\tau = M\int_0^u u\,du = \tfrac{1}{2}Mu^2 \qquad (2\text{-}9)$$

where τ is a variable of integration.

2-3 ROTATING SYSTEMS

Most electric motors are of rotating type. Consider a lever, pivoted and free to move as shown in Fig. 2-3a. When an external force f is applied in a *perpendicular* direction at a radius r from the pivot, then the torque acting on the lever is

$$\begin{array}{ccc} T & = f & r \\ [Nm] & [N] & [m] \end{array} \qquad (2\text{-}10)$$

which acts in a counter-clockwise direction, considered here to be positive.

▲ **Example 2-1**   In Fig. 2-3a, a mass M is hung from the tip of the lever. Calculate the holding torque required to keep the lever from turning, as a function of angle θ in the range of 0 to 90 degrees. Assume that $M = 0.5\,kg$ and $r = 0.3\,m$.

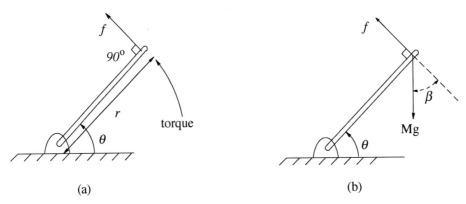

Figure 2-3 (a) Pivoted Lever; (b) holding torque for the lever.

Solution   The gravitational force on the mass is shown in Fig. 2-3b. For the lever to be stationary, the net force perpendicular to the lever must be zero, i.e.

$$f = M g \, \cos \beta$$

where $g = 9.8 \, m/s^2$ is the gravitational acceleration. Note in Fig. 2-3b that $\beta = \theta$. The holding torque T_h must be

$$T_h = f r = M \, g r \cos \theta .$$

Substituting the numerical values,

$$T_h = 0.5 \times 9.8 \times 0.3 \times \cos \theta = 1.47 \cos \theta \; Nm .$$ ▲

In electric machines, the various forces shown by arrows in Fig. 2-4 are produced due to electromagnetic interactions. The definition of torque in Eq. 2-10 correctly describes the resulting electromagnetic torque T_{em} that causes the rotation of the motor and the mechanical load connected to it by a shaft.

In a rotational system, the angular acceleration due to a net torque acting on it is determined by its moment-of-inertia J. The example below shows how to calculate the moment-of-inertia J of a rotating solid cylindrical mass.

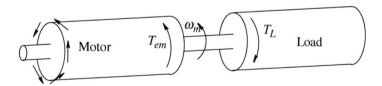

Figure 2-4 Torque in an electric motor.

▲ **Example 2-2**

    (a) Calculate the moment-of-inertia J of a solid cylinder that is free to rotate about its axis, as shown in Fig. 2-5a, in terms of its mass M and the radius r_1.

(b) Given that a solid steel cylinder has radius $r_1 = 6cm$, length $\ell = 18cm$, and the material density $\rho = 7.85 \times 10^3 kg/m^3$, calculate its moment-of-inertia J.

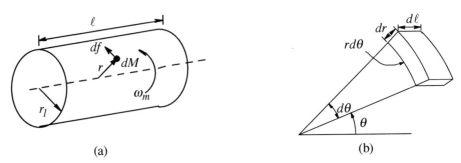

(a)   (b)

Figure 2-5 Calculation of the inertia, J_{cyl}, of a solid cylinder.

Solution (a) From Newton's Law of Motion, in Fig. 2-5a, to accelerate a differential mass dM at a radius r, the net differential force df required in a perpendicular (tangential) direction, from Eq. 2-1, is

$$(dM)(\frac{du}{dt}) = df \qquad (2\text{-}11)$$

where the linear speed u in terms of the angular speed ω_m (in rad/s) is

$$u = r\,\omega_m. \qquad (2\text{-}12)$$

Multiplying both sides of Eq. 2-11 by the radius r, recognizing that $(r\,df)$ equals the net differential torque dT and using Eq. 2-12,

$$r^2\,dM\,\frac{d}{dt}\omega_m = dT. \qquad (2\text{-}13)$$

The same angular acceleration $\frac{d}{dt}\omega_m$ is experienced by all elements of the cylinder. With the help of Fig. 2-5b, the differential mass dM in Eq. 2-13 can be expressed as

$$dM = \rho \underbrace{rd\theta}_{arc} \underbrace{dr}_{height} \underbrace{d\ell}_{length} \qquad (2\text{-}14)$$

where ρ is the material density in kg/m^3. Substituting dM from Eq. 2-14 into Eq. 2-13,

$$\rho \, (r^3 dr \, d\theta \, d\ell) \frac{d}{dt} \omega_m = dT. \qquad (2\text{-}15)$$

The net torque acting on the cylinder can be obtained by integrating over all differential elements in terms of r, θ, and ℓ as

$$\rho \, (\int_0^{r_1} r^3 dr \int_0^{2\pi} d\theta \int_0^{\ell} d\ell) \frac{d}{dt} \omega_m = T. \qquad (2\text{-}16)$$

Carrying out the triple integration yields

$$\underbrace{(\frac{\pi}{2} \rho \, \ell \, r_1^4)}_{J_{cyl}} \frac{d}{dt} \omega_m = T \qquad (2\text{-}17)$$

or

$$J_{cyl} \frac{d\omega_m}{dt} = T \qquad (2\text{-}18)$$

where the quantity within the brackets in Eq. 2-17 is called the moment-of-inertia J, which for a solid cylinder is

$$J_{cyl} = \frac{\pi}{2} \rho \, \ell \, r_1^4. \qquad (2\text{-}19)$$

Since the mass of the cylinder in Fig. 2-5a is $M = \rho(\pi \, r_1^2)\ell$, the moment-of-inertia in Eq. 2-19 can be written as

$$J_{cyl} = \frac{1}{2}M r_1^2 . \tag{2-20}$$

(b)   Substituting $r_1 = 6cm$, length $\ell = 18\,cm$, and $\rho = 7.85x10^3\,kg/m^3$ in Eq. 2-19, the moment-of-inertia J_{cyl} of the cylinder in Fig. 2-5a is

$$J_{cyl} = \frac{\pi}{2} \times 7.85 \times 10^3 \times 0.18 \times (0.06)^4 = 0.029\,kg \cdot m^2 . \qquad \blacktriangle$$

The net torque T_J acting on the rotating body of inertia J causes it to accelerate. Similar to systems with linear motion where $f_M = Ma$, Newton's Law in rotational systems becomes

$$T_J = J\alpha \tag{2-21}$$

where the angular acceleration $\alpha (= d\omega / dt)$ in rad / s^2 is

$$\alpha = \frac{d\omega_m}{dt} = \frac{T_J}{J} \tag{2-22}$$

which is similar to Eq. 2-18 in the previous example. In MKS units, a torque of $1\,Nm$, acting on an inertia of $1\,kg \cdot m^2$ results in an angular acceleration of $1\,rad / s^2$.

In systems such as the one shown in Fig. 2-6a, the motor produces an electromagnetic torque T_{em}. The bearing friction and wind resistance (drag) can

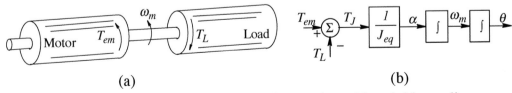

(a)   (b)

Figure 2-6 Motor and load torque interaction with a rigid coupling.

be combined with the load torque T_L opposing the rotation. In most systems, we can assume that the rotating part of the motor with inertia J_M is rigidly coupled (without flexing) to the load inertia J_L. The net torque, the difference between the electromagnetic torque developed by the motor and the load torque opposing it, causes the combined inertias of the motor and the load to accelerate in accordance with Eq. 2-22:

$$\frac{d}{dt}\omega_m = \frac{T_J}{J_{eq}} \tag{2-23}$$

where the net torque $T_J = T_{em} - T_L$ and the equivalent combined inertia $J_{eq} = J_M + J_L$.

▲ **Example 2-3** In Fig. 2-6a, each structure has the same inertia as the cylinder in Example 2-2. The load torque T_L is negligible. Calculate the required electromagnetic torque, if the speed is to increase linearly from rest to 1,800 rpm in $5\,s$.

Solution Using the results of Example 2-2, the combined inertia of the system is

$$J_{eq} = 2\times0.029 = 0.058\,kg \cdot m^2 .$$

The angular acceleration is

$$\frac{d}{dt}\omega_m = \frac{\Delta\omega_m}{\Delta t} = \frac{(1800/60)2\pi}{5} = 37.7\,rad/s^2 .$$

Therefore, from Eq. 2-23,

$$T_{em} = 0.058\times37.7 = 2.19\,Nm . \qquad\qquad ▲$$

Eq. 2-23 shows that the net torque is the quantity that causes acceleration, which in turn leads to changes in speed and position. Integrating the acceleration $\alpha(t)$ with respect to time,

$$\text{Speed } \omega_m(t) = \omega_m(0) + \int_0^t \alpha(\tau)d\tau \qquad (2\text{-}24)$$

where $\omega_m(0)$ is the speed at t=0 and τ is a variable of integration. Further integrating $\omega_m(t)$ in Eq. 2-24 with respect to time yields

$$\theta(t) = \theta(0) + \int_0^t \omega_m(\tau)d\tau \qquad (2\text{-}25)$$

where $\theta(0)$ is the position at $t = 0$, and τ is again a variable of integration. Eqs. 2-23 through 2-25 indicate that torque is the fundamental variable for controlling speed and position. Eqs. 2-23 through 2-25 can be represented in a block-diagram form, as shown in Fig. 2-6b.

▲ **Example 2-4** Consider that the rotating system shown in Fig. 2-6a, with the combined inertia $J_{eq} = 2 \times 0.029 = 0.058 \ kg \cdot m^2$, is required to have the angular speed profile shown in Fig. 2-1b. The load torque is zero. Calculate and plot, as functions of time, the electromagnetic torque required from the motor and the change in position.

Solution   In the plot of Fig. 2-1b, the magnitude of the acceleration and the deceleration is 100 rad/s². During the intervals of acceleration and deceleration, since $T_L = 0$,

$$T_{em} = T_J = J_{eq} \frac{d\omega_m}{dt} = \pm 5.8 \ Nm$$

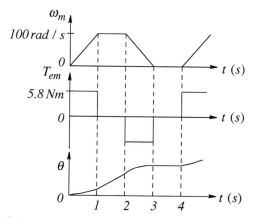

Figure 2-7 Speed, torque and angle variations with time.

as shown in Fig. 2-7. During intervals with a constant speed, no torque is required. Since the position θ is the time-integral of speed, the resulting change of position (assuming that the initial position is zero) is also plotted in Fig. 2-7. ▲

In a rotational system shown in Fig. 2-8, if a net torque T causes the cylinder to rotate by a differential angle $d\theta$, the differential work done is

$$dW = T d\theta \tag{2-26}$$

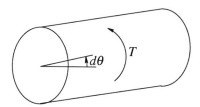

Figure 2-8 Torque, work and power.

If this differential rotation takes place in a differential time dt, the power can be expressed as

$$p = \frac{dW}{dt} = T\frac{d\theta}{dt} = T\omega_m \tag{2-27}$$

where $\omega_m = d\theta/dt$ is the angular speed of rotation. Substituting for T from Eq. 2-21 into Eq. 2-27,

$$p = J\frac{d\omega_m}{dt}\omega_m \qquad (2\text{-}28)$$

Integrating both sides of Eq. 2-28 with respect to time, assuming that the speed ω_m and the kinetic energy W at time $t = 0$ are both zero, the kinetic energy stored in the rotating mass of inertia J is

$$W = \int_0^t p(\tau)d\tau = J\int_0^t \omega_m \frac{d\omega_m}{d\tau}d\tau = J\int_0^{\omega_m} \omega_m\, d\omega_m = \tfrac{1}{2}J\omega_m^2 \qquad (2\text{-}29)$$

This stored kinetic energy can be recovered by making the power $p(t)$ reverse direction, that is, by making $p(t)$ negative.

▲ **Example 2-5**   In Example 2-3, calculate the kinetic energy stored in the combined inertia at a speed of 1,800 rpm.

Solution   From Eq. 2-29,

$$W = \frac{1}{2}(J_L + J_M)\omega_m^2 = \frac{1}{2}(0.029 + 0.029)\left(2\pi\frac{1800}{60}\right)^2 = 1030.4\ J\ .\quad ▲$$

2-4   FRICTION

Friction within the motor and the load acts to oppose rotation. Friction occurs in the bearings that support rotating structures. Moreover, moving objects in air encounter windage or drag. In vehicles, this drag is a major force that must be overcome. Therefore, friction and windage can be considered as opposing forces or torque that must be overcome. The frictional torque is generally nonlinear in nature. We are all familiar with the need for a higher force (or torque) in the beginning (from rest) to set an object in motion. This friction at zero speed is called stiction. Once in motion, the friction may consist of a component called

Coulomb friction which remains independent of speed magnitude (it always opposes rotation), as well as another component called viscous friction, which increases linearly with speed.

In general, the frictional torque T_f in a system consists of all of the aforementioned components. An example is shown in Fig. 2-9; this friction characteristic may be linearized for an approximate analysis by means of the dotted line. With this approximation, the characteristic is similar to that of viscous friction in which

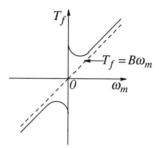

Figure 2-9 Actual and linearized friction characteristics.

$$T_f = B\omega_m \tag{2-30}$$

where B is the coefficient of viscous friction or viscous damping.

▲ **Example 2-6** The aerodynamic drag force in automobiles can be estimated as $f_L = 0.046 C_w A u^2$, where the drag force is in N, C_w is the drag coefficient (a unit-less quantity), A is the vehicle cross-sectional area in m², and u is the sum of the vehicle speed and headwind in km/h [4]. If A = 1.8 m² for each of the vehicles in Fig. 2-10a and 2-10b with C_w = 0.3 and C_w = 0.5 respectively,

(a) $C_w = 0.3$ (b) $C_w = 0.5$

Figure 2-10 Drag forces for different vehicles.

calculate the drag force and the power required to overcome it at the speeds of 50 km/h, and 100 km/h.

Solution   The drag force is $f_L = 0.046 C_w A u^2$ and the power required at the constant speed, from Eq. 2-6, is $P = f_L u$ where the speed is expressed in m/s. Table 2-1 lists the drag force and the power required at various speeds for the two vehicles. Since the drag force F_L depends on the square of the speed, the power depends on the cube of the speed.

Table 2-1

Vehicle	$u =$ 50 km/h		$u =$ 100 km/h	
C_w=0.3	$f_L = 62.06N$	$P = 0.86kW$	$f_L = 248.2N$	$P = 6.9kW$
C_w=0.5	$f_L = 103.4N$	$P = 1.44kW$	$f_L = 413.7N$	$P = 11.5kW$

Traveling at 50 km/h compared to 100 km/h requires $1/8^{th}$ the power, but it takes twice as long to reach the destination. Therefore, the energy required at 50 km/h would be $1/4^{th}$ that at 100 km/h.   ▲

2-5   TORSIONAL RESONANCES

In Fig. 2-6, the shaft connecting the motor with the load was assumed to be of infinite stiffness, that is, the two were rigidly connected. In reality, any shaft will twist (flex) as it transmits torque from one end to the other. In Fig. 2-11, the torque T_{shaft} available to be transmitted by the shaft is

$$T_{shaft} = T_{em} - J_M \frac{d\omega_m}{dt}$$ (2-31)

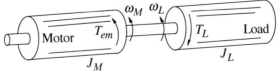

Figure 2-11 Motor and load torque interaction with a rigid coupling.

This torque at the load-end overcomes the load torque and accelerates it,

$$T_{shaft} = T_L + J_L \frac{d\omega_L}{dt} \tag{2-32}$$

The twisting or the flexing of the shaft, in terms of the angles at the two ends, depends on the shaft torsional or the compliance coefficient K:

$$(\theta_M - \theta_L) = \frac{T_{shaft}}{K} \tag{2-33}$$

where θ_M and θ_L are the angular rotations at the two ends of the shaft. If K is infinite, $\theta_M = \theta_L$. For a shaft of finite compliance, these two angles are not equal and the shaft acts as a spring. This compliance in the presence of energy stored in the masses and inertias of the system can lead to resonance conditions at certain frequencies. This phenomenon is often termed torsional resonance. Such resonances should be avoided or kept low, otherwise they can lead to fatigue and failure of the mechanical components.

2-6   ELECTRICAL ANALOGY

An analogy with electrical circuits can be very useful when analyzing mechanical systems. A commonly used analogy, though not a unique one, is to relate mechanical and electrical quantities as shown in Table 2–2.

Table 2-2 Torque–Current Analogy

Mechanical System	Electrical System
Torque (T)	Current (i)
Angular speed (ω_m)	Voltage (v)
Angular displacement (θ)	Flux linkage (ψ)
Moment of inertia (J)	Capacitance (C)
Spring constant (K)	1/inductance (1/L)
Damping coefficient (B)	1/resistance (1/R)
Coupling ratio (n_M/n_L)	Transformer ratio (n_L/n_M)

Note: The coupling ratio is discussed later in this chapter.

For the mechanical system shown in Fig. 2-11, Fig. 2-12a shows the electrical analogy, where each inertia is represented by a capacitor from its node to a reference (ground) node. In this circuit, we can write equations similar to Eqs. 2-31 through 2-33. Assuming that the shaft is of infinite stiffness, the inductance representing it becomes zero, and the resulting circuit is shown in Fig. 2-12b, where $\omega_m = \omega_M = \omega_L$. The two capacitors representing the two inertias can now be combined to result in a single equation similar to Eq. 2-23.

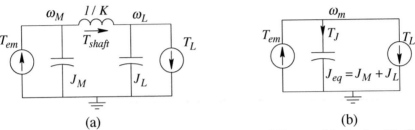

(a) (b)

Figure 2-12 Electrical analogy: (a) shaft of finite stiffness; (b) shaft of infinite stiffness.

▲ **Example 2-7** In an electric-motor drive similar to that shown in Fig. 2-6a, the combined inertia is $J_{eq} = 5 \times 10^{-3} \, kg \cdot m^2$. The load torque opposing rotation is mainly due to friction, and can be described as $T_L = 0.5 \times 10^{-3} \omega_L$. Draw the electrical equivalent circuit and plot the electromagnetic torque required from the motor to bring the system linearly from rest to a speed of 100 rad/s in 4 s, and then to maintain that speed.

Solution The electrical equivalent circuit is shown in Fig. 2-13a. The inertia is represented by a capacitor of $5 \, mF$, and the friction by a

resistance $R = \dfrac{1}{0.5 \times 10^{-3}} = 2000 \, \Omega$. The linear acceleration is $\dfrac{100}{4} = 25 \, rad/s^2$,

which in the equivalent electrical circuit corresponds to $\dfrac{dv}{dt} = 25 \, \dfrac{V}{s}$. Therefore,

during the acceleration period, $v(t) = 25t$. Thus, the capacitor current during the linear acceleration interval is

$$i_c(t) = C\frac{dv}{dt} = 125.0 \; mA \qquad\qquad 0 \le t < 4s \qquad\qquad \text{(2-34a)}$$

and the current through the resistor is

$$i_R(t) = \frac{v(t)}{R} = \frac{25t}{2000} = 12.5t \; mA \qquad\qquad 0 \le t < 4s \qquad\qquad \text{(2-34b)}$$

Therefore,

$$T_{em}(t) = (125.0 + 12.5t) \times 10^{-3} \; Nm \qquad\qquad 0 \le t < 4s \qquad\qquad \text{(2-34c)}$$

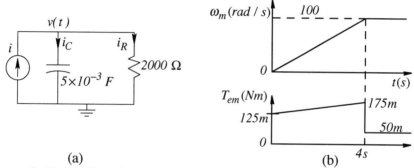

(a)   (b)
Figure 2-13 (a) Electrical equivalent; (b) torque and speed variation.

Beyond the acceleration stage, the electromagnetic torque is required only to overcome friction, which equals $50 \times 10^{-3} \; Nm$, as plotted in Fig. 2-13b. ▲

2-7 COUPLING MECHANISMS

Wherever possible, it is preferable to couple the load directly to the motor, to avoid the additional cost of the coupling mechanism and of the associated power losses. In practice, coupling mechanisms are often used for the following reasons:

- a rotary motor is driving a load which requires linear motion
- the motors are designed to operate at higher rotational speeds (to reduce their physical size) compared to the speeds required of the mechanical loads

- the axis of rotation needs to be changed

There are various types of coupling mechanisms. For conversion between rotary and linear motions, it is possible to use conveyor belts (belt and pulley), rack-and-pinion or a lead-screw type of arrangement. For rotary-to-rotary motion, various types of gear mechanisms are employed.

The coupling mechanisms have the following disadvantages:
- additional power loss
- introduction of nonlinearity due to a phenomenon called backlash
- wear and tear

2-7-1   Conversion between Linear and Rotary Motion

In many systems, a linear motion is achieved by using a rotating-type motor, as shown in Fig. 2-14.

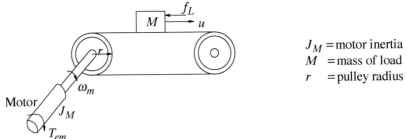

J_M = motor inertia
M = mass of load
r = pulley radius

Figure 2-14 Combination of rotary and linear motion.

In such a system, the angular and the linear speeds are related by the radius r of the drum:

$$u = r\,\omega_m \qquad (2\text{-}35)$$

To accelerate the mass M in Fig. 2-14 in the presence of an opposing force f_L, the force f applied to the mass, from Eq. 2-1, must be

$$f = M\frac{du}{dt} + f_L \qquad (2\text{-}36)$$

This force is delivered by the motor in the form of a torque T, which is related to f, using Eq. 2-35, as

$$T = r \cdot f = r^2 M \frac{d\omega_m}{dt} + r f_L \tag{2-37}$$

Therefore, the electromagnetic torque required from the motor is

$$T_{em} = J_M \frac{d\omega_m}{dt} + \underbrace{r^2 M \frac{d\omega_m}{dt} + r f_L}_{due\,to\,load} \tag{2-38}$$

▲ **Example 2-8** In the vehicle of Example 2-6 with $C_w = 0.5$, assume that each wheel is powered by its own electric motor that is directly coupled to it. If the wheel diameter is 60 *cm*, calculate the torque and the power required from each motor to overcome the drag force, when the vehicle is traveling at a speed of 100 *km/h*.

Solution In Example 2-6, the vehicle with $C_w = 0.5$ presented a drag force $f_L = 413.7\ N$ at the speed $u = 100\ km/h$. The force required from each of the four motors is $f_M = \dfrac{f_L}{4} = 103.4\ N$. Therefore, the torque required from each motor is

$$T_M = f_M\, r = 103.4 \times \frac{0.6}{2} = 31.04\ Nm .$$

From Eq. 2-35,

$$\omega_m = \frac{u}{r} = (\frac{100 \times 10^3}{3600}) \frac{1}{(0.6/2)} = 92.6\ rad/s .$$

Therefore, the power required from each motor is

$$T_M \omega_m = 2.87\ kW . \qquad\qquad ▲$$

2-7-2 Gears

For matching speeds, Fig. 2-15 shows a gear mechanism where the shafts are assumed to be of infinite stiffness and the masses of the gears are ignored. We will further assume that there is no power loss in the gears. Both gears must have the same linear speed at the point of contact. Therefore, their angular speeds are related by their respective radii r_1 and r_2 such that

$$r_1 \omega_M = r_2 \omega_L \qquad (2\text{-}39)$$

and

$$\omega_M T_1 = \omega_L T_2 \qquad \text{(assuming no power loss)} \qquad (2\text{-}40)$$

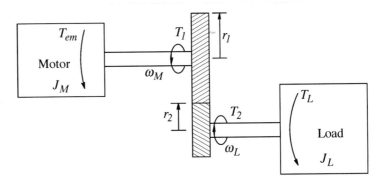

Fig. 2-15 Gear mechanism for coupling the motor to the load.

Combining Eqs. 2-39 and 2-40,

$$\frac{r_1}{r_2} = \frac{\omega_L}{\omega_M} = \frac{T_1}{T_2} \qquad (2\text{-}41)$$

where T_1 and T_2 are the torques at the ends of the gear mechanism, as shown in Fig. 2-15. Expressing T_1 and T_2 in terms of T_{em} and T_L in Eq. 2-41,

$$(T_{em} - J_M \frac{d\omega_M}{dt}) \underbrace{\frac{\omega_M}{\omega_L}}_{T_1} = \underbrace{(T_L + J_L \frac{d\omega_L}{dt})}_{T_2} \qquad (2\text{-}42)$$

From Eq. 2-42, the electromagnetic torque required from the motor is

$$T_{em} = \underbrace{[J_M + (\frac{\omega_L}{\omega_M})^2 J_L]}_{J_{eq}} \frac{d\omega_M}{dt} + (\frac{\omega_L}{\omega_M}) T_L \qquad (\text{note: } \frac{d\omega_L}{dt} = \frac{d\omega_M}{dt} \frac{\omega_L}{\omega_M}) \qquad (2\text{-}43)$$

where the equivalent inertia at the motor side is

$$J_{eq} = J_M + \left(\frac{\omega_L}{\omega_M}\right)^2 J_L = J_M + \left(\frac{r_1}{r_2}\right)^2 J_L \qquad (2\text{-}44)$$

2-7-2-1   Optimum Gear Ratio

Eq. 2-43 shows that the electromagnetic torque required from the motor to accelerate a motor-load combination depends on the gear ratio. In a basically inertial load where T_L can be assumed to be negligible, T_{em} can be minimized, for a given load-acceleration $\frac{d\omega_L}{dt}$, by selecting an optimum gear ratio $(r_1/r_2)_{opt.}$. The derivation of the optimum gear ratio shows that the load inertia "seen" by the motor should equal the motor inertia, that is, in Eq. 2-44

$$J_M = \left(\frac{r_1}{r_2}\right)^2_{opt.} J_L \quad or \quad (\frac{r_1}{r_2})_{opt.} = \sqrt{\frac{J_M}{J_L}} \qquad (2\text{-}45a)$$

and, consequently,

$$J_{eq} = 2 J_M \qquad (2\text{-}45b)$$

With the optimum gear ratio, in Eq. 2-43, using $T_L = 0$, and using Eq. 2-41,

$$\left(T_{em} \right)_{opt.} = \frac{2\,J_M}{\left(\frac{r_1}{r_2} \right)_{opt.}} \frac{d\omega_L}{dt} \qquad (2\text{-}46)$$

Similar calculations can be made for other types of coupling mechanisms (see homework problems).

2-8 TYPES OF LOADS

Load torques normally act to oppose rotation. In practice, loads can be classified into the following categories [5]:

1. Centrifugal (Squared) Torque
2. Constant Torque
3. Squared Power
4. Constant Power

2-8-1 Centrifugal Loads

Centrifugal loads such as fans and blowers require torque that varies with speed^2 and load power that varies with speed^3, as shown in Fig. 2-16.

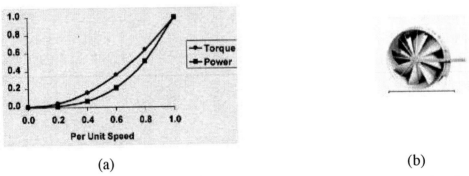

(a)   (b)

Figure 2-16 (a) Characteristics of centrifugal loads; (b) fan – example of a centrifugal load [5].

2-8-2 Constant-Torque Loads

In constant-torque loads such as conveyors, hoists, cranes, and elevators, torque remains constant with speed and the load power varies linearly with speed as shown in Fig. 2-17.

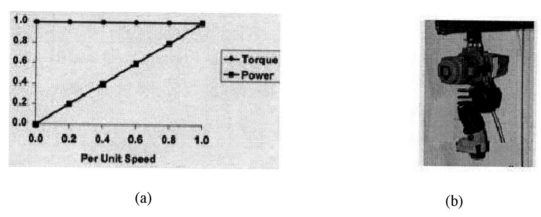

(a)   (b)

Figure 2-17 (a) Characteristics of constant-torque loads; (b) hoist – example of a constant-torque load [5].

2-8-3 Squared-Power Loads

In squared-power loads such as compressors and rollers, torque varies linearly with speed and the load power varies with speed^2 as shown in Fig. 2-18.

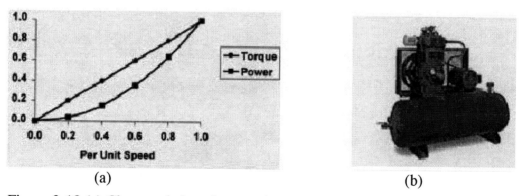

(a)   (b)

Figure 2-18 (a) Characteristics of squared-power loads; (b) compressor – example of a squared-power load [5].

2-8-4 Constant-Power Loads

In constant-power loads such as winders and unwinders, the torque beyond a certain speed range varies inversely with speed and the load power remains constant with speed, as shown in Fig. 2-19.

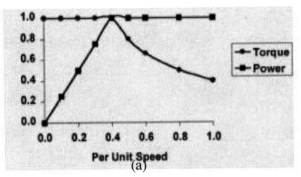
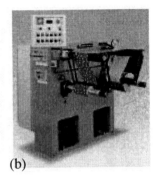

(b)

Figure 2-19 (a) Characteristics of constant-power loads; (b) winder – example of a constant-power load [5].

2-9 FOUR-QUADRANT OPERATION

In many high-performance systems, drives are required to operate in all four quadrants of the torque-speed plane, as shown in Fig. 2-20b. The motor drives the load in the forward direction in quadrant 1, and in the reverse direction in quadrant 3. In both of these quadrants, the average power is positive and flows from the motor to the mechanical load. In order to control the load speed rapidly, it may be necessary to operate the system in the regenerative braking mode, where the direction of power is reversed so that it flows from the load into the motor, and usually into the utility (through the power-processing unit). In quadrant 2, the speed is positive but the torque produced by the motor is negative. In quadrant 4, the speed is negative and the motor torque is positive.

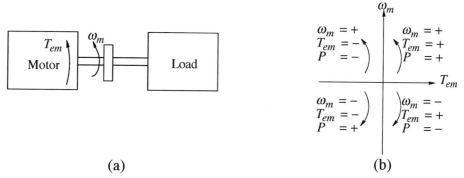

(a)   (b)

Figure 2-20 Four-quadrant requirement in drives.

2-10   STEADY STATE AND DYNAMIC OPERATIONS

As discussed in section 2-8, each load has its own torque-speed characteristic. For high performance drives, in addition to the steady state operation, the dynamic operation - how the operating point changes with time - is also important.   The change of speed of the motor-load combination should be accomplished rapidly and without any oscillations (which otherwise may destroy the load).   This requires a good design of the closed-loop controller, as discussed in Chapter 8, which deals with control of drives.

SUMMARY/REVIEW QUESTIONS

1. What are the MKS units for force, torque, linear speed, angular speed, speed and power?
2. What is the relationship between force, torque and power?
3. Show that torque is the fundamental variable in controlling speed and position.
4. What is the kinetic energy stored in a moving mass and a rotating mass?
5. What is the mechanism for torsional resonances?
6. What are the various types of coupling mechanisms?
7. What is the optimum gear ratio to minimize the torque required from the motor for a given load-speed profile as a function of time?
8. What are the torque-speed and the power-speed profiles for various types of loads?

REFERENCES

1. H. Gross (ed.), *Electric Feed Drives for Machine Tools*, Siemens and Wiley, New York, 1983.
2. *DC Motors and Control ServoSystem – An Engineering handbook*, 5th ed., Electro-Craft Corporation, Hopkins, MN, 1980.
3. M. Spong and M. Vidyasagar, Robot Dynamics and Control, Wiley & Sons, 1989.
4. Bosch, *Automotive Handbook*, Robert Bosch GmbH, 1993.
5. T. Nondahl, Proceedings of the NSF/EPRI-Sponsored Faculty Workshop on "Teaching of Power Electronics," June 25-28, 1998, University of Minnesota.

PROBLEMS

2-1   A constant torque of 5 *Nm* is applied to an unloaded motor at rest at time t = *0*. The motor reaches a speed of 1800 *rpm* in 4 *s*. Assuming the damping to be negligible, calculate the motor inertia.

2-2   Calculate the inertia if the cylinder in Example 2-2 is hollow, with the inner radius $r_2 = 3$ *cm*.

2-3   A vehicle of mass 1,400 *kg* is traveling at a speed of 50 *km/hr*. What is the kinetic energy stored in its mass? Calculate the energy that can be recovered by slowing the vehicle to a speed of 10 *km/hr*.

Belt-and-Pulley System

2-4   Consider the belt and pulley system in Fig 2-14. Inertias other than that shown in the figure are negligible. The pulley radius $r = 0.09$ *m* and the motor inertia $J_M = 0.01$ $kg \cdot m^2$. Calculate the torque T_{em} required to accelerate a load of 1.0 *kg* from rest to a speed of 1 *m/s* in a time of 5 *s*. Assume the motor torque to be constant during this interval.

2-5   For the belt and pulley system shown in Fig. 2-14, $M = 0.02$ *kg*. For a motor with inertia $J_M = 40$ $g \cdot cm^2$, determine the pulley radius that minimizes the torque required from the motor for a given load-speed profile. Ignore damping and the load force f_L.

Gears

2-6   In the gear system shown in Fig. 2-15, the gear ratio $n_L / n_M = 3$ where n equals the number of teeth in a gear. The load and motor inertia are $J_L = 10 \ kg \cdot m^2$ and $J_M = 1.2 \ kg \cdot m^2$. Damping and the load-torque T_L can be neglected. For the load-speed profile shown in Fig. 2-1b, draw the profile of the electromagnetic torque T_{em} required from the motor as a function of time.

2-7   In the system of Problem 2-6, assume a triangular speed profile of the load with equal acceleration and deceleration rates (starting and ending at zero speed). Assuming a coupling efficiency of 100%, calculate the time needed to rotate the load by an angle of $30°$ if the magnitude of the electromagnetic torque (positive or negative) from the motor is 500 Nm.

2-8   The vehicle in Example 2-8 is powered by motors that have a maximum speed of 6000 rpm. Each motor is coupled to the wheel using a gear mechanism. (a) Calculate the required gear ratio if the vehicle's maximum speed is 150 km/hr, and (b) calculate the torque required from each motor at the maximum speed.

2-9   Consider the system shown in Fig. 2-15. For $J_M = 40 \ g \cdot cm^2$ and $J_L = 60 \ g \cdot cm^2$, what is the optimum gear ratio to minimize the torque required from the motor for a given load-speed profile? Neglect damping and external load torque.

Lead-Screw Mechanism

2-10   Consider the lead-screw drive shown in Fig. P2-10. Derive the following equation in terms of pitch s, where $\dot{u}_L =$ linear acceleration of the load, J_M = motor inertia, J_s = screw arrangement inertia, and the coupling ratio $n = \dfrac{s}{2\pi}$:

$$T_{em} = \frac{\dot{u}_L}{n}\left[J_M + J_s + n^2 \left(M_T + M_W \right) \right] + n F_L$$

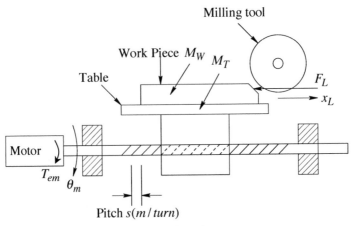

Figure P2-10 Lead-screw system.

SIMULATION PROBLEMS

2-11   Making an electrical analogy, solve Problem 2-4.

2-12   Making an electrical analogy, solve Problem 2-6.

CHAPTER 3

REVIEW OF BASIC ELECTRIC CIRCUITS

3-1   INTRODUCTION

The purpose of this chapter is to review elements of the basic electric circuit theory that are essential to the study of electric drives: the use of phasors to analyze circuits in sinusoidal steady state, the reactive power, the power factor, and the analysis of three-phase circuits.

In this book, we will use MKS units and the IEEE-standard letters and graphic symbols whenever possible. The lowercase letters v and i are used to represent instantaneous values of voltages and currents that vary as functions of time. They may or may not be shown explicitly as functions of time t. A current's positive direction is indicated by an arrow, as shown in Fig. 3-1. Similarly, the voltage polarities must be indicated. The voltage v_{ab} refers to the voltage of node "a" with respect to node "b," thus $v_{ab} = v_a - v_b$.

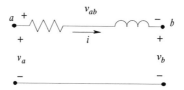

Figure 3-1 Conventions for currents and voltages.

3-2   PHASOR REPRESENTATION IN SINUSOIDAL STEADY STATE

In linear circuits with sinusoidal voltages and currents of frequency f applied for a long time to reach steady state, all circuit voltages and currents are at a frequency $f(=\omega/2\pi)$. To analyze such circuits, calculations are simplified by means of phasor-domain analysis. The use of phasors also provides a deeper insight (with relative ease) into circuit behavior.

In the phasor domain, the time-domain variables $v(t)$ and $i(t)$ are transformed into phasors which are represented by the complex variables $\overline{V}$ and $\overline{I}$. Note that these phasors are expressed by uppercase letters with a bar "-" on top. In a complex (real and imaginary) plane, these phasors can be drawn with a magnitude and an angle.

A co-sinusoidal time function is taken as a reference phasor; for example, the voltage expression in Eq. 3-1 below is represented by a phasor, which is entirely real with an angle of zero degrees:

$$v(t) = \hat{V}\cos\omega t \qquad\qquad \Leftrightarrow \qquad \overline{V} = \hat{V}\angle 0 \qquad\qquad (3\text{-}1)$$

Similarly,

$$i(t) = \hat{I}\cos(\omega t - \phi) \qquad\qquad \Leftrightarrow \qquad \overline{I} = \hat{I}\angle -\phi \qquad\qquad (3\text{-}2)$$

where "^" indicates the peak amplitude. These voltage and current phasors are drawn in Fig. 3-2. We should note the following in Eqs. 3-1 and 3-2: we have chosen the peak values of voltages and currents to represent the phasor magnitudes, and the frequency ω is implicitly associated with each phasor. Knowing this frequency, a phasor expression can be re-transformed into a time-domain expression.

Using phasors, we can convert differential equations into easily solved algebraic equations containing complex variables. Consider the circuit of Fig. 3-3a in a sinusoidal steady state with an applied voltage at a frequency $f(=\omega/2\pi)$. In

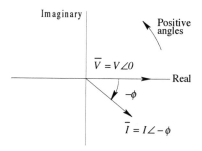

Figure 3-2 Phasor diagram.

order to calculate the current in this circuit, remaining in time domain, we would be required to solve the following differential equation:

$$Ri(t) + L\frac{di(t)}{dt} + \frac{1}{C}\int i(t) \bullet dt = \hat{V}\cos(\omega t) \qquad (3\text{-}3)$$

Using phasors, we can redraw the circuit of Fig. 3-3a in Fig. 3-3b, where the inductance L is represented by $j\omega L$ and the capacitance C is signified by $-j(\frac{1}{\omega C})$. In the phasor-domain circuit, the impedance Z of the series-connected elements is obtained by the impedance triangle of Fig. 3-3c as

$$Z = R + jX_L - jX_c \qquad (3\text{-}4)$$

where

$$X_L = \omega L, \text{ and } \quad X_c = \frac{1}{\omega C} \qquad (3\text{-}5)$$

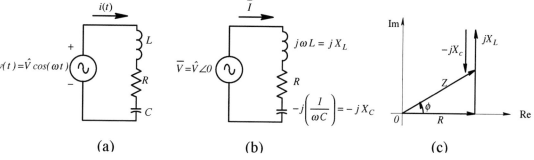

(a)   (b)   (c)

Figure 3-3 (a) Time domain circuit; (b) phasor domain circuit; (c) impedance triangle.

This impedance can be expressed as

$$Z = |Z| \angle \varphi \qquad (3\text{-}6a)$$

where

$$|Z| = \sqrt{R^2 + \left(\omega L - \frac{1}{\omega C}\right)^2} \quad \text{and} \quad \phi = \tan^{-1}\left[\frac{\left(\omega L - \frac{1}{\omega C}\right)}{R}\right] \qquad (3\text{-}6b)$$

It is important to recognize that while Z is a complex quantity, it is <u>not</u> a phasor and does <u>not</u> have a corresponding time-domain expression.

▲ **Example 3-1** Calculate the impedance seen from the terminals of the circuit in Fig. 3-4 under a sinusoidal steady state at a frequency $f = 60 Hz$.

Solution
$$Z = j0.1 + (\text{-}j5.0 \| 2.0).$$

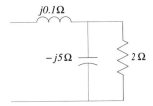

Figure 3-4 Impedance network.

$$Z = j0.1 + \frac{\text{-}j10}{(2\text{-}j5)} = 1.72 - j0.59 = 1.82 \angle -18.9° \ \Omega. \qquad ▲$$

Using the impedance in Eq. 3-6, the current in Fig. 3-3b can be obtained as

$$\overline{I} = \frac{\overline{V}}{Z} = \left(\frac{\hat{V}}{|Z|}\right) \angle -\phi \qquad (3\text{-}7)$$

where $\hat{I} = \dfrac{\hat{V}}{|Z|}$ and ϕ is as calculated from Eq. 3-6b. Using Eq. 3-2, the current can be expressed in the time domain as

$$i(t) = \frac{\hat{V}}{|Z|}\cos(\omega t - \phi) \tag{3-8}$$

In the impedance triangle of Fig. 3-3c, a positive value of the phase angle ϕ implies that the current lags behind the voltage in the circuit of Fig. 3-3a. Sometimes, it is convenient to express the inverse of the impedance, which is called admittance:

$$Y = \frac{1}{Z} \tag{3-9}$$

The phasor-domain procedure for solving $i(t)$ is much easier than solving the differential-integral equation given by Eq. 3-3 (see homework problems 3-3 and 3-4).

▲ **Example 3-2** Calculate the current $\overline{I}_1$ and $i_1(t)$ in the circuit of Fig. 3-5 if the applied voltage has an rms value of $120V$ and a frequency of $60\,Hz$. Assume $\overline{V}_1$ to be the reference phasor.

Solution For an rms value of $120V$, the peak amplitude is $\hat{V}_1 = \sqrt{2} \times 120 = 169.7V$. With $\overline{V}_1$ as the reference phasor, it can be written as $\overline{V}_1 = 169.7\angle 0^0 V$. Impedance of the circuit seen from the applied voltage terminals is

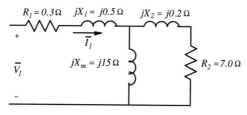

Figure 3-5 Example 3-2.

$$Z = (R_1 + jX_1) + (jX_m) \| (R_2 + jX_2)$$

$$= (0.3 + j0.5) + \frac{(j15)(7 + j0.2)}{(j15) + (7 + j0.2)} = (5.92 + j3.29) = 6.78\angle 29° \ \Omega.$$

$$\overline{I}_1 = \frac{\overline{V}_1}{Z} = \frac{169.7\angle 0°}{6.78\angle 29°} = 25.0\angle -29° A. \ \text{Therefore,}$$

$$i_1(t) = 25.0\cos(\omega t - 29°) A.$$

The rms value of this current is $\dfrac{25.0}{\sqrt{2}} = 17.7\ A.$ ▲

3-2-1 Power, Reactive Power, and Power Factor

Consider the generic circuit of Fig. 3-6 in a sinusoidal steady state. Each sub-circuit may consist of passive (R-L-C) elements and active voltage and current sources. Based on the arbitrarily chosen voltage polarity and the current direction shown in Fig. 3-6, the instantaneous power $p(t) = v(t)i(t)$ is delivered by sub-circuit 1 and absorbed by sub-circuit 2. This is because in sub-circuit 1 the positively-defined current is coming out of the positive-polarity terminal (the same as in a generator). On the other hand, the positively-defined current is entering the positive-polarity terminal in sub-circuit 2 (the same as in a load). A negative value of $p(t)$ reverses the roles of sub-circuit 1 and sub-circuit 2.

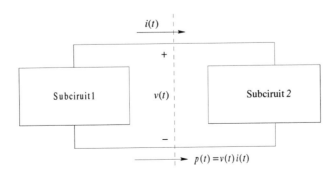

Figure 3-6 A generic circuit divided into two sub-circuits.

Under a sinusoidal steady state condition at a frequency f, the complex power S, the reactive power Q, and the power factor express how "effectively" the real (average) power P is transferred from one sub-circuit to the other.

If $v(t)$ and $i(t)$ are in phase, $p(t) = v(t)i(t)$, as shown in Fig. 3-7a, pulsates at twice the steady state frequency. But, at all times, $p(t) \geq 0$, and therefore the power always flows in one direction: from sub-circuit 1 to sub-circuit 2. Now consider the waveforms of Fig. 3-7b, where the $i(t)$ waveform lags behind the $v(t)$ waveform by a phase angle $\phi(t)$. Now, $p(t)$ becomes negative during a time interval of (ϕ / ω) during each half-cycle. A negative instantaneous power implies power flow in the opposite direction. This back-and-forth flow of power indicates that the real (average) power is not optimally transferred from one sub-circuit to the other, as is the case in Fig. 3-7a.

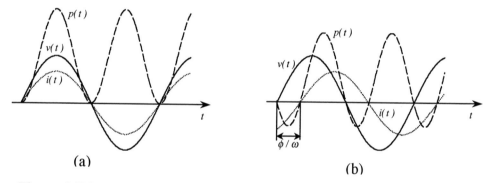

(a)   (b)

Figure 3-7 Instantaneous power with sinusoidal currents and voltages.

The circuit of Fig. 3-6 is redrawn in Fig. 3-8a in the phasor domain. The voltage and the current phasors are defined by their magnitudes and phase angles as

$$\overline{V} = \hat{V} \angle \phi_v \qquad \text{and} \qquad \overline{I} = \hat{I} \angle \phi_i \qquad\qquad (3\text{-}10)$$

In Fig. 3-8b, it is assumed that $\phi_v = 0$ and that ϕ_i has a negative value. To express real, reactive and complex powers, it is convenient to use the rms voltage value V and the rms current value I, where

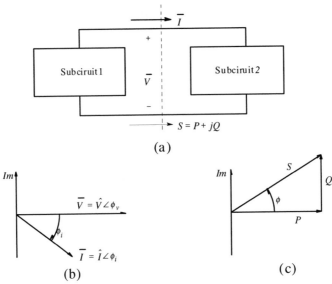

Figure 3-8 (a) Power transfer in phasor domain; (b) phasor diagram; (c) power triangle.

$$V = \frac{1}{\sqrt{2}}\hat{V} \quad \text{and} \quad I = \frac{1}{\sqrt{2}}\hat{I} \tag{3-11}$$

The complex power S is defined as

$$S = \frac{1}{2}\overline{V}\,\overline{I}^* \qquad (\text{* indicates complex conjugate}) \tag{3-12}$$

Therefore, substituting the expressions for voltage and current into Eq. 3-12, and noting that $\overline{I}^* = \hat{I}\angle -\phi_i$, in terms of the rms values of Eq. 3-11,

$$S = V\angle\phi_v\, I\angle -\phi_i = V\,I\angle(\phi_v - \phi_i) \tag{3-13}$$

The difference between the two phase angles is defined as

$$\phi = \phi_v - \phi_i \tag{3-14}$$

Therefore,

$$S = V\,I\angle\phi = P + jQ \tag{3-15}$$

where

$$P = V I \cos\phi \qquad (3-16)$$

and

$$Q = V I \sin\phi \qquad (3-17)$$

The power triangle corresponding to Fig. 3-8b is shown in Fig. 3-8c. From Eq. 3-15, the magnitude of S, also called the "apparent power," is

$$|S| = \sqrt{P^2 + Q^2} \qquad (3-18)$$

and

$$\phi = \tan^{-1}\left(\frac{Q}{P}\right) \qquad (3-19)$$

The above quantities have the following units: P: W (Watts); Q: Var (Volt-Amperes Reactive) assuming by convention that an inductive load draws positive vars; $|S|$: VA (Volt-amperes); finally, ϕ_v, ϕ_i, ϕ: radians, measured positively in a counter-clockwise direction with respect to the reference axis (drawn horizontally from left to right).

The physical significance of the apparent power $|S|$, P, and Q should be understood. The cost of most electrical equipment such as generators, transformers, and transmission lines is proportional to $|S|(= VI)$, since their electrical insulation level and the magnetic core size depend on the voltage V and the conductor size depends on the current I. The real power P has physical significance since it represents the useful work being performed plus the losses. In most situations, it is desirable to have the reactive power Q be zero.

To support the above discussion, another quantity called the power factor is defined. The power factor is a measure of how effectively a load draws real power:

$$\text{power factor} = \frac{P}{|S|} = \frac{P}{VI} = \cos\phi \qquad (3\text{-}20)$$

which is a dimension-less quantity. Ideally, the power factor should be 1.0 (that is, Q should be zero) in order to draw real power with a minimum current magnitude and hence minimize losses in electrical equipment and transmission and distribution lines. An inductive load draws power at a lagging power factor where the current lags behind the voltage. Conversely, a capacitive load draws power at a leading power factor where the load current leads the load voltage.

▲ **Example 3-3** Calculate P, Q, S, and the power factor of operation at the terminals in the circuit of Fig. 3-5 in Example 3-2. Draw the power triangle.

Solution

$$P = V_1 I_1 \cos\phi = 120 \times 17.7 \cos 29^0 = 1857.7 \ W$$

$$Q = V_1 I_1 \sin\phi = 120 \times 17.7 \times \sin 29^0 = 1029.7 \ VAR$$

$$|S| = V_1 I_1 = 120 \times 17.7 = 2124 \ VA$$

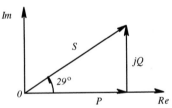

Figure 3-9 Power Triangle.

From Eq. 3-19, $\phi = \tan^{-1}\dfrac{Q}{P} = 29^0$. The power triangle is shown in Fig. 3-9. Note that the angle S in the power triangle is the same as the impedance angle ϕ in Example 3-2.   ▲

Also note the following for the inductive impedance in the above example: 1) The impedance is Z = $|Z| \angle\phi$, where ϕ is positive. 2) The current lags the voltage by the impedance angle ϕ. This corresponds to a lagging power factor of operation. 3) In the power triangle, the impedance angle ϕ relates P, Q, and S. 4) An inductive impedance, when applied a voltage, draws a positive reactive power (vars). If the impedance were to be capacitive, the phase angle ϕ would be negative and the impedance would draw a negative reactive power (in other words, the impedance would supply a positive reactive power).

3-3   THREE-PHASE CIRCUITS

Basic understanding of three-phase circuits is just as important in the study of electric drives as in power systems. Nearly all electricity is generated by means of three-phase ac generators. Figure 3-10 shows a one-line diagram of a three-phase transmission and distribution system. Generated voltages (usually between 22 and 69 kV) are stepped up by means of transformers to 230 kV to 500 kV level for transferring power over transmission lines from the generation site to load centers. Most motor loads above a few kW in power rating operate from three-phase voltages. In most ac motor drives, the input to the drive may be a single-phase or a three-phase line-frequency ac. However, motors are almost always supplied by three-phase, adjustable frequency ac, with the exception of the small, two-phase fan motors used in electronic equipment.

The most common configurations of three-phase ac circuits are wye-connections and delta connections. We will investigate both of these under sinusoidal steady state conditions. In addition, we will assume a balanced condition, which implies that all three voltages are equal in magnitude and displaced by 120^0 ($2\pi/3$ radians) with respect to each other.

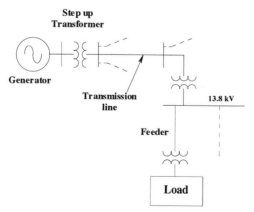

Figure 3-10 One-line diagram of a three phase transmission and distribution system.

Consider the wye-connected source and the load shown in the phasor domain in Fig. 3-11.

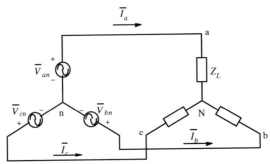

Figure 3-11 Y-connected source and load.

The phase sequence is commonly assumed to be $a-b-c$, which is considered a positive sequence. In this sequence, the phase "a" voltage leads the phase "b" voltage by 120^0, and phase "b" leads phase "c" by 120^0 ($2\pi/3$ radians), as shown in Fig. 3-12.

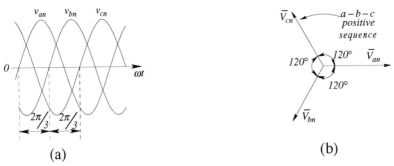

Figure 3-12 Three phase voltages in time and phasor domain.

This applies to both the time domain and the phasor domain. Notice that in the $a-b-c$ sequence voltages plotted in Fig. 3-12a, first v_{an} reaches its positive peak, and then v_{bn} reaches its positive peak $2\pi/3$ radians later, and so on. We can represent these voltages in the phasor form as

$$\overline{V}_{an} = \hat{V}_s\angle 0^0, \quad \overline{V}_{bn} = \hat{V}_s\angle -120^0, \quad \text{and} \quad \overline{V}_{cn} = \hat{V}_s\angle -240^0 \tag{3-21}$$

where $\hat{V}_s$ is the phase-voltage amplitude and the phase "a" voltage is assumed to be the reference (with an angle of zero degrees). For a balanced set of voltages given by Eq. 3-21, at any instant, the sum of these phase voltages equals zero:

$$\overline{V}_{an} + \overline{V}_{bn} + \overline{V}_{cn} = 0 \qquad \text{and} \qquad v_{an}(t) + v_{bn}(t) + v_{cn}(t) = 0 \qquad (3\text{-}22)$$

3-3-1 Per-Phase Analysis

A three-phase circuit can be analyzed on a per-phase basis, provided that it has a balanced set of source voltages and equal impedances in each of the phases. Such a circuit was shown in Fig. 3-11. In such a circuit, the source neutral "n" and the load neutral "N" are at the same potential. Therefore, "hypothetically" connecting these with a zero impedance wire, as shown in Fig. 3-13, does not change the original three-phase circuit, which can now be analyzed on a per-phase basis.

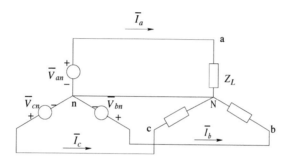

Figure 3-13 Hypothetical wire connecting source and load neutrals.

Selecting phase "a" for this analysis, the per-phase circuit is shown in Fig. 3-14a. If $Z_L = |Z_L|\angle\phi$, using the fact that in a balanced three-phase circuit, phase quantities are displaced by 120^0 with respect to each other, we find that

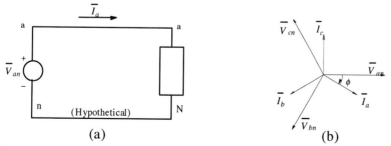

(a) (b)

Figure 3-14 (a) Single phase equivalent circuit; (b) phasor diagram.

$$\overline{I}_a = \frac{\overline{V}_{an}}{Z_L} = \frac{\hat{V}_s}{|Z_L|} \angle -\phi,$$

$$\overline{I}_b = \frac{\overline{V}_{bn}}{Z_L} = \frac{\hat{V}_s}{|Z_L|} \angle (-\frac{2\pi}{3} - \phi), \text{ and} \qquad (3\text{-}23)$$

$$\overline{I}_c = \frac{\overline{V}_{cn}}{Z_L} = \frac{\hat{V}_s}{|Z_L|} \angle (-\frac{4\pi}{3} - \phi)$$

The three-phase voltages and currents are shown in Fig. 3-14b. The total real and reactive powers in a balanced three-phase circuit can be obtained by multiplying the per-phase values by a factor of 3. The power factor is the same as its per-phase value.

▲ **Example 3-4**   In the balanced circuit of Fig. 3-11, the rms phase voltages equal $120V$ and the load impedance $Z_L = 5\angle 30^0\Omega$. Calculate the power factor of operation and the total real and reactive power consumed by the three-phase load.

Solution   Since the circuit is balanced, only one of the phases, for example phase "a," needs to be analyzed:

$$\overline{V}_{an} = \sqrt{2} \times 120\angle 0^0 V$$

$$\overline{I}_a = \frac{\overline{V}_{an}}{Z_L} = \frac{\sqrt{2} \times 120\angle 0^\circ}{5\angle 30^\circ} = \sqrt{2} \times 24\angle -30^0 A$$

The rms value of the current is $24A$. The power factor can be calculated as

power factor $= \cos 30^0 = 0.866$ (lagging).

The total real power consumed by the load is

$$P = 3 \, V_{an} I_a \cos\phi = 3 \times 120 \times 24 \times \cos 30^0 = 7482 \; W \, .$$

The total reactive power "consumed" by the load is

$$Q = 3 \; V_{an} I_a \sin \phi = 3 \times 120 \times 24 \times \sin 30^0 = 4320 \, VAR .$$ ▲

3-3-2 Line-to-Line Voltages

In the balanced wye-connected circuit of Fig. 3-11, it is often necessary to consider the line-to-line voltages, such as those between phases "a" and "b," and so on. Based on the previous analysis, we can refer to both neutral points "n" and "N" by a common term "n," since the potential difference between n and N is zero. Therefore, in Fig. 3-11,

$$\overline{V}_{ab} = \overline{V}_{an} - \overline{V}_{bn}, \quad \overline{V}_{bc} = \overline{V}_{bn} - \overline{V}_{cn}, \quad \text{and} \quad \overline{V}_{ca} = \overline{V}_{cn} - \overline{V}_{an} \tag{3-24}$$

as shown in the phasor diagram of Fig. 3-15. Either using Eq. 3-24, or graphically from Fig. 3-15, we can show that

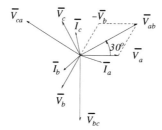

Figure 3-15 Line-to-line voltages in a balanced system.

$$\overline{V}_{ab} = \sqrt{3} \hat{V}_s \angle \frac{\pi}{6}$$

$$\overline{V}_{bc} = \sqrt{3} \hat{V}_s \angle (\frac{\pi}{6} - \frac{2\pi}{3}) = \sqrt{3} \hat{V}_s \angle - \frac{\pi}{2} \tag{3-25}$$

$$\overline{V}_{ca} = \sqrt{3} \hat{V}_s \angle (\frac{\pi}{6} - \frac{4\pi}{3}) = \sqrt{3} \hat{V}_s \angle - \frac{7\pi}{6}$$

Comparing Eqs. 3-21 and 3-25, we see that the line-to-line voltages have an amplitude of $\sqrt{3}$ times the phase voltage amplitude:

$$\hat{V}_{LL} = \sqrt{3}\hat{V}_s \qquad\qquad (3\text{-}26)$$

and $\overline{V}_{ab}$ leads $\overline{V}_{an}$ by $\pi/6$ radians (30^0).

3-3-3 Delta-Connected Loads

In ac-motor drives, the three motor phases may be connected in a delta configuration. Therefore, we will consider the circuit of Fig. 3-16 where the load is connected in a delta configuration. Under a totally balanced condition, it is possible to replace the delta-connected load with an equivalent wye-connected load similar to that in Fig. 3-11. We can then apply a per-phase analysis using Fig. 3-14.

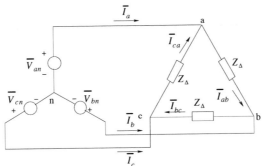

Figure 3-16 Delta connected load.

Consider the delta-connected load impedances of Fig. 3-17a in a three-phase circuit. In terms of the currents drawn, these are equivalent to the wye-connected impedances of Fig. 3-17b, where

$$Z_y = \frac{Z_\Delta}{3} \qquad\qquad (3\text{-}27)$$

The wye-connected equivalent circuit in Fig. 3-17b is easy to analyze on a per phase basis.

(a)   (b)

Figure 3-17 Delta-Wye transformation.

SUMMARY/REVIEW QUESTIONS

1. Why is it important to always indicate the directions of currents and the polarities of voltages?

2. What are the meanings of $i(t)$, $\hat{I}$, I, and $\bar{I}$?

3. In a sinusoidal waveform voltage, what is the relationship between the peak and the rms values?

4. How are currents, voltages, resistors, capacitors, and inductors represented in the phasor domain? Express and draw the following as phasors, assuming both ϕ_v and ϕ_i to be positive:

$$v(t) = \hat{V}\cos(\omega t + \phi_v) \quad \text{and} \quad i(t) = \hat{I}\cos(\omega t + \phi_i).$$

5. How is the current flowing through impedance $|Z|\angle\phi$ related to the voltage across it, in magnitude and phase?

6. What are real and reactive powers? What are the expressions for these in terms of rms values of voltage and current and the phase difference between the two?

7. What is complex power S? How are real and reactive powers related to it? What are the expressions for S, P, and Q, in terms of the current and voltage phasors? What is the power triangle? What is the polarity of the reactive power drawn by an inductive/capacitive circuit?

8. What are balanced three-phase systems? How can their analyses be simplified? What is the relation between line-to-line and phase voltages in terms of magnitude and phase? What are wye and delta connections?

REFERENCE

Any introductory textbook on Electric Circuits.

PROBLEMS

3-1   Calculate the rms values of currents with the waveforms shown in Fig. P3-1.

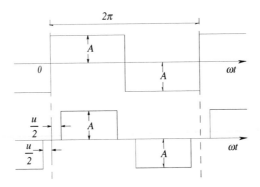

Figure P3-1 Current waveforms.

3-2   Express the following voltages as phasors: (a)
$v_1(t) = \sqrt{2} \times 100 \cos(\omega t - 30^0)$ V and (b) $v_2(t) = \sqrt{2} \times 100 \cos(\omega t + 30^0)$ V.

3-3   The series R-L-C circuit of Fig. 3-3a is in a sinusoidal steady state at a frequency of 60 Hz. V=120 V, $R = 1.5$ Ω, L= 20 mH, and C=100 μF. Calculate $i(t)$ in this circuit by solving the differential equation Eq. 3-3.

3-4   Repeat Problem 3-3 using the phasor-domain analysis.

3-5   In a linear circuit in sinusoidal steady state with only one active source $\overline{V} = 90 \angle 30^o$ V, the current in a branch is $\overline{I} = 5 \angle 15^o$ A. Calculate the current in the same branch if the source voltage were to be $100 \angle 0^0 V$.

3-6   In the circuit of Fig. 3-5 in Example 3-2, show that the real and reactive powers supplied at the terminals equal the sum of their individual components, that is $P = \sum_k I_k^2 R_k$ and $Q = \sum_k I_k^2 X_k$.

3-7   An inductive load connected to a 120-V (rms), 60-Hz ac source draws 5 kW at a power factor of 0.8. Calculate the capacitance required in parallel with the load in order to bring the combined power factor to 0.95 (lagging).

3-8   In the circuit of Fig. P3-8, $\overline{V}_1 = \sqrt{2} \times 100 \angle 0 V$ and $X_L = 0.5 \ \Omega$. Show $\overline{V}_1, \overline{V}_2$, and $\overline{I}$ on a phasor diagram and calculate P_1 and Q_1 for the following values of $\overline{I}$: (a) $\sqrt{2} \times 10 \angle 0 A$, (b) $\sqrt{2} \times 10 \angle 180^o A$, (c) $\sqrt{2} \times 10 \angle 90^o A$, and (d) $\sqrt{2} \times 10 \angle -90^o A$.

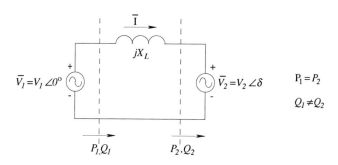

Figure P3-8 Power flow with AC sources.

3-9   A balanced three-phase inductive load is supplied in steady state by a balanced three-phase voltage source with a phase voltage of 120 V rms. The load draws a total of 10 kW at a power factor of 0.9. Calculate the rms value of the phase currents and the magnitude of the per-phase load impedance, assuming a wye-connected load. Draw a phasor diagram showing all three voltages and currents.

3-10   A positive sequence (a-b-c), balanced, wye-connected voltage source has the phase-a voltage given as $\overline{V}_a = \sqrt{2} \times 100 \angle 30^o V$. Obtain the time-domain voltages $v_a(t)$, $v_b(t)$, $v_c(t)$, and $v_{ab}(t)$.

3-11   Repeat Problem 3-9, assuming a delta-connected load.

SIMULATION PROBLEMS

3-12   Repeat Problem 3-3 in sinusoidal steady state by means of computer simulation.

3-13   Repeat Problem 3-9 in sinusoidal steady state by means of computer simulation.

3-14   Repeat Problem 3-11 in sinusoidal steady state by means of computer simulation.

CHAPTER 4

BASIC UNDERSTANDING OF SWITCH-MODE POWER ELECTRONIC CONVERTERS IN ELECTRIC DRIVES

4-1   INTRODUCTION

As discussed in Chapter 1, electric drives require power-processing units (PPUs) to efficiently convert line-frequency utility input in order to supply motors with voltages and currents of appropriate form and frequency. Similar to linear amplifiers, power-processing units amplify the input control signals. However, unlike linear amplifiers, PPUs in electric drives use switch-mode power electronics principles to achieve high energy efficiency and low cost, size, and weight. In this chapter, we will examine the basic switch-mode principles, topologies, and control for the processing of electrical power in an efficient and controlled manner.

4-2   OVERVIEW OF POWER PROCESSING UNITS (PPUs)

Fig. 4-1 shows in block-diagram form the structure of commonly used PPUs. The structure consists of a diode rectifier followed by a filter capacitor to convert line-frequency ac into dc. The switch-mode (a term we will soon define) converter,

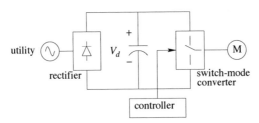

Figure 4-1 Block diagram of PPUs.

under the direction of the controller, supplies the motor with voltages and currents of the appropriate form (ac or dc).

4-2-1 Rectifier

In the block-diagram of Fig. 4-1, the role of the rectifier is to convert line-frequency ac (single-phase or three-phase) into a dc voltage, without any control over its magnitude. The capacitor across the dc output of the rectifier acts as a filter that reduces the ripple in the output voltage V_d, which we will assume to be a constant dc for our discussion in this chapter. The energy efficiency of this sub-block can be very high, approximately 99%.

The rectifier-capacitor combination can be viewed as a peak-charging circuit. Therefore, waveforms of the current drawn from the utility source are highly distorted. A further discussion of these rectifiers is left to Chapter 16, where the techniques of drawing power from the utility by means of sinusoidal currents at a unity power factor are described. Ways of making the power flow bi-directional (that is, also back into the utility system) are also discussed in Chapter 16.

4-2-2 Switch-Mode Converters

The dc voltage V_d (assumed to be constant) produced by the rectifier-capacitor combination is used as the input voltage to the switch-mode converter in Fig. 4-1. The task of this converter, depending on the motor type, is to deliver an adjustable-magnitude dc or sinusoidal ac to the motor by amplifying the signal from the controller by a constant gain. The power flow through the switch-mode converter must be able to reverse. In switch-mode converters, as their name implies, transistors are operated as switches: either fully on or fully off. The switch-mode converters used for dc- and ac-motor drives can be simply illustrated, as in Figs. 4-2a and 4-2b, respectively, where each bi-positional switch constitutes a pole. The dc-dc converter for dc-motor drives in Fig. 4-2a consists of two such poles, whereas the dc-to-three-phase ac converter shown in Fig. 4-2b for ac-motor drives consists of three such poles.

Typically, PPU efficiencies exceed 95% and can exceed 98% in very large power ratings. Therefore, the energy efficiency of adjustable-speed drives is comparable to that of conventional line-fed motors; thus systems with adjustable-speed drives can achieve much higher overall *system* efficiencies (compared to their conventional counterparts) in many applications discussed in Chapter 1.

4-3   ANALYSIS OF SWITCH-MODE CONVERTERS

It is sufficient to concentrate on one of the poles, for example pole-A, in the converter topologies of Fig. 4-2. Redrawn in Figure 4-3a, a pole can be considered to be the building block of switch-mode converters. Each pole consists of a bi-positional switch (either up or down) whose realization by means of two transistors and two diodes is described later. This pole, shown in Fig. 4-3a, is a 2-port: on one side there is a voltage port across the capacitor, whose voltage V_d cannot change instantaneously; on the other side there is a current port with a series inductor whose current i_A also cannot change instantaneously.

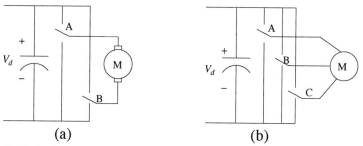

Figure 4-2 Switch mode converters for (a) dc- and (b) ac-motor drives.

4-3-1   Pulse-Width Modulation (PWM) to Synthesize the Output Voltage

The objective of the converter pole in Fig. 4-3a is to achieve the output voltage (at the current port) such that its *average* is of the desired value. As we will examine in detail in this chapter, the pole has a constant gain by which it amplifies the control voltage $v_{c,A}$ to result in the average output voltage. The way to accomplish this is stated as follows and is mathematically derived later in this chapter.

The bi-positional switch "chops" the input dc voltage V_d into a train of voltage pulses, shown by the v_{AN} waveform in Fig. 4-3b, by switching up or down at a constant repetition rate (called switching frequency f_s), typically in a range of a few *kHz* up to 50 *kHz*. The *average* value of this waveform depends on the pulse width or duration (when v_{AN} equals V_d), within each switching time-period T_s ($=1/f_s$). However, the pulse width, as discussed later, depends on the control voltage $v_{c,A}$. (Since the control voltage modulates the pulse width, this process is called pulse-width modulation or PWM.) Hence, the *average* output voltage of the pole in Fig. 4-3a depends on the control voltage - amplified by a constant gain by this pole. In spite of the pulsating (discontinuous) nature of the instantaneous

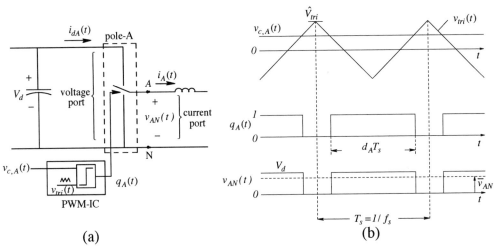

Figure 4-3 (a) Pole-A; (b) waveforms during a switching

output voltage $v_{AN}(t)$, the series inductance at the output of the pole ensures that the output current $i_A(t)$ remains smooth (continuous).

To modulate the width of the voltage pulses at the current port, inexpensive pulse-width-modulation integrated circuits (PWM-IC) are available. In these ICs, as shown in Fig. 4-3a, the control voltage $v_{c,A}$ is compared with a triangular waveform signal. The signal-level control voltage $v_{c,A}$ is generated by the feedback controller responsible for ensuring that the drive delivers the commanded torque, speed, and position to the load. (The design of this controller is discussed in Chapter 8.) The triangular waveform signal $v_{tri}(t)$, shown in Figs. 4-3a and 4-3b, is generated internally in the PWM-IC. The frequency f_s of the triangular waveform establishes the switching frequency of the converter. Both f_s and the amplitude $\hat{V}_{tri}$ of the triangular waveform signal are usually kept constant.

4-3-2   Analysis of a Pole as the Building Block

As Fig. 4-3a shows, the control voltage $v_{c,A}(t)$ is compared with an internally generated triangular waveform $v_{tri}(t)$. Based on the comparator output in Fig. 4-3a, the gate drive (not shown) causes the switch of the pole to be in the "up" position if $v_{c,A}(t) > v_{tri}(t)$; otherwise the switch will be in the "down" position. The comparator output can be described mathematically by means of a switching function $q_A(t)$, shown in Fig. 4-3b, which assumes two values: 1 or 0. Comparison of the signal-level waveforms, $v_{c,A}$ and v_{tri}, results in the mathematical switching function $q_A(t)$, which dictates the output voltage of the pole in the following manner:

$$\begin{aligned} \text{If } v_{c,A}(t) > v_{tri}(t) &\Rightarrow q_A(t) = 1 \Rightarrow \text{ switch "up"} \Rightarrow v_{AN}(t) = V_d \\ \text{otherwise,} \quad & q_A(t) = 0 \Rightarrow \text{ switch "down"} \Rightarrow v_{AN}(t) = 0 \end{aligned} \tag{4-1}$$

From Eq. 4-1, the output voltage can be expressed simply as

$$v_{AN}(t) = q_A(t)V_d \qquad (4\text{-}2)$$

In the pole of Fig. 4-3a, the current at the voltage port, i_{dA}, equals i_A in the "up" position of the switch; otherwise it is zero. Hence, the mathematical switching function $q_A(t)$ relates the output current $i_A(t)$ to $i_{dA}(t)$ as follows:

$$i_{dA}(t) = q_A(t)i_A(t) \qquad (4\text{-}3)$$

Eqs. 4-2 and 4-3 confirm that in the two-port of Fig. 4-3a, the dependent variables $v_{AN}(t)$ and $i_{dA}(t)$ are related to the respective independent variables V_d and $i_A(t)$ by the switching function $q_A(t)$.

4-3-3   Average Representation of the Pole

In Fig. 4-3b, we will define the duty-ratio d_A of pole-A as the ratio of the pulse width (the interval during which $q_A(t)=1$ and the switch is in the "up" position) to the switching time-period T_s. With the assumption that the voltage V_d is constant, the average value of the output voltage, shown dotted in Fig. 4-3b, can be obtained by integrating v_{AN} over one switching time-period and then dividing the integral by T_s:

$$\overline{v}_{AN} = \frac{1}{T_s} \int_{T_s} v_{AN}(t)\,dt = \frac{1}{T_s}\left[\int_0^{d_A T_s} V_d \cdot d\tau + \int_{d_A T_s}^{T_s} 0 \cdot d\tau \right] = d_A V_d \qquad (4\text{-}4)$$

where the bar "-" on top of the v in $\overline{v}_{AN}$ indicates that $\overline{v}_{AN}$ is the average value of the output voltage during the switching cycle. This average voltage linearly depends on the duty-ratio d_A. But how does $\overline{v}_{AN}$ depend on the control voltage $v_{c,A}$? We can answer this question if we can determine how the duty-ratio d_A depends on the control voltage. In Fig. 4-3b, notice that if $v_{c,A}(t) = \hat{V}_{tri}$, the switch will be in the "up" position during the entire switching time-period. Hence, we can write that if

$$v_{c,A}(t) = \hat{V}_{tri} \quad \Rightarrow \quad d_A = 1 \quad \Rightarrow \quad \overline{v}_{AN} = V_d \tag{4-5a}$$

In contrast, if $v_{c,A}(t) = -\hat{V}_{tri}$, the switch will be in the "down" position during the entire switching time-period; thus, if

$$v_{c,A}(t) = -\hat{V}_{tri} \quad \Rightarrow \quad d_A = 0 \quad \Rightarrow \quad \overline{v}_{AN} = 0 \tag{4-5b}$$

In the linear range, the control voltage remains within the positive and the negative peaks of the triangular waveform $(-\hat{V}_{tri} \leq v_{c,A} \leq \hat{V}_{tri})$, resulting in piecewise-linear waveforms. Hence, we can utilize the results of the two operating points obtained above to derive a general relationship between the control voltage and the switch duty-ratio. Notice from Eqs. 4-5a and 4-5b that the duty-ratio changes by unity for a change in the control voltage of $2\hat{V}_{tri}$ (from $-\hat{V}_{tri}$ to $\hat{V}_{tri}$). This defines the slope of this relationship as

$$\frac{\Delta d_A}{\Delta v_{C,A}} = \underbrace{\left(\frac{1}{2\hat{V}_{tri}} \right)}_{slope} \tag{4-6a}$$

which allows us to express the linear relationship between the duty-ratio and the control voltage as

$$d_A = \underbrace{\left(\frac{1}{2\hat{V}_{tri}} \right)}_{slope} v_{c,A} + offset \qquad \left(-\hat{V}_{tri} \leq v_{c,A} \leq \hat{V}_{tri} \right) \tag{4-6b}$$

By substituting the results of one of the operating points (for example from Eq. 4-5a, $v_{c,A} = \hat{V}_{tri}$ corresponds to $d_A = 1$) in Eq. 4-6b, the offset can be calculated as $1/2$. Substituting the value of the offset into Eq. 4-6b, we have the relationship in the linear range of the control voltage variation:

$$d_A = \frac{1}{2} + \frac{1}{2}\frac{v_{c,A}}{\hat{V}_{tri}} \qquad (0 \le d_A \le 1) \qquad \text{(4-7)}$$

Substituting for d_A from Eq. 4-7 into Eq. 4-4,

$$\overline{v}_{AN} = \underbrace{\left(\frac{V_d}{2}\right)}_{dc\ offset} + \underbrace{\left(\frac{V_d}{2\hat{V}_{tri}}\right)}_{k_{pole}} v_{c,A} \qquad \text{(4-8)}$$

Eq. 4-8 shows that the average output voltage of the converter pole has an offset of $V_d/2$ and that the pole amplifies the input control signal $v_{c,A}$ by a constant gain of

$$k_{pole} = \frac{V_d}{2\hat{V}_{tri}} \qquad \text{(4-9)}$$

Combining Eqs. 4-7 and 4-8 confirms Eq. 4-4, which shows that the average output voltage at the current port can be controlled by the duty-ratio d_A (which, in turn, depends on the control voltage). Usually (for example, in synthesizing a sinusoidal ac output, which is described later in this chapter) the control voltage continuously varies with time, but much more slowly compared to the switching frequency waveform of v_{tri}. Therefore, the duty-ratio in Eq. 4-7 and the average output voltage in Eq. 4-8 can be treated as continuous functions of time: $d_A(t)$ and $\overline{v}_{AN}(t)$. This allows us to express Eq. 4-4 as

$$\overline{v}_{AN}(t) = d_A(t)V_d \qquad \text{(4-10)}$$

While designing these systems, we should be mindful of the fact that the instantaneous output voltage, in addition to its average value, contains a ripple component at the high switching frequency. Due to the motor inductance shown in Fig. 4-3a at the current port, the resulting current i_A is relatively smooth - a continuous function of time.

▲ **Example 4-1** In a switch-mode converter pole-A, $V_d = 300V$, $\hat{V}_{tri} = 5V$, and $f_s = 20\,kHz$. Calculate the values of the control signal $v_{c,A}$ and the pole duty-ratio d_A for the following values of the average output voltage: (a) $\overline{v}_{AN} = 250V$ and (b) $\overline{v}_{AN} = 50V$.

Solution   From Eq. 4-8,

$$\overline{v}_{AN} = \frac{V_d}{2} + \left(\frac{V_d}{2\hat{V}_{tri}}\right) v_{c,A}(t) = 150 + \left(\frac{150}{5}\right) v_{c,A}(t).$$

Therefore,

$$v_{c,A}(t) = \frac{\left(\overline{v}_{AN} - 150\right)}{30}$$

and from Eq. 4-7,

$$d_A = \frac{1}{2} + \frac{1}{2\hat{V}_{tri}} v_{c,A}(t) = 0.5 + 0.1 \times v_{c,A}(t).$$

In the above equations, substituting for $\overline{v}_{AN}$ yields

(a) for $\overline{v}_{AN} = 250$ V, $v_{c,A}(t) = 3.333$ V, and $d_A = 0.833$.

(b) for $\overline{v}_{AN} = 50$ V, $v_{c,A}(t) = -3.333$ V, and $d_A = 0.167$.

▲

4-3-3-1   Currents $\overline{i}_A(t)$ and $\overline{i}_{dA}(t)$

Due to the series inductance at the current port, the waveform of the current $i_A(t)$ is relatively smooth and consists of linear segments as shown in Fig. 4-4a.

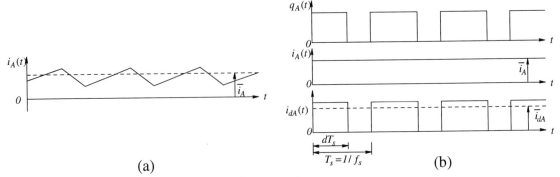

(a)

(b)

Figure 4-4 Current waveforms at the two ports.

Relative to the average value $\bar{i}_A(t)$, shown dotted in Fig. 4-4a, the peak-to-peak ripple in $i_A(t)$ must be kept low, which otherwise would result in excessive power losses and torque pulsations within the motor, as will be discussed in Chapter 15. As a first-order approximation, we can neglect this ripple, allowing us to assume that the instantaneous current $i_A(t)$ equals its average value $\bar{i}_A(t)$, as shown in Fig. 4-4b. In accordance with Eq. 4-3, the $i_{dA}(t)$ waveform is also shown in Fig.

4-4b. Therefore, following the averaging procedure that led to Eqs. 4-4 and 4-10, we can derive the expression for the average value $\bar{i}_{dA}$ in terms of $\bar{i}_A$ in Fig. 4-4b:

$$\bar{i}_{dA}(t) = d_A(t) \cdot \bar{i}_A(t) \qquad (4\text{-}11)$$

This average value is shown by a dotted line in Fig. 4-4b. It is possible to show that the relationship in Eq. 4-11 is also valid in the presence of the ripple in $i_A(t)$; this ripple is neglected only for the sake of simplifying the discussion (see homework problem 4-2).

4-3-3-2 Average Representation of a Pole by an Ideal Transformer

Eqs. 4-10 and 4-11 show that the average voltages and currents at the two ports of a pole are each related by the duty-ratio d_A. Therefore, the switching pole redrawn in Fig. 4-5a can be represented on an average basis by means of an ideal transformer shown in Fig. 4-5b, where the voltages and the currents on the two sides are related by the turns-ratio, similar to Eqs. 4-10 and 4-11.

The turns-ratio $1:d_A(t)$ of this electronic transformer can be varied continuously with time, recognizing that $d_A(t)$ in Eq. 4-7 depends on the input control signal $v_{c,A}(t)$. Note that this is not a real transformer, and it is possible to transmit dc as well as ac voltages and currents across it.

This simple transformer equivalent circuit allows us to concentrate on the average quantities that are of primary interest. However, once again, we should not lose sight of the fact that we are dealing with a switch-mode converter where, within every switching-cycle, the instantaneous output voltage $v_{AN}(t)$ and the input current i_{dA} are pulsating and are discontinuous functions of time.

4-4   CONVERTER POLE AS A TWO-QUADRANT CONVERTER

In the converter pole of Fig. 4-5a, the voltages V_d and v_{AN} cannot reverse polarity, but the currents i_A and i_{dA} *can* reverse their direction. This fact makes the pole in Fig. 4-5a a two-quadrant converter, as discussed below. To achieve a four-quadrant operation (where the output voltage as well as the output current can reverse) necessitates using two or three such poles, as shown in the converters of Fig. 4-2.

To examine the two-quadrant operation, let us consider the converter pole connected to the circuit of Fig. 4-6a, which consists of a voltage source E_a in series with an inductance L_a and a resistance R_a at the current port. In Chapter 7

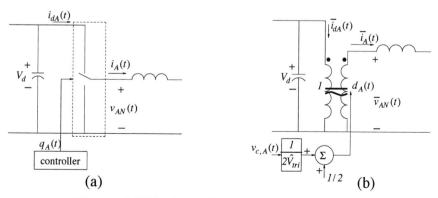

(a)   (b)

Figure 4-5 Ideal transformer equivalent of a single pole.

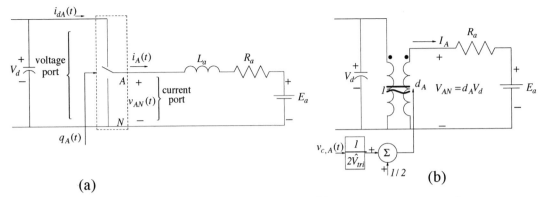

(a)

(b)

Figure 4-6 (a) Two-quadrant converter; (b) average representation.

we will see that a dc motor operating in steady state can be represented by this equivalent circuit where E_a ($< V_d$) is the induced dc voltage, called back-emf, in series with the internal inductance L_a and the resistance R_a.

In examining this two-quadrant operation, we are not interested in the ripple components. Therefore, we will make use of the average representation. In fact, we will assume that the system is operating in a dc steady state; that is, the control voltage, and hence the average output voltage and E_a are not changing with time. In this dc steady state, as shown in Fig. 4-6b, the average quantities are represented by uppercase letters, where

$$I_A = \frac{V_{AN} - E_a}{R_a} = \frac{d_A V_d - E_a}{R_a} \qquad (4\text{-}12)$$

Given that $E_a < V_d$, which is always the case, it is possible to control d_A (and hence V_{AN}) to make I_A positive or negative (i.e., to make it flow in either direction).

4-4-1   Buck Mode of Operation

The positive I_A (with $V_{AN} > E_a$) corresponds to the average power flow in the direction considered to be positive. Under these conditions, the converter is in the "buck" mode of operation. In this mode, the input voltage V_d is "bucked" by the converter to produce a lower voltage, and the power flows from the higher voltage V_d to the side of the lower voltage V_{AN} (and E_a).

4-4-2 Boost Mode of Operation

By adjusting the switch duty-ratio d_A such that $V_{AN} < E_a$, I_A reverses direction and the average power flow is from a smaller voltage E_a (and V_{AN}) to a larger voltage V_d, thus implying a "boost" mode of operation. In either mode, the average representation of the switching converter pole, shown in Fig. 4-6b by an ideal transformer, is valid.

The above discussion shows that the converter pole of Fig. 4-6a is capable of operating in both modes: buck and boost, a fact that is further illustrated by the following example. The ripple in the output current is illustrated by Example 4-3.

▲ **Example 4-2** In the 2-quadrant converter of Fig. 4-6a, $V_d = 100V$, $E_a = 75V$, and $R_a = 0.5\Omega$. In dc steady state, calculate V_{AN} and d_A if (a) $I_A = 5$ A, and (b) $I_A = -5$ A.

Solution
(a) For $I_A = 5$ A, from Eq. 4-12,

$$V_{AN} = E_a + R_a I_A = 77.5V \qquad \text{and} \qquad d_A = \frac{V_{AN}}{V_d} = 0.775$$

The waveforms of $v_{AN}(t)$, V_{AN} and E_a are shown in Fig. 4-7a.

(b) For $I_A = -5$ A, from Eq. 4-12,

$$V_{AN} = E_a + R_a I_A = 72.5V \qquad \text{and} \qquad d_A = \frac{V_{AN}}{V_d} = 0.725.$$

The waveforms of $v_{AN}(t)$, V_{AN}, and E_a are shown in Fig. 4-7b. ▲

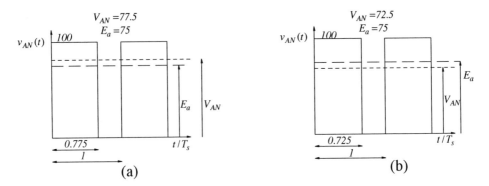

Figure 4-7 Waveforms of $v_{AN(t)}$, V_{AN} and E_a

▲ **Example 4-3** In Example 4-2, with $I_A = 5\ A$, calculate the peak-to-peak ripple in $i_A(t)$ if $L_a = 1\ mH$ and $f_s = 20\ kHz$.

Solution The pulsating output voltage waveform of $v_{AN}(t)$ in Fig. 4-7a can be expressed as the sum of its average (dc) component V_{AN} and the ripple component $v_{ripple}(t)$:

$$v_{AN}(t) = V_{AN} + v_{ripple}(t) .$$ (4-13)

The ripple-component waveform repeats with the same frequency as the switching frequency and contains components at the switching frequency and its multiples. The voltage in Eq. 4-13 is applied to the linear circuit, as shown in Fig. 4-8a.

To analyze this circuit, we can draw it at the dc and the ripple frequency, as shown by Figs. 4-8b and 4-8c, respectively, and then apply the principle of superposition. In Fig. 4-8a,

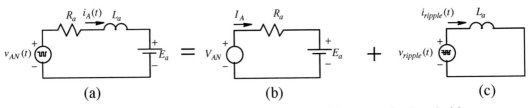

Figure 4-8 Application of superposition to calculate $i_A(t)$.

4-14

$$i_A(t) = I_A + i_{ripple}(t) \tag{4-14}$$

where I_A in the dc circuit of Example 4-2 is given as 5 A. In the ripple-frequency circuit of Fig. 4-8c, the reactance of the inductor L_a at the switching frequency and at its multiples is much larger than R_a; therefore, it is reasonable to neglect R_a. The ripple voltage is plotted in Fig. 4-9a. Since $v_{ripple}(t)$ has a zero average value, the same will be true for $i_{ripple}(t)$ in Fig. 4-8c. During the interval dT_s, $v_{ripple}(=V_d - V_{AN})$ appears across the inductor in Fig. 4-8c. Therefore, the peak-to-peak ripple in the output current can be calculated as follows, where $T_s = 1/f_s = 50\mu s$:

$$\Delta i_A(p-p) = \frac{V_d - V_{AN}}{L_a} d_A T_s = \frac{100 - 77.5}{1000\mu} 0.775 \times 50\mu = 0.87\,A \tag{4-15}$$

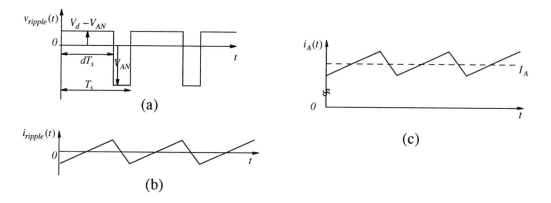

Figure 4-9 Waveforms for $v_{ripple}(t), i_{ripple}(t)$ and $i_A(t)$.

The waveform for $i_{ripple}(t)$ is plotted in Fig. 4-9b. Note that its average value is zero. Using Eq. 4-14, the total current $i_A(t)$ is plotted in Fig. 4-9c. ▲

4-5 IMPLEMENTATION OF BI-POSITIONAL SWITCHES

So far we have assumed a hypothetical bi-positional switch, which gives the converter pole a bi-directional power flow capability by operating in the buck or the boost mode. This bi-positional switch is realized as shown in Fig. 4-10a, where the gate-drive circuitry is omitted for simplification. In the transistors shown, if gated on, the current can only flow in the direction of the arrow.

The transistor-diode combination, shown on the left side in Fig. 4-10a, facilitates the buck mode of operation when i_A is positive. The transistor-diode combination on the right side in Fig. 4-10a facilitates the boost mode of operation when i_A is negative. The previously defined switching function $q_A(t)$ should now be considered a set of two complementary signals in the sense that

$$q_A^+(t) = q_A(t) \tag{4-16a}$$

and

$$q_A^-(t) = \text{the complement of } q_A(t) = 1 - q_A(t) \tag{4-16b}$$

where $q_A^+ (= q_A)$ through the gate drive controls the upper transistor, gating it to be fully *on* when $q_A^+ = 1$, otherwise *off*. Similarly, $q_A^- (= 1 - q_A)$ controls the bottom transistor. A small blanking time between the two complementary gate signals, introduced to avoid "shoot-through," is neglected in the idealized discussion here, the details of which are covered in power electronics courses.

Power dissipation in transistors is kept low by operating them as switches, fully *on* or fully *off*, even when the switching frequencies range from approximately 2 *kHz* in large motor drives to 50 *kHz* in very small drives. In Fig. 4-10b, the collector current i_c is plotted as a function of the voltage V_{CE} across one of the

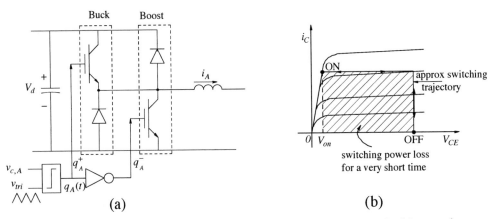

Figure 4-10 (a) Bi-positional switch using transistors; (b) switching trajectory.

transistors, for various values of the gate voltages. Controlling the gate voltage dictates the state of the transistor: *on* or *off*. During the transition from one state to the other, the transistor voltage and the current are simultaneously high, making instantaneous power dissipation in the transistor large. However, since the transition is complete in typically much less than one μs, the average power loss due to the switching of transistors is kept small. In the on-state, when the transistor is conducting current, the voltage drop V_{on} across the transistor is ~1 V, resulting in only a small amount of conduction losses.

4-6 SWITCH-MODE CONVERTERS FOR DC- AND AC-MOTOR DRIVES

The converters used in dc and three-phase ac motor drives consist of two poles, and three poles, respectively, as shown in Fig. 4-2. By using the average representation of a pole discussed earlier, we can quickly describe the basic principles underlying the operation of these converters.

4-6-1 Converters for DC-Motor Drives (Four-Quadrant Capability)

The dc-drive converter with two poles is shown in Fig. 4-11a, where $v_c(t)$ is the control voltage delivered by the feedback controller.

For pole-A, the control voltage is the same as $v_c(t)$; that is, $v_{c,A}(t) = v_c(t)$. For pole-B, the control voltage is made equal to the negative of $v_c(t)$; that is, $v_{c,B}(t) = -v_c(t)$. Comparing these control voltages with the same triangular waveform results in the switching functions $q_A(t)$ and $q_B(t)$, as well as the following duty-ratios for the two poles:

$$d_A(t) = \frac{1}{2} + \frac{1}{2}\frac{v_c(t)}{\hat{V}_{tri}} \quad \text{and} \quad d_B(t) = \frac{1}{2} - \frac{1}{2}\frac{v_c(t)}{\hat{V}_{tri}} \tag{4-17}$$

The converter, in terms of average quantities, is shown in Fig. 4-11b, where

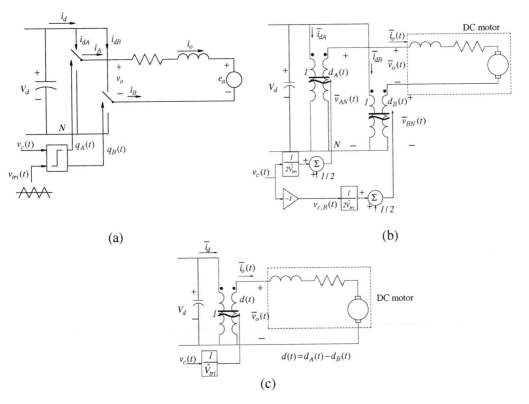

Figure 4-11 (a) Switching converter for dc-dc motor drives; (b) and (c) its average representation.

$$\overline{v}_{AN}(t) = \frac{V_d}{2} + \frac{V_d}{2\hat{V}_{tri}} v_c(t) \qquad \text{and} \qquad \overline{v}_{BN}(t) = \frac{V_d}{2} - \frac{V_d}{2\hat{V}_{tri}} v_c(t) \qquad (4\text{-}18)$$

At the output terminals, the output voltage is the difference between the pole output voltages. Therefore, as illustrated in Fig. 4-11c,

$$\overline{v}_o(t) = \overline{v}_{AN}(t) - \overline{v}_{BN}(t) = \underbrace{\left(\frac{V_d}{\hat{V}_{tri}} \right)}_{k_{PWM}} v_c(t)$$

or

$$\overline{v}_o(t) = k_{PWM} v_c(t) \qquad (4\text{-}19)$$

where, in a dc-dc converter for dc-motor drives, the constant gain $\overline{v}_o / v_c$ is

$$k_{PWM} = \frac{V_d}{\hat{V}_{tri}} \qquad (4\text{-}20)$$

For determining the turns-ratio in the combined representation of two poles in Fig. 4-11c, we can define a duty-ratio $d(t)$ where

$$d(t) = d_A(t) - d_B(t) = \frac{v_c(t)}{\hat{V}_{tri}} \qquad (-1 \le d(t) \le 1) \qquad (4\text{-}21)$$

The duty-ratios d_A and d_B are limited to the range 0 to 1 by their physical definition, but the derived duty ratio $d(t)$ can range from -1 to $+1$.

Eqs. 4-19 and 4-20 show that the dc-dc converter amplifies the control voltage by a constant gain k_{PWM} to produce an average output voltage. This average output voltage can be positive or negative, depending on the control voltage. Although we have not specifically discussed the output current in the converter of Fig. 4-11, we know from our previous discussion that the current through a pole can flow in either direction. Therefore, in the converter of Fig. 4-11 consisting of two poles, the current can flow in either direction, independent of the polarity of the output

voltage. This gives the converter a four-quadrant capability to drive a dc machine in forward or reverse direction, in motoring as well as in regenerative braking mode.

4-6-2 Converters for Three-Phase AC-Motor Drives

The ac-drive converter with three poles is shown in Fig. 4-12a, where the feedback controller determines the amplitude $\hat{V}_c$ and the frequency f_1 of the control voltage. This information is used in the PWM-IC to generate three control voltages:

$$v_{c,A}(t) = \hat{V}_c \sin(\omega_1 t) \quad v_{c,B}(t) = \hat{V}_c \sin(\omega_1 t - 120^0) \quad v_{c,C}(t) = \hat{V}_c \sin(\omega_1 t - 240^0) \,(4\text{-}22)$$

Comparing these control voltages with the same triangular waveform results in the switching functions $q_A(t)$, $q_B(t)$, and $q_C(t)$ with the following duty-ratios for the three poles:

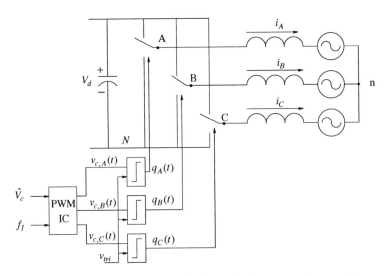

Figure 4-12 (a) Switch mode inverter for ac drives.

$$d_A(t) = \frac{1}{2} + \frac{1}{2}\frac{\hat{V}_c}{\hat{V}_{tri}}\sin(\omega_1 t)$$

$$d_B(t) = \frac{1}{2} + \frac{1}{2}\frac{\hat{V}_c}{\hat{V}_{tri}}\sin(\omega_1 t - 120^0) \qquad (4\text{-}23)$$

$$d_C(t) = \frac{1}{2} + \frac{1}{2}\frac{\hat{V}_c}{\hat{V}_{tri}}\sin(\omega_1 t - 240^0)$$

The converter, in terms of the average quantities, is shown in Fig. 4-12b, where

$$\overline{v}_{AN}(t) = \frac{V_d}{2} + \frac{V_d}{2}\frac{\hat{V}_c}{\hat{V}_{tri}}\sin(\omega_1 t)$$

$$\overline{v}_{BN}(t) = \frac{V_d}{2} + \frac{V_d}{2}\frac{\hat{V}_c}{\hat{V}_{tri}}\sin(\omega_1 t - 120^0) \qquad (4\text{-}24)$$

$$\overline{v}_{CN}(t) = \frac{V_d}{2} + \frac{V_d}{2}\frac{\hat{V}_c}{\hat{V}_{tri}}\sin(\omega_1 t - 240^0)$$

In the above analysis, the phase angle for phase-A is arbitrarily assumed to be zero; in fact, it can be whatever value is desired. We should also note that the dc-offsets of Eq. 4-24 also cancel each other in the line-to-line voltages v_{AB}, v_{BC}, and v_{CA}.

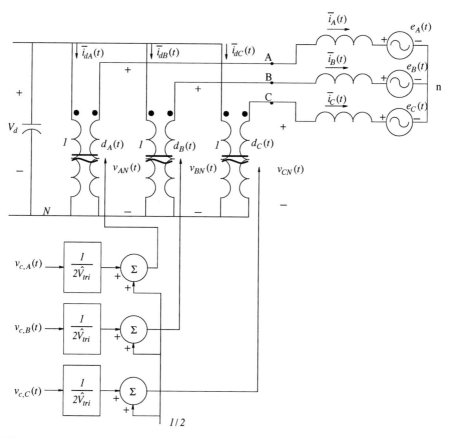

Figure 4-12 (b) Average representation of the three-phase converter.

Under a balanced sinusoidal operating condition, we can show that the *average* potential at the load-neutral "n" is the same as the mid-point of the dc bus, that is, $\overline{v}_{nN} = V_d/2$. Therefore, the average voltages appearing across each phase of the load (from phase to load-neutral) are similar to those in Eq. 4-24, except without the dc-offset of $V_d/2$:

$$\overline{v}_{An}(t) = \underbrace{\left(\frac{V_d}{2\hat{V}_{tri}}\right)}_{k_{pole}} \hat{V}_c \sin(\omega_1 t) = k_{pole} v_{c,A}(t) \tag{4-25a}$$

$$\overline{v}_{Bn}(t) = \underbrace{\left(\frac{V_d}{2\hat{V}_{tri}}\right)}_{k_{pole}} \hat{V}_c \sin(\omega_1 t - 120^0) = k_{pole} v_{c,B}(t) \tag{4-25b}$$

$$\bar{v}_{Cn}(t) = \left(\frac{V_d}{2\hat{V}_{tri}}\right)\hat{V}_c \sin(\omega_1 t - 240^0) = k_{pole}v_{c,C}(t) \qquad (4\text{-}25c)$$

$$\underbrace{\quad\quad\quad}_{k_{pole}}$$

where $k_{pole} = \dfrac{V_d}{2\hat{V}_{tri}}$ (as given by Eq. 4-9) is the gain by which each pole amplifies

its control voltage. Eq. 4-25 shows that the converter for ac-motor drives generates three-phase sinusoidal voltages of the desired frequency and amplitude.

4-7 POWER SEMICONDUCTOR DEVICES

Electric drives owe their market success, in part, to rapid improvements in power semiconductor devices and control ICs. Switch-mode power electronic converters require diodes and transistors, which are controllable switches that can be turned on and off by applying a small voltage to their gates. These power devices are characterized by the following quantities:

1.   Voltage Rating is the maximum voltage that can be applied across a device in its *off*-state, beyond which the device "breaks down" and an irreversible damage occurs.

2.   Current Rating is the maximum current (expressed as instantaneous, average, and/or rms) that a device can carry, beyond which excessive heating within the device destroys it.

3.   Switching Speeds are the speeds with which a device can make a transition from its *on*-state to *off*-state, or vice versa. Small switching times associated with fast-switching devices result in low switching losses, or considering it differently, fast-switching devices can be operated at high switching frequencies.

4.   *On*-State Voltage is the voltage drop across a device during its on-state while conducting a current. The smaller this voltage is, the smaller the on-state power loss.

4-7-1 Device Ratings

Available power devices range in voltage ratings of several kV (up to 9 kV) and current ratings of several kA (up to 5 kA). Moreover, these devices can be connected in series and parallel to satisfy any voltage and current requirements. Their switching speeds range from a fraction of a microsecond to a few microseconds, depending on their other ratings. In general, higher power devices switch more slowly than their low power counterparts. The *on*-state voltage is usually in the range of 1 to 3 volts.

4-7-2 Power Diodes

Power diodes are available in voltage ratings of several kV (up to 9 kV) and current ratings of several kA (up to 5 kA). The on-state voltage drop across these diodes is usually of the order of 1 V. Switch-mode converters used in motor drives require fast-switching diodes. On the other hand, the diode rectification of line-frequency ac can be accomplished by slower switching diodes, which have a slightly lower *on*-state voltage drop.

4-7-3 Controllable Switches

Transistors are controllable switches which are available in several forms: Bipolar-Junction Transistors (BJTs), metal-oxide-semiconductor field-effect transistors (MOSFETs), Gate Turn Off (GTO) thyristors, and insulated-gate bipolar transistor (IGBTs). In switch-mode converters for motor-drive applications, there are two devices which are primarily used: MOSFETs at low power levels and IGBTs in power ranges extending to MW levels. The following subsections provide a brief overview of their characteristics and capabilities.

4-7-3-1 MOSFETs

In applications at voltages below 200 volts and switching frequencies in excess of 50 kHz, MOSFETs are clearly the device of choice because of their low *on*-state losses in low voltage ratings, their fast switching speeds, and their ease of control. The circuit symbol of an n-channel MOSFET is shown in Fig. 4-13a. It consists of three terminals: drain (D), source (S), and gate (G). The main current flows between the drain and the source terminals. MOSFET i-v characteristics for various gate voltage values are shown in Fig. 4-13b; it is fully *off* and approximates an open switch when the gate-source voltage is zero. To turn the MOSFET *on* completely, a positive gate-to-source voltage, typically in a range of 10 to 15 volts, must be applied. This gate-source voltage should be continuously applied in order to keep the MOSFET in its *on*-state.

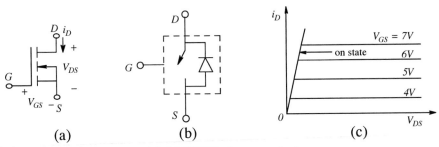

Figure 4-13 MOSFET characteristics.

4-7-3-2 Insulated-Gate Bipolar Transistors (IGBTs)

IGBTs combine the ease of control of MOSFETs with low *on*-state losses, even at fairly high voltage ratings. Their switching speeds are sufficiently fast for switching frequencies up to 30 *kHz*. Therefore, they are used in a vast voltage and power range - from a fractional *kW* to many *MW*.

The circuit symbol for an IGBT is shown in Fig. 4-14a and the *i-v* characteristics are shown in Fig. 4-14b. Similar to MOSFETs, IGBTs have a high impedance gate, which requires only a small amount of energy to switch the device. IGBTs have a small *on*-state voltage, even in devices with large blocking-voltage ratings (for example, V_{on} is approximately 2 *V* in 1200-V devices). IGBTs can be designed to block negative voltages, but most commercially available IGBTs, by design to improve other properties, cannot block any appreciable reverse-polarity voltage (similar to MOSFETs).

Insulated-gate bipolar transistors have turn-on and turn-off times on the order of 1 microsecond and are available as modules in ratings as large as 3.3 *kV* and 1200 *A*. Voltage ratings of up to 5 *kV* are projected.

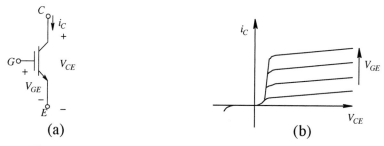

Figure 4-14 IGBT symbol and characteristics.

4-7-4   "Smart Power" Modules including Gate Drivers

A gate-drive circuitry, shown as a block in Fig. 4-15, is required as an intermediary to interface the control signal coming from a microprocessor or an analog control integrated circuit (IC) to the power semiconductor switch. Such gate-drive circuits require many components, passive as well as active. An electrical isolation may also be needed between the control-signal circuit and the circuit in which the power switch is connected. The gate-driver ICs, which include all of these components in one package, have been available for some time.

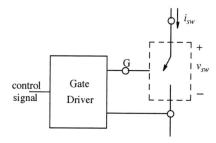

Figure 4-15 Block diagram of gate-drive circuit.

Lately, "Smart Power" modules, also called Power Integrated Modules (PIMs), have become available. Smart power modules combine more than one power switch and diode, along with the required gate-drive circuitry, into a single module. These modules also include fault protection and diagnostics. Such modules immensely simplify the design of power electronic converters.

4-7-5 Cost of MOSFETs and IGBTs

As these devices evolve, their relative cost continues to decline. The cost of single devices in 1999 was approximately 0.25 $/A for 600-V devices and 0.50 $/A for 1200-V devices. Power modules for the 3 kV class of devices cost approximately 1 $/A.

SUMMARY/REVIEW QUESTIONS

1. What is the function of PPUs?
2. What are the sub-blocks of PPUs?
3. What are the roles of the rectifier and the filter-capacitor sub-blocks?
4. Qualitatively, how does a switch-mode amplifier differ from a linear amplifier?
5. Why does operating transistors as switches result in much smaller losses compared to operating them in their linear region?
6. How is a bi-positional switch realized in a converter pole?
7. What is the gain of each converter pole?
8. How does a switch-mode converter pole approach the output of a linear amplifier?
9. What is the meaning of $\overline{v}_{AN}(t)$?
10. How is the pole output voltage made linearly proportional to the input control signal?
11. What is the physical significance of the duty-ratio, for example $d_A(t)$?
12. How is pulse-width-modulation (PWM) achieved and what is its function?
13. Instantaneous quantities on the two sides of the converter pole, for example pole-A, are related by the switching signal $q_A(t)$. What relates the average quantities on the two sides?
14. What is the equivalent model of a switch-mode pole in terms of its average quantities?
15. How is a switch-mode dc-dc converter which can achieve an output voltage of either polarity and an output current flowing in either direction realized?
16. What is the frequency content of the output voltage waveform in dc-dc converters?

17. In a dc-drive converter, how is it possible to keep the ripple in the output current small, despite the output voltage pulsating between 0 and V_d, or 0 and $-V_d$, during each switching cycle?

18. What is the frequency content of the input dc current? Where does the pulsating ripple component of the dc-side current flow through?

19. How is bi-directional power flow achieved through a converter pole?

20. What makes the average of the dc-side current in a converter pole related to the average of the output current by its duty-ratio?

21. How are three-phase, sinusoidal ac output voltages synthesized from a dc voltage input?

22. What are the voltage and current ratings and the switching speeds of various power semiconductor devices?

REFERENCES

1. N. Mohan, T. Undeland, and W. P. Robbins, *Power Electronics: Converters, Applications and Design*, 2nd edition, 1995, John Wiley & Sons, New York, NY.

2. N. Mohan, Power Electronics: *Computer Simulation, Analysis and Education using PSpice*, January 1998, distributed through www.mnpere.com.

3. Proceedings of the NSF-Faculty Workshop, *Teaching of First Courses on Power Electronics*, University of Minnesota, June 25-28, 1998.

4. N. Mohan, A 4-1/2 hour video course on *Power Electronics (parts 1 and 2, approximately 2 hours long)*, distributed through www.mnpere.com.

PROBLEMS

4-1 In a switch-mode converter pole-A, $V_d = 150V$, $\hat{V}_{tri} = 5V$, and $f_s = 20\,kHz$. Calculate the values of the control signal $v_{c,A}$ and the pole duty-ratio d_A during which the switch is in its top position, for the following values of the average output voltage: $\overline{v}_{AN} = 125V$ and $\overline{v}_{AN} = 50V$.

4-2 In a converter pole, the $i_A(t)$ waveform is as shown in Fig. 4-4a. Including the ripple, show that the relationship of Eq. 4-11 is valid.

4-3   A switch-mode dc-dc converter uses a PWM-controller IC which has a triangular waveform signal at 25 kHz with $\hat{V}_{tri} = 3$ V. If the input dc source voltage $V_d = 150V$, calculate the gain k_{PWM} of this switch-mode amplifier.

4-4   In a switch-mode dc-dc converter, $\dfrac{v_c}{\hat{V}_{tri}} = 0.8$ with a switching frequency $f_s = 20\,kHz$ and $V_d = 150V$. Calculate and plot the ripple in the output voltage $v_o(t)$.

4-5   A switch-mode dc-dc converter is operating at a switching frequency of 20 kHz, and V_d = 150 V. The average current being drawn by the dc motor is 8.0 A. In the equivalent circuit of the dc motor, E_a = 100 V, R_a = 0.25 Ω, and L_a = 4 mH. (a) Plot the output current and calculate the peak-to-peak ripple and (b) plot the dc-side current.

4-6   In Problem 4-5, the motor goes into regenerative braking mode. The average current being supplied by the motor to the converter during braking is 8.0 A. Plot the voltage and current waveforms on both sides of this converter. Calculate the average power flow into the converter.

4-7   In Problem 4-5, calculate $\overline{i}_{dA}$, $\overline{i}_{dB}$, and $\overline{i}_d(=I_d)$.

4-8   Repeat Problem 4-5 if the motor is rotating in the reverse direction, with the same current draw and the same induced emf E_a value of the opposite polarity.

4-9   Repeat Problem 4-8 if the motor is braking while it has been rotating in the reverse direction. It supplies the same current and produces the same induced emf E_a value of the opposite polarity.

4-10 Repeat problem 4-5 if a bi-polar voltage switching is used in the dc-dc converter. In such a switching scheme, the two bi-positional switches are operated in such a manner that when switch-A is in the top position, switch-B is in its bottom position, and vice versa. The switching signal for pole-A is derived by comparing the control voltage (as in Problem 4-5) with the triangular waveform.

4-11 Plot $d_A(t)$ if the output voltage of the converter pole-A is

$$\overline{v}_{AN}(t) = \frac{V_d}{2} + 0.85\frac{V_d}{2}\sin(\omega_1 t), \text{ where } \omega_1 = 2\pi \times 60\, rad/s.$$

4-12 In the three-phase dc-ac inverter of Fig. 4-12a, $V_d = 300V$, $\hat{V}_{tri} = 1V$, $\hat{V}_c = 0.75V$, and $f_1 = 45\,Hz$. Calculate and plot $d_A(t), d_B(t), d_C(t)$, $\overline{v}_{AN}(t), \overline{v}_{BN}(t), \overline{v}_{CN}(t)$, and $\overline{v}_{An}(t)$, $\overline{v}_{Bn}(t)$, and $\overline{v}_{Cn}(t)$.

4-13 In the balanced three-phase dc-ac inverter shown in Fig. 4-12b, the phase-A average output voltage is $\overline{v}_{An}(t) = \frac{V_d}{2}0.75\sin(\omega_1 t)$, where $V_d = 300V$ and $\omega_1 = 2\pi \times 45\, rad/s$. The inductance L in each phase is 5 mH. The ac-motor internal voltage in phase A can be represented as $e_A(t) = 106.14\sin(\omega_1 t - 6.6^0)V$, assuming this internal voltage to be purely sinusoidal. (a) Calculate and plot $d_A(t)$, $d_B(t)$, and $d_C(t)$, (b) sketch $\overline{i}_A(t)$, and (c) sketch $\overline{i}_{dA}(t)$.

4-14 In Problem 4-13, calculate and plot $\overline{i}_d(t)$, which is the average dc current drawn from the dc capacitor bus in Fig. 4-12b.

SIMULATION PROBLEMS

4-15 In a switch-mode converter pole-A, $V_d = 300V$ and $\hat{V}_{tri} = 5V$. The values of f_s are specified below. The control voltage $v_c(t)$ is a sine wave, with an amplitude $\hat{V}_c = 3.75V$ and $f_1 = 60\,Hz$. With respect to a hypothetical mid-point "o" of the dc input bus voltage, the idealized pole output is given as $\overline{v}_{Ao}(t) = \underbrace{\frac{V_d/2}{\hat{V}_{tri}}}_{k_{pole}} v_c(t)$. Now, assume that the control voltage has a discrete and constant value during each switching-frequency time-period T_s. This value equals the value of the control voltage at the beginning of each T_s. Based on these discrete values of the control voltage, calculate the average value $\bar{v}_{Ao,k}$ over every k-th switching time-period. Plot $\bar{v}_{Ao}(t)$ and $\bar{v}_{Ao,k}$. In a separate figure, plot the difference of these two output voltage values. Repeat this procedure for two values of switching frequency, where both values are chosen to be extremely low (for modern power semiconductor devices) for ease of plotting: (a) $f_s = 900\,Hz$ and (b) $f_s = 1.8\,kHz$. Which switching-frequency value leads to a better approximation of the idealized output? What would you expect if the switching frequency is increased to 18 kHz?

4-16 Simulate a two-quadrant pole of Fig. 4-6a in dc steady state. The nominal values are as follows: $V_d = 200\ V$, $R_a = 0.37\,\Omega$, $L_a = 1.5\ mH$, $E_a = 136\ V$, $\hat{V}_{tri} = 1\ V$, and $v_{c,A} = 0.416\ V$. The switching frequency $f_s = 20\,kHz$. In dc steady state, the average output current is $I_A = 10\,A$. (a) Obtain the plot of $v_{AN}(t)$, $i_A(t)$, and $i_{dA}(t)$, (b) obtain the peak-peak ripple in $i_A(t)$ and compare it with its value obtained analytically, and (c) obtain the average values of $i_A(t)$ and $i_{dA}(t)$, and show that these two averages are related by the duty-ratio d_A.

4-17 Repeat Problem 4-16 by calculating the value of the control voltage such that the converter pole is operating in the boost mode, with $I_A = -10\,A$.

DC-DC Converters

4-18 Simulate the dc-dc converter of Fig. 4-11a in dc steady state. The nominal values are as follows: $V_d = 200\ V$, $R_a = 0.37\,\Omega$, $L_a = 1.5\ mH$, $\hat{V}_{tri} = 1V$, and $v_{c,A} = 0.416\ V$. The switching frequency $f_s = 20\,kHz$. In the dc steady state, the average output current is $I_A = 10\,A$. (a) Obtain the plot of $v_o(t)$, $i_o(t)$, and $i_d(t)$, (b) obtain the peak-peak ripple in $i_o(t)$ and compare it with its value obtained analytically, and (c) obtain the average values of $i_o(t)$ and $i_d(t)$, and show that these two averages are related by the duty-ratio d in Eq. 4-21.

4-19 In Problem 4-18, apply a step-increase in the control voltage to 0.6 V at 0.5 ms and observe the output current response.

4-20 Repeat Problem 4-19 with each converter pole represented on its average basis.

DC-to-Three-Phase AC Inverters

4-21 Simulate the three-phase ac inverter on an average basis for the system described in Problem 4-13. Obtain the various waveforms.

4-22 Repeat Problem 4-21 for a corresponding switching circuit and compare the switching waveforms with the average waveforms in Problem 4-21.

CHAPTER 5

MAGNETIC CIRCUITS

5-1   INTRODUCTION

The purpose of this chapter is to review some of the basic concepts associated with magnetic circuits and to develop an understanding of transformers, which is needed for the study of ac motors and generators.

5-2   MAGNETIC FIELD PRODUCED BY CURRENT-CARRYING CONDUCTORS

When a current i is passed through a conductor, a magnetic field is produced. The direction of the magnetic field depends on the direction of the current. As shown in Fig. 5-1a, the current through a conductor, perpendicular and *into* the paper plane, is represented by "$\times$"; this current produces magnetic field in a clockwise direction. Conversely, the current *out of* the paper plane, represented by a dot, produces magnetic field in a counter-clockwise direction, as shown in Fig. 5-1b.

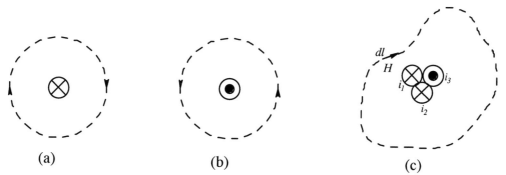

(a)   (b)   (c)

Figure 5-1 Magnetic field; Ampere's Law.

5-2-1 Ampere's Law

The magnetic-field intensity H produced by current-carrying conductors can be obtained by means of Ampere's Law, which in its simplest form states that, at anytime, the line (contour) integral of the magnetic field intensity along *any* closed path equals the total current enclosed by this path. Therefore, in Fig. 5-1c,

$$\oint Hd\ell = \Sigma i \tag{5-1}$$

where $\oint$ represents a contour or a closed-line integration. Note that the scalar H in Eq. 5-1 is the component of the magnetic field intensity (a vector field) in the direction of the differential length $d\ell$ along the closed path. Alternatively, we can express the field intensity and the differential length to be vector quantities, which will require a dot product on the left side of Eq. 5-1.

▲ **Example 5-1** Consider the coil in Fig. 5-2, which has $N = 25$ turns. The toroid on which the coil is wound has an inside diameter $ID = 5\,cm$ and an outside diameter $OD = 5.5\,cm$. For a current $i = 3\,A$, calculate the field intensity H along the mean-path length within the toroid.

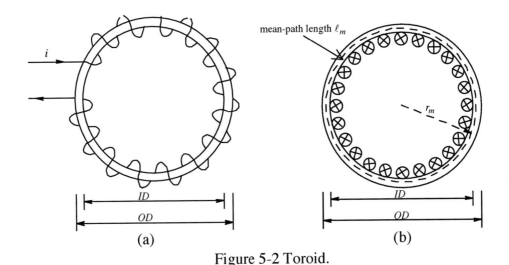

Figure 5-2 Toroid.

Solution   Due to symmetry, the magnetic field intensity H_m along a circular contour within the toroid is constant.   In Fig. 5-2, the mean radius $r_m = \frac{1}{2}(\frac{OD+ID}{2})$. Therefore, the mean path of length $\ell_m (= 2\pi r_m = 0.165\,m)$ encloses the current i N-times, as shown in Fig. 5-2b. Therefore, from Ampere's Law in Eq. 5-1, the field intensity along this mean path is

$$H_m = \frac{Ni}{\ell_m}$$ (5-2)

which for the given values can be calculated as

$$H_m = \frac{25 \times 3}{0.165} = 454.5\ A/m.$$

If the width of the toroid is much smaller than the mean radius r_m, it is reasonable to assume a uniform H_m throughout the cross-section of the toroid.   ▲

The field intensity in Eq. 5-2 has the units of [A/m], noting that "turns" is a unit-less quantity. The product Ni is commonly referred to as the ampere-turns or mmf F that produces the magnetic field. The current in Eq. 5-2 may be dc, or time varying. If the current is time varying, the relationship in Eq. 5-2 is valid on an instantaneous basis; that is, $H_m(t)$ is related to $i(t)$ by N/ℓ_m.

5-3   FLUX DENSITY B AND THE FLUX ϕ

At any instant of time t for a given H-field, the density of flux lines, called the flux density B (in units of $[T]$ for Tesla) depends on the permeability μ of the material on which this H-field is acting. In air,

$$B = \mu_o H \qquad \mu_o = 4\pi \times 10^{-7} \left[\frac{henries}{m}\right]$$ (5-3)

where μ_o is the permeability of air or free space.

5-3-1   Ferromagnetic Materials

Ferromagnetic materials guide magnetic fields and, due to their high permeability, require small ampere-turns (a small current for a given number of turns) to produce the desired flux density. These materials exhibit the multi-valued nonlinear behavior shown by their *B-H* characteristics in Fig. 5-3a. Imagine that the toroid in Fig. 5-2 consists of a ferromagnetic material such as silicon steel. If the current through the coil is slowly varied in a sinusoidal manner with time, the corresponding H-field will cause one of the hysteresis loops shown in Fig. 5-3a to be traced. Completing the loop once results in a net dissipation of energy within the material, causing power loss referred as the hysteresis loss.

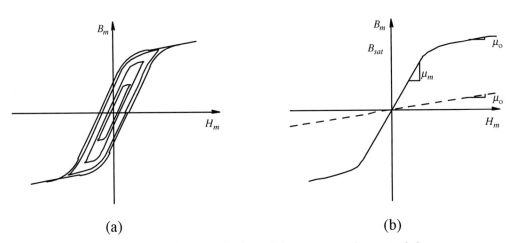

(a)   (b)

Figure 5-3 *B-H* characteristics of ferromagnetic materials.

Increasing the peak value of the sinusoidally-varying *H*-field will result in a bigger hysteresis loop. Joining the peaks of the hysteresis loop, we can approximate the *B-H* characteristic by the single curve shown in Fig. 5-3b. At low values of magnetic field, the *B-H* characteristic is assumed to be linear with a constant slope, such that

$$B_m = \mu_m H_m \tag{5-4a}$$

where μ_m is the permeability of the ferromagnetic material. Typically, the μ_m of a material is expressed in terms of a permeability μ_r relative to the permeability of air:

$$\mu_m = \mu_r \mu_o \qquad\qquad (\mu_r = \frac{\mu_m}{\mu_o}) \qquad\qquad\qquad (5\text{-}4b)$$

In ferromagnetic materials, the μ_m can be several thousand times larger than the μ_o.

In Fig. 5-3b, the linear relationship (with a constant μ_m) is approximately valid until the "knee" of the curve is reached, beyond which the material begins to saturate. Ferromagnetic materials are often operated up to a maximum flux density, slightly above the "knee" of $1.6\ T$ to $1.8\ T$, beyond which many more ampere-turns are required to increase flux density only slightly. In the saturated region, the incremental permeability of the magnetic material approaches μ_o, as shown by the slope of the curve in Fig. 5-3b.

In this course, we will assume that the magnetic material is operating in its linear region and therefore its characteristic can be represented by $B_m = \mu_m H_m$, where μ_m remains constant.

5-3-2 Flux ϕ

Magnetic flux lines form closed paths, as shown in Fig. 5-4's toroidal magnetic core, which is surrounded by the current-carrying coil. The flux in the toroid can be calculated by selecting a circular area A_m in a plane perpendicular to the direction of the flux lines. As discussed in Example 5-1, it is reasonable to assume a uniform H_m and hence a uniform flux-density B_m throughout the core cross-section. Substituting for H_m from Eq. 5-2 into Eq. 5-4a,

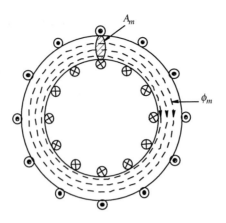

Figure 5-4 Toroid with flux ϕ_m.

$$B_m = \mu_m \frac{Ni}{\ell_m} \qquad (5\text{-}5)$$

where B_m is the density of flux lines in the core. Therefore, making the assumption of a uniform B_m, the flux ϕ_m can be calculated as

$$\phi_m = B_m A_m \qquad (5\text{-}6)$$

where flux has the units of Weber [Wb]. Substituting for B_m from Eq. 5-5 into Eq. 5-6,

$$\phi_m = A_m \left(\mu_m \frac{Ni}{\ell_m} \right) = \frac{Ni}{\underbrace{\left(\dfrac{\ell_m}{\mu_m A_m} \right)}_{\Re_m}} \qquad (5\text{-}7)$$

where Ni equals the ampere-turns (or mmf F) applied to the core, and the term within the brackets on the right side is called the reluctance $\Re_m$ of the magnetic core. From Eq. 5-7

$$\Re_m = \frac{\ell_m}{\mu_m A_m} [A/Wb] \qquad (5\text{-}8)$$

Eq. 5-7 makes it clear that the reluctance has the units $[A/Wb]$. Eq. 5-8 shows that the reluctance of a magnetic structure, for example the toroid in Fig. 5-4, is linearly proportional to its magnetic path length and inversely proportional to both its cross-sectional area and the permeability of its material.

Eq. 5-7 shows that the amount of flux produced by the applied ampere-turns F ($= Ni$) is inversely proportional to the reluctance $\Re$; this relationship is analogous to Ohm's Law ($I = V / R$) in electric circuits in dc steady state.

5-3-3 Flux Linkage

If all turns of a coil, for example the one in Fig. 5-4, are linked by the same flux ϕ, then the coil has a flux linkage λ, where

$$\lambda = N\phi \tag{5-9}$$

▲ **Example 5-2** In Example 5-1, the core consists of a material with $\mu_r = 2000$. Calculate the flux density B_m and the flux ϕ_m.

Solution   In Example 5-1, we calculated that $H_m = 454.5 \, A/m$. Using Eqs. 5-4a and 5-4b,

$$B_m = 4\pi \times 10^{-7} \times 2000 \times 454.5 = 1.14 \, T.$$

The width of the toroid is $\dfrac{OD - ID}{2} = 0.25 \times 10^{-2} \, m$. Therefore, the cross-sectional area of the toroid is

$$A_m = \frac{\pi}{4}(0.25 \times 10^{-2})^2 = 4.9 \times 10^{-6} \, m^2.$$

Hence, from Eq. 5-6, assuming that the flux density is uniform throughout the cross-section,

$$\phi_m = 1.14 \times 4.9 \times 10^{-6} = 5.59 \times 10^{-6} \, Wb .$$ ▲

5-4   MAGNETIC STRUCTURES WITH AIR GAPS

In the magnetic structures of electric machines, the flux lines have to cross two air gaps. To study the effect of air gaps, let us consider the simple magnetic structure of Fig. 5-5 consisting of an N-turn coil on a magnetic core made up of iron. The objective is to establish a desired magnetic field in the air gap of length ℓ_g by controlling the coil current i. We will assume the magnetic field intensity H_m to be uniform along the mean path length ℓ_m in the magnetic core. The magnetic field intensity in the air gap is denoted as H_g. From Ampere's Law in Eq. 5-1, the line integral along the mean path within the core and in the air gap yields the following equation:

$$H_m \ell_m + H_g \ell_g = Ni \tag{5-10}$$

Applying Eq. 5-3 to the air gap and Eq. 5-4a to the core, the flux densities corresponding to H_m and H_g are

$$B_m = \mu_m H_m \quad \text{and} \quad B_g = \mu_o H_g \tag{5-11}$$

In terms of the flux densities of Eq. 5-11, Eq. 5-10 can be written as

$$\frac{B_m}{\mu_m} \ell_m + \frac{B_g}{\mu_o} \ell_g = Ni \tag{5-12}$$

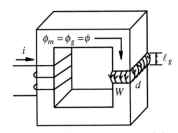

Figure 5-5 Magnetic structure with air gap.

Since flux lines form closed paths, the flux crossing any perpendicular cross-sectional area in the core is the same as that crossing the air gap (neglecting the leakage flux, which is discussed later on). Therefore,

$$\phi = A_m B_m = A_g B_g \tag{5-13}$$

or

$$B_m = \frac{\phi}{A_m} \quad \text{and} \quad B_g = \frac{\phi}{A_g} \tag{5-14}$$

Generally, flux lines bulge slightly around the air gap, as shown in Fig. 5-5. This bulging is called the *fringing effect,* which can be accounted for by estimating the air gap area A_g, which is done by increasing each dimension in Fig. 5-5 by the length of the air gap:

$$A_g = (W + \ell_g)(d + \ell_g) \tag{5-15}$$

Substituting flux densities from Eq. 5-14 into Eq. 5-12,

$$\phi(\frac{\ell_m}{A_m \mu_m} + \frac{\ell_g}{A_g \mu_o}) = Ni \tag{5-16}$$

In Eq. 5-16, we can recognize from Eq. 5-8 that the two terms within the parenthesis equal the reluctances of the core and of the air gap, respectively. Therefore, the effective reluctance $\Re$ of the whole structure in the path of the flux lines is the sum of the two reluctances:

$$\Re = \Re_m + \Re_g \tag{5-17}$$

Substituting from Eq. 5-17 into Eq. 5-16, where Ni equals the applied mmf F,

$$\phi = \frac{F}{\Re} \tag{5-18}$$

Eq. 5-18 allows ϕ to be calculated for the applied ampere-turns (mmf F). Then B_m and B_g can be calculated from Eq. 5-14.

▲ **Example 5-3** In the structure of Fig. 5-5, all flux lines in the core are assumed to cross the air gap. The structure dimensions are as follows: core cross-sectional area $A_m = 20 \, cm^2$, mean path length $\ell_m = 40 \, cm$, $\ell_g = 2 \, mm$, and $N = 75$ turns. In the linear region, the core permeability can be assumed to be constant, with $\mu_r = 4500$. The coil current $i(=30A)$ is below the saturation level. Ignore the flux fringing effect. Calculate the flux density in the air gap, (a) including the reluctance of the core as well as that of the air gap and (b) ignoring the core reluctance in comparison to the reluctance of the air gap.

Solution From Eq. 5-8,

$$\mathfrak{R}_m = \frac{\ell_m}{\mu_o \mu_r A_m} = \frac{40 \times 10^{-2}}{4\pi \times 10^{-7} \times 4500 \times 20 \times 10^{-4}} = 3.54 \times 10^4 \, \frac{A}{Wb}.$$

and

$$\mathfrak{R}_g = \frac{\ell_g}{\mu_o A_g} = \frac{2 \times 10^{-3}}{4\pi \times 10^{-7} \times 20 \times 10^{-4}} = 79.57 \times 10^4 \, \frac{A}{Wb}$$

(a)   Including both reluctances, from Eq. 5-16,

$$\phi_g = \frac{Ni}{\mathfrak{R}_m + \mathfrak{R}_g} \quad \text{and}$$

$$B_g = \frac{\phi_g}{A_g} = \frac{Ni}{(\mathfrak{R}_m + \mathfrak{R}_g) A_g} = \frac{75 \times 30}{(79.57 + 3.54) \times 10^4 \times 20 \times 10^{-4}} = 1.35 \, T.$$

(b)   Ignoring the core reluctance, from Eq. 5-16,

$$\phi_g = \frac{Ni}{\mathfrak{R}_g} \quad \text{and}$$

$$B_g = \frac{\phi_g}{A_g} = \frac{Ni}{\mathfrak{R}_g A_g} = \frac{75 \times 30}{79.57 \times 10^4 \times 20 \times 10^{-4}} = 1.41\ T\ .$$ ▲

This example shows that the reluctance of the air gap dominates the flux and the flux density calculations; thus we can often ignore the reluctance of the core in comparison to that of the air gap.

5-5   INDUCTANCES

At any instant of time in the coil of Fig. 5-6a, the flux linkage of the coil (due to flux lines entirely in the core) is related to the current i by a parameter defined as the inductance L_m:

$$\lambda_m = L_m i \tag{5-19}$$

where the inductance $L_m (= \lambda_m / i)$ is constant if the core material is in its linear operating region.   The coil inductance in the linear magnetic region can be calculated by multiplying all the factors shown in Fig. 5-6b, which are based on earlier equations:

$$L_m = \underbrace{\left(\frac{N}{\ell_m}\right)}_{\text{Eq. 5-2}} \underbrace{\mu_m}_{\text{Eq. 5-4a}} \underbrace{A_m}_{\text{Eq. 5-6}} \underbrace{N}_{\text{Eq. 5-9}} = \frac{N^2}{\left(\dfrac{\ell_m}{\mu_m A_m}\right)} = \frac{N^2}{\mathfrak{R}_m} \tag{5-20}$$

Eq. 5-20 indicates that the inductance L_m is strictly a property of the magnetic circuit (i.e., the core material, the geometry, and the number of turns), provided

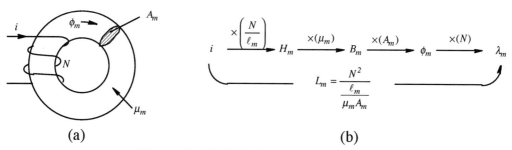

(a)   (b)

Figure 5-6 Coil Inductance.

that the operation is in the linear range of the magnetic material, where the slope of its *B-H* characteristic can be represented by a constant μ_m.

▲ **Example 5-4** In the rectangular toroid of Fig. 5-7, $w = 5\ mm$, $h = 15\ mm$, the mean path length $\ell_m = 18\ cm$, $\mu_r = 5000$, and $N = 100$ turns. Calculate the coil inductance L_m, assuming that the core is unsaturated.

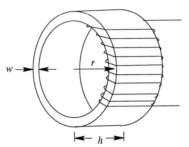

Figure 5-7 Rectangular toroid.

Solution From Eq. 5-8,

$$\mathfrak{R}_m = \frac{\ell_m}{\mu_m A_m} = \frac{0.18}{5000 \times 4\pi \times 10^{-7} \times 5 \times 10^{-3} \times 15 \times 10^{-3}} = 38.2 \times 10^4 \ \frac{A}{Wb}.$$

Therefore, from Eq. 5-20,

$$L_m = \frac{N^2}{\mathfrak{R}_m} = 26.18\ mH.$$ ▲

5-5-1 Magnetic Energy Storage in Inductors

Energy in an inductor is stored in its magnetic field. From the study of electric circuits, we know that at anytime, with a current i, the energy stored in the inductor is

$$W = \frac{1}{2} L_m i^2 \ [J]$$ (5-21)

where $[J]$, for Joules, is a unit of energy. Initially assuming a structure without an air gap, such as in Fig. 5-6a, we can express the energy storage in terms of flux density, by substituting into Eq. 5-21 the inductance from Eq. 5-20 and the current from the Ampere's Law in Eq. 5-2:

$$W_m = \frac{1}{2} \frac{N^2}{\frac{\ell_m}{\mu_m A_m}} \underbrace{(H_m \ell_m / N)^2}_{i^2} = \frac{1}{2} \frac{(H_m \ell_m)^2}{\frac{\ell_m}{\mu_m A_m}} = \frac{1}{2} \frac{B_m^2}{\mu_m} \underbrace{A_m \ell_m}_{volume} \quad [J] \tag{5-22a}$$

where $A_m \ell_m = volume$, and in the linear region $B_m = \mu_m H_m$. Therefore, from Eq. 5-22a, the energy density in the core is

$$w_m = \frac{1}{2} \frac{B_m^2}{\mu_m} \tag{5-22b}$$

Similarly, the energy density in the air gap depends on μ_o and the flux density in it. Therefore, from Eq. 5-22b, the energy density in any medium can be expressed as

$$w = \frac{1}{2} \frac{B^2}{\mu} \quad [J/m^3] \tag{5-23}$$

In electric machines, where air gaps are present in the path of the flux lines, the energy is primarily stored in the air gaps. This is illustrated by the following example.

▲ **Example 5-5** In Example 5-3 part (a), calculate the energy stored in the core and in the air gap and compare the two.

Solution In Example 5-3 part (a), $B_m = B_g = 1.35T$. Therefore, from Eq. 5-23,

$$w_m = \frac{1}{2} \frac{B_m^2}{\mu_m} = 161.1 \ J/m^3$$

and

$$w_g = \frac{1}{2}\frac{B_g^{\,2}}{\mu_o} = 0.725 \times 10^6 \ J/m^3.$$

Therefore,

$$\frac{w_g}{w_m} = \mu_r = 4500.$$

Based on the given cross-sectional areas and lengths, the core volume is 200 times larger than that of the air gap. Therefore, the ratio of the energy storage is

$$\frac{W_g}{W_m} = \frac{w_g}{w_m} \times \frac{(volume)_g}{(volume)_m} = \frac{4500}{200} = 22.5 \qquad \blacktriangle$$

5-6   FARADAY'S LAW: INDUCED VOLTAGE IN A COIL DUE TO TIME-RATE OF CHANGE OF FLUX LINKAGE

In our discussion so far, we have established in magnetic circuits relationships between the electrical quantity i and the magnetic quantities H, B, ϕ, and λ. These relationships are valid under dc (static) conditions, as well as at any instant when these quantities are varying with time. We will now examine the voltage across the coil under time-*varying* conditions. In the coil of Fig. 5-8, Faraday's Law dictates that the time-rate of change of flux-linkage equals the voltage across the coil at any instant:

$$e(t) = \frac{d}{dt}\lambda(t) = N\frac{d}{dt}\phi(t) \qquad\qquad (5\text{-}24)$$

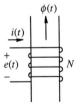

Figure 5-8 Voltage polarity and direction of flux and current.

This assumes that all flux lines link all N-turns such that $\lambda = N\phi$. The polarity of the emf $e(t)$ and the direction of $\phi(t)$ in the above equation are yet to be justified.

The above relationship is valid, no matter what is causing the flux to change. One possibility is that a second coil is placed on the same core. When the second coil is supplied by a time-varying current, mutual coupling causes the flux ϕ through the coil shown in Fig. 5-8 to change with time. The other possibility is that a voltage $e(t)$ is applied across the coil in Fig. 5-8, causing the change in flux, which can be calculated by integrating both sides of Eq. 5-24 with respect to time:

$$\phi(t) = \phi(0) + \frac{1}{N}\int_0^t e(\tau) \cdot d\tau \qquad (5\text{-}25)$$

where $\phi(0)$ is the initial flux at $t = 0$ and τ is a variable of integration.

Recalling the Ohm's Law equation $v = Ri$, the current direction through a resistor is defined to be into the terminal chosen to be of the positive polarity. This is the passive sign convention. Similarly, in the coil of Fig. 5-8, we can establish the voltage polarity and the flux direction in order to apply Faraday's Law, given by Eqs. 5-24 and 5-25. If the flux direction is given, we can establish the voltage polarity as follows: first determine the direction of a hypothetical current that will produce flux in the same direction as given. Then, the positive polarity for the voltage is at the terminal which this hypothetical current is entering. Conversely, if the voltage polarity is given, imagine a hypothetical current entering the positive-polarity terminal. This current, based on how the coil is wound, for example in Fig. 5-8, determines the flux direction for use in Eqs. 5-24 and 5-25. Following these rules to determine the voltage polarity and the flux direction is easier than applying Lenz's Law (not discussed here).

▲ **Example 5-6** In the structure of Fig. 5-8, the flux $\phi_m (= \hat{\phi}_m \sin \omega t)$ linking the coil is varying sinusoidally with time, where $N = 300$ turns, $f = 60\,Hz$, and the cross-sectional area $A_m = 10\,cm^2$. The peak flux density $\hat{B}_m = 1.5\,T$. Calculate the expression for the induced voltage with the polarity shown in Fig. 5-8. Plot the flux and the induced voltage as functions of time.

Solution   From Eq. 5-6,

$$\hat{\phi}_m = \hat{B}_m A_m = 1.5 \times 10 \times 10^{-4} = 1.5 \times 10^{-3} \; Wb \, .$$

From Faraday's Law in Eq. 5-24,

$$e(t) = \omega N \hat{\phi}_m \cos \omega t = 2\pi \times 60 \times 300 \times 1.5 \times 10^{-3} \times \cos \omega t = 169.65 \cos \omega t \; V \, .$$

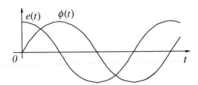

Figure 5-9 Waveforms of flux and induced voltage.

The waveforms are plotted in Fig. 5-9.   ▲

Example 5-6 illustrates that the voltage is induced due to $d\phi / dt$, regardless of whether any current flows in that coil. In the following subsection, we will establish the relationship between $e(t), \phi(t)$, and $i(t)$.

5-6-1   Relating $e(t), \phi(t)$, and $i(t)$

In the coil of Fig. 5-10a, an applied voltage $e(t)$ results in $\phi(t)$, which is dictated by the Faraday's Law equation in the integral form, Eq. 5-25. But what about the current drawn by the coil to establish this flux? Rather than going back to Ampere's Law, we can express the coil flux linkage in terms of its inductance and current using Eq. 5-19:

$$\lambda(t) = Li(t) \tag{5-26}$$

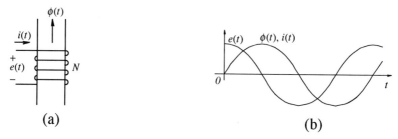

(a)   (b)

Figure 5-10 Voltage, current, and flux.

Assuming that the entire flux links all N turns, the coil flux linkage $\lambda(t) = N\phi(t)$. Substituting this into Eq. 5-26 gives

$$\phi(t) = \frac{L}{N}i(t) \tag{5-27}$$

Substituting for $\phi(t)$ from Eq. 5-27 into Faraday's Law in Eq. 5-24 results in

$$e(t) = N\frac{d\phi}{dt} = L\frac{di}{dt} \tag{5-28}$$

Eqs. 5-27 and 5-28 relate $i(t)$, $\phi(t)$, and $e(t)$; all of these are plotted in Fig. 5-10b.

▲ **Example 5-7** In Example 5-6, the coil inductance is $50\,mH$. Calculate the expression for the current $i(t)$ in Fig. 5-10b.

Solution From Eq. 5-27,

$$i(t) = \frac{N}{L}\phi(t) = \frac{300}{50\times10^{-3}}1.5\times10^{-3}\sin\omega t = 9.0\sin\omega t\ A. \qquad ▲$$

5-7   LEAKAGE AND MAGNETIZING INDUCTANCES

Just as conductors guide currents in electric circuits, magnetic cores guide *flux* in *magnetic circuits*. But there is an important difference. In electric circuits, the conductivity of copper is approximately 10^{20} times higher than that of air, allowing leakage currents to be neglected at dc or at low frequencies such as 60 Hz. In magnetic circuits, however, the permeabilities of magnetic materials are only around 10^4 times greater than that of air. Because of this relatively low ratio, the core window in the structure of Fig. 5-11a has "leakage" flux lines, which do not reach their intended destination - the air gap. Note that the coil shown in Fig. 5-11a is drawn schematically. In practice, the coil consists of multiple layers and the core is designed to fit as snugly to the coil as possible, thus minimizing the unused "window" area.

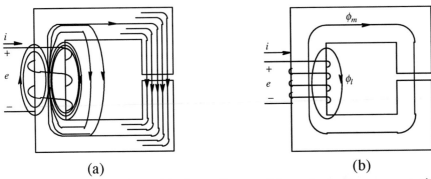

(a)   (b)

Figure 5-11 (a) Magnetic and leakage fluxes; (b) equivalent representation of magnetic and leakage fluxes.

The leakage effect makes accurate analysis of magnetic circuits more difficult, so that it requires sophisticated numerical methods, such as finite element analysis. However, we can account for the effect of leakage fluxes by making certain approximations. We can divide the total flux ϕ into two parts: the magnetic flux ϕ_m, which is completely confined to the core and links all N turns, and the leakage flux, which is partially or entirely in air and is represented by an "equivalent" leakage flux ϕ_ℓ, which also links all N turns of the coil but does not follow the entire magnetic path, as shown in Fig. 5-11b. Thus,

$$\phi = \phi_m + \phi_\ell \tag{5-29}$$

where ϕ is the equivalent flux which links all N turns. Therefore, the total flux linkage of the coil is

$$\lambda = N\phi = \underbrace{N\phi_m}_{\lambda_m} + \underbrace{N\phi_\ell}_{\lambda_\ell} = \lambda_m + \lambda_\ell \tag{5-30}$$

The total inductance (called the self-inductance) can be obtained by dividing both sides of Eq. 5-30 by the current i:

$$\underbrace{\frac{\lambda}{i}}_{L_{self}} = \underbrace{\frac{\lambda_m}{i}}_{L_m} + \underbrace{\frac{\lambda_\ell}{i}}_{L_\ell} \tag{5-31}$$

Therefore,

$$L_{self} = L_m + L_\ell \tag{5-32}$$

where L_m is often called the *magnetizing inductance* due to ϕ_m in the magnetic core, and L_ℓ is called the *leakage inductance* due to the leakage flux ϕ_ℓ. From Eq. 5-32, the total flux linkage of the coil can be written as

$$\lambda = (L_m + L_\ell)i \tag{5-33}$$

Hence, from Faraday's Law in Eq. 5-24,

$$e(t) = L_\ell \frac{di}{dt} + \underbrace{L_m \frac{di}{dt}}_{e_m(t)} \tag{5-34}$$

This results in the circuit of Fig. 5-12a. In Fig. 5-12b, the voltage drop due to the leakage inductance can be shown separately so that the voltage induced in the coil is solely due to the magnetizing flux. The coil resistance R can then be added in series to complete the representation of the coil.

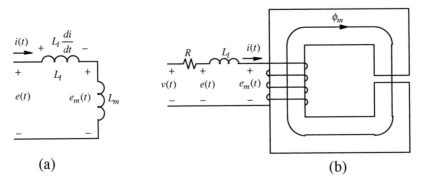

(a)　　　　　　　　　　　　　　　　　(b)

Figure 5-12 (a) Circuit representation;
(b) leakage inductance separated from the core.

5-7-1 Mutual Inductances

Most magnetic circuits, such as those encountered in electric machines and transformers, consist of multiple coils. In such circuits, the flux established by the current in one coil partially links the other coil or coils. This phenomenon can be described mathematically by means of mutual inductances, as examined in circuit theory courses. Mutual inductances are also needed to develop mathematical models for dynamic analysis of electric machines. Since it is not the objective of this book, we will not elaborate any further on the topic of mutual inductances. Rather, we will use simpler and more intuitive means to accomplish the task at hand.

5-8   TRANSFORMERS

Electric machines consist of several mutually-coupled coils where a portion of the flux produced by one coil (winding) links other windings. A transformer consists of two or more tightly-coupled windings where almost all of the flux produced by one winding links the other windings. Transformers are essential for transmission and distribution of electric power. They also facilitate the understanding of ac motors and generators very effectively.

To understand the operating principles of transformers, consider a single coil, also called a winding of N_1 turns, as shown in Fig. 5-13a. Initially, we will assume that the resistance and the leakage inductance of this winding are both zero; the

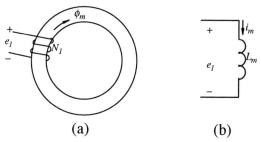

(a)   (b)

Figure 5-13 Magnetizing inductance of a single coil.

second assumption implies that all of the flux produced by this winding is confined to the core. Applying a time-varying voltage e_1 to this winding results in a flux $\phi_m(t)$. From Faraday's Law:

$$e_1(t) = N_1 \frac{d\phi_m}{dt} \tag{5-35}$$

where $\phi_m(t)$ is completely dictated by the time-integral of the applied voltage, as given below (where it is assumed that the flux in the winding is initially zero):

$$\phi_m(t) = \frac{1}{N_1} \int_0^t e_1(\tau) \cdot d\tau \tag{5-36}$$

The current $i_m(t)$ drawn to establish this flux depends on the magnetizing inductance L_m of this winding, as depicted in Fig. 5-13b.

A second winding of N_2 turns is now placed on the core, as shown in Fig. 5-14a. A voltage is induced in the second winding due to the flux $\phi_m(t)$ linking it. From Faraday's Law,

$$e_2(t) = N_2 \frac{d\phi_m}{dt} \tag{5-37}$$

Eqs. 5-35 and 5-37 show that in each winding, the volts-per-turn are the same, due to the same $d\phi_m / dt$:

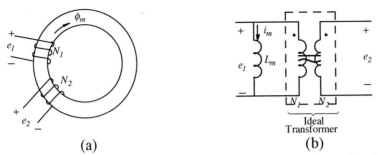

Figure 5-14 (a) Core with two coils; (b) equivalent circuit.

$$\frac{e_1(t)}{N_1} = \frac{e_2(t)}{N_2} \qquad (5\text{-}38)$$

We can represent the relationship of Eq. 5-38 in Fig. 5-14b by means of a hypothetical circuit component called the "ideal transformer," which relates the voltages in the two windings by the turns-ratio N_1 / N_2:

$$\frac{e_1(t)}{e_2(t)} = \frac{N_1}{N_2} \qquad (5\text{-}39)$$

The dots in Fig. 5-14b convey the information that the winding voltages will be of the same polarity at the dotted terminals with respect to their undotted terminals. For example, if ϕ_m is increasing with time, the voltages at both dotted terminals will be positive with respect to the corresponding undotted terminals. The advantage of using this dot convention is that the winding orientations on the core need not be shown in detail.

A load such an R-L combination is now connected across the secondary winding, as shown in Fig. 5-15a. A current $i_2(t)$ will now flow through the R-L combination. The resulting ampere-turns $N_2 i_2$ will tend to change the core flux ϕ_m but *cannot* because $\phi_m(t)$ is completely dictated by the applied voltage $e_1(t)$, as given in Eq. 5-36. Therefore, additional current i_2' in Fig. 5-15b is drawn by winding 1 in order to compensate (or nullify) $N_2 i_2$, such that

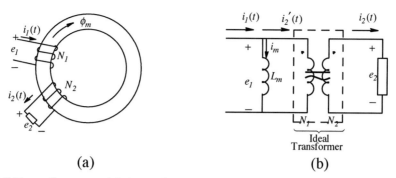

Figure 5-15 Transformer with impedance on the secondary; (b) equivalent circuit.

$$N_1 i_2' = N_2 i_2 \tag{5-40}$$

or

$$\frac{i_2'(t)}{i_2(t)} = \frac{N_2}{N_1} \tag{5-41}$$

This is the second property of the "ideal transformer." Thus, the total current drawn from the terminals of winding 1 is

$$i_1(t) = i_m(t) + i_2'(t) \tag{5-42}$$

In Fig. 5-15, the resistance and the leakage inductance associated with winding 2 appear in series with the R-L load. Therefore, the induced voltage e_2 differs from the voltage v_2 at the winding terminals by the voltage drop across the winding resistance and the leakage inductance, as depicted in Fig. 5-16. Similarly, the applied voltage v_1 differs from the emf e_1 (induced by the time-rate of change of the flux ϕ_m) by the voltage drop across the resistance and the leakage inductance of winding 1.

5-8-1 Core Losses

We can model core losses due to hysteresis and eddy currents by connecting a resistance R_{he} in parallel with L_m, as shown in Fig. 5-16. The loss due to the hysteresis-loop in the B-H characteristic was discussed earlier. Another source of core loss is due to eddy currents. All magnetic materials have a finite electrical resistivity (ideally, it should be infinite). As discussed in section 5-6, which dealt with Faraday's voltage induction law, time-varying fluxes induce voltages in the core, which result in circulating (eddy) currents within the core to oppose these flux changes (and partially neutralize them).

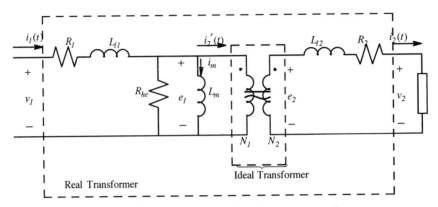

Figure 5-16 Equivalent circuit of a real transformer.

In Fig. 5-17a, an increasing flux ϕ will set up many current loops (due to induced voltages that oppose the change in core flux), which result in losses. The primary means of limiting the eddy-current losses is to make the core out of steel laminations which are insulated from each other by means of thin layers of varnish, as shown in Fig. 5-17b. A few laminations are shown to illustrate how insulated laminations reduce eddy-current losses. Because of the insulation between laminations, the current is forced to flow in much smaller loops within each lamination. Laminating the core reduces the flux and the induced voltage more than it reduces the effective resistance to the currents within a lamination, thus reducing the overall losses. For 50- or 60-Hz operation, lamination thicknesses are typically 0.2 to 1 mm.

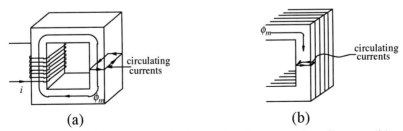

(a)   (b)

Figure 5-17 (a) Eddy currents induced by time varying fluxes; (b) core with insulated laminations.

5-8-2 Real versus Ideal Transformer Models

Consider the equivalent circuit of a real transformer, shown in Fig. 5-16. If we ignore all of the parasitics, such as the leakage inductances and the losses, and if we assume that the core permeability is infinite (thus $L_m = \infty$), then the equivalent circuit of the real transformer reduces to exactly that of the ideal transformer.

5-8-3 Determining Transformer Model Parameters

In order to utilize the transformer equivalent circuit of Fig. 5-16, we need to determine the values of its various parameters. We can obtain these by means of two tests: 1) an open-circuit test and 2) a short-circuit test.

5-8-3-1 Open-Circuit Test

In this test, one of the windings, for example winding 2, is kept open as shown in Fig. 5-18, while winding 1 is applied its rated voltage. The rms input voltage V_{oc}, the rms current I_{oc} and the average power P_{oc} are measured, where the subscript "oc" refers to the open-circuit condition. Under the open-circuit condition, the winding current is very small and is determined by the large magnetizing impedance. Therefore, the voltage drop across the leakage impedance can be neglected, as shown in Fig. 5-18. In terms of the measured quantities, R_{he} can be calculated as follows:

$$R_{he} = \frac{V_{oc}^{\,2}}{P_{oc}} \tag{5-43}$$

The magnitude of the open-circuit impedance in Fig. 5-18 can be calculated as

$$\left| Z_{oc} \right| = \frac{X_m R_{he}}{\sqrt{R_{he}^{\,2} + X_m^2}} = \frac{V_{oc}}{I_{oc}} \tag{5-44}$$

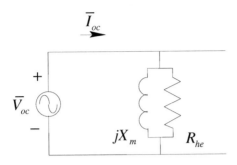

Figure 5-18 Open-circuit test.

Using the measured values V_{oc}, I_{oc}, and R_{he} calculated from Eq. 5-43, we can calculate the magnetizing reactance X_m from Eq. 5-44.

5-8-3-2 Short-Circuit Test

In this test, one of the windings, for example winding 1, is short-circuited, as shown in Fig. 5-19a. A small voltage is then applied to winding 2 and adjusted so that the current in each winding is approximately equal to its rated value. Under this short-circuited condition, the magnetizing reactance X_m and the core-loss resistance R_{he} can be neglected in comparison to the leakage impedance of winding 1, as shown in Fig. 5-19a. In this circuit, the rms voltage V_{sc}, the rms current I_{sc}, and the average power P_{sc} are measured, where the subscript "sc" represents the short-circuited condition.

In terms of voltages, currents, and the turns-ratio defined in Fig. 5-19a,

$$\frac{\overline{E}_2}{\overline{E}_1} = \frac{N_2}{N_1} \qquad \text{and} \qquad \frac{\overline{I}_{sc}}{\overline{I}_1} = \frac{N_1}{N_2} \tag{5-45}$$

Therefore,

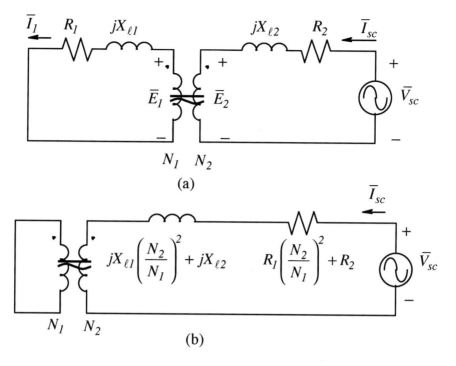

Figure 5-19 Short-circuit test.

$$\frac{\bar{E}_2}{\bar{I}_{sc}} = \frac{\dfrac{N_2}{N_1}\bar{E}_1}{\dfrac{N_1}{N_2}\bar{I}_1}$$

$$= \left(\frac{N_2}{N_1}\right)^2 \frac{\bar{E}_1}{\bar{I}_1} \tag{5-46}$$

Notice that in Eq. 5-46, from Fig. 5-19a

$$\frac{\bar{E}_1}{\bar{I}_1} = R_1 + jX_{\ell1} \tag{5-47}$$

Therefore, substituting Eq. 5-47 into Eq. 5-46,

$$\frac{\bar{E}_2}{\bar{I}_{sc}} = \left(\frac{N_2}{N_1}\right)^2 (R_1 + jX_{\ell1}) \tag{5-48}$$

This allows the equivalent circuit under short-circuited condition in Fig. 5-19a to be drawn as in Fig. 5-19b, where the parasitic components of coil 1 have been moved to coil 2's side and included with coil 2's parasitic components. Having transferred the winding 1 leakage impedance to the side of winding 2, we can effectively replace the ideal transformer portion of Fig. 5-19b with a short. Thus, in terms of the measured quantities,

$$R_2 + \left(\frac{N_2}{N_1}\right)^2 R_1 = \frac{P_{sc}}{I_{sc}^2} \qquad (5\text{-}49)$$

Transformers are designed to produce approximately equal I^2R losses (copper losses) in each winding. This implies that the resistance of a winding is inversely proportional to the square of its rated current. In a transformer, the rated currents are related to the turns-ratio as

$$\frac{I_{1,rated}}{I_{2,rated}} = \frac{N_2}{N_1} \qquad (5\text{-}50)$$

where the turns-ratio is either explicitly mentioned on the name-plate of the transformer or it can be calculated from the ratio of the rated voltages. Therefore,

$$\frac{R_1}{R_2} = \left(\frac{I_{2,rated}}{I_{1,rated}}\right)^2 = \left(\frac{N_1}{N_2}\right)^2$$

or

$$R_1\left(\frac{N_2}{N_1}\right)^2 = R_2 \qquad (5\text{-}51)$$

Substituting Eq. 5-51 into Eq. 5-49,

$$R_2 = \frac{1}{2}\frac{P_{sc}}{I_{sc}^2} \qquad (5\text{-}52)$$

and R_1 can be calculated from Eq. 5-51.

The leakage reactance in a winding is approximately proportional to the square of its number of turns. Therefore,

5-28

$$\frac{X_{\ell 1}}{X_{\ell 2}} = \left(\frac{N_1}{N_2}\right)^2 \qquad \text{or} \qquad \left(\frac{N_2}{N_1}\right)^2 X_{\ell 1} = X_{\ell 2} \tag{5-53}$$

Using Eqs. 5-51 and 5-53 in Fig. 5-19b,

$$\left|Z_{sc}\right| = \sqrt{\left(2R_2\right)^2 + \left(2X_{\ell 2}\right)^2} = \frac{V_{sc}}{I_{sc}} \tag{5-54}$$

Using the measured values V_{sc} and I_{sc}, and R_2 calculated from Eq. 5-52, we can calculate $X_{\ell 2}$ from Eq. 5-54 and $X_{\ell 1}$ from Eq. 5-53.

5-9   PERMANENT MAGNETS

Many electric machines other than induction motors consist of permanent magnets in smaller ratings. However, the use of permanent magnets will undoubtedly extend to machines of higher power ratings, because permanent magnets provide a "free" source of flux, which otherwise has to be created by current-carrying windings that incur i^2R losses in winding resistance. The higher efficiency and the higher power density offered by permanent-magnet machines are very attractive. In recent years, significant advances have been made in Nd-Fe-B material, which has a very attractive magnetic characteristic, shown in comparison to other permanent-magnet materials in Fig. 5-20. Nd-Fe-B magnets offer high flux density operation, high energy densities, and a high ability to resist demagnetization. Decrease in their manufacturing cost, coupled with advances in operation at high temperatures, will allow their application at much higher power ratings than at present.

In the subsequent chapters, as we discuss permanent-magnet machines, it is adequate for us to treat them as a source of flux, which otherwise would have to be established by current-carrying windings.

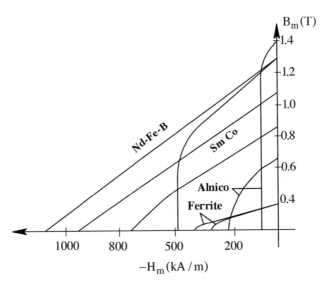

Figure 5-20 Characteristics of various permanent magnet materials.

SUMMARY/REVIEW QUESTIONS

1. What is the role of magnetic circuits? Why are magnetic materials with very high permeabilities desirable? What is the permeability of air? What is the typical range of the relative permeabilities of ferromagnetic materials like iron?

2. Why can "leakage" be ignored in electric circuits but not in magnetic circuits?

3. What is Ampere's Law and what quantity is usually calculated by using it?

4. What is the definition of the mmf F?

5. What is meant by "magnetic saturation"?

6. What is the relationship between ϕ and B?

7. How can magnetic reluctance $\mathfrak{R}$ be calculated? What field quantity is calculated by dividing the mmf F by the reluctance $\mathfrak{R}$?

8. In magnetic circuits with an air gap, what usually dominates the total reluctance in the flux path: the air gap or the rest of the magnetic structure?

9. What is the meaning of the flux linkage λ of a coil?

10. Which law allows us to calculate the induced emf? What is the relationship between the induced voltage and the flux linkage?

11. How is the polarity of the induced emf established?

12. Assuming sinusoidal variations with time at a frequency f, how are the rms value of the induced emf, the peak of the flux linking a coil, and the frequency of variation f related?

13. How does the inductance L of a coil relate Faraday's Law to Ampere's Law?

14. In a linear magnetic structure, define the inductance of a coil in terms of its geometry.

15. What is leakage inductance? How can the voltage drop across it be represented separate from the emf induced by the main flux in the magnetic core?

16. In linear magnetic structures, how is energy storage defined? In magnetic structures with air gaps, where is energy mainly stored?

17. What is the meaning of "mutual inductance"?

18. What is the role of transformers? How is an ideal transformer defined? What parasitic elements must be included in the model of an ideal transformer for it to represent a real transformer?

19. What are the advantages of using permanent magnets?

REFERENCES

1. G. R. Slemon, *Electric Machines and Drives,* Addison-Wesley, 1992.
2. Fitzgerald, Kingsley, and Umans, *Electric Machinery*, 5th edition, McGraw Hill, 1990.

PROBLEMS

5-1 In Example 5-1, calculate the field intensity within the core: a) very close to the inside diameter and b) very close to the outside diameter. c) Compare the results with the field intensity along the mean path.

5-2 In Example 5-1, calculate the reluctance in the path of flux lines if $\mu_r = 2000$.

5-3 Consider the core of dimensions given in Example 5-1. The coil requires an inductance of $25\,\mu H$. The maximum current is $3\,A$ and the maximum flux density is not to exceed $1.3\,T$. Calculate the number of turns N and the relative permeability μ_r of the magnetic material that should be used.

5-4   In Problem 5-3, assume the permeability of the magnetic material to be infinite. To satisfy the conditions of maximum flux density and the desired inductance, a small air gap is introduced. Calculate the length of this air gap (neglecting the effect of flux fringing) and the number of turns N.

5-5   In Example 5-4, calculate the maximum current beyond which the flux density in the core will exceed 0.3 T.

5-6   The rectangular toroid of Fig. 5-7 in Example 5-4 consists of a material whose relative permeability can be assumed to be infinite. The other parameters are as given in Example 5-4. An air gap of 0.05 mm length is introduced. Calculate (a) the coil inductance L_m assuming that the core is unsaturated and (b) the maximum current beyond which the flux density in the core will exceed 0.3 T.

5-7   In Problem 5-6, calculate the energy stored in the core and in the air gap at the flux density of 0.3 T.

5-8   In the structure of Fig. 5-11a, $L_m = 200$ mH, $L_l = 1$ mH, and $N=100$ turns. Ignore the coil resistance. A steady state voltage is applied, where $\overline{V} = \sqrt{2}\times120\angle0V$ at a frequency of 60 Hz. Calculate the current $\overline{I}$ and i(t).

5-9   A transformer is designed to step down the applied voltage of 120 V (rms) to 24 V (rms) at 60 Hz. Calculate the maximum rms voltage that can be applied to the high-side of this transformer without exceeding the rated flux density in the core if this transformer is used in a power system with a frequency of 50 Hz.

5-10 Assume the transformer in Fig. 5-15a to be ideal. Winding 1 is applied a sinusoidal voltage in steady state with $\overline{V}_1 = \sqrt{2}\times120V\angle0^o$ at a frequency f=60 Hz. $N_1 / N_2 = 3$. The load on winding 2 is a series combination of R and L with $Z_L = (5 + j3)\Omega$. Calculate the current drawn from the voltage source.

5-11 Consider the transformer shown in Fig. 5-15a, neglecting the winding resistances, leakage inductances, and the core loss. $N_1 / N_2 = 3$. For a voltage of 120 V (rms) at a frequency of 60 Hz applied to winding 1, the magnetizing current is 1.0 A (rms). If a load of 1.1 Ω at a power factor of 0.866 (lagging) is connected to the secondary winding, calculate $\overline{I}_1$.

5-12   In Problem 5-11, the core of the transformer now consists of a material with a μ_r that is one-half of that in Problem 5-11. Under the operating conditions listed in Problem 5-11, what are the core flux density and the magnetizing current? Compare these values to those in Problem 5-11. Calculate $\overline{I}_1$.

5-13   A 2400 / 240 V, 60-Hz transformer has the following parameters in the equivalent circuit of Fig. 5-16: the high-side leakage impedance is $(1.2 + j\ 2.0)$ Ω, the low-side leakage impedance is $(0.012 + j\ 0.02)$ Ω, and X_m at the high-side is 1800 Ω. Neglect R_{he}. Calculate the input voltage if the output voltage is 240 V (rms) and supplying a load of 1.5 Ω at a power factor of 0.9 (lagging).

5-14   Calculate the equivalent-circuit parameters of a transformer, if the following open-circuit and short-circuit test data is given for a 60-Hz, 50-kVA, 2400:240 V distribution transformer:

open-circuit test with high-side open:

$$V_{OC} = 240\ V,\ I_{OC} = 5.0\ A,\ P_{OC} = 400\ W,$$

short-circuit test with low-side shorted:

$$V_{SC} = 90\ V,\ I_{SC} = 20\ A,\ P_{SC} = 700W.$$

CHAPTER 6

BASIC PRINCIPLES OF ELECTROMECHANICAL ENERGY CONVERSION

6-1 INTRODUCTION

Electric machines, as motors, convert electrical power input into mechanical output, as shown in Fig. 6-1. These machines may be operated solely as generators, but they also enter the generating mode when slowing down (during regenerative braking) where the power flow is reversed. In this chapter, we will briefly look at the basic structure of electric machines and the fundamental principles of the electromagnetic interactions that govern their operation. We will limit our discussion to rotating machines, although the same principles apply to linear machines.

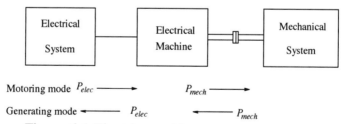

Figure 6-1 Electric machine as an energy converter.

6-2 BASIC STRUCTURE

We often describe electric machines by viewing a cross-section, as if the machine is "cut" by a plane perpendicular to the shaft axis and viewed from one side, as shown in Fig. 6-2a. Because of symmetry, this cross-section can be taken anywhere along the shaft axis. The simplified cross-section in Fig. 6-2b shows

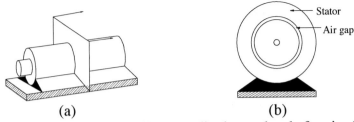

Figure 6-2 Motor construction (a) "cut" perpendicular to the shaft axis; (b) cross-section seen from one side.

that all machines have a stationary part, called the stator, and a rotating part, called the rotor, separated by an air gap, thereby allowing the rotor to rotate freely on a shaft, supported by bearings. The stator is firmly affixed to a foundation to prevent it from turning.

In order to require small ampere-turns to create flux lines shown crossing the air gap in Fig. 6-3a, both the rotor and the stator are made up of high permeability ferromagnetic materials and the length of the air gap is kept as small as possible. In machines with ratings under 10 *kW* in ratings, a typical length of the air gap is about 1 *mm*, which is shown highly exaggerated for ease of drawing.

The stator-produced flux distribution in Fig. 6-3a is shown for a 2-pole machine where the field distribution corresponds to a combination of a single north pole and a single south pole. Often there are more than 2 poles, for example 4 or 6. The flux-distribution in a 4-pole machine is represented in Fig. 6-3b. Due to complete symmetry around the periphery of the airgap, it is sufficient to consider only one pole pair consisting of adjacent north and south poles. Other pole pairs have identical conditions of magnetic fields and currents.

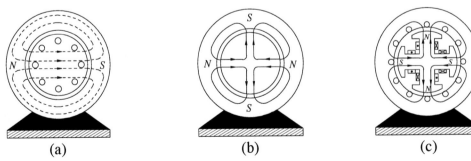

Figure 6-3 Structure of machines.

If the rotor and the stator are perfectly round, the air gap is uniform and the magnetic reluctance in the path of flux lines crossing the air gap is uniform. Machines with such structures are called non-salient pole machines. Sometimes, the machines are purposely designed to have saliency so that the magnetic reluctance is unequal along various paths, as shown in Fig. 6-3c. Such saliency results in what is called the reluctance torque, which may be the primary or a significant means of producing the torque.

We should note that to reduce eddy-current losses, the stator and the rotor often consist of laminations of silicon steel, which are insulated from each other by a layer of thin varnish. These laminations are stacked together, perpendicular to the shaft axis. Conductors which run parallel to the shaft axis may be placed in slots cut into these laminations to place. Readers are urged to purchase a used dc motor and an induction motor and then take them apart to look at their construction.

6-3   PRODUCTION OF MAGNETIC FIELD

We will now examine how coils produce magnetic fields in electric machines. For illustration, a concentrated coil of N_S turns is placed in two stator slots 180^0 (called full-pitch) apart, as shown in Fig. 6-4a. The rotor is present without its electrical circuit. We will consider only the magnetizing flux lines that completely cross the two air gaps, and at present ignore the leakage flux lines. The flux lines *in the air gap* are radial, that is, in a direction which goes through

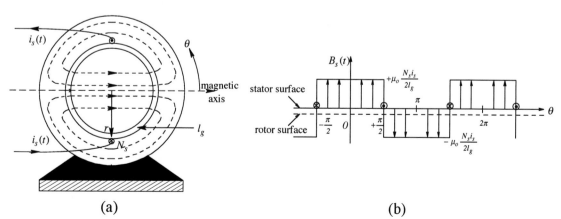

Figure 6-4 Production of magnetic field.

the center of the machine. Associated with the radial flux lines, the field intensity in the air gap is also in a radial direction; it is assumed it to be positive ($+H_S$) if it is away from the center of the machine, otherwise negative ($-H_S$). The subscript "s" (for stator) refers to the field intensity *in the air gap* due to the stator. We will assume the permeability of iron to be infinite, hence the H-fields in the stator and the rotor are zero. Applying Ampere's Law along any of the closed paths shown in Fig. 6-4a, at any instant of time t,

$$\underbrace{H_s \ell_g}_{\text{outward}} - \underbrace{(-H_s)\ell_g}_{\text{inward}} = N_s i_s \qquad \text{or} \qquad H_s = \frac{N_s i_s}{2\ell_g} \qquad\qquad (6\text{-}1)$$

where a negative sign is associated with the integral in the inward direction, because while the path of integration is inward, the field intensity is measured outward. The total mmf acting along any path shown in Fig. 6-4a is $N_s i_s$. Having assumed the permeability of the stator and the rotor iron to be infinite, by symmetry, half of the total ampere-turns ($\frac{N_s i_s}{2}$) are "consumed" or "acting" in making the flux lines cross each air gap length. Hence, the mmf F_s acting on each air gap is

$$F_s = \frac{N_s i_s}{2} \qquad\qquad (6\text{-}2)$$

Substituting for $\frac{N_s i_s}{2}$ from Eq. 6-2 into Eq. 6-1,

$$F_s = H_s \ell_g \qquad\qquad (6\text{-}3)$$

Associated with H_s in the air gap is the flux density B_s, which using Eq. 6-1 can be written as

$$B_s = \mu_o H_s = \mu_o \frac{N_s i_s}{2\ell_g} \qquad\qquad (6\text{-}4)$$

All field quantities (H_s, F_s, and B_s) directed away from the center of the machine are considered positive. Figure 6-4b shows the "developed" view, as if the circular cross-section in Fig. 6-4a were flat. Note that the field distribution is a square wave. From Eqs. 6-1, 6-2, and 6-4, it is clear that all three stator-produced field quantities (H_s, F_s, and B_s) are proportional to the instantaneous value of the stator current $i_s(t)$ and are related to each other by constants. Therefore, in Fig. 6-4b, the square wave plot of B_s distribution at an instant of time also represents H_s and B_s distributions at that time, plotted on different scales.

In the structure of Fig. 6-4a, the axis through $\theta = 0^0$ is referred to as the magnetic axis of the coil or winding that is producing this field. The magnetic axis of a winding goes through the center of the machine in the direction of the flux lines produced by a positive value of the winding current and is perpendicular to the plane in which the winding is located.

▲ **Example 6-1** In Fig 6-4a, consider a concentrated coil with $N_s = 25$ turns, and air gap length $\ell_g = 1$ *mm*. The mean radius (at the middle of the air gap) is $r = 15$ *cm*, and the length of the rotor is $\ell = 35$ *cm*. At an instant of time t, the current $i_s = 20\,A$. (a) Calculate the H_s, F_s, and B_s distributions in the air gap as a function of θ, and (b) calculate the total flux crossing the air gap.

Solution
(a)   Using Eq. 6-2,

$$F_s = \frac{N_s i_s}{2} = 250\,A{\cdot}turns \ .$$

From Eq. 6-1,

$$H_s = \frac{N_s i_s}{2\ell_g} = 2.5 \times 10^5 \, A/m \ .$$

Finally, using Eq. 6-4,

$$B_s = \mu_o H_s = 0.314\,T\,.$$

Plots of the field distributions are similar to those shown in Fig. 6-4b.

(b) The flux crossing the rotor is $\phi_s = \int B \cdot dA$, calculated over half of the curved cylindrical surface A. The flux density is uniform and the area A is one-half of the circumference times the rotor length: $A = \dfrac{1}{2}(2\pi r)\ell = 0.165\,m^2$. Therefore,

$$\phi_s = B_s \cdot A = 0.0518\,Wb\,.$$ ▲

Note that the length of the air gap in electrical machines is extremely small, typically one to two *mm*. Therefore, we will use the radius r at the middle of the air gap to also represent the radius to the conductors located in the rotor and the stator slots.

6-4 BASIC PRINCIPLES OF OPERATION

There are two basic principles that govern electric machines' operation to convert between electric energy and mechanical work:

1) A force is produced on a current-carrying conductor when it is subjected to an *externally-established* magnetic field.
2) An emf is induced in a conductor moving in a magnetic field.

6-4-1 Electromagnetic Force

Consider the conductor of length ℓ shown in Fig. 6-5a. The conductor is carrying a current i and is subjected to an *externally-established* magnetic field of a uniform flux-density B perpendicular to the conductor length. A force f_{em} is exerted on the conductor due to the electromagnetic interaction between the external magnetic field and the conductor current. The magnitude of this force is given as

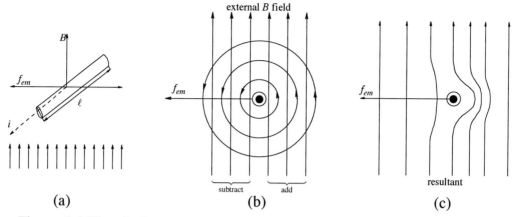

(a)   (b)   (c)

Figure 6-5 Electric force on a current-carrying conductor in a magnetic field.

$$\underbrace{f_{em}}_{[Nm]} = \underbrace{B}_{[T]} \underbrace{i}_{[A]} \underbrace{\ell}_{[m]} \tag{6-5}$$

As shown in Fig. 6-5a, the direction of the force is perpendicular to the directions of both i and B. To obtain the direction of this force, we will superimpose the flux lines produced by the conductor current, which are shown in Fig. 6-5b. The flux lines add up on the right side of the conductor and subtract on the left side, as shown in Fig. 6-5c. Therefore, the force f_{em} acts *from the higher concentration of flux lines to the lower concentration*, that is, from right to left in this case.

▲ **Example 6-2** In Fig. 6-6a, the conductor is carrying a current into the paper plane in the presence of an external, uniform field. Determine the direction of the electromagnetic force.

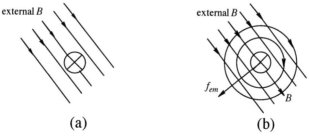

(a)   (b)

Figure 6-6 Figure for Example 6-2.

Solution The flux lines are clockwise and add up on the upper-right side, hence the resulting force shown in Fig. 6-6b. ▲

6-4-2 Induced EMF

In Fig. 6-7a, a conductor of length ℓ is moving to the right at a speed u. The B-field is uniform and is perpendicularly directed into the paper plane. The magnitude of the induced emf at any instant of time is then given by

$$\underset{[V]}{e} = \underset{[T]}{B} \underset{[m]}{l} \underset{[m/s]}{u} \tag{6-6}$$

The polarity of the induced emf can be established as follows: due to the conductor motion, the force on a charge q (positive, or negative in the case of an electron) within the conductor can be written as

$$f_q = q(\mathbf{u} \times \mathbf{B}) \tag{6-7}$$

where the speed and the flux density are shown by bold letters to imply that these are vectors and their cross product determines the force. Since $\mathbf{u}$ and $\mathbf{B}$ are orthogonal to each other, as shown in Fig. 6-7b, the force on a positive charge is upward. Similarly, the force on an electron will be downwards. Thus, the upper end will have a positive potential with respect to the lower end. This induced emf across the conductor is independent of the current that would flow if a closed path were to be available (as would normally be the case). With the current flowing, the voltage across the conductor will be the induced-emf $e(t)$ in Eq. 6-6 minus the voltage drops across the conductor resistance and inductance.

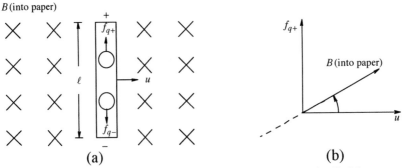

Figure 6-7 Conductor moving in a magnetic field.

▲ **Example 6-3** In Figs. 6-8a and 6-8b, the conductors perpendicular to the paper plane are moving in the directions shown, in the presence of an external, uniform B-field. Determine the polarity of the induced emf.

(a)   (b)

Figure 6-8 Example 6-3.

Solution   The vectors representing **u** and **B** are shown. In accordance with Eq. 6-7, the top side of the conductor in Fig. 6-8a is positive. The opposite is true in Fig. 6-8b.   ▲

6-4-3 Magnetic Shielding of Conductors in Slots

The current-carrying conductors in the stator and the rotor are often placed in slots, which shield the conductors magnetically. As a consequence, the force is mainly exerted on the iron around the conductor. It can be shown, although we will not prove it here, that this force has the same magnitude and direction as it would in the absence of the magnetic shielding by the slot. Since our aim in this course is not to design but rather to utilize electric machines, we will completely ignore the effect of the magnetic shielding of conductors by slots in our subsequent discussions. The same argument applies to the calculation of induced emf and its direction using Eqs. 6-6 and 6-7.

6-5   APPLICATION OF THE BASIC PRINCIPLES

Consider the structure of Fig. 6-9a, where we will assume that the stator has established a uniform field B_s in the radial direction through the air gap. An N_r-turn coil is located on the rotor at a radius r. We will consider the force and the torque acting on the rotor in the counter-clockwise direction to be positive.

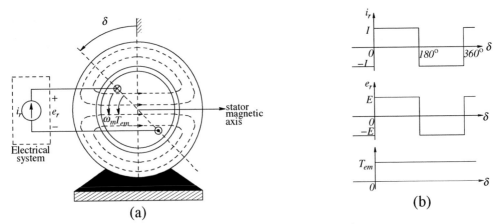

Figure 6-9 Motoring mode.

A current i_r is passed through the rotor coil, which is subjected to a stator-established field B_s in Fig. 6-9a. The coil inductance is assumed to be negligible. The current magnitude I is constant but its direction (details are discussed in Chapter 7) is controlled such that it depends on the location δ of the coil, as plotted in Fig. 6-9b. In accordance with Eq. 6-5, the force on both sides of the coil results in an electromagnetic torque on the rotor in a counter-clockwise direction, where

$$f_{em} = B_s(N_r I)\ell \qquad (6\text{-}8)$$

Thus,

$$T_{em} = 2f_{em}r = 2B_s(N_r I)\ell r \qquad (6\text{-}9)$$

As the rotor turns, the current direction is changed every half-cycle, resulting in a torque that remains constant, as given by Eq. 6-9. This torque will accelerate the mechanical load connected to the rotor shaft, resulting in a speed ω_m. Note that an equal but opposite torque is experienced by the stator. This is precisely the reason for affixing the stator to the foundation - to prevent the stator from turning.

Due to the conductors moving in the presence of the stator field, in accordance with Eq. 6-6, the magnitude of the induced emf at any instant of time in each conductor of the coil is

$$E_{cond} = B_s \ell \underbrace{r\omega_m}_{u} \tag{6-10}$$

Thus, the magnitude of the induced emf in the rotor coil with $2N_r$ conductors is

$$E = 2N_r B_s \ell r\omega_m \tag{6-11}$$

The waveform of the emf e_r, with the polarity indicated in Fig. 6-9a, is similar to that of i_r, as plotted in Fig. 6-9b.

6-6   ENERGY CONVERSION

In this idealized system which has no losses, we can show that the electrical input power P_{el} is converted into the mechanical output power P_{mech}. Using the waveforms of i_r, e_r, and T_{em} in Fig. 6-9b at any instant of time,

$$P_{el} = e_r i_r = (2N_r B_s \ell r\omega_m)I \tag{6-12}$$

and

$$P_{mech} = T_{em}\omega_m = (2B_s N_r I\ell r)\omega_m \tag{6-13}$$

Thus,

$$P_{mech} = P_{el} \tag{6-14}$$

The above relationship is valid in the presence of losses. The power drawn from the electrical source is P_{el}, in Eq. 6-12, plus the losses in the electrical system. The mechanical power available at the shaft is P_{mech}, in Eq. 6-13, minus the losses in the mechanical system. These losses are briefly discussed in section 6-7.

▲ **Example 6-4**   The machine shown in Fig. 6-9a has a radius of 15 *cm* and the length of the rotor is 35 *cm*. The rotor coil has $N_r = 15$ turns, and $B_s = 1.3T$ (uniform). The current i_r, as plotted in Fig. 6-9b, has a magnitude $I = 10$ A. $\omega_m = 100 \, rad/s$. Calculate and plot T_{em} and the induced emf e_r. Also, calculate the power being converted.

Solution   Using Eq. 6-9, the electromagnetic torque on the rotor will be in a counter-clockwise direction and of a magnitude

$$T_{em} = 2B_s(N_r I)\ell r = 2 \times 1.3 \times 15 \times 10 \times 0.35 \times 0.15 = 20.5\,Nm$$

The electromagnetic torque will have the waveform shown in Fig. 6-9b. At a speed of $\omega_m = 100\,rad/s$, the electrical power absorbed for conversion into mechanical power is

$$P = \omega_m T_{em} = 100 \times 20.5 \approx 2\,kW \qquad\qquad ▲$$

6-6-1 Regenerative Braking

At a speed ω_m, the rotor inertia, including that of the connected mechanical load, has stored kinetic energy. This energy can be recovered and fed back into the electrical system shown in Fig. 6-10a. In so doing, the current is so controlled as to have the waveform plotted in Fig. 6-10b, as a function of the angle δ. Notice that the waveform of the induced voltage remains unchanged. In this regenerative case, due to the reversal of the current direction (compared to that in the motoring mode), the torque T_{em} is in the clockwise direction (opposing the rotation), and shown to be negative in Fig. 6-10b. Now the input power P_{mech} from the mechanical side equals the output power P_{el} into the electrical system. This direction of power flow represents the generator mode of operation.

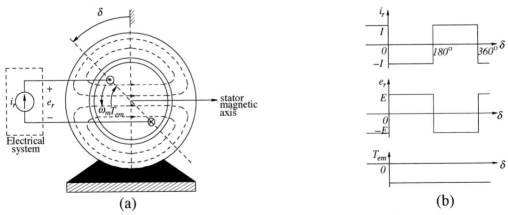

(a)   (b)

Figure 6-10 Regenerative braking mode.

6-7   POWER LOSSES AND ENERGY EFFICIENCY

As indicated in Fig. 6-11, any electric drive has inherent power losses, which are converted into heat. These losses, which are complex functions of the speed and the torque of the machine, are discussed in Chapter 15. If the output power of the drive is P_o, then the input power to the motor in Fig. 6-11 is

$$P_{in,motor} = P_o + P_{loss,motor} \qquad\qquad (6\text{-}15)$$

At any operating condition, let $P_{loss,motor}$ equal all of the losses in the motor. Then the energy efficiency of the motor is

$$\eta_{motor} = \frac{P_o}{P_{in,motor}} = \frac{P_o}{P_o + P_{loss,motor}} \qquad\qquad (6\text{-}16)$$

In the power-processing unit of an electric drive, power losses occur due to current conduction and switching within the power semiconductor devices. Similar to Eq. 6-16, we can define the energy efficiency of the PPU as η_{PPU}. Therefore, the overall efficiency of the drive is such that

$$\eta_{drive} = \eta_{motor} \times \eta_{PPU} \qquad\qquad (6\text{-}17)$$

Energy efficiencies of drives depend on many factors which we will discuss in Chapter 15. The energy efficiency of small to medium sized electric motors ranges from 85 to 93 percent, while that of power-processing units ranges from 93 to 97 percent. Thus, from Eq. 6-17, the overall energy efficiency of drives is in

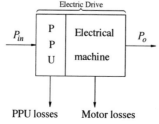

Figure 6-11 Power losses and energy efficiency.

the approximate range of 80 to 90 percent.

6-8   MACHINE RATINGS

Machine ratings specify the limits of speed and torque at which a machine can operate. Usually they are specified for the continuous duty operation. These limits may be higher for intermittent duty and for dynamic operation during brief periods of accelerations and decelerations. Power loss in a machine raises its temperature above the temperature of its surroundings, which is often referred to as the ambient temperature. The ambient temperature is usually taken to be $40°C$. Machines are classified based on the temperature rise that they can tolerate. The temperature should not exceed the limit specified by the machine class. As a rule of thumb, operation at $10°C$ above the limit reduces the motor life expectancy by 50 percent.

The name-plate on the machine usually specifies the continuous-duty, full-load operating point in terms of the full-load torque, called the rated torque, and the full-load speed, called the rated speed. The product of these two values specifies the full-load power, or the rated power:

$$P_{rated} = \omega_{rated} T_{rated} \qquad\qquad (6-18)$$

The maximum speed of a motor is limited due to structural reasons such as the capability of the bearings and the rotor to withstand high speeds. The maximum torque that a motor can deliver is limited by the temperature rise within the motor. In all machines, higher torque output results in larger power losses. The temperature rise depends on power losses as well as cooling. In self-cooled machines, the cooling is not as effective at lower speeds; this reduces the machine torque capability at lower speeds. The torque-speed capability of electrical machines can be specified in terms of a safe operating area (SOA), as shown in Fig. 6-12. The torque capability declines at lower speeds due to insufficient cooling. An expanded area, both in terms of speed and torque, is usually possible for intermittent duty and during brief periods of acceleration and deceleration.

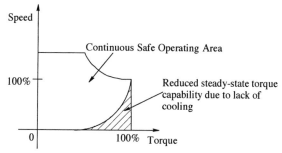

Figure 6-12 Safe Operating Area for electric machines.

In addition to the rated power and speed, the name-plate also specifies the rated voltage, the rated current (at full-load), and in the case of ac machines, the power factor at full load and the rated frequency of operation.

SUMMARY/REVIEW QUESTIONS

1. What is the role of electric machines? What do the motoring-mode and the generating-mode of operations mean?

2. What are the definitions of stator and rotor?

3. Why do we use high permeability ferromagnetic materials for stators and rotors in electric machines? Why are these constructed by stacking laminations together, rather than as a solid structure?

4. What is the approximate air gap length in machines with less than 10 kW ratings?

5. What are multi-pole machines? Why can such machines be analyzed by considering only one pair of poles?

6. Assuming the permeability of iron to be infinite, where is the mmf produced by machine coils "consumed"? What law is used to calculate the field quantities, such as flux density, for a given current through a coil? Why is it important to have a small air gap length?

7. What are the two basic principles of operation for electric machines?

8. What is the expression for force acting on a current-carrying conductor in an externally established B-field? What is its direction?

9. What is slot shielding and why can we choose to ignore it?

10. How do we express the induced emf in a conductor "cutting" an externally established B-field? How do we determine the polarity of the induced emf?

11.   How do electrical machines convert energy from one form to another?

12.   What are various loss mechanisms in electric machines?

13.   How is electrical efficiency defined and what are typical values of efficiencies for the machines, the power-processing units, and the overall drives?

14.   What is the end-result of power losses in electric machines?

15.   What is meant by the various ratings on the name-plates of machines?

REFERENCES

1.   A. E. Fitzgerald, C. Kingsley and S. Umans, *Electric machinery*, 5th edition, McGraw-Hill, Inc., 1990.

2.   G. R. Slemon, *Electric Machines and Drives*, Addison-Wesley, 1992.

PROBLEMS

6-1   Assume the field distribution for the machine shown in Fig. P6-1 to be radially uniform. The magnitude of the air gap flux density is B_s, the rotor length is ℓ, and the rotational speed of the motor is ω_m. (a) Plot the emf $e_{11'}$ induced in the coil as a function of θ for two values of i_a: 0 A and 10 A. (b) In the position shown, the current i_a in the coil 11' equals I_o. Calculate the torque acting on the coil in this position for two values of instantaneous speed ω_m: 0 rad/s and 100 rad/s.

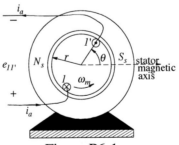

Figure P6-1

6-2   Figure P6-2 shows a primitive machine with a rotor producing a uniform magnetic field such that the air-gap flux density in the radial direction is of the magnitude B_r. Plot the induced emf $e_{11'}$ as a function of θ. The length of the rotor is ℓ and the radius at the air gap is r.

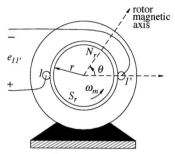
Figure P6-2

6-3   In the primitive machine shown in Fig. P6-3, the air-gap flux density B_s has a sinusoidal distribution given by $B_S = \hat{B}\cos\theta$. The rotor length is ℓ. (a) Given that the rotor is rotated at a speed of ω_m, plot as a function of θ the emf $e_{11'}$ induced and the torque T_{em} acting on the coil if $i_a = I$. (b) In the position shown, the current i_a in the coil equals I. Calculate P_{el}, the electrical power input to the machine, and P_{mech}, the mechanical power output of the machine, if $\omega_m = 60 \ rad/s$.

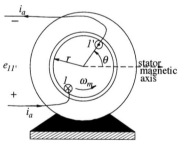
Figure P6-3

6-4   In the machine shown in Fig. P6-4, the air-gap flux density B_r has a sinusoidal distribution given by $B_r = \hat{B} \cos\alpha$, where α is measured with respect to the rotor magnetic axis. Given that the rotor is rotating at an angular speed ω_m and the rotor length is ℓ, plot the emf $e_{11'}$ induced in the coil as a function of θ.

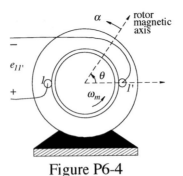

Figure P6-4

6-5 In the machine shown in Fig. P6-5, the air gap flux density B_s is constant and equal to B_{max} in front of the pole faces, and is zero elsewhere. The direction of the B-field is from left (north pole) to right (south pole). The rotor is rotating at an angular speed of ω_m and the length of the rotor is ℓ. Plot the induced emf $e_{11'}$ as a function of θ. What should be the waveform of i_a that produces an optimum electromagnetic torque T_{em}?

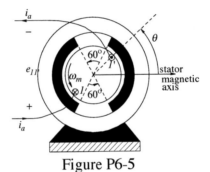

Figure P6-5

6-6 As shown in Fig. P6-6, a rod in a uniform magnetic field is free to slide on two rails. The resistance of the rod and the rails are negligible. Electrical continuity between the rails and the rod is assumed, so a current can flow

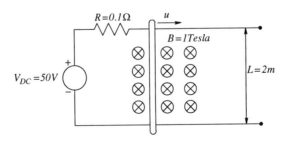

Figure P6-6

through the rod. A damping force, F_d, tending to slow down the rod, is proportional to the square of the rod's speed as follows: $F_d = k_f u^2$ where $k_f = 1500$. Assume that the inductance in this circuit can be ignored. Find the steady state speed u of the rod, assuming the system extends endlessly to the right.

6-7 Consider Fig. P6-7. Plot the mmf distribution in the air gap as a function of θ for $i_a = I$. Assume each coil has a single turn.

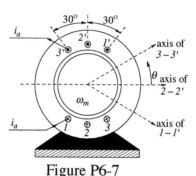

Figure P6-7

6-8 In Fig. P6-8, the stator coil has N_s turns and the rotor coil has N_r turns. Each coil produces in the air gap a uniform, radial flux density B_s and B_r, respectively. In the position shown, calculate the torque experienced by both the rotor coil and the stator coil, due to the currents i_s and i_r flowing through these coils. Show that the torque on the stator is equal in magnitude but opposite in direction to that experienced by the rotor.

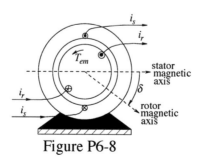

Figure P6-8

CHAPTER 7

DC-MOTOR DRIVES AND ELECTRONICALLY-COMMUTATED MOTOR DRIVES

7-1 INTRODUCTION

Historically, dc-motor drives have been the most popular drives for speed and position control applications. They owe this popularity to their low cost and ease of control. Their demise has been prematurely predicted for many years. However, they are losing their market share to ac drives due to wear in their commutator and brushes, which require periodic maintenance. Another factor in the decline of the market share of dc drives is cost. Figure 7-1 shows the cost distribution within dc drives in comparison to ac drives at present and in the future. In inflation-adjusted dollars, the costs of ac and dc motors are expected to remain nearly constant. For power processing and control, ac drives require more complex electronics (PPUs), making them at present more expensive than in dc-motor drives. However, the cost of drive electronics (PPUs) continues to decrease. Therefore, ac drives are gaining market share over dc drives.

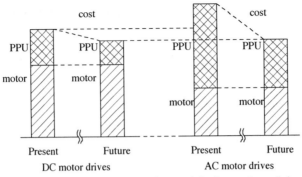

Figure 7-1 Cost distribution with dc and ac drives.

There are two important reasons to learn about dc drives. First, a number of such drives are currently in use and this number keeps increasing. Second, the control of ac-motor drives emulates the operating principles of dc-motor drives. Therefore, knowledge of dc-motor drives forms the first step in learning how to control ac drives.

In a dc-motor drive, dc voltage and current are supplied by a power-processing unit to the dc motor, as shown in the block diagram of Fig. 7-2. There are two designs of dc machines: stators consisting of either permanent magnets or a field winding. The power-processing units can also be classified into two categories: switch-mode power converters that operate at a high switching frequency, as discussed in Chapter 4, or line-commutated, thyristor converters, which are discussed later in Chapter 16. In this chapter, our focus will be on small servo-drives, which usually consist of permanent-magnet motors supplied by switch-mode power electronic converters.

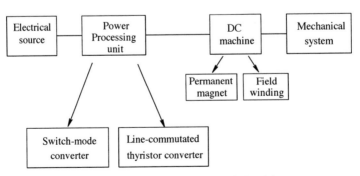

Figure 7-2 Classification of dc drives.

At the end of this chapter, a brief discussion of Electronically-Commutated Motors (ECM) is included as a way of reinforcing the concept of current commutation, as well as a way of introducing an important class of motor drives which do not have the problem of wear in commutator and brushes.

7-2   THE STRUCTURE OF DC MACHINES

Figure 7-3 shows a cut-away view of a dc motor. It shows a permanent-magnet stator, a rotor which carries the armature winding, a commutator, and the brushes. In dc machines, the stator establishes a uniform flux ϕ_f in the air gap in the radial direction (the subscript "f" is for field). If permanent magnets like those shown in the cross-section of Fig. 7-4a are used, the air gap flux density established by the stator remains constant (it cannot be changed). A field winding whose current can be varied can be used to achieve an additional degree of control over the air gap flux density, as shown in Fig. 7-4b.

Figs. 7-3 and 7-5 show that the rotor slots contain a winding, called the armature winding, which handles electrical power for conversion to (or from) mechanical power at the rotor shaft. In addition, there is a commutator affixed to the rotor. On its outer surface, the commutator contains copper segments which are

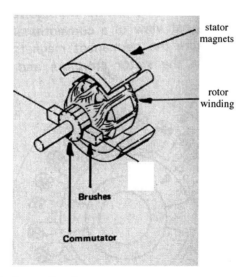

Figure 7-3 Exploded view of a dc motor; source: Engineering Handbook by Electro-Craft Corp [5].

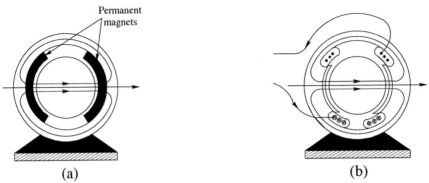

Permanent magnets

(a)   (b)

Figure 7-4 Cross-sectional view of magnetic field produced by stator.

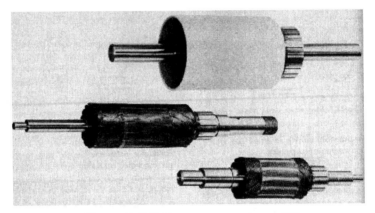

Figure 7-5 DC motor armatures [5].

electrically insulated from each other by means of mica or plastic. The coils of the armature winding are connected to these commutator segments so that a stationary dc source can supply voltage and current to the rotating cummutator by means of stationary carbon brushes which rest on top of the commutator. The wear due to the mechanical contact between the commutator and the brushes requires periodic maintenance, which is the main drawback of dc machines.

7-3   OPERATING PRINCIPLES OF DC MACHINES

The basic principle that governs the production of a steady electromagnetic torque has already been introduced in Chapter 6. A rotor coil in a uniform radial field established by the stator was supplied with a current, which reversed direction every half-cycle of rotation. The induced emf in the coil also alternated every half-cycle.

In practice, this reversal of current can be realized in the dc machine (still primitive) shown in Fig. 7-6a, using two commutator segments (s1 and s2) and two brushes (b1 and b2). Using the notations commonly adopted in the context of dc machines, the armature quantities are indicated by the subscript "a", and the density of the stator-established flux (that crosses the two air gaps) is called the field flux density B_f, whose distribution as function of θ in Fig. 7-6b is plotted in Fig. 7-6c. In the plot of Fig. 7-6c, the uniform flux density B_f in the air gap is assumed to be positive under the south pole and negative under the north pole. There is also a small "neutral" zone where the flux density is small and is changing from one polarity to the other.

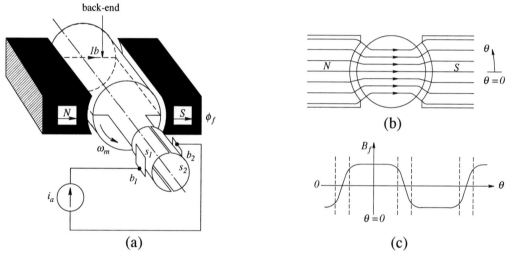

Figure 7-6 Flux density in the air gap.

We will see how the commutator and the brushes in the primitive (non-practical) machine of Fig. 7-6a convert a dc current i_a supplied by a stationary source into an alternating current in the armature coil. The cross-sectional view of this primitive machine, looking from the front, is represented in Fig. 7-7. For the position of the coil at $\theta = 0°$ shown in Fig. 7-7a, the coil current $i_{1-1'}$ is positive and a counter-clockwise force is produced on each conductor. Figure 7-7b shows the cross-section when the rotor has turned counter-clockwise by $\theta = 90°$. The brushes are wider than the insulation between the commutator segments. Therefore, in this elementary machine, the current i_a flows through the

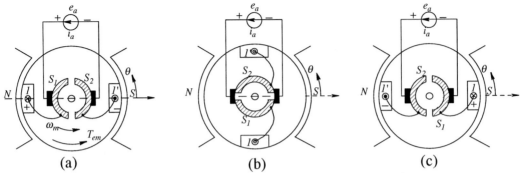

Figure 7-7 Torque production and commutator action.

commutator segments and no current flows through the conductors. In this region, the coil undergoes "commutation" where its current direction reverses as the rotor turns further. Fig. 7-7c shows the cross-section at the rotor position $\theta = 180°$. Compared to Fig. 7-7a at $\theta = 0°$, the roles of conductors 1 and $1'$ are interchanged; hence at $\theta = 180°$, $i_{1-1'}$ is negative and the same counter-clockwise torque as at $\theta = 0°$ is produced.

The above discussion shows how the commutator and brushes convert a dc current at the armature terminals of the machine into a current that alternates every half-cycle through the armature coil. In the armature coil, the induced emf also alternates every half-cycle and is "rectified" at the armature terminals. The current and the induced emf in the coil are plotted in Fig. 7-8a as a function of the rotor position θ. The torque on the rotor and the induced emf appearing at the brush terminals are plotted in Figs. 7-8b and 7-8c where their average values are indicated by the dotted lines. Away from the "neutral zone," the torque and the induced emf expressions, in accordance with Chapter 6, are as follows:

$$T_{em} = (2B_f \ell r)i_a \qquad\qquad (7\text{-}1)$$

and

$$e_a = (2B_f \ell r)\omega_m \qquad\qquad (7\text{-}2)$$

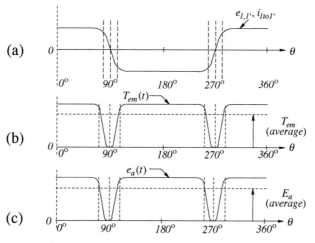

Figure 7-8 Waveforms for the motor in Fig. 7-7.

where ℓ is effective conductor length and r is the radius. Notice the pronounced dip in the torque and the induced emf waveforms. These waveforms are improved by having a large number of distributed coils in the armature, as illustrated in the following example.

▲ **Example 7-1** Consider the elementary dc machine shown in Fig. 7-9 whose stator poles produce a uniform, radial flux density B_f in the air gap. The armature winding consists of 4 coils {1-1', 2-2', 3-3', and 4-4'} in 4 rotor slots. A dc current i_a is applied to the armature as shown. Assume the rotor speed to be ω_m (rad/s). Plot the induced emf across the brushes and the electromagnetic torque T_{em} as a function of the rotor position θ.

Solution   Fig. 7-9 shows three rotor positions measured in a counter-clockwise (CCW) direction: $\theta = 0, 45°$ and $90°$. This figure shows how coils 1 and 3 go through current commutation. At $\theta = 0^o$, the currents are from 1 to 1' and from 3' to 3. At $\theta = 45^o$, the currents in these coils are zero. At $\theta = 90°$, the two currents have reversed direction. The total torque and the induced emf at the brush terminals are plotted in Fig. 7-10.   ▲

If we compare the torque T_{em} and the emf e_a waveforms of the 4-coil winding in Fig. 7-10 to those for the 1-coil winding in Fig. 7-8, it is clear that pulsations in

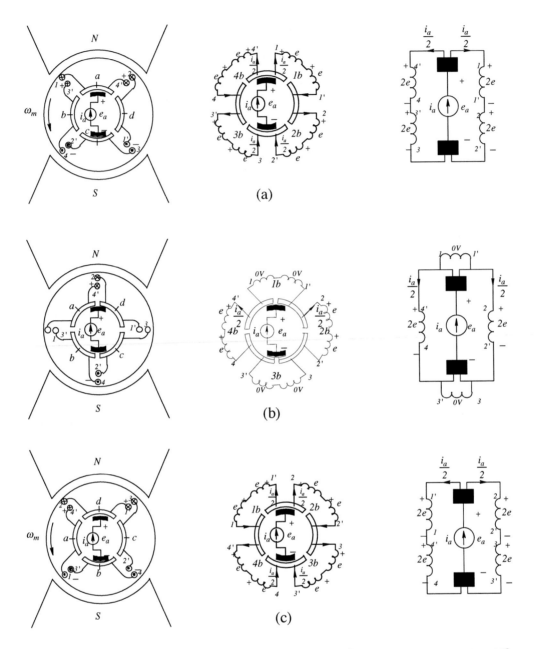

Figure 7-9 The dc machine in Example 7-1 (a) at $\theta = 0°$;(b) CCW rotation by 45°; (c) CCW rotation by 90°.

the torque and in the induced emf are reduced by increasing the number of coils and slots. Practical dc machines consist of a large number of coils in their armature windings. Therefore, we can neglect the effect of the coils in the "neutral" zone undergoing current commutation, and the armature can be

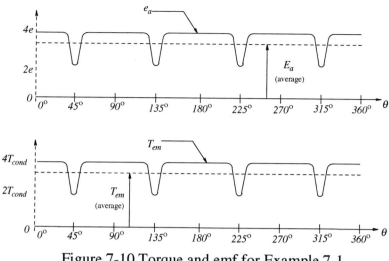

Figure 7-10 Torque and emf for Example 7-1.

represented as shown in Fig. 7-11. The following conclusions regarding the commutator action can be drawn:

- The armature current i_a supplied through the brushes divides equally between two circuits connected in parallel. Each circuit consists of half of the total conductors, which are connected in series. All conductors under a pole have currents in the same direction. The respective forces produced on each conductor are in the same direction and add up to yield the total torque. The direction of the armature current i_a determines the direction of currents through the conductors. (The current direction is independent of the direction of rotation.) Therefore, the direction of the electromagnetic torque produced by the machine also depends on the direction of i_a.

- The induced voltage in each of the two parallel armature circuits, and therefore across the brushes, is the sum of the voltages induced in all conductors connected in series. All conductors under a pole have induced emfs of the same polarity. The polarity of these induced emfs depends on the direction of rotation. (The emf polarity is independent of the current direction.)

7-9

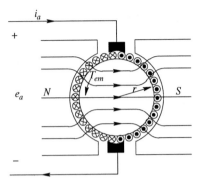

Figure 7-11 DC machine schematic representation.

We can now calculate the net torque produced and the emf induced. In the dc machine represented in Fig. 7-11, let there be a total of n_a conductors, each of length l, placed in a uniform and radial flux density B_f. Then, the electromagnetic torque produced by a current $\dfrac{i_a}{2}$ can be calculated by multiplying the force per conductor by the number of conductors and the radius r :

$$T_{em} = \left(n_a \ell r B_f\right)\frac{i_a}{2} \qquad\qquad (7\text{-}3)$$

In a machine, the values of n_a, ℓ and r are fixed. The flux density B_f also has a fixed value in a permanent-magnet machine. Therefore, we can write the torque expression as

$$T_{em} = k_T i_a \qquad \text{where} \quad k_T = \left(\frac{n_a}{2}\ell r\right)B_f \; [\frac{Nm}{A}] \qquad\qquad (7\text{-}4)$$

This expression shows that the magnitude of the electromagnetic torque produced is linearly proportional to the armature current i_a. The constant k_T is called the "Motor Torque Constant" and is given in motor specification sheets. From the discussion in Chapter 6, we know that we can reverse the direction of the electromagnetic torque by reversing i_a.

At a speed of ω_m (rad/s), the induced emf e_a across the brushes can be calculated by multiplying the induced emf per conductor by $n_a/2$, which is the number of conductors in series in each of the two parallel connected armature circuits. Thus,

$$e_a = \left(\frac{n_a}{2} \ell r B_f \right) \omega_m \qquad (7\text{-}5)$$

Using the same arguments as before for the torque, we can write the induced voltage expression as

$$e_a = k_E \, \omega_m \qquad \text{where} \qquad k_E = \left(\frac{n_a}{2} \ell r \right) B_f \quad [\frac{V}{rad/s}] \qquad (7\text{-}6)$$

This shows that the magnitude of the induced emf across the brushes is linearly proportional to the rotor speed ω_m. It also depends on the constant k_E, which is called the "Motor Voltage Constant" and is specified in motor specification sheets. The polarity of this induced emf is reversed if the rotational speed ω_m is reversed.

We should note that in any dc machine, the torque constant k_T and the voltage constant k_E are exactly the same, as shown by Eqs. 7-4 and 7-6, provided that we use the MKS units:

$$k_T = k_E = \left(\frac{n_a}{2} \ell r \right) B_f \qquad (7\text{-}7)$$

7-3-1 Armature Reaction

Figure 7-12a shows the flux lines ϕ_f produced by the stator. The armature winding on the rotor, with i_a flowing through it, also produces flux lines, as shown in Fig. 7-12b. These two sets of flux lines - ϕ_f and the armature flux ϕ_a - are at a right angle to each other. Assuming that the magnetic circuit does not

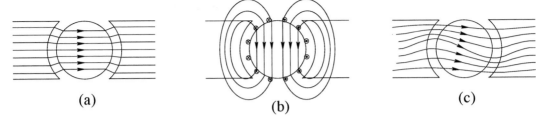

(a)　　　　　　　　(b)　　　　　　　　(c)

Figure 7-12 Effect of armature reaction.

saturate, we can superimpose the two sets of flux lines and show the combined flux lines in the air gap as in Fig. 7-12c. The fluxes ϕ_a and ϕ_f add in certain portions and subtract in the other portions. If the magnetic saturation is neglected as we have assumed, then due to the symmetry of the machine, the effect of an increased torque produced by conductors under higher flux density is canceled out by decreased torque produced by conductors under lower flux density. The same holds true for the induced emf e_a. Therefore, the calculations of the torque T_{em} and the induced emf e_a in the previous section remain valid.

If ϕ_a is so high that the net flux may saturate portions of the magnetic material in its path, then the superposition of the previous section is not valid. In that case, at high values of ϕ_a the net flux in the air gap near the saturated magnetic portions will be reduced compared to its value obtained by superposition. This will result in degradation in the torque produced by the given armature current. This effect is commonly called "saturation due to armature reaction." In our discussion we can neglect magnetic saturation and other ill-effects of armature reaction because in permanent-magnet machines the mmf produced by the armature winding results in a small ϕ_a. This is because there is a high magnetic reluctance in the path of ϕ_a. In field-wound dc machines, countermeasures can be taken: the mmf produced by the armature winding can be neutralized by passing the armature current in the opposite direction through a compensating winding placed on the pole faces of the stator, and through the commutating-pole windings, as shown in Fig. 7-13.

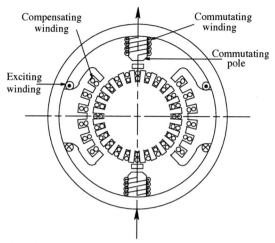

Figure 7-13 Compensating and commutating windings.

7-4   DC-MACHINE EQUIVALENT CIRCUIT

It is often convenient to discuss a dc machine in terms of its equivalent circuit of Fig. 7-14a, which shows conversion between electrical and mechanical power. In this figure, an armature current i_a is flowing. This current produces the electromagnetic torque $T_{em}(= k_T i_a)$ necessary to rotate the mechanical load at a speed of ω_m. Across the armature terminals, the rotation at the speed of ω_m induces a voltage, called the back-emf $e_a(= k_E \omega_m)$.

On the electrical side, the applied voltage v_a overcomes the back-emf e_a and causes the current i_a to flow. Recognizing that there is a voltage drop across both

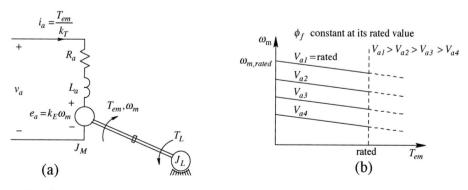

Figure 7-14 (a) Equivalent circuit of a dc motor; (b) steady state characteristics.

the armature winding resistance R_a (which includes the voltage drop across the carbon brushes) and the armature winding inductance L_a, we can write the equation of the electrical side as

$$v_a = e_a + R_a i_a + L_a \frac{di_a}{dt} \qquad (7\text{-}8)$$

On the mechanical side, the electromagnetic torque produced by the motor overcomes the mechanical-load torque T_L to produce accelaration:

$$\frac{d\omega_m}{dt} = \frac{1}{J_{eq}}(T_{em} - T_L) \qquad (7\text{-}9)$$

where J_{eq} is the total effective value of the combined inertia of the dc machine and the mechanical load.

Note that the equations of the electric system and the mechanical system are coupled. The back-emf e_a in the electrical-system equation (Eq. 7-8) depends on the mechanical speed ω_m. The torque T_{em} in the mechanical-system equation (Eq. 7-9) depends on the electrical current i_a. The electrical power absorbed from the electrical source by the motor is converted into mechanical power and vice versa. In steady state, with a voltage V_a applied to the armature terminals, and a load-torque T_L supplied as well,

$$I_a = \frac{T_{em}(=T_L)}{k_T} \qquad (7\text{-}10)$$

Also,

$$\omega_m = \frac{E_a}{k_E} = \frac{V_a - R_a I_a}{k_E} \qquad (7\text{-}11)$$

The steady state torque-speed characteristics for various values of V_a are plotted in Fig. 7-14b.

▲ **Example 7-2**   A permanent-magnet dc motor has the following parameters: $R_a = 0.35\Omega$ and $k_E = k_T = 0.5$ in MKS units. For a torque of up to 8 Nm, plot its steady state torque-speed characteristics for the following values of V_a: 100V, 75V, and 50V.

Solution   Let's consider the case of $V_a = 100V$. Ideally, at no-load (zero torque), from Eq. 7-10, $I_a = 0$. Therefore, from Eq. 7-11, the no-load speed is

$$\omega_m = \frac{V_a}{k_E} = \frac{100}{0.5} = 200 \, rad \, / \, s \, .$$

At a torque of 8 Nm, from Eq. 7-10, $I_a = \dfrac{8 \, Nm}{0.5} = 16 \, A$. Again using Eq. 7-11,

$$\omega_m = \frac{100 - 0.35 \times 16}{0.5} = 188.8 \, rad \, / \, s \, .$$

The torque-speed characteristic is a straight line, as shown in Fig. 7-15.

Similar characteristics can be drawn for the other values of V_a: 75V and 50V.   ▲

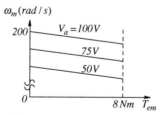

Figure 7-15 Example 7-2.

7-5   VARIOUS OPERATING MODES IN DC-MOTOR DRIVES

The major advantage of a dc-motor drive is the ease with which torque and speed can be controlled. A dc drive can easily be made to operate as a motor or as a generator in forward or reverse direction of rotation. In our prior discussions, the dc machine was operating as a motor in a counter-clockwise direction (which we will consider to be the forward direction). In this section, we will see how a dc machine can be operated as a generator during regenerative braking and how its speed can be reversed.

7-5-1   Regenerative Braking

Today, dc machines are seldom used as generators per se, but they operate in the generator mode in order to provide braking. For example, regenerative braking is used to slow the speed of a dc-motor-driven electric vehicle (most of which use brushless-dc motor drives, discussed in Chapter 10, but the principle of regeneration is the same) by converting kinetic energy associated with the inertia of the vehicle into electrical energy, which is fed into the batteries.

Initially, let's assume that a dc machine is operating in steady state as a motor and rotating in the forward direction as shown in Fig. 7-16a. A positive armature voltage v_a, which overcomes the back-emf e_a, is applied and the current i_a flows to supply the load torque. The polarities of the induced emfs and the directions of the currents in the armature conductors are also shown.

One way of slowing down this dc-motor-driven electric vehicle is to apply mechanical brakes. However, a better option is to let the dc machine go into the generator mode by reversing the direction in which the electromagnetic torque

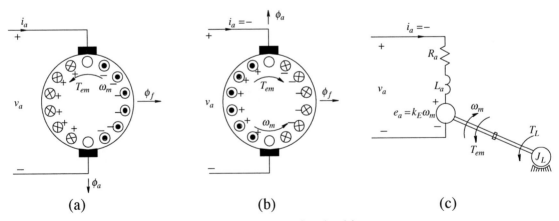

Figure 7-16 Regenerative braking.

T_{em} is produced. This is accomplished by reversing the direction of the armature current, which is shown to have a negative value in Fig. 7-16b. Since the machine is still turning in the same direction (forward and counter-clockwise), the induced back-emf e_a remains positive. The armature-current direction can be reversed by decreasing the applied voltage v_a in comparison to the back-emf e_a (that is, $v_a < e_a$). The current reversal through the conductors causes the torque to reverse and oppose the rotation. Now, the power from the mechanical system (energy stored in the inertia) is converted and supplied to the electrical system. The equivalent circuit of Fig. 7-16c in the generator mode shows the power being supplied to the electrical source (batteries, in the case of electrical vehicles).

Note that the torque $T_{em} (= k_T i_a)$ depends on the armature current i_a. Therefore, the torque will change as quickly as i_a is changed. DC motors for servo applications are designed with a low value of the armature inductance L_a; therefore, i_a and T_{em} can be controlled very quickly.

▲ **Example 7-3**   Consider the dc motor of Example 7-2 whose moment-of-inertia $J_m = 0.02 \, kg \cdot m^2$. Its armature inductance L_a can be neglected for slow changes. The motor is driving a load of inertia $J_L = 0.04 \, kg \cdot m^2$. The steady state operating speed is 300 rad/s. Calculate and plot the $v_a(t)$ that is required to bring this motor to a halt as quickly as possible, without exceeding the armature current of 12 A.

Solution   In order to bring the system to a halt as quickly as possible, the maximum allowed current should be supplied, that is $i_a = -12 \, A$. Therefore, $T_{em} = k_E i_a = -6 \, Nm$. The combined equivalent inertia is $J_{eq} = 0.06 \, kg \cdot m^2$. From Eq. 7-9 for the mechanical system,

$$\frac{d\omega_m}{dt} = \frac{1}{0.06}(-6.0) = -100 \, rad/s .$$

Therefore, the speed will reduce to zero in 3 s in a linear fashion, as plotted in Fig. 7-17.

At time $t = 0^+$,

$$E_a = k_E \omega_m = 150V \text{ and}$$

$$V_a = E_a + R_a I_a = 150 + 0.35(-12) = 145.8V.$$

Both e_a and v_a linearly decrease with time, as shown in Fig. 7-17. ▲

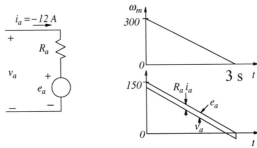

Figure 7-17 Example 7-3.

7-5-2 Operating in the Reverse Direction

Applying a reverse–polarity dc voltage to the armature terminals makes the armature current flow in the opposite direction. Therefore, the electromagnetic torque and the motor speed will also be reversed. Just as for the forward direction, regenerative braking is possible during rotation in the reverse direction.

7-5-3 Four-Quadrant Operation

As illustrated in Fig. 7-18, a dc machine can be easily operated in all four quadrants of its torque-speed plane. For example, starting with motoring in the forward direction, it can be made to go into the other quadrants of operation by reversing the armature current and then reversing the applied armature voltage.

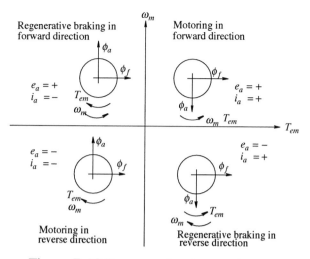

Figure 7-18 Four-quadrant operation.

7-6   FLUX WEAKENING IN WOUND-FIELD MACHINES

In dc machines with a wound field, the field flux ϕ_f and the flux density B_f can be controlled by adjusting the field-winding current I_f. This changes the machine torque-constant and the voltage-constant given by Eqs. 7-4 and 7-6, both of which can be written explicitly in terms of B_f as

$$k_T = k_t B_f \tag{7-12}$$

and

$$k_E = k_e B_f \tag{7-13}$$

where the constants k_t and k_e are also equal to each other.

Below the rated speed, we will always keep the field flux at its rated value so that the torque constant k_T is at its maximum value, which minimizes the current required to produce the desired torque, thus minimizing $i^2 R$ losses. At the rated field flux, the induced back-emf reaches its rated value at the rated speed. What if we wish to operate the machine at speeds higher than the rated value? This would require a terminal voltage higher than the rated value. To work around this, we can reduce the field flux, which allows the motor to be operated at speeds higher than the rated value without exceeding the rated value of the terminal voltage. This mode of operation is called the flux-weakening mode. Since the armature current is not allowed to exceed its rated value, the torque capability drops off as shown in Fig. 7-19 due to the reduction of the torque constant k_T in Eq. 7-12.

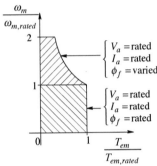

Figure 7-19 Field weakening in wound field machines.

7-7 POWER-PROCESSING UNITS IN DC DRIVES

In dc drives, the power-processing unit provides dc voltage and current to the armature of the dc machine. In general, this unit should be very energy efficient and should have a low cost. Depending on its application, the dc drive may be required to respond quickly and may also be operated in all 4-quadrants of Fig. 7-18. Therefore, both v_a and i_a must be adjustable and reversible and independent of each other.

In most cases, the power-processing unit shown in Fig. 7-2 is an interface between the electric utility and the dc machine (notable exceptions are vehicles supplied by batteries). Therefore, the power processor must draw power from the utility without causing or being susceptible to power quality problems. Ideally, the power flow through the PPU should be reversible into the utility system. The PPU should provide voltage and current to the dc machine with waveforms as close to a dc as possible. Deviations from a pure dc in the current waveform result in additional losses within the dc machine.

Power-processing units that utilize switch-mode conversion have already been discussed in Chapter 4. Their block diagram is repeated in Fig. 7-20. The "front-end" of such units is usually a diode-rectifier bridge (which will be discussed in detail in Chapter 16). It is possible to replace the diode-rectifier "front-end" with a switch-mode converter to make the power flow *into* the utility during regenerative braking (also discussed in Chapter 16). The design of the feedback controller for dc drives will be discussed in detail in Chapter 8.

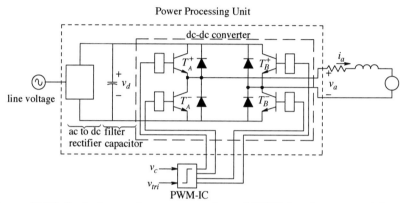

Figure 7-20 Switch-mode converter based PPU for dc-motor drives.

7-8   ELECTRONICALLY-COMMUTATED (TRAPEZOIDAL WAVEFORM, BRUSH-LESS DC) MOTOR DRIVES

Earlier in this chapter, we have seen that the role of the commutator and the brushes is to reverse the direction of current through a conductor based on its location. The current through a conductor is reversed as it moves from one pole to the other. In brush-type dc motors discussed previously, the field flux is created by permanent magnets (or a field winding) on the stator, while the power-handling armature winding is on the rotor.

In contrast, in Electronically-Commutated Motors (ECM), the commutation of current is provided electronically based on the positional information obtained from a sensor. These are "inside-out" machines where the magnetic field is established by the permanent magnets located on the rotor and the power handling winding is placed on the stator, as shown in Fig. 7-21a. The block diagram of the drive, including the PPU and the position sensor, is shown in Fig. 7-21b. The stator in Fig. 7-21a contains three-phase windings, which are displaced by 120 degrees. We will concentrate only on phase-a, because the roles of the other two phases are identical. The phase-a winding spans 60 degrees on each side, thus a total of 120 degrees, as shown in Fig. 7-21a. It is connected in a wye-arrangement with the other phases, as shown in Fig. 7-21b. It is distributed uniformly in slots, with a total of $2N_s$ conductors, where all of the conductors of the winding are in series. We will assume that the rotor produces a uniform flux density B_f distribution of flux lines crossing the air gap, rotating at a speed ω_m in a counter-clockwise direction. The flux-density distribution established by the rotor is rotating but the conductors of the stator windings are stationary. The principle of the induced emf $e = B\ell u$ discussed in Chapter 6 is valid here as well. This is confirmed by the example below.

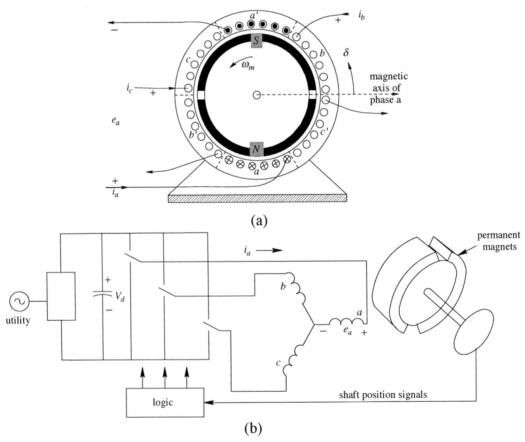

(a)

(b)

Figure 7-21 ECM drive.

▲ **Example 7-4** Show that the principle $e = B\ell u$ applies to situations in which the conductors are stationary but the flux-density distribution is rotating.

Solution   In Fig. 7-21a, take a conductor from the top group and one from the bottom group at 180 degrees, forming a coil, as shown in Fig. 7-22a. Fig. 7-22b shows that the flux linkage of the coil is changing as a function of the rotor position δ (with $\delta = 0$ at the position shown in Fig. 7-22a). The peak flux linkage of the coil occurs at $\delta = \dfrac{\pi}{2}$ radians ;

$$\hat{\lambda}_{coil} = (\pi r l)B_f \tag{7-14}$$

where ℓ is the rotor length and r is the radius. From Faraday's Law, the coil voltage equals the rate of change of the flux linkage. Therefore, recognizing that $\dfrac{d\delta}{dt} = \omega_m$,

$$e_{coil} = \frac{d\lambda_{coil}}{dt} = \frac{d\lambda_{coil}}{d\delta}\frac{d\delta}{dt} = \frac{(\pi r \ell)B_f}{\pi/2}\omega_m = 2\underbrace{B_f \ell r \omega_m}_{e_{cond}} \qquad 0 \le \delta \le \frac{\pi}{2} \tag{7-15}$$

where

$$e_{cond} = B_f \ell \underbrace{r \omega_m}_{u} = B_f \ell u . \tag{7-16}$$

This proves that we can apply $e = B\ell u$ to calculate the conductor voltage.

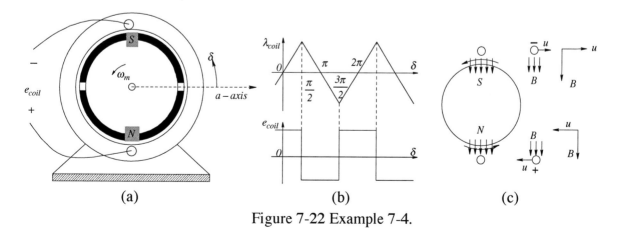

Figure 7-22 Example 7-4.

Using Fig. 7-22c, we will obtain the polarity of the induced emf in the conductors, without calculating the flux linkage and then its time-rate-of-change. We will assume that the flux-density distribution is stationary but that the conductor is moving in the opposite direction, as shown in the right side of Fig. 7-22c. Applying the rule discussed earlier regarding determining the voltage polarity shows that the polarity of the induced emf is negative in the top conductor and positive in the bottom conductor. This results in the coil voltage (with the polarity indicated in Fig. 7-22a) to be as shown in Fig. 7-22b.   ▲

7-8-1   Induced EMF

Returning to the machine of Fig. 7-21a, using the principle $e = B\ell u$ for each conductor, the total induced emf in the rotor position shown in Fig. 7-21a is

$$e_a = 2N_s B_f \ell r \omega_m \qquad\qquad (7\text{-}17)$$

Up to a 60-degree movement of the rotor in the counter-clockwise direction, the induced voltage in phase-a will be the same as that calculated by using Eq. 7-17. Beyond 60 degrees, some conductors in the top are "cut" by the north pole and the others by the south pole. The same happens in the bottom group of conductors. Therefore, the induced emf e_a linearly decreases during the next 60-degree interval, reaching an opposite polarity but the same magnitude as that given by Eq. 7-17. This results in a trapezoidal waveform for e_a as a function of δ, plotted in Fig. 7-23. The other phases have similar induced waveforms, displaced by 120 degrees with respect to each other. Notice that during every 60-degree interval, two of the phases have emf waveforms that are flat. We will discuss shortly in section 7-8-2 that during each 60-degree interval, the two phases with the flat emf waveforms are effectively connected in series and the current through them is controlled, while the third phase is open. Therefore, the phase-phase back-emf is twice that of Eq. 7-17:

$$e_{ph-ph} = 2(2N_s B_f \ell r \omega_m) \qquad\qquad (7\text{-}18)$$

or

$$e_{ph-ph} = k_E \omega_m \quad \text{where} \quad k_E = 4 N_s B_f \ell r \qquad (7\text{-}19)$$

k_E is the voltage constant in $V/(rad/s)$.

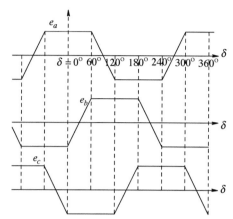

Figure 7-23 Induced emf in the three phases.

7-8-2 Electromagnetic Torque

Let's assume that phase-a in Fig. 7-21a has a constant current $i_a = I$ while the rotor is rotating. The forces, and hence the torque developed by the phase-a conductors, can be calculated using $f = B\ell i$, as shown in Fig. 7-24a. The torque on the rotor is in the opposite (counter-clockwise) direction. The torque $T_{em,a}$ on the rotor due to phase-a, with a constant current $i_a (= I)$, is plotted in Fig. 7-24b as a function of δ. Notice that it has the same waveform as the induced voltages, becoming negative when the conductors are "cut" by the opposite pole flux. Similar torque functions are plotted for the other two phases. For each phase, the torque functions with a negative value of current are also plotted by dotted waveforms; the reason for doing so is described in the next paragraph.

Our objective is to produce a net electromagnetic torque which does not fluctuate with the rotor position. Therefore, how should the currents in the three windings be controlled, in view of the torque waveforms in Fig. 7-24b for $+I$ and $-I$? First, let's assume that the three-phase windings are wye-connected, as shown in Fig. 7-21b. Then in the waveforms of Fig. 7-24b, during each 60-degree interval, we will pick the torque waveforms that are positive and have a flat-top. The phases are indicated in Fig. 7-24c, where we notice that during each 60-degree

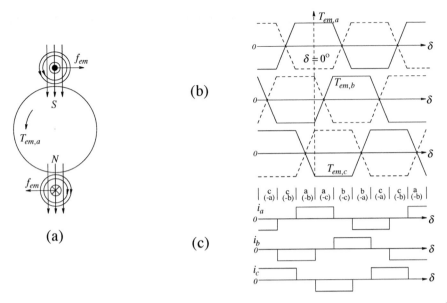

Figure 7-24 (a) Force directions for phase-a conductors; (b) Torque waveforms; (c) phase currents for a constant torque.

interval, we will require one phase to have a current $+I$ (indicated by +), the other to have $-I$ (indicated by -), and the third to have a zero current (open). These currents satisfy Kirchhoff's Current Law in the wye-connected phase windings. The net electromagnetic torque developed by combining the two phases can be written as

$$T_{em} = 2 \times \underbrace{2 N_s B_f \ell r I}_{each\ phase} \qquad (7\text{-}20)$$

or

$$T_{em} = k_T I \quad where \quad k_T = 4 N_s B_f \ell r \qquad (7\text{-}21)$$

k_T is the torque constant in *Nm/A*. Notice from Eqs. 7-19 and 7-21 that in MKS units, $k_E = k_T = 4 N_s B_f \ell r$.

In the switch-mode inverter of Fig. 7-21b, we can obtain these currents by pulse-width-modulating only two poles in each 60-degree interval, as depicted in Fig. 7-25a. The current can be regulated to be of the desired magnitude by the hysteresis-control method depicted in Fig. 7-25b. During interval 1, having pole-

a in the top position and pole-*b* in the bottom position causes the current through phases *a* and *b* to build up. When this current tends to exceed the upper threshold, the pole positions are reversed, causing the current to decline. When the current tends to fall below the lower threshold, the pole positions are reversed causing the current to once again increase. This allows the current to be maintained within a narrow band around the desired value. (It should be noted that in practice, to decrease the current, we can move both poles to the top position or to the bottom position and the current will decrease due to the back-emf e_{ph-ph} associated with phases *a* and *b* connected in series.)

7-8-3 Torque Ripple

Our previous discussion would suggest that the torque developed by this motor is smooth, provided that the ripple in the current depicted in Fig. 7-25c can be kept to a minimum. In practice, there is a significant torque fluctuation every 60-degrees of rotation due to the imperfections of the flux-density distribution and the difficulty of providing rectangular pulses of phase currents, which need to be timed accurately based on the rotor position sensed by a mechanical transducer connected to the rotor shaft. We will briefly look at such position sensors in Chapter 17. However, it is possible to eliminate the sensor, making such drives sensorless by mathematical calculations based on the measured voltage of the phase that is open. In applications where a smooth torque is needed, the trapezoidal-emf brush-less dc motors are replaced with sinusoidal-waveform brush-less motors, which are discussed in Chapter 10.

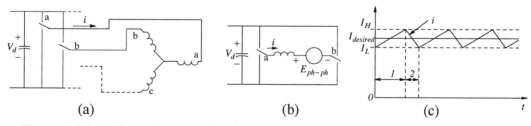

Figure 7-25 (a) Two phases conducting; (b) equivalent circuit; (c) hysteresis current

SUMMARY/REVIEW QUESTIONS

1. What is the breakdown of costs in dc-motor drives relative to ac-motor drives?
2. What are the two broad categories of dc motors?
3. What are the two categories of power-processing units?
4. What is the major drawback of dc motors?
5. What are the roles of commutator and brushes?
6. What is the relationship between the voltage-constant and the torque-constant of a dc motor? What are their units?
7. Show the dc-motor equivalent circuit. What does the armature current depend on? What does the induced back-emf depend on?
8. What are the various modes of dc-motor operation? Explain these modes in terms of the directions of torque, speed, and power flow.
9. How does a dc-motor torque-speed characteristic behave when a dc motor is applied with a constant dc voltage under an open-loop mode of operation?
10. What additional capability can be achieved by flux weakening in wound-field dc machines?
11. What are various types of field windings?
12. Show the safe operating area of a dc motor and discuss its various limits.
13. Assuming a switch-mode power-processing unit, show the applied voltage waveform and the induced emf for all four modes (quadrants) of operation.
14. What is the structure of trapezoidal-waveform electronically-commutated motors?
15. How can we justify applying the equation $e = B\ell u$ in a situation where the conductor is stationary but the flux-density distribution is moving?
16. How is the current controlled in a switch-mode inverter supplying ECM?
17. What is the reason for torque ripple in ECM drives?

REFERENCES

1. N. Mohan, T. Undeland, and W. P. Robbins, *Power Electronics: Converters, Applications and Design*, 2nd edition, 1995, John Wiley & Sons, New York, NY.

2. N. Mohan, *Power Electronics: Computer Simulation, Analysis and Education using PSpice Schematics*, January 1998.

3. A. E. Fitzgerald, C. Kingsley and S. Umans, *Electric Machinery*, 5th edition, McGraw-Hill, Inc., 1990.

4. G. R. Slemon, *Electric Machines and Drives,* Addison-Wesley, 1992.

5. Engineering Handbook, Electro-Craft Corporation.

6. T. Jahns, *Variable Frequency Permanent Magnet AC Machine Drives*, Power Electronics and Variable Frequency Drives, (edited by B. K. Bose), IEEE Press, 1997.

PROBLEMS

Permanent-Magnet DC-Motor Drives

7-1   Consider a permanent-magnet dc motor with the following parameters: $R_a = 0.35 \ \Omega$, $L_a = 1.5 \ mH$, $k_E = 0.5 \ V/(rad/s)$, $k_T = 0.5 \ Nm/A$, and $J_m = 0.02 \ kg \cdot m^2$. The rated torque of this motor is 4 Nm. Plot the steady state torque-speed characteristics for $V_a = 100 \ V$, 60 V, and 30 V.

7-2   The motor in Problem 7-1 is driving a load whose torque requirement remains constant at 3 Nm, independent of speed. Calculate the armature voltage V_a to be applied in steady state, if this load is to be driven at 1,500 *rpm*.

7-3   The motor in Problem 7-1 is driving a load at a speed of 1,500 *rpm*. At some instant, it goes into regenerative braking. Calculate the armature voltage v_a at that instant, if the current i_a is not to exceed 10 A in magnitude. Assume that the inertia is large and thus the speed changes very slowly.

7-4   The motor in Problem 7-1 is supplied by a switch-mode dc-dc converter which has a dc-bus voltage of 200 V. The switching frequency $f_s = 25$ *kHz*. Calculate and plot the waveforms for $v_a(t)$, e_a, $i_a(t)$, and $i_d(t)$ under the following conditions:

(a) Motoring in forward direction at a speed of 1,500 *rpm*, supplying a load of 3 *Nm*.

(b) Regenerative braking from conditions in (a), with a current of 10 *A*.

(c) Motoring in reverse direction at a speed of 1,500 *rpm*, supplying a load of 3 *Nm*.

(d) Regenerative braking from conditions in (c), with a current of 10 *A*.

7-5   The motor in Problem 7-1 is driving a load at a speed of 1,500 *rpm*. The load inertia is 0.04 $kg \cdot m^2$ and it requires a torque of 3 *Nm*. In steady state, calculate the peak-to-peak ripple in the armature current and speed if it is supplied by the switch-mode dc-dc converter of Problem 7-4.

7-6   In Problem 7-5, what is the additional power loss in the armature resistance due to the ripple in the armature current? Calculate this as a percentage of the loss if the motor was supplied by a pure dc source.

7-7   The motor in Problem 7-1 is driving a load at a speed of 1,500 *rpm*. The load is purely inertial with an inertia of 0.04 $kg \cdot m^2$. Calculate the energy recovered by slowing it down to 750 *rpm* while keeping the current during regenerative braking at 10 *A*.

7-8   A permanent-magnet dc motor is to be started from rest. $R_a = 0.35\ \Omega$, $k_E = 0.5$ $V /(rad/s)$, $k_T = 0.5$ *Nm/A*, and $J_m = 0.02$ $kg \cdot m^2$. This motor is driving a load of inertia $J_L = 0.04$ $kg \cdot m^2$, and a load torque $T_L = 2$ *Nm*. The motor current must not exceed 15 *A*. Calculate and plot both the voltage v_a, which must be applied to bring this motor to a steady state speed of 300 *rad/s* as quickly as possible, and the speed, as functions of time. Neglect the effect of L_a.

7-9   The dc motor of Problem 7-1 is operating in steady state with a speed of 300 *rad/s*. The load is purely inertial with an inertia of 0.04 $kg \cdot m^2$. At some instant, its speed is to decrease linearly and reverse to 100 *rad/s* in a total of 4 *s*. Neglect L_a and friction. Calculate and plot the required current and the resulting voltage v_a that should be applied to the armature terminals of this machine. As intermediate steps, calculate and plot e_a, the required electromagnetic torque T_{em} from the motor, and the current i_a.

7-10   The permanent-magnet dc motor of Example 7-3 is to be started under a loaded condition. The load-torque T_L is linearly proportional to speed and equals 4 *Nm* at a speed of 300 *rad/s*. Neglect L_a and friction. The motor current must not exceed 15 *A*. Calculate and plot the voltage v_a, which must be applied to bring this motor to a steady state speed of 300 *rad/s* as quickly as possible.

Wound-Field DC-Motor Drives

7-11 Assume that the dc-motor of Problem 7-1 has a wound field. The rated speed is 2,000 *rpm*. Assume that the motor parameters are somehow kept the same as in Problem 7-1 with the rated field current of 1.5 *A*. As a function of speed, show the capability curve by plotting the torque and the field current I_f, if the speed is increased up to twice its rated value.

7-12 A wound-field dc motor is driving a load whose torque requirement increases linearly with speed and reaches 5 *Nm* at a speed of 1,400 *rpm*. The armature terminal voltage is held to its rated value. At the rated B_f, the no-load speed is 1,500 *rpm* and the speed while driving the load is 1,400 *rpm*. If B_f is reduced to 0.8 times its rated value, calculate the new steady state speed.

ECM Drives

7-13 In an ECM drive, $k_E = k_T = 0.75$ in MKS units. Plot the phase currents and the induced-emf waveforms, as a function of δ, if the motor is operating at a speed of 100 *rad/s* and delivering a torque of 6 *Nm*.

7-14 By drawing waveforms similar to those in Figs. 7-23, 7-24b, and 7-24c, show how regenerative braking can be achieved in ECM drives.

CHAPTER 8

DESIGNING FEEDBACK CONTROLLERS FOR MOTOR DRIVES

8-1 INTRODUCTION

Many applications, such as robotics and factory automation, require precise control of speed and position. In such applications, a feedback control, as illustrated by Fig. 8-1, is used. This feedback control system consists of a power-processing unit (PPU), a motor, and a mechanical load. The output variables such as torque and speed are sensed and are fed back to be compared with the desired (reference) values. The error between the reference and the actual values are amplified to control the power-processing unit to minimize or eliminate this error. A properly designed feedback controller makes the system insensitive to disturbances and changes in the system parameters.

The objective of this chapter is to discuss the design of motor-drive controllers. A dc-motor drive is used as an example, although the same design concepts can be applied in controlling brushless-dc motor drives and vector-controlled induction-motor drives. In the following discussion, it is assumed that the power-

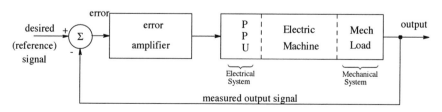

Fig 8-1 Feedback controlled drive.

processing unit is of a switch-mode type and has a very fast response time. A permanent-magnet dc machine with a constant field flux ϕ_f is assumed.

8-2   CONTROL OBJECTIVES

The control system in Fig. 8-1 is shown simplified in Fig. 8-2, where $G_p(s)$ is the Laplace-domain transfer function of the plant consisting of the power-processing unit, the motor, and the mechanical load. $G_c(s)$ is the controller transfer function.   In response to a desired (reference) input $X^*(s)$, the output of the system is $X(s)$, which (ideally) equals the reference input. The controller $G_c(s)$ is designed with the following objectives in mind:

- a zero steady state error.
- a good dynamic response (which implies both a fast transient response, for example to a step-change in the input, and a small settling time with very little overshoot).

To keep the discussion simple, a unity feedback will be assumed. The open-loop transfer function (including the forward path and the unity feedback path) $G_{OL}(s)$ is

$$G_{OL}(s) = G_c(s)G_p(s) \tag{8-1}$$

The closed-loop transfer function $\dfrac{X(s)}{X^*(s)}$ in a unity feedback system is

$$G_{CL}(s) = \frac{G_{OL}(s)}{1+G_{OL}(s)} \tag{8-2}$$

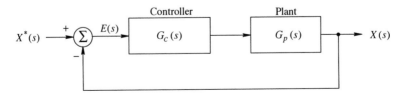

Fig 8-2 Simplified control system representation.

In order to define a few necessary control terms, we will consider a generic Bode plot of the open-loop transfer function $G_{OL}(s)$ in terms of its magnitude and phase angle, shown in Fig. 8-3a as a function of frequency. The frequency at which the gain equals unity (that is $|G_{OL}(s)| = 0db$) is defined as the crossover frequency f_c (angular frequency ω_c). At the crossover frequency, the phase delay introduced by the open-loop transfer function must be less than 180^0 in order for the closed-loop feedback system to be stable. Therefore, at f_c, the phase angle $\phi_{OL}|_{f_c}$ of the open-loop transfer function, measured with respect to -180^0, is defined as the Phase Margin (PM):

$$\text{Phase Margin (PM)} = \phi_{OL}|_{f_c} - (-180^0) = \phi_{OL}|_{f_c} + 180^0 \qquad (8\text{-}3)$$

Note that $\phi_{OL}|_{f_c}$ has a negative value. For a satisfactory dynamic response without oscillations, the phase margin should be greater than 45^0, preferably close to 60^0.

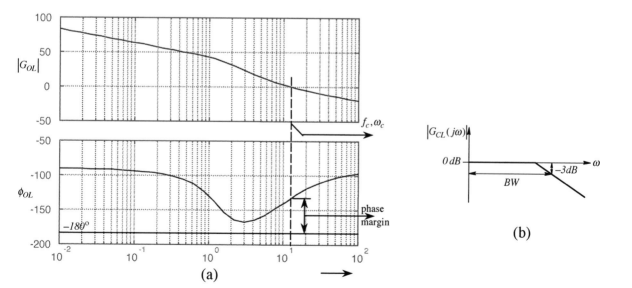

Figure 8-3 (a) Phase Margin; (b) bandwidth.

The magnitude of the closed-loop transfer function is plotted in Fig. 8-3b (idealized by the asymptotes), in which the bandwidth is defined as the frequency at which the gain drops to (−3 dB). As a first-order approximation in many practical systems,

$$\text{Closed-loop bandwidth} \approx f_c \qquad\qquad (8\text{-}4)$$

For a fast transient response by the control system, for example a response to a step-change in the input, the bandwidth of the closed-loop should be high. From Eq. 8-4, this requirement implies that the crossover frequency f_c (of the open-loop transfer function shown in Fig. 8-3a) should be designed to be high.

▲ **Example 8-1** In a unity feedback system, the open-loop transfer function is given as $G_{OL}(s) = \dfrac{k_{OL}}{s}$, where $k_{OL} = 2\times 10^3\, rad\,/\,s$. (a) Plot the open-loop transfer function. What is the crossover frequency? (b) Plot the closed-loop transfer function and calculate the bandwidth. (c) Calculate and plot the time-domain closed-loop response to a step-change in the input.

Solution
(a) The open-loop transfer function is plotted in Fig. 8-4a, which shows that the crossover frequency $\omega_c = k_{OL} = 2\times 10^3\, rad\,/\,s$.

(b) The closed-loop transfer function, from Eq. 8-2, is $G_{CL}(s) = \dfrac{1}{1+s\,/\,k_{OL}}$. This closed-loop transfer function is plotted in Fig. 8-4b, which shows that the

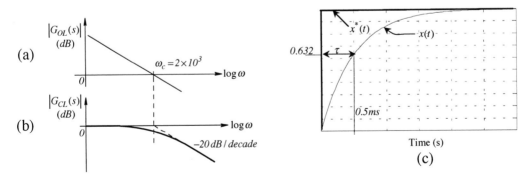

Figure 8-4 (a) Gain magnitude of a first-order system open loop; (b) gain magnitude of a closed loop; (c) step response.

bandwidth is exactly equal to the ω_c calculated in part a.

(c) For a step change, $X^*(s) = \dfrac{1}{s}$. Therefore,

$$X(s) = \frac{1}{s}\frac{1}{1+s/k_{OL}} = \frac{1}{s} - \frac{1}{1+s/k_{OL}}.$$

The Laplace-inverse transform yields

$$x(t) = (1-e^{-t/\tau})u(t) \quad \text{where } \tau = \frac{1}{k_{OL}} = 0.5\,ms.$$

The time response is plotted in Fig. 8-4c. We can see that a higher value of k_{OL} results in a higher bandwidth and a smaller time-constant τ, leading to a faster response. ▲

8-3 CASCADE CONTROL STRUCTURE

In the following discussion, a cascade control structure such as that shown in Fig. 8-5 is used. The cascade control structure is commonly used for motor drives because of its flexibility. It consists of distinct control loops; the innermost current (torque) loop is followed by the speed loop. If position needs to be controlled accurately, the outermost position loop is superimposed on the speed loop. Cascade control requires that the bandwidth (speed of response) increase towards the inner loop, with the torque loop being the fastest and the position loop being the slowest. The cascade control structure is widely used in industry.

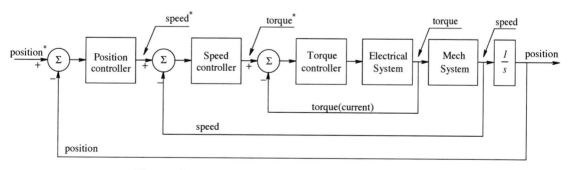

Figure 8-5 Cascade control of a motor drive.

8-4   STEPS IN DESIGNING THE FEEDBACK CONTROLLER

Motion control systems often must respond to large changes in the desired (reference) values of the torque, speed, and position. They must reject large, unexpected load disturbances. For large changes, the overall system is often nonlinear. This nonlinearity comes about because the mechanical load is often highly nonlinear. Additional nonlinearity is introduced by voltage and current limits imposed by the power-processing unit and the motor. In view of the above, the following steps for designing the controller are suggested:

1.   The first step is to assume that, around the steady-state operating point, the input reference changes and the load disturbances are all small. In such a small-signal analysis, the overall system can be assumed to be linear around the steady-state operating point, thus allowing the basic concepts of linear control theory to be applied.

2.   Based on the linear control theory, once the controller has been designed, the entire system can be simulated on a computer under large-signal conditions to evaluate the adequacy of the controller. The controller must be "adjusted" as appropriate.

8-5   SYSTEM REPRESENTATION FOR SMALL-SIGNAL ANALYSIS

For ease of the analysis described below, the system in Fig. 8-5 is assumed to be linear and the steady-state operating point is assumed to be zero for all of the system variables. This linear analysis can be then extended to nonlinear systems and to steady-state operating conditions other than zero. The control system in Fig. 8-5 is designed with the highest bandwidth (associated with the torque loop), which is one or two orders of magnitude smaller than the switching frequency f_s.

As a result, in designing the controller, the switching-frequency components in various quantities are of no consequence. Therefore, we will use the average variables discussed in Chapter 4, where the switching-frequency components were eliminated.

The Average Representation of the Power-Processing Unit (PPU)

For the purpose of designing the feedback controller, we will assume that the dc-bus voltage V_d within the PPU shown in Fig. 8-6a is constant. Following the averaging analysis in Chapter 4, the average representation of the switch-mode converter is shown in Fig. 8-6b. In terms of the dc-bus voltage V_d and the triangular-frequency waveform peak $\hat{V}_{tri}$, the average output voltage $\overline{v}_a(t)$ of the converter is linearly proportional to the control voltage:

$$\overline{v}_a(t) = k_{PWM} v_c(t) \qquad (k_{PWM} = \frac{V_d}{\hat{V}_{tri}}) \qquad (8\text{-}5)$$

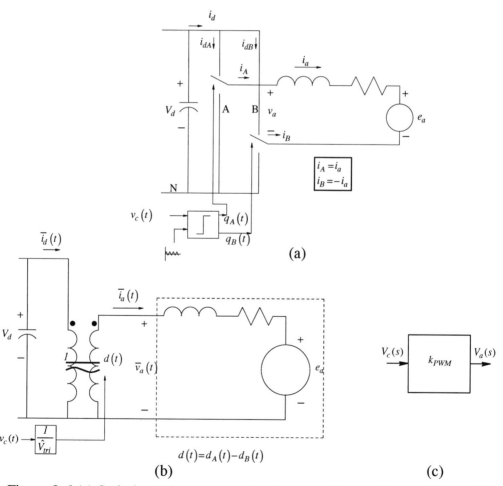

Figure 8-6 (a) Switch-mode converter for dc motor drives; (b) average model of the switch-mode converter; (c) linearized representation.

where k_{PWM} is the gain constant of the PWM converter. Therefore, in Laplace domain, the PWM controller and the dc-dc switch-mode converter can be represented simply by a gain-constant k_{PWM}, as shown in Fig. 8-6c:

$$V_a(s) = k_{PWM} V_c(s) \tag{8-6}$$

where $V_a(s)$ is the Laplace transform of $\overline{v}_a(t)$, and $V_c(s)$ is the Laplace transform of $v_c(t)$. The above representation is valid in the linear range, where $-\hat{V}_{tri} \leq v_c \leq \hat{V}_{tri}$.

8-5-2 The Modeling of the DC Machine and the Mechanical Load

The dc motor and the mechanical load are modeled as shown by the equivalent circuit in Fig. 8-7a, in which the speed $\omega_m(t)$ and the back-emf $e_a(t)$ are assumed not to contain switching-frequency components. The electrical and the mechanical equations corresponding to Fig. 8-7a are

$$\overline{v}_a(t) = e_a(t) + R_a \overline{i}_a(t) + L_a \frac{d}{dt} \overline{i}_a(t), \qquad e_a(t) = k_E \omega_m(t) \tag{8-7}$$

and

$$\frac{d}{dt} \omega_m(t) = \frac{\overline{T}_{em}(t) - T_L}{J_{eq}}, \qquad \overline{T}_{em}(t) = k_T \overline{i}_a(t) \tag{8-8}$$

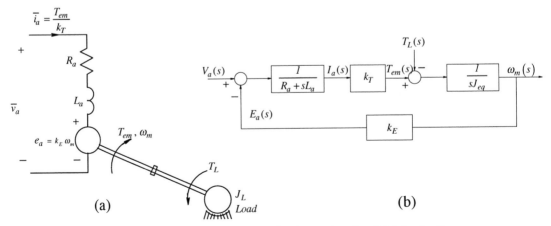

(a)

(b)

Fig 8-7 DC motor and mechanical load (a) equivalent circuit; (b) block diagram.

where the equivalent load inertia $J_{eq}(=J_M+J_L)$ is the sum of the motor inertia and the load inertia, and the damping is neglected (it could be combined with the load torque T_L). In the simplified procedure presented here, the controller is designed to follow the changes in the torque, speed, and position reference values (and hence the load torque in Eq. 8-8 is assumed to be absent). Eqs. 8-7 and 8-8 can be expressed in the Laplace domain as

$$V_a(s) = E_a(s) + (R_a + sL_a)I_a(s) \qquad (8\text{-}9)$$

or

$$I_a(s) = \frac{V_a(s) - E_a(s)}{R_a + sL_a}, \qquad E_a(s) = k_E\omega_m(s) \qquad (8\text{-}10)$$

We can define the Electrical Time Constant τ_e as

$$\tau_e = \frac{L_a}{R_a} \qquad (8\text{-}11)$$

Therefore, Eq. 8-10 can be written in terms of τ_e as

$$I_a(s) = \frac{1/R_a}{1 + \dfrac{s}{1/\tau_e}}\{V_a(s) - E_a(s)\}, \qquad E_a(s) = k_E\omega_m(s) \qquad (8\text{-}12)$$

From Eq. 8-8, assuming the load torque to be absent in the design procedure,

$$\omega_m(s) = \frac{T_{em}(s)}{sJ_{eq}}, \qquad T_{em}(s) = k_T I_a(s) \qquad (8\text{-}13)$$

Eqs. 8-10 and 8-13 can be combined and represented in block-diagram form, as shown in Fig. 8-7b.

8-6   CONTROLLER DESIGN

The controller in the cascade control structure shown in Fig. 8-5 is designed with the objectives discussed in section 8-2 in mind. In the following section, a simplified design procedure is described.

8-6-1 PI Controllers

Motion control systems often utilize a proportional-integral (PI) controller, as shown in Fig. 8-8. The input to the controller is the error $E(s) = X^*(s) - X(s)$, which is the difference between the reference input and the measured output.

In Fig. 8-8, the proportional controller produces an output proportional to the error input:

$$V_{c,p}(s) = k_p E(s) \qquad\qquad (8\text{-}14)$$

where k_p is the proportional-controller gain. In torque and speed loops, proportional controllers, if used alone, result in a steady-state error in response to step-change in the input reference. Therefore, they are used in combination with the integral controller described below.

In the integral controller shown in Fig. 8-8, the output is proportional to the integral of the error $E(s)$, expressed in the Laplace domain as

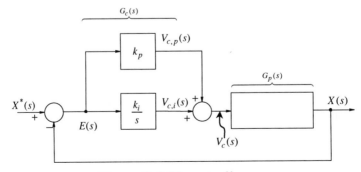

Figure 8-8 PI controller.

$$V_{c,i}(s) = \frac{k_i}{s} E(s) \qquad (8-15)$$

where k_i is the integral-controller gain. Such a controller responds slowly because its action is proportional to the time integral of the error. The steady-state error goes to zero for a step-change in input because the integrator action continues for as long as the error is not zero.

In motion-control systems, the P controllers in the position loop and the PI controllers in the speed and torque loop are often adequate. Therefore, we will not consider differential (D) controllers. As shown in Fig. 8-8, $V_c(s) = V_{c,p}(s) + V_{c,i}(s)$. Therefore, using Eqs. 8-14 and 8-15, the transfer function of a PI controller is

$$\frac{V_c(s)}{E(s)} = (k_p + \frac{k_i}{s}) = \frac{k_i}{s}[1 + \frac{s}{k_i / k_p}] \qquad (8-16)$$

8-7 EXAMPLE OF A CONTROLLER DESIGN

In the following discussion, we will consider the example of a permanent-magnet dc-motor supplied by a switch-mode PWM dc-dc converter. The system parameters are given as follows in Table 8-1:

Table 8-1 DC-Motor Drive System

System Parameter	Value
R_a	$2.0\,\Omega$
L_a	$5.2\,mH$
J_{eq}	$152 \times 10^{-6}\,kg \cdot m^2$
B	0
K_E	$0.1\,V / (rad / s)$
k_T	$0.1\,Nm / A$
V_d	$60V$
$\hat{V}_{tri}$	$5V$
f_s	$33\,kHz$

We will design the torque, speed, and position feedback controllers (assuming a unity feedback) based on the small-signal analysis, in which the load nonlinearity and the effects of the limiters can be ignored.

8-7-1   The Design of the Torque (Current) Control Loop

As mentioned earlier, we will begin with the innermost loop in Fig. 8-9a (utilizing the transfer function block diagram of Fig. 8-7b to represent the motor-load combination, Fig. 8-6c to represent the PPU, and Fig. 8-8 to represent the PI controller).

In permanent-magnet dc motors in which ϕ_f is constant, the current and the torque are proportional to each other, related by the torque constant k_T. Therefore, we will consider the current to be the control variable because it is more convenient to use. Notice that there is a feedback in the current loop from

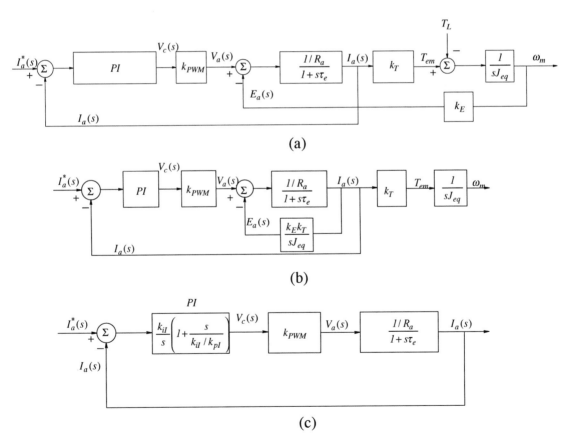

(a)

(b)

(c)

Fig. 8-9 Design of the torque control loop.

the output speed. This feedback dictates the induced back-emf. Neglecting T_L, and considering the current to be the output, $E_a(s)$ can be calculated in terms of $I_a(s)$ in Fig. 8-9a as $E_a(s) = \dfrac{k_T k_E}{s J_{eq}} I_a(s)$. Therefore, Fig. 8-9a can be redrawn as shown in Fig. 8-9b. Notice that the feedback term depends inversely on the inertia J_{eq}. Assuming that the inertia is sufficiently large to justify neglecting the feedback effect, we can simplify the block diagram, as shown in Fig. 8-9c.

The current-controller in Fig. 8-9c is a proportional-integral (PI) error amplifier with the proportional gain k_{pI} and the integral gain k_{iI}. Its transfer function is given by Eq. 8-16. The subscript "I" refers to the current loop. The open-loop transfer function $G_{I,OL}(s)$ of the simplified current loop in Fig. 8-9c is

$$G_{I,OL}(s) = \underbrace{\frac{k_{iI}}{s}\left[1 + \frac{s}{k_{iI}/k_{pI}}\right]}_{PI-controller} \underbrace{k_{PWM}}_{PPU} \underbrace{\frac{1/R_a}{1 + \dfrac{s}{1/\tau_e}}}_{motor} \tag{8-17}$$

To select the gain constants of the PI controller in the current loop, a simple design procedure, which results in a phase margin of 90 degrees, is suggested as follows:

- Select the zero (k_{iI}/k_{pI}) of the PI controller to cancel the motor pole at $(1/\tau_e)$ due to the electrical time-constant τ_e of the motor. Under these conditions,

$$\frac{k_{iI}}{k_{pI}} = \frac{1}{\tau_e} \qquad \text{or} \qquad k_{pI} = \tau_e k_{iI} \tag{8-18}$$

Cancellation of the pole in the motor transfer function renders the open-loop transfer function to be

$$G_{I,OL}(s) = \frac{k_{I,OL}}{s} \tag{8-19a}$$

where

$$k_{I,OL} = \frac{k_{iI} k_{PWM}}{R_a} \tag{8-19b}$$

- In the open-loop transfer function of Eq. 8-19a, the crossover frequency $\omega_{cI} = k_{I,OL}$. We will select the crossover frequency $f_{cI} (= \omega_{cI} / 2\pi)$ of the current open-loop to be approximately one to two orders of magnitude smaller than the switching frequency of the power-processing unit in order to avoid interference in the control loop from the switching-frequency noise. Therefore, at the selected crossover frequency, from Eq. 8-19b,

$$k_{iI} = \frac{\omega_{cI} R_a}{k_{PWM}} \tag{8-20}$$

This completes the design of the torque (current) loop, as illustrated by the example below, where the gain constants k_{pI} and k_{iI} can be calculated from Eqs. 8-18 and 8-20.

▲ **Example 8-2**   Design the current loop for the example system of Table 8-1, assuming that the crossover frequency is selected to be 1 *kHz*.

Solution   From Eq. 8-20, for $\omega_{cI} = 2\pi \times 10^3 \, rad \, / \, s$,

$$k_{iI} = \frac{\omega_{cI} R_a}{k_{PWM}} = 1050.0$$

and, from Eq. 8-18,

$$k_{pI} = k_{iI} \tau_e = k_{iI} \frac{L_a}{R_a} = 2.73 \, .$$

The open-loop transfer function is plotted in Fig. 8-10a, which shows that the crossover frequency is 1 *kHz*, as assumed previously. The closed-loop transfer function is plotted in Fig. 8-10b.

▲

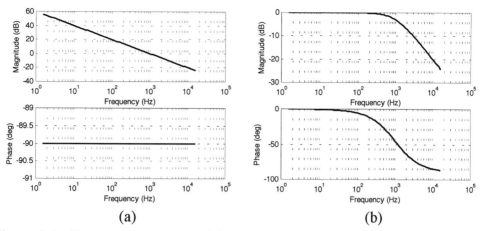

(a)   (b)

Figure 8-10 Frequency response of the current loop (a) open loop; (b) closed loop.

8-7-2   The Design of the Speed Loop

We will select the bandwidth of the speed loop to be one order of magnitude smaller than that of the current (torque) loop. Therefore, the closed-current loop can be assumed to be ideal for design purposes and represented by unity, as shown in Fig. 8-11. The speed controller is of the proportional-integral (PI) type. The resulting open-loop transfer function $G_{\Omega,OL}(s)$ of the speed loop in the block diagram of Fig. 8-11 is as follows, where the subscript "Ω" refers to the speed loop:

$$G_{\Omega,OL}(s) = \underbrace{\frac{k_{i\Omega}}{s}[1 + s/(k_{i\Omega}/k_{p\Omega})]}_{PI\ controller}\ \underbrace{1}_{current\ loop}\ \underbrace{\frac{k_T}{sJ_{eq}}}_{torque+inertia} \tag{8-21}$$

Eq. 8-21 can be rearranged as

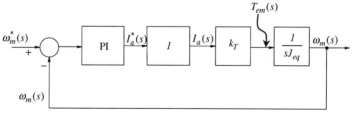

Fig 8-11 Block diagram of the speed loop.

8-15

$$G_{\Omega,OL}(s) = (\frac{k_{i\Omega}k_T}{J_{eq}})\frac{1+s/(k_{i\Omega}/k_{p\Omega})}{s^2} \tag{8-22}$$

This shows that the open-loop transfer function consists of a double pole at the origin. At low frequencies in the Bode plot, this double pole at the origin causes the magnitude to decline at the rate of -40 db per decade while the phase angle is at -180^0. We can select the crossover frequency $\omega_{c\Omega}$ to be one order of magnitude smaller than that of the current loop. Similarly, we can choose a reasonable value of the phase margin $\phi_{pm,\Omega}$. Therefore, Eq. 8-22 yields two equations at the crossover frequency:

$$\left|(\frac{k_{i\Omega}k_T}{J_{eq}})\frac{1+s/(k_{i\Omega}/k_{p\Omega})}{s^2}\right|_{s=j\omega_{c\Omega}} = 1 \tag{8-23}$$

and

$$\angle(\frac{k_{i\Omega}k_T}{J_{eq}})\frac{1+s/(k_{i\Omega}/k_{p\Omega})}{s^2}\bigg|_{s=j\omega_{c\Omega}} = -180^0 + \phi_{pm,\Omega} \tag{8-24}$$

The two gain constants of the PI controller can be calculated by solving these two equations, as illustrated by the following example.

▲ **Example 8-3**   Design the speed loop controller, assuming the speed loop crossover frequency to be one order of magnitude smaller than that of the current loop in Example 8-2; that is, $f_{c\Omega} = 100\,Hz$, and thus $\omega_{c\Omega} = 628\,rad/s$. The phase margin is selected to be 60^0.

Solution   In Eqs. 8-23 and 8-24, substituting $k_T = 0.1\,Nm/A$, $J_{eq} = 152 \times 10^{-6}\,kg \cdot m^2$, and $\phi_{PM,\Omega} = 60^o$ at the crossover frequency, where $s = j\omega_{c\Omega} = j628$, we can calculate that $k_{p\Omega} = 0.827$ and $k_{i\Omega} = 299.7$. The open- and the closed-loop transfer functions are plotted in Figs. 8-12a and 8-12b.   ▲

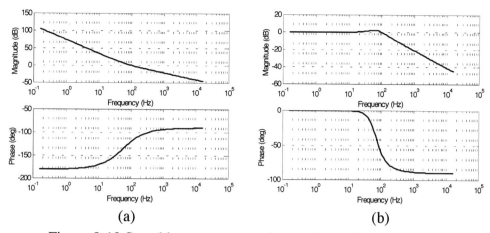

Figure 8-12 Speed loop response (a) open loop; (b) closed loop.

8-7-3 The Design of the Position Control Loop

We will select the bandwidth of the position loop to be one order of magnitude smaller than that of the speed loop. Therefore, the speed loop can be idealized and represented by unity, as shown in Fig. 8-13. For the position controller, it is adequate to have only a proportional gain $k_{p\theta}$ because of the presence of a true

integrator $\left(\dfrac{1}{s}\right)$ in Fig. 8-13 in the open-loop transfer function. This integrator

will reduce the steady state error to zero for a step-change in the reference position. With this choice of the controller, and with the closed–loop response of the speed loop assumed to be ideal, the open-loop transfer function $G_{\theta,OL}(s)$ is

$$G_{\theta,OL}(s) = \frac{k_\theta}{s}$$

(8-25)

Therefore, selecting the crossover frequency $\omega_{c\theta}$ of the open-loop allows k_θ to be calculated as

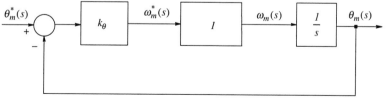

Fig 8-13 Block diagram of position loop.

$$k_\theta = \omega_{c\theta} \tag{8-26}$$

▲ **Example 8-4** For the example system of Table 8-1, design the position-loop controller, assuming the position-loop crossover frequency to be one order of magnitude smaller than that of the speed loop in Example 8-3 (that is, $f_{c\theta} = 10\,Hz$ and $\omega_{c\theta} = 62.8\,rad/s$).

Solution   From Eq. 8-26, $k_\theta = \omega_{c\theta} = 62.8\,rad/s$.

The open- and the closed-loop transfer functions are plotted in Figs. 8-14a and 8-14b.   ▲

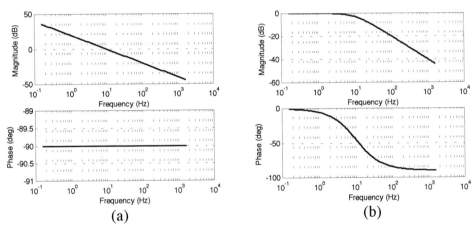

(a)   (b)

Figure 8-14 Position loop response (a) open loop; (b) closed loop.

8-8   THE ROLE OF FEED-FORWARD

Although simple to design and implement, a cascaded control consisting of several inner loops is likely to respond to changes more slowly than a control system in which all of the system variables are processed and acted upon simultaneously. In industrial systems, approximate reference values of inner-loop variables are often available. Therefore, these reference values are fed forward, as shown in Fig. 8-15. The feed-forward operation can minimize the disadvantage of the slow dynamic response of cascaded control.

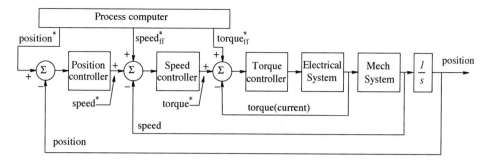

Figure 8-15 Control system with feedforward.

8-9   THE EFFECTS OF LIMITS

As pointed out earlier, one of the benefits of cascade control is that the intermediate variables such as torque (current) and the control signal to the PWM-IC can be limited to acceptable ranges by putting limits on their reference values. This provides safety of operation for the motor, for the power electronics converter within the power processor, and for the mechanical system as well.

As an example, in the original cascade control system discussed earlier, limits can be placed on the torque (current) reference, which is the output of the speed PI controller, as seen in Fig. 8-15.   Similarly, as shown in Fig. 8-16a, a limit inherently exists on the control voltage (applied to the PWM-IC chip), which is the output of the torque/current PI controller.

Similarly, a limit inherently exists on the output of the PPU, whose magnitude cannot exceed the input dc-bus voltage V_d. For a large change in reference or a large disturbance, the system may reach such limits.   This makes the system nonlinear and introduces further delay in the loop when the limits are reached. For example, a linear controller may demand a large motor current in order to meet a sudden load torque increase, but the current limit will cause the current loop to meet this increased load torque demand slower than is otherwise possible. This is the reason that after the controller is designed based on the assumptions of linearity, its performance in the presence of such limits should be thoroughly simulated.

8-10   ANTI-WINDUP (NON-WINDUP) INTEGRATION

In order for the system to maintain stability in the presence of limits, special attention should be paid to the controllers with integrators, such as the PI controller shown in Fig. 8-16b. In the anti-windup integrator of Fig. 8-16b, if the controller output reaches its limit, then the integrator action is turned off by shorting the input of the integrator to ground, if the saturation increases in the same direction.

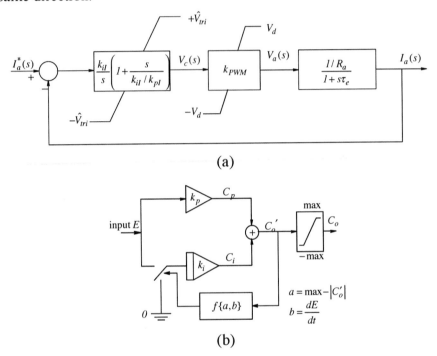

(a)

(b)

Figure 8-16 (a) Limits on the PI controller; (b) PI with anti-windup.

SUMMARY/REVIEW QUESTIONS

1. What are the various blocks of a motor drive?
2. What is a cascaded control and what are its advantages?
3. Draw the average models of a PWM controller and a dc-dc converter.
4. Draw the dc-motor equivalent circuit and its representation in Laplace domain. Is this representation linear?
5. What is the transfer function of a proportional-integral (PI) controller?
6. Draw the block diagram of the torque loop.
7. What is the rationale for neglecting the feedback from speed in the torque loop?

8. Draw the simplified block diagram of the torque loop.

9. Describe the procedure for designing the PI controller in the torque loop.

10. How would we have designed the PI controller of the torque loop if the effect of the speed were not ignored?

11. What allows us to approximate the closed torque loop by unity in the speed loop?

12. What is the procedure for designing the PI controller in the speed loop?

13. How would we have designed the PI controller in the speed loop if the closed torque-loop were not approximated by unity?

14. Draw the position-loop block diagram.

15. Why do we only need a P controller in the position loop?

16. What allows us to approximate the closed speed loop by unity in the position loop?

17. Describe the design procedure for determining the controller in the position loop.

18. How would we have designed the position controller if the closed speed loop were not approximated by unity?

19. Draw the block diagram with feed-forward. What are its advantages?

20. Why are limiters used and what are their effects?

21. What is the integrator windup and how can it be avoided?

REFERENCES

1. M. Kazmierkowski and H. Tunia, "Automatic Control of Converter-Fed Drives," Elsevier, 1994, 559 pages.

2. M. Kazmierkowski, R. Krishnan and F. Blaabjerg, "Control of Power Electronics," Academic Press, 2002, 518 pages.

3. W. Leonard, "Control of Electric Drives," Springer-Verlag, New York, 1985.

PROBLEMS AND SIMULATIONS

8-1   In a unity feedback system, the open-loop transfer function is of the form

$G_{OL}(s) = \dfrac{k}{1 + s/\omega_p}$. Calculate the bandwidth of the closed-loop transfer

function. How does the bandwidth depend on k and ω_p?

8-2   In a feedback system, the forward path has a transfer function of the form $G(s) = k/(1 + s/\omega_p)$, and the feedback path has a gain of k_{fb} which is less than unity. Calculate the bandwidth of the closed-loop transfer function. How does the bandwidth depend on k_{fb}?

8-3   In designing the torque loop of Example 8-2, include the effect of the back-emf, shown in Fig. 8-9a. Design a PI controller for the same open-loop crossover frequency and for a phase margin of 60 degrees. Compare your results with those in Example 8-2.

8-4   In designing the speed loop of Example 8-3, include the torque loop by a first-order transfer function based on the design in Example 8-2. Design a PI controller for the same open-loop crossover frequency and the same phase margin as in Example 8-3 and compare results.

8-5   In designing the position loop of Example 8-4, include the speed loop by a first-order transfer function based on the design in Example 8-3. Design a P-type controller for the same open-loop crossover frequency as in Example 8-4 and for a phase margin of 60 degrees. Compare your results with those in Example 8-4.

8-6   In an actual system in which there are limits on the voltage and current that can be supplied, why and how does the initial steady-state operating point make a difference for large-signal disturbances?

8-7   Obtain the time response of the system designed in Example 8-3, in terms of the change in speed, for a step-change of the load-torque disturbance.

8-8   Obtain the time response of the system designed in Example 8-4, in terms of the change in position, for a step-change of the load-torque disturbance.

8-9   In the example system of Table 8-1, the maximum output voltage of the dc-dc converter is limited to 60 V. Assume that the current is limited to 8 A in magnitude. How do these two limits impact the response of the system to a large step-change in the reference value?

8-10   In Example 8-3, design the speed-loop controller, without the inner current loop, as shown in Fig. P8-10, for the same crossover frequency and phase margin as in Example 8-3. Compare results with the system of Example 8-3.

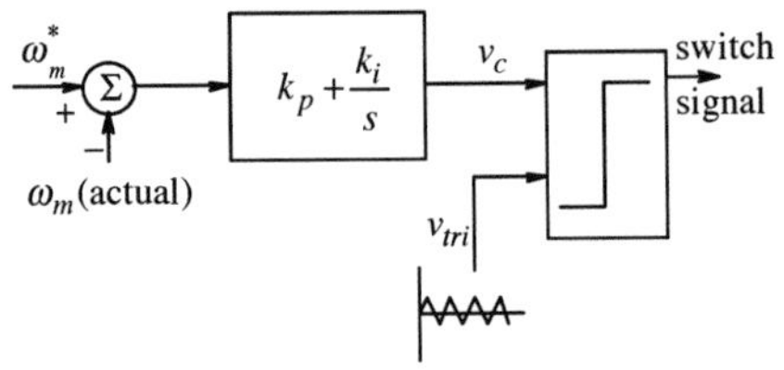

Figure P8-10

CHAPTER 9

INTRODUCTION TO AC MACHINES AND SPACE VECTORS

9-1   INTRODUCTION

The market share of ac drives is growing at the expense of brush-type dc motor drives. In ac drives, motors are primarily of two types: induction motors, which are the workhorses of the industry, and the sinusoidal-waveform, permanent-magnet synchronous motors, which are mostly used for high performance applications in small power ratings. The purpose of this chapter is to introduce the tools necessary to analyze the operation of these ac machines in later chapters.

Generally, three-phase ac voltages and currents supply all of these machines. The stators of the induction and the synchronous machines are similar and consist of 3-phase windings. However, the rotor construction makes the operation of these two machines different. In the stator of these machines, each phase winding (a winding consists of a number of coils connected in series) produces a sinusoidal field distribution in the air gap. The field distributions due to three phases are displaced by 120 degrees ($2\pi / 3$ radians) in space with respect to each other, as indicated by their magnetic axes (defined in Chapter 6 for a concentrated coil) in the cross-section of Fig. 9-1 for a 2-pole machine, the simplest case. In this chapter, we will learn to represent sinusoidal field distributions in the air gap with space vectors which will greatly simplify our analysis.

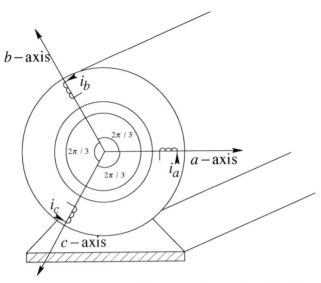

Figure 9-1 Magnetic axes of the three phases in a 2-pole machine.

9-2   SINUSOIDALLY-DISTRIBUTED STATOR WINDINGS

In the following description, we will assume a 2-pole machine (with $p=2$). This analysis is later generalized to multi-pole machines by means of Example 9-2.

In ac machines, windings for each phase ideally should produce a sinusoidally-distributed, radial field (F, H, and B) in the air gap. Theoretically, this requires a sinusoidally-distributed winding in each phase. In practice, this is approximated in a variety of ways discussed in References [1] and [2]. To visualize this sinusoidal distribution, consider the winding for phase a, shown in Fig. 9-2a, where, in the slots, the number of turns-per-coil for phase-a progressively increases away from the magnetic axis, reaching a maximum at $\theta = 90^0$. Each coil, such as the coil with sides 1 and 1', spans 180 degrees where the current into coil-side 1 returns in 1' through the end-turn at the back of the machine. This coil (1,1') is connected in series to coil-side 2 of the next coil (2,2'), and so on. Graphically, such a winding for phase-a can be drawn as shown in Fig. 9-2b, where bigger circles represent higher conductor densities, noting that all of the conductors in the winding are in series and hence carry the same current.

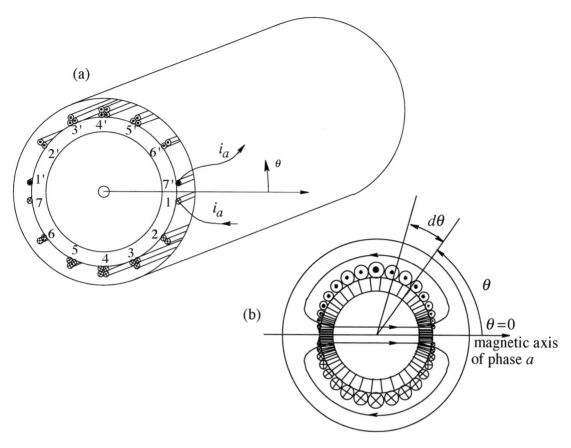

Figure 9-2 Sinusoidally-distributed winding for phase-*a*.

In Fig. 9-2b, in phase *a,* the conductor density $n_s(\theta)$, in terms of the number of conductors per radian angle, is a sinusoidal function of the angle θ, and can be expressed as

$$n_s(\theta) = \hat{n}_s \sin\theta \quad [no.\, of\, conductors\,/\, rad] \qquad 0 < \theta < \pi \qquad (9\text{-}1)$$

where $\hat{n}_s$ is the maximum conductor density, which occurs at $\theta = \dfrac{\pi}{2}$. If the phase winding has a total of N_s turns (that is, $2N_s$ conductors), then each winding-half, from $\theta = 0$ to $\theta = \pi$, contains N_s conductors. To determine $\hat{n}_s$ in Eq. 9-1 in terms of N_s, note that a differential angle $d\theta$ at θ in Fig. 9-2b contains $n_s(\theta) \cdot d\theta$ conductors. Therefore, the integral of the conductor density in Fig. 9-2b, from $\theta = 0$ to $\theta = \pi$, equals N_s conductors:

$$\int_{0}^{\pi} n_s(\theta)\, d\theta = N_s \qquad\qquad (9\text{-}2)$$

Substituting the expression for $n_s(\theta)$ from Eq. 9-1, the integral in Eq. 9-2 yields

$$\int_{0}^{\pi} n_s(\theta)\, d\theta = \int_{0}^{\pi} \hat{n}_s \sin\theta\, d\theta = 2\hat{n}_s \qquad\qquad (9\text{-}3)$$

Equating the right-sides of Eqs. 9-2 and 9-3,

$$\hat{n}_s = \frac{N_s}{2} \qquad\qquad (9\text{-}4)$$

Substituting $\hat{n}_s$ from Eq. 9-4 into Eq. 9-1 yields the sinusoidal conductor-density distribution in the phase-a winding as

$$n_s(\theta) = \frac{N_s}{2}\sin\theta \qquad 0 \le \theta \le \pi \qquad\qquad (9\text{-}5)$$

In a multi-pole machine (with $p > 2$), the peak conductor density remains the same, $N_s / 2$, as in Eq. 9-5 for a 2-pole machine. (This is shown in Example 9-2 and the homework problem 9-4.)

Rather than restricting the conductor density expression to a region $0 < \theta < \pi$, we can interpret the negative of the conductor density in the region $\pi < \theta < 2\pi$ in Eq. 9-5 as being associated with carrying the current in the opposite direction, as indicated in Fig. 9-2b.

In this discussion, we will consider only the magnetizing flux lines that completely cross the two air gaps. That means that, at present, we will ignore the leakage flux lines. To obtain the air gap field (mmf, flux density and the magnetic field intensity) distribution caused by the winding current, we will make use of the symmetry in Fig. 9-3. The radially-oriented fields in the air gap at angles θ and $(\theta + \pi)$ are equal in magnitude but opposite in direction. We will

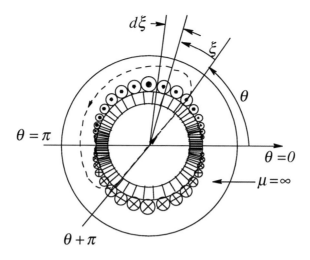

Figure 9-3 Calculation of air gap field distribution.

assume the field direction away from the center of the machine to be positive. Therefore, the magnetic field-intensity *in the air gap*, established by the current i_a (hence the subscript "*a*") at positions θ and $(\theta + \pi)$ will be equal in magnitude but of opposite sign: $H_a(\theta + \pi) = -H_a(\theta)$. To exploit this symmetry, we will apply Ampere's Law to a closed path shown in Fig. 9-3 through angles θ and $(\theta + \pi)$. We will assume the magnetic permeability of the rotor and the stator iron to be infinite and hence the *H*-field in iron to be zero. In terms of $H_a(\theta)$, application of Ampere's Law along the closed path in Fig. 9-3, at any instant of time *t*, results in

$$\underbrace{H_a \ell_g}_{\text{outward}} - \underbrace{(-H_a)\ell_g}_{\text{inward}} = \int_0^\pi i_a \cdot n_s(\theta + \xi) \cdot d\xi \qquad (9\text{-}6)$$

where ℓ_g is the length of each air gap and a negative sign is associated with the integral in the inward direction because, while the path of integration is inward, the field intensity is measured outwardly. On the right side of Eq. 9-6, $n_s(\xi) \cdot d\xi$ is the number of turns enclosed in the differential angle $d\xi$ at angle ξ, as measured in Fig. 9-3. In Eq. 9-6, integration from 0 to π yields the total number of conductors enclosed by the chosen path, including the "negative" conductors that carry current in the opposite direction. Substituting the conductor density expression from Eq. 9-5 into Eq. 9-6,

$$2H_a(\theta)\ell_g = \frac{N_s}{2}i_a\int_0^\pi sin(\theta+\xi)\cdot d\xi = N_s\,i_a\cos\theta$$

or

$$H_a(\theta) = \frac{N_s}{2\ell_g}i_a\cos\theta \qquad\qquad (9\text{-}7)$$

Using Eq. 9-7, the radial flux density $B_a(\theta)$ and the mmf $F_a(\theta)$ acting on the air gap at an angle θ can be written as

$$B_a(\theta) = \mu_o H_a(\theta) = (\frac{\mu_o N_s}{2\ell_g})i_a\cos\theta \qquad\qquad (9\text{-}8)$$

$$F_a(\theta) = \ell_g\,H_a(\theta) = \frac{N_s}{2}i_a\cos\theta \qquad\qquad (9\text{-}9)$$

The co-sinusoidal field distributions in the air gap due to a positive value of i_a

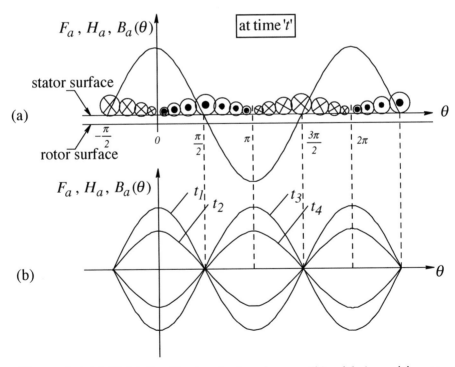

Figure 9-4 (a) Field distribution in the air gap; (b) with i_a positive at t_1 and t_2, and negative at t_3 and t_4.

(with the direction as defined in Figs. 9-2a and 9-2b), given by Eqs. 9-7 through 9-9, are plotted in the developed view of Fig. 9-4a. The angle θ is measured in the counter-clockwise direction with respect to the phase-*a* magnetic axis. The radial field distributions in the air gap peak along the phase-*a* magnetic axis, and at any instant of time, their amplitudes are linearly proportional to the value of i_a at that time. Fig. 9-4b shows field distributions in the air gap due to positive and negative values of i_a at various times. Notice that regardless of the positive or the negative current in phase-*a*, the flux-density distribution produced by it in the air gap always has its peak (positive or negative) along the phase-*a* magnetic axis.

▲ **Example 9-1** In the sinusoidally-distributed winding of phase-*a*, shown in Fig. 9-3, $N_s = 100$ and the current $i_a = 10A$. The air gap length $\ell_g = 1mm$. Calculate the ampere-turns enclosed and the corresponding *F*, *H*, and *B* fields for the following Ampere's Law integration paths: (a) through θ equal to 0^0 and 180^0 as shown in Fig. 9-5a and (b) through θ equal to 90^0 and 270^0 as shown in Fig. 9-5b.

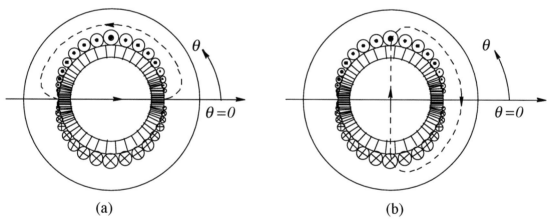

(a) (b)

Figure 9-5 Paths corresponding to Example 9-1.

Solution

(a) At $\theta = 0^0$, from Eqs. 9-7 through 9-9,

$$H_a\big|_{\theta=0} = \frac{N_s}{2\ell_g} i_a \cos(\theta) = 5 \times 10^5 \ A/m,$$

$$B_a\big|_{\theta=0} = \mu_o H_a\big|_{\theta=0} = 0.628 \, T \text{, and}$$

$$F_a\big|_{\theta=0} = \ell_g H_a\big|_{\theta=0} = 500 \, A \cdot turns.$$

All the field quantities reach their maximum magnitude at $\theta = 0^0$ and $\theta = 180^0$, because the path through them encloses all of the conductors that are carrying current in the same direction.

(b) From Eqs. 9-7 through 9-9, at $\theta = 90^0$,

$$H_a\big|_{\theta=90^0} = \frac{N_s}{2\ell_g} i_a \cos(\theta) = 0 \, A/m, \quad B_a\big|_{\theta=90^0} = 0, \quad \text{and} \quad F_a\big|_{\theta=90^0} = 0.$$

Half of the conductors enclosed by this path, as shown in Fig. 9-5b, carry current in a direction opposite that of the other half. The net effect is the cancellation of all of the field quantities in the air gap at 90 and 270 degrees. ▲

We should note that there is a limited number of total slots along the stator periphery, and each phase is allotted only a fraction of the total slots. In spite of these limitations, the field distribution can be made to approach a sinusoidal distribution in space, as in the ideal case discussed above. Since machine design is not our objective, we will leave the details for the interested reader to investigate in References [1] and [2].

▲ **Example 9-2** Consider the phase-*a* winding for a 4-pole stator (*p=4*) as shown in Fig. 9-6a. All of the conductors are in series. Just like in a 2-pole machine, the conductor density is a sinusoidal function. The total number of turns per-phase is N_s. Obtain the expressions for the conductor density and the field distribution, both as functions of position.

Solution We will define an electrical angle θ_e in terms of the actual (mechanical) angle θ:

$$\theta_e = \frac{p}{2}\theta \quad \text{where} \quad \theta_e = 2\theta \, (p=4 \, poles) \tag{9-10}$$

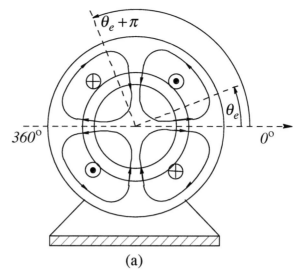

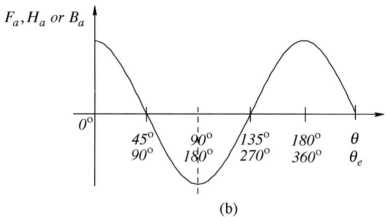

(b)

Figure 9-6 Phase a of a 4-pole machine.

Skipping a few steps (left as homework problem 9-4), we can show that, in terms of θ_e, the conductor density in phase-a of a p-pole stator ideally should be

$$n_s(\theta_e) = \frac{N_s}{2}\sin\theta_e. \qquad (p \geq 2) \qquad (9\text{-}11)$$

To calculate the field distribution, we will apply Ampere's Law along the path through θ_e and $(\theta_e + \pi)$, shown in Fig. 9-6a, and we will make use of symmetry. The procedure is similar to that used for a 2-pole machine (the intermediate steps are skipped here and left as homework problem 9-5). The results for a multi-pole machine ($p \geq 2$) are as follows:

$$H_a(\theta_e) = \frac{N_s}{p\,\ell_g} i_a \cos\theta_e \qquad\qquad\qquad\qquad (9\text{-}12a)$$

$$B_a(\theta_e) = \mu_o H_a(\theta_e) = (\frac{\mu_o N_s}{p\,\ell_g}) i_a \cos\theta_e \qquad\qquad (9\text{-}12b)$$

and

$$F_a(\theta_e) = \ell_g\, H_a(\theta_e) = \frac{N_s}{p} i_a \cos\theta_e. \qquad\qquad (9\text{-}12c)$$

These distributions are plotted in Fig. 9-6b for a 4-pole machine. Notice that one complete cycle of distribution spans 180 mechanical degrees; therefore, this distribution is repeated twice around the periphery in the air gap. ▲

9-2-1 Three-Phase, Sinusoidally-Distributed Stator Windings

In the previous section, we focused only on phase-a, which has its magnetic axis along $\theta = 0^0$. There are two more identical sinusoidally-distributed windings for phases b and c, with magnetic axes along $\theta = 120^0$ and $\theta = 240^0$, respectively, as represented in Fig. 9-7a. These three windings are generally connected in a wye-arrangement by connecting terminals a', b', and c' together, as shown in Fig. 9-7b. Field distributions in the air gap due to currents i_b and i_c are identical in

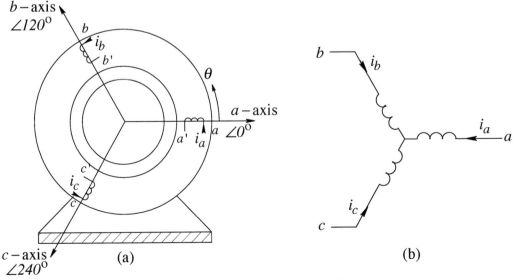

Figure 9-7 Three-phase windings.

shape to those in Figs. 9-4a and 9-4b, due to i_a, but they peak along their respective phase-*b* and phase-*c* magnetic axes.

By Kirchhoff's Current Law, in Fig. 9-7b,

$$i_a(t) + i_b(t) + i_c(t) = 0 \qquad\qquad (9\text{-}13)$$

▲ **Example 9-3**   At any instant of time t, the stator windings of the 2-pole machine shown in Fig. 9-7b have $i_a = 10\,A$, $i_b = -7\,A$, and $i_c = -3\,A$. The air gap length $\ell_g = 1\,mm$ and each winding has $N_s = 100$ turns. Plot the flux density, as a function of θ, produced by each current, and the resultant flux density $B_s(\theta)$ in the air gap due to the combined effect of the three stator currents at this time. Note that the subscript "s" (which refers to the stator) includes the effect of all three stator phases on the air gap field distribution.

Solution   From Eq. 9-8, the peak flux density produced by any phase current i is

$$\hat{B} = \frac{\mu_o N_s}{2\ell_g} i = \frac{4\pi \times 10^{-7} \times 100}{2 \times 1 \times 10^{-3}} i = 0.0628\, i \ [T].$$

The flux-density distributions are plotted as functions of θ in Fig. 9-8 for the given values of the three phase currents. Note that B_a has its positive peak at $\theta = 0^o$, B_b has its negative peak at $\theta = 120^o$, and B_c has its negative peak at $\theta = 240^o$. Applying the principle of superposition under the assumption of a linear magnetic circuit, adding together the flux-density distributions produced by each phase at every angle θ yields the combined stator-produced flux density distribution $B_s(\theta)$, plotted in Fig. 9-8.   ▲

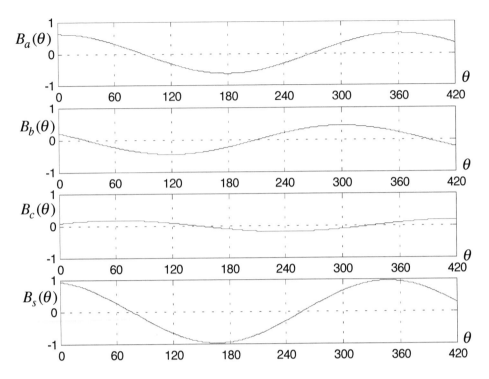

Figure 9-8 Waveforms of flux density.

9-3 THE USE OF SPACE VECTORS TO REPRESENT SINUSOIDAL FIELD DISTRIBUTIONS IN THE AIR GAP

In linear ac circuits in a sinusoidal steady state, all voltages and currents vary sinusoidally with time. These sinusoidally time-varying voltages and currents are represented by phasors $\overline{V}$ and $\overline{I}$ for ease of calculations. These phasors are expressed by complex numbers, as discussed in Chapter 3.

Similarly, in ac machines, at any instant of time t, sinusoidal space distributions of fields (B, H, F) in the air gap can be represented by space vectors. At any instant of time t, in representing a field distribution in the air gap with a space vector, we should note the following:

- The peak of the field distribution is represented by the amplitude of the space vector.

- Where the field distribution has its *positive* peak, the angle θ, measured with respect to the phase-*a* magnetic axis (by convention chosen as the reference axis), is represented by the orientation of the space vector.

Similar to phasors, space vectors are expressed by complex numbers. The space vectors are denoted by a "$\rightarrow$" on top, and their time dependence is usually explicitly shown.

Let us first consider phase-*a*. In Fig. 9-9a, at any instant of time t, the mmf produced by the sinusoidally-distributed phase-*a* winding has a co-sinusoidal shape (distribution) in space; that is, this distribution always peaks along the phase-*a* magnetic axis, and elsewhere it varies with the cosine of the angle θ away from the magnetic axis. The amplitude of this co-sinusoidal spatial distribution depends on the phase current i_a, which varies with time. Therefore, as shown in Fig. 9-9a, at any time t, the mmf distribution due to i_a can be represented by a space vector $\overrightarrow{F_a}(t)$:

$$\overrightarrow{F_a}(t) = \frac{N_s}{2} i_a(t) \angle 0^0 \qquad (9\text{-}14)$$

The amplitude of $\overrightarrow{F_a}(t)$ is $(N_s/2)$ times $i_a(t)$, and $\overrightarrow{F_a}(t)$ is always oriented along the phase-*a* magnetic axis at the angle of 0^0. The phase-*a* magnetic axis is always used as the reference axis. A representation similar to the mmf distribution can be used for the flux-density distribution.

In a similar manner, at any time t, the mmf distributions produced by the other two phase windings can also be represented by space vectors oriented along their respective magnetic axes at 120^0 and 240^0, as shown in Fig. 9-9a for negative values of i_b and i_c. In general, at any instant of time, we have the following three space vectors representing the respective mmf distributions:

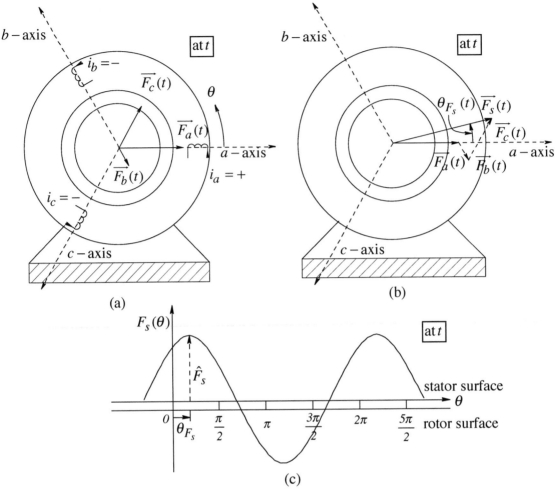

Figure 9-9 Representation of MMF space vector in a machine.

$$\overrightarrow{F_a}(t) = \frac{N_s}{2} i_a(t) \angle 0^0$$

$$\overrightarrow{F_b}(t) = \frac{N_s}{2} i_b(t) \angle 120^0 \qquad (9\text{-}15)$$

$$\overrightarrow{F_c}(t) = \frac{N_s}{2} i_c(t) \angle 240^0$$

Note that the sinusoidal distribution of mmf in the air gap at any time t is a consequence of the sinusoidally distributed windings. As shown in Fig. 9-9a for a positive value of i_a and negative values of i_b and i_c (such that $i_a + i_b + i_c = 0$), each of these vectors is pointed along its corresponding magnetic axis, with its amplitude depending on the winding current at that time. Due to the three stator currents, the resultant stator mmf distribution is represented by a resultant space vector which is obtained by vector addition in Fig. 9-9b:

$$\overrightarrow{F}_s(t) = \overrightarrow{F}_a(t) + \overrightarrow{F}_b(t) + \overrightarrow{F}_c(t) = \hat{F}_s \angle \theta_{F_s} \qquad (9\text{-}16a)$$

where $\hat{F}_s$ is the space vector amplitude and θ_{F_s} is the orientation (with the a-axis as the reference). The space vector $\overrightarrow{F}_s(t)$ represents the mmf distribution in the air gap at this time t due to all three phase currents; $\hat{F}_s$ represents the peak amplitude of this distribution and θ_{F_s} is the angular position at which the positive peak of the distribution is located. The subscript "s" refers to the combined mmf due to all three phases of the stator. The space vector $\overrightarrow{F}_s$ at this time in Fig. 9-9b represents the mmf distribution in the air gap, which is plotted in Fig. 9-9c.

Expressions similar to $\overrightarrow{F}_s(t)$ in Eq. 9-16a can be derived for the space vectors representing the combined-stator flux-density and the field-intensity distributions:

$$\overrightarrow{B}_s(t) = \overrightarrow{B}_a(t) + \overrightarrow{B}_b(t) + \overrightarrow{B}_c(t) = \hat{B}_s \angle \theta_{B_s} \qquad (9\text{-}16b)$$

and

$$\overrightarrow{H}_s(t) = \overrightarrow{H}_a(t) + \overrightarrow{H}_b(t) + \overrightarrow{H}_c(t) = \hat{H}_s \angle \theta_{H_s} \qquad (9\text{-}16c)$$

How are these three field distributions, represented by space vectors defined in Eqs. 9-16a through 9-16c, related to each other? This question is answered by Eqs. 9-21a and 9-21b in section 9-4-1.

▲ **Example 9-4**   In a 2-pole, three-phase machine, each of the sinusoidally-distributed windings has $N_s = 100$ turns. The air gap length $\ell_g = 1.5mm$. At a time t, $i_a = 10\,A$, $i_b = -10\,A$, and $i_c = 0\,A$. Using space vectors, calculate and plot the resultant flux density distribution in the air gap at this time.

Solution   From Eqs. 9-15 and 9-16, noting that mathematically $1\angle 0^0 = \cos\theta + j\sin\theta$,

$$\overrightarrow{F_s}(t) = \frac{N_s}{2}\left(i_a\angle 0^0 + i_b\angle 120^0 + i_c\angle 240^0\right)$$

$$= 50 \times \left\{10 + (-10)(\cos 120^0 + j\sin 120^0) + (0)(\cos 240^0 + j\sin 240^0)\right\}$$

$$= 50 \times 17.32\angle - 30^o = 866\angle - 30^0 \ A \cdot turns.$$

From Eqs. 9-8 and 9-9, $B_a(\theta) = \left(\mu_0 / \ell_g\right)F_a(\theta)$. The same relationship applies to the field quantities due to all three stator phase currents being applied simultaneously; that is, $B_s(\theta) = \left(\mu_0 / \ell_g\right)F_s(\theta)$. Therefore, at any instant of time t,

$$\overrightarrow{B_s}(t) = \frac{\mu_0}{\ell_g}\overrightarrow{F_s}(t) = \frac{4\pi \times 10^{-7}}{1.5 \times 10^{-3}}866\angle - 30^0 = 0.73\angle - 30^0 \ T.$$

This space vector is drawn in Fig. 9-10a. The flux density distribution has a peak value of 0.73 T and the positive peak is located at $\theta = -30^0$, as shown in Fig. 9-10b. Elsewhere, the radial flux density in the air gap, due to the combined action of all three phase currents, is cosinusoidally distributed. ▲

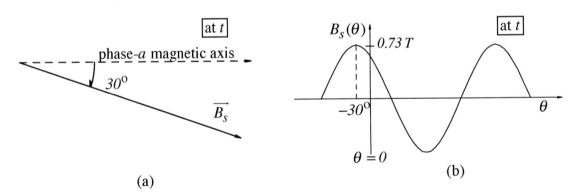

(a)   (b)

Figure 9-10 (a) Resultant flux-density space vector; (b) flux-density distribution.

9-4 SPACE-VECTOR REPRESENTATION OF COMBINED TERMINAL CURRENTS AND VOLTAGES

At any time t, we can measure the phase quantities, such as the voltage $v_a(t)$ and the current $i_a(t)$, at the terminals. Since there is no easy way to show that phase currents and voltages are distributed in space at any given time, we will NOT assign space vectors to physically represent these phase quantities. Rather, at any instant of time t, we will define space vectors to mathematically represent the combination of phase voltages and phase currents. These space vectors are defined to be the sum of their phase components (at that time) multiplied by their respective phase-axis orientations. Therefore, at any instant of time t, the stator current and the stator voltage space vectors are defined, in terms of their phase components (shown in Fig. 9-11a), as

$$\vec{i}_s(t) = i_a(t)\angle 0^0 + i_b(t)\angle 120^0 + i_c(t)\angle 240^0 = \hat{I}_s(t)\angle\theta_{i_s}(t) \qquad (9\text{-}17)$$

and

$$\vec{v}_s(t) = v_a(t)\angle 0^0 + v_b(t)\angle 120^0 + v_c(t)\angle 240^0 = \hat{V}_s(t)\angle\theta_{v_s}(t) \qquad (9\text{-}18)$$

where the subscript "s" refers to the combined quantities of the stator. We will see later on that this mathematical description is of immense help in understanding the operation and control of ac machines.

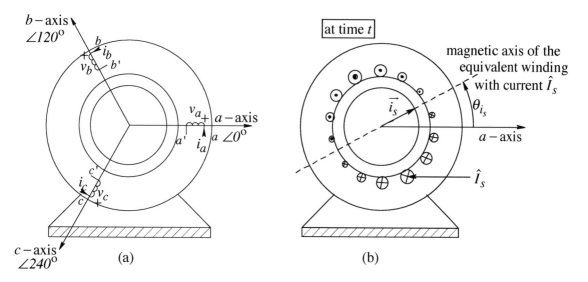

Figure 9-11 (a) Phase voltages and currents; (b) physical interpretation of stator current space vector.

9-4-1 Physical Interpretation of the Stator Current Space Vector $\vec{i}_s(t)$

The stator current space vector $\vec{i}_s(t)$ can be easily related to the stator mmf space vector $\vec{F}_s$. Multiplying both sides of Eq. 9-17 by $(N_s/2)$ gives

$$\frac{N_s}{2}\vec{i}_s(t) = \underbrace{\frac{N_s}{2}i_a(t)\angle 0^0}_{\vec{F}_a(t)} + \underbrace{\frac{N_s}{2}i_b(t)\angle 120^0}_{\vec{F}_b(t)} + \underbrace{\frac{N_s}{2}i_c(t)\angle 240^0}_{\vec{F}_c(t)} \qquad (9\text{-}19a)$$

Using Eq. 9-16, the sum of the mmf space vectors for the three phases is the resultant stator space vector. Therefore,

$$\frac{N_s}{2}\vec{i}_s(t) = \vec{F}_s(t) \qquad (9\text{-}19b)$$

Thus,

$$\vec{i}_s(t) = \frac{\vec{F}_s(t)}{(N_s/2)} \qquad \text{where} \quad \hat{I}_s(t) = \frac{\hat{F}_s(t)}{(N_s/2)} \quad \text{and} \quad \theta_{i_s}(t) = \theta_{F_s}(t) \qquad (9\text{-}20)$$

Eq. 9-20 shows that the vectors $\vec{i}_s(t)$ and $\vec{F}_s(t)$ are related only by a scalar constant $(N_s/2)$. Therefore, they have the same orientation and their amplitudes are related by $(N_s/2)$. At any instant of time t, Eq. 9-20 has the following interpretation:

> The combined mmf distribution in the air gap produced by i_a, i_b, and i_c flowing through their respective sinusoidally-distributed phase windings (each with N_s turns) is the same as that produced in Fig. 9-11b by a current $\hat{I}_s$ flowing through an equivalent sinusoidally-distributed stator winding with its axis oriented at $\theta_{i_s}(t)$. This equivalent winding also has N_s turns.

As we will see later on, the above interpretation is very useful – it allows us to obtain, at any instant of time, the combined torque acting on all three phase windings by calculating the torque acting on this single equivalent winding with a current $\hat{I}_s$.

Next, we will use $\vec{i}_s(t)$ to relate the field quantities produced due to the combined effects of the three stator phase winding currents. Eqs. 9-7 through 9-9 show that the field distributions H_a, B_a, and F_a, produced by i_a flowing through the phase-a winding, are related by scalar constants. This will also be true for the combined fields in the air gap caused by the simultaneous flow of i_a, i_b, and i_c, since the magnetic circuit is assumed to be unsaturated and the principle of superposition applies. Therefore, we can write expressions for $\overline{B}_s(t)$ and $\overline{H}_s(t)$ in terms of $\vec{i}_s(t)$ which are similar to Eq. 9-19b for $\overline{F}_s(t)$ (which is repeated below),

$$\overline{F}_s(t) = \frac{N_s}{2}\vec{i}_s(t)$$

$$\overline{H}_s(t) = \frac{N_s}{2\ell_g}\vec{i}_s(t) \qquad \text{(rotor-circuit electrically open-circuited)} \qquad (9\text{-}21a)$$

$$\overline{B}_s(t) = \frac{\mu_o N_s}{2\ell_g}\vec{i}_s(t)$$

The relationships in Eq. 9-21a show that these stator space vectors (with the rotor circuit electrically open-circuited) are collinear (that is, they point in the same direction) at any instant of time. Eq. 9-21 also yields the relationship between the peak values as

$$\hat{F}_s = \frac{N_s}{2}\hat{I}_s$$

$$\hat{H}_s = \frac{N_s}{2\ell_g}\hat{I}_s \qquad \text{(rotor-circuit electrically open-circuited)} \qquad (9\text{-}21b)$$

$$\hat{B}_s = \frac{\mu_o N_s}{2\ell_g}\hat{I}_s$$

▲ **Example 9-5** For the conditions in an ac machine in Example 9-4 at a given time t, calculate $\vec{i}_s(t)$. Show the equivalent winding and the current necessary to produce the same mmf distribution as the three phase windings combined.

Solution In Example 9-4, $i_a = 10A$, $i_b = -10A$, and $i_c = 0A$. Therefore, from Eq. 9-17,

$$\vec{i}_s = i_a\angle 0^0 + i_b\angle 120^0 + i_c\angle 240^0 = 10 + (-10)\angle 120^0 + (0)\angle 240^0 = 17.32\angle -30^0 \ A.$$

The space vector $\vec{i}_s$ is shown in Fig. 9-12a.

Since the $\vec{i}_s$ vector is oriented at $\theta = -30^o$ with respect to the phase-a magnetic axis, the equivalent sinusoidally-distributed stator winding has its magnetic axis at an angle of -30° with respect to the phase-a winding, as shown in Fig. 9-12b. The current required in the equivalent stator winding to produce the equivalent mmf distribution is the peak current $\hat{I}_s = 17.32A$. ▲

9-4-2 Phase Components of Space Vectors $\vec{i}_s(t)$ and $\vec{v}_s(t)$

If the three stator windings in Fig. 9-13a are connected in a wye arrangement, the sum of their currents is zero at any instant of time t by Kirchhoff's Current Law: $i_a(t) + i_b(t) + i_c(t) = 0$. Therefore, as shown in Fig. 9-13b, at any time t, a space

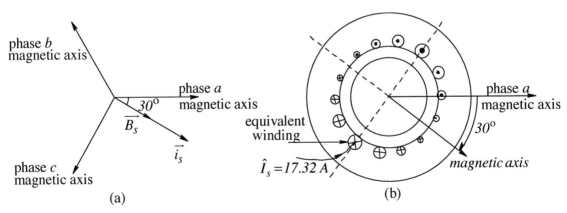

Figure 9-12 (a) Stator current space vector; (b) the equivalent winding.

vector is constructed from a unique set of phase components, which can be obtained by multiplying the projection of the space vector along the three axes by 2/3. (We should note that if the phase currents were not required to add up to zero, there would be an infinite number of phase component combinations.)

This graphical procedure is based on the mathematical derivations described below. First, let us consider the relationship

$$1\angle\theta = e^{j\theta} = \cos\theta + j\sin\theta \tag{9-22}$$

The real part in the above equation is

$$\text{Re}(1\angle\theta) = \cos\theta \tag{9-23}$$

Therefore, mathematically, we can obtain the phase components of a space vector such as $\vec{i}_s(t)$ as follows: multiply both sides of the $\vec{i}_s(t)$ expression in Eq. 9-17 by $1\angle 0^0$, $1\angle -120^0$, and $1\angle -240^0$, respectively. Equate the real parts on both sides and use the condition that $i_a(t) + i_b(t) + i_c(t) = 0$.

To obtain i_a:

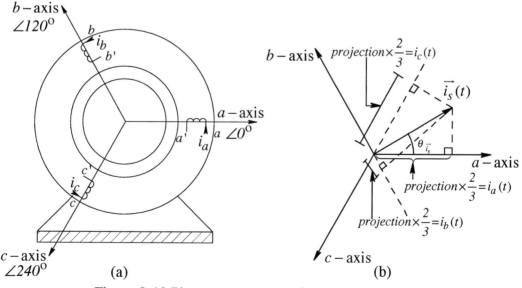

Figure 9-13 Phase components of a space vector.

$$\text{Re}[\vec{i}_s \angle 0^0] = i_a + \underbrace{\text{Re}[i_b \angle 120^0]}_{-\frac{1}{2}i_b} + \underbrace{\text{Re}[i_c \angle 240^0]}_{-\frac{1}{2}i_c} = \frac{3}{2}i_a$$

(9-24a)

$$\therefore i_a = \frac{2}{3}\text{Re}[\vec{i}_s \angle 0^0] = \frac{2}{3}\text{Re}[\hat{I}_s \angle \theta_{i_s}] = \frac{2}{3}\hat{I}_s \cos\theta_{i_s}$$

To obtain i_b :

$$\text{Re}[\vec{i}_s \angle -120^0] = \underbrace{\text{Re}[i_a \angle -120^0]}_{-\frac{1}{2}i_a} + i_b + \underbrace{\text{Re}[i_c \angle 120^0]}_{-\frac{1}{2}i_c} = \frac{3}{2}i_b$$

(9-24b)

$$\therefore i_b = \frac{2}{3}\text{Re}[\vec{i}_s \angle -120^0] = \frac{2}{3}\text{Re}[\hat{I}_s \angle(\theta_{i_s} - 120^o)] = \frac{2}{3}\hat{I}_s \cos(\theta_{i_s} - 120^o)$$

To obtain i_c :

$$\text{Re}[\vec{i}_s \angle -240^0] = \underbrace{\text{Re}[i_a \angle -240^0]}_{-\frac{1}{2}i_a} + \underbrace{\text{Re}[i_b \angle -120^0]}_{-\frac{1}{2}i_b} + i_c = \frac{3}{2}i_c$$

(9-24c)

$$\therefore i_c = \frac{2}{3}\text{Re}[\vec{i}_s \angle -240^0] = \frac{2}{3}\text{Re}[\hat{I}_s \angle(\theta_{i_s} - 240^o)] = \frac{2}{3}\hat{I}_s \cos(\theta_{i_s} - 240^o)$$

Since $i_a(t) + i_b(t) + i_c(t) = 0$, it can be shown that the same uniqueness applies to components of all space vectors such as $\vec{v}_s(t)$, $\vec{B}_s(t)$, and so on for both the stator and the rotor.

▲ **Example 9-6** In an ac machine at a given time, the stator voltage space vector is given as $\vec{v}_s = 254.56\angle 30^0\,V$. Calculate the phase voltage components at this time.

Solution   From Eq. 9-24,

$$v_a = \frac{2}{3}\text{Re}\{\vec{v}_s \angle 0^0\} = \frac{2}{3}\text{Re}\{254.56\angle 30^0\} = \frac{2}{3}\times 254.56\cos 30^\circ = 146.97\,V,$$

$$v_b = \frac{2}{3}\text{Re}\{\vec{v}_s \angle -120^0\} = \frac{2}{3}\text{Re}\{254.56\angle -90^0\} = \frac{2}{3}\times 254.56\cos(-90^\circ) = 0\,V,\text{ and}$$

$$v_c = \frac{2}{3}\text{Re}\{\vec{v}_s \angle -240^0\} = \frac{2}{3}\text{Re}\{254.56\angle -210^0\} = \frac{2}{3}\times 254.56\cos(-210^\circ) = -146.97\,V$$

▲

9-5 BALANCED SINUSOIDAL STEADY-STATE EXCITATION (ROTOR OPEN-CIRCUITED)

So far, our discussion has been in very general terms where voltages and currents are not restricted to any specific form. However, we are mainly interested in the normal mode of operation, that is, balanced three-phase, sinusoidal steady state conditions. Therefore, we will assume that a balanced set of sinusoidal voltages at a frequency $f\ (=\dfrac{\omega}{2\pi})$ in steady state is applied to the stator, with the rotor assumed to be open-circuited. We will initially neglect the stator winding resistances R_s and the leakage inductances $L_{\ell s}$.

In steady state, applying voltages to the windings in Fig. 9-14a (under rotor open-circuit condition) results in magnetizing currents. These magnetizing currents are

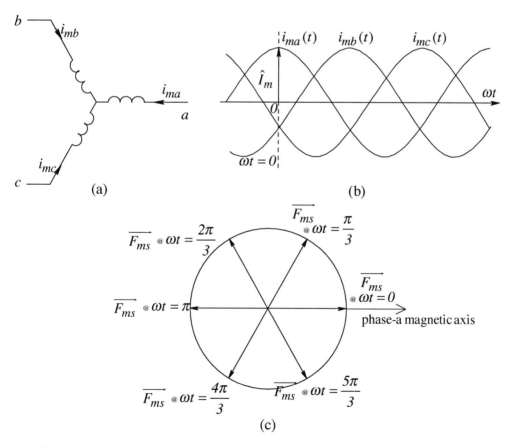

Figure 9-14 (a) Windings; b) magnetizing currents; (c) rotating mmf space vector.

indicated by adding "*m*" to the subscripts in the following equation, and are plotted in Fig. 9-14b

$$i_{ma} = \hat{I}_m \cos \omega t, \quad i_{mb} = \hat{I}_m \cos\left(\omega t - 2\pi/3\right), \text{and} \quad i_{mc} = \hat{I}_m \cos\left(\omega t - 4\pi/3\right) \qquad (9\text{-}25)$$

where $\hat{I}_m$ is the peak value of the magnetizing currents and the time origin is chosen to be at the positive peak of $i_{ma}(t)$.

9-5-1   Rotating Stator MMF Space Vector

Substituting into Eq. 9-17 the expressions in Eq. 9-25 for the magnetizing currents varying sinusoidally with time, the stator magnetizing current space vector is

$$\overrightarrow{i_{ms}}(t) = \hat{I}_m \left[\cos\omega t \angle 0^0 + \cos(\omega t - 2\pi/3)\angle 120^0 + \cos(\omega t - 4\pi/3)\angle 240^0 \right] \qquad (9\text{-}26)$$

The expression within the square bracket in Eq. 9-26 simplifies to $\dfrac{3}{2}\angle\omega t$ (see homework problem 9-8) and Eq. 9-26 becomes

$$\overrightarrow{i_{ms}}(t) = \underbrace{\frac{3}{2}\hat{I}_m}_{\hat{I}_{ms}} \angle\omega t = \hat{I}_{ms}\angle\omega t \quad \text{where} \quad \hat{I}_{ms} = \frac{3}{2}\hat{I}_m \qquad (9\text{-}27)$$

From Eq. 9-21a,

$$\overrightarrow{F_{ms}}(t) = \frac{N_s}{2}\overrightarrow{i_{ms}}(t) = \hat{F}_{ms}\angle\omega t \quad \text{where} \quad \hat{F}_{ms} = \frac{N_s}{2}\hat{I}_{ms} = \frac{3}{2}\frac{N_s}{2}\hat{I}_m \qquad (9\text{-}28)$$

Similarly, using Eq. 9-21a again,

$$\overrightarrow{B_{ms}}(t) = (\frac{\mu_o N_s}{2\ell_g})\overrightarrow{i_{ms}}(t) \quad \text{where} \quad \hat{B}_{ms} = (\frac{\mu_o N_s}{2\ell_g})\hat{I}_{ms} = \frac{3}{2}(\frac{\mu_o N_s}{2\ell_g})\hat{I}_m \qquad (9\text{-}29)$$

Note that if the peak flux density $\hat{B}_{ms}$ in the air gap is to be at its rated value in Eq. 9-29, then the $\hat{I}_{ms}$ and hence the peak value of the magnetizing current $\hat{I}_m$ in each phase must also be at their rated values.

Under sinusoidal steady-state conditions, the stator-current, the stator-mmf, and the air gap flux-density space vectors have constant amplitudes ($\hat{I}_{ms}$, $\hat{F}_{ms}$, and $\hat{B}_{ms}$). As shown by $\overrightarrow{F_{ms}}(t)$ in Fig. 9-14c, all of these space vectors rotate with time at a constant speed, called the synchronous speed ω_{syn}, in the counter-clockwise direction, which in a 2-pole machine is equal to the frequency $\omega (= 2\pi f)$ of the voltages and currents applied to the stator:

$$\omega_{syn} = \omega \quad (p = 2) \tag{9-30}$$

▲ **Example 9-7** With the rotor electrically open-circuited in a 2-pole ac machine, voltages are applied to the stator, and result in the magnetizing currents plotted in Fig. 9-15a. Sketch the direction of the flux lines at the instants $\omega t = 0^{o}, 60^{o}, 120^{o}, 180^{o}, 240^{o}$, and 300°. Show that one electrical cycle results in the rotation of the flux orientation by one revolution, in accordance with Eq. 9-30 for a 2-pole machine.

Solution At $\omega t = 0$, $i_{ma} = \hat{I}_m$ and $i_{mb} = i_{mc} = -(1/2)\hat{I}_m$. The current directions for the three windings are indicated in Fig. 9-15b, where the circles for phase-*a* are shown larger due to twice as much current in them compared to the other two phases. The resulting flux orientation is shown as well. A Similar procedure is followed at other instants, as shown in Figs. 9-15c through 9-15g. These drawings clearly show that in a 2-pole machine, the electrical excitation through one cycle of the electrical frequency $f (= \omega / 2\pi)$ results in the rotation of the flux orientation, and hence of the space vector $\overrightarrow{B_{ms}}$, by one revolution in space. Therefore, $\omega_{syn} = \omega$, as expressed in Eq. 9-30. ▲

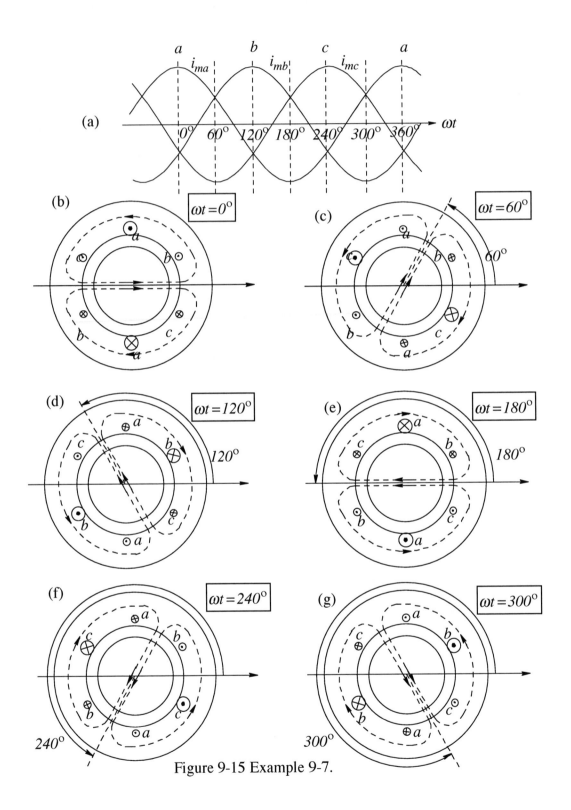

(a)

(b) $\omega t = 0°$

(c) $\omega t = 60°$

(d) $\omega t = 120°$

(e) $\omega t = 180°$

(f) $\omega t = 240°$

(g) $\omega t = 300°$

Figure 9-15 Example 9-7.

9-5-2   Rotating Stator MMF Space Vector in Multi-Pole Machines

In the previous section, we considered a 2-pole machine. In general, in a p-pole machine, a balanced sinusoidal steady state, with currents and voltages at a frequency $f(=\dfrac{\omega}{2\pi})$, results in an mmf space vector that rotates at a speed

$$\omega_{syn} = \frac{\omega}{p/2} \qquad\qquad (\frac{p}{2} = \text{pole-pairs}) \qquad\qquad (9\text{-}31)$$

This can be illustrated by considering a p-pole machine and repeating the procedure outlined in Example 9-7 for a 2-pole machine (this is left as homework problem 9-11).

In the space vectors for multi-pole machines, the three magnetic axes can be drawn as in a 2-pole machine (similar to the space vector diagrams of Fig. 9-9b or 9-13b, for example), except now the axes are separated by 120 degrees (electrical), where the electrical angles are defined by Eq. 9-10. Therefore, one complete cycle of electrical excitation causes the space vector, at the synchronous speed given in Eq. 9-31, to rotate by 360 degrees (electrical); that is, in the space vector diagram, the space vector returns to the position that it started from. This corresponds to a rotation by an angle of $360/(p/2)$ mechanical degrees, which is exactly what happens within the machine. However, in general (special situations will be pointed out), since no additional insight is gained by this multi-pole representation, it is best to analyze a multi-pole machine as if it were a 2-pole machine.

9-5-3   The Relationship between Space Vectors and Phasors in Balanced Three-Phase Sinusoidal Steady State ($\left.\overrightarrow{v_s}\right|_{t=0} \Leftrightarrow \overline{V}_a$ and $\left.\overrightarrow{i_{ms}}\right|_{t=0} \Leftrightarrow \overline{I}_{ma}$)

In Fig. 9-14b, note that at $\omega t = 0$, the magnetizing current i_{ma} in phase-a is at its positive peak. Corresponding to this time $\omega t = 0$, the space vectors $\overrightarrow{i_{ms}}$, $\overrightarrow{F_{ms}}$, and $\overrightarrow{B_{ms}}$ are along the a-axis in Fig. 9-14c. Similarly, at $\omega t = 2\pi/3\ rad$ or 120^0, i_{mb} in phase-b reaches its positive peak. Correspondingly, the space vectors $\overrightarrow{i_{ms}}$, $\overrightarrow{F_{ms}}$, and $\overrightarrow{B_{ms}}$ are along the b-axis, 120^0 ahead of the a-axis. Therefore, we can conclude that under a balanced three-phase sinusoidal steady state, when a phase voltage (or a phase current) is at its positive peak, the combined stator voltage (or current) space vector will be oriented along that phase axis. This can also be stated as follows: when a combined stator voltage (or current) space vector is oriented along the magnetic axis of any phase, at that time, that phase voltage (or current) is at its positive peak value.

We will make use of the information in the above paragraph. Under a balanced three-phase sinusoidal steady state, let us arbitrarily choose some time as the origin $t = 0$ in Fig. 9-16a such that the current i_{ma} reaches its positive peak at a later time $\omega t = \alpha$. The phase-a current can be expressed as

$$i_{ma}(t) = \hat{I}_m \cos(\omega t - \alpha) \tag{9-32}$$

which is represented by a phasor below and shown in the phasor diagram of Fig. 9-16b:

$$\overline{I}_{ma} = \hat{I}_m \angle -\alpha \tag{9-33a}$$

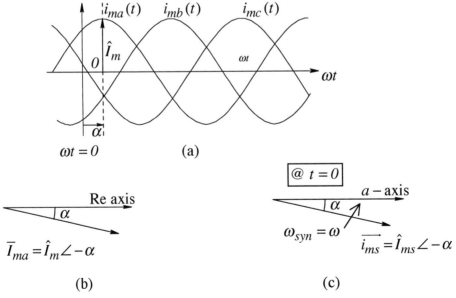

Figure 9-16 Relationship between space vectors and phasors in balanced sinusoidal steady state.

The phase-a current $i_{ma}(t)$ reaches its positive peak at $\omega t = \alpha$. Therefore, at time $t = 0$, the $\overrightarrow{i_{ms}}$ space vector will be as shown in Fig. 9-16c, behind the magnetic axis of phase-a by an angle α, so that it will be along the a-axis at a later time $\omega t = \alpha$, when i_{ma} reaches its positive peak. Therefore, at time $t = 0$,

$$\overrightarrow{i_{ms}}\Big|_{t=0} = \hat{I}_{ms} \angle -\alpha \quad \text{where} \quad \hat{I}_{ms} = \frac{3}{2}\hat{I}_m \tag{9-33b}$$

Combining Eqs. 9-33a and 9-33b,

$$\overrightarrow{i_{ms}}\Big|_{t=0} = \frac{3}{2}\overline{I}_{ma} \tag{9-34}$$

where the left side mathematically represents the combined current space vector at time $t = 0$ and in the right side $\overline{I}_{ma}$ is the phase-a current phasor representation. In sinusoidal steady state, Eq. 9-34 illustrates an important relationship between space vectors and phasors which we will use very often:

1. The orientation of the phase-a voltage (or current) phasor is the same as the orientation of the combined stator voltage (or current) space vector at time $t = 0$.

2. The amplitude of the combined stator voltage (or current) space vector is larger than that of the phasor amplitude by a factor of $3/2$.

Note that knowing the phasors for phase-a is sufficient, as the other phase quantities are displaced by 120 degrees with respect to each other and have equal magnitudes. This concept will be used in the following section.

9-5-4 Induced Voltages in Stator Windings

In the following discussion, we will ignore the resistance and the leakage inductance of the stator windings, shown wye-connected in Fig. 9-17a. Neglecting all losses, under the condition that there is no electrical circuit or excitation in the rotor, the stator windings appear purely inductive. Therefore, in each phase, the phase voltage and the magnetizing current are related as

$$e_{ma} = L_m \frac{di_{ma}}{dt}, \quad e_{mb} = L_m \frac{di_{mb}}{dt}, \quad \text{and} \quad e_{mc} = L_m \frac{di_{mc}}{dt} \qquad (9\text{-}35)$$

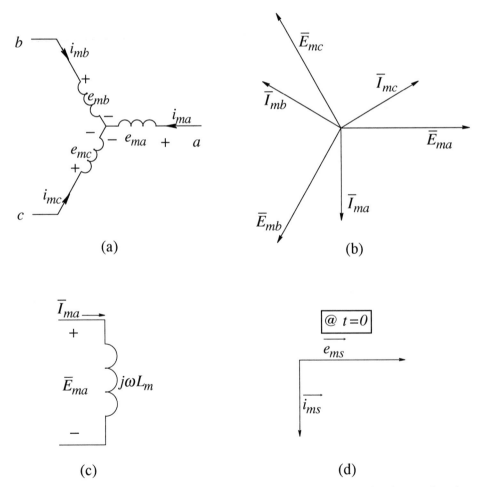

Figure 9-17 Winding current and induced emf (a) individual windings; (b) phasors; (c) per-phase equivalent circuit; (d) space vectors.

where L_m is the magnetizing inductance of the three-phase stator, which in terms of the machine parameters can be calculated as (see homework problems 9-13 and 9-14)

$$L_m = \frac{3}{2}\left[\frac{\pi\mu_o r\ell}{\ell_g}\left(\frac{N_s}{2}\right)^2\right] \tag{9-36}$$

where r is the radius, ℓ is the rotor length, and ℓ_g is the air gap length. The combination of quantities within the square bracket is the single-phase self-inductance $L_{m,1-phase}$ of each of the stator phase windings in a 2-pole machine:

$$L_{m,1-phase} = \frac{\pi\mu_o r\ell}{\ell_g}\left(\frac{N_s}{2}\right)^2 \tag{9-37}$$

Due to mutual coupling between the three phases, L_m given in Eq. 9-36 is larger than $L_{m,1-phase}$ by a factor of 3/2:

$$L_m = \frac{3}{2}L_{m,1-phase} \tag{9-38}$$

Under a balanced sinusoidal steady state, assuming that i_{ma} peaks at $\omega t = 90^o$, we can draw the three-phase phasor diagram shown in Fig. 9-17b, where

$$\overline{E}_{ma} = (j\omega L_m)\overline{I}_{ma} \tag{9-39}$$

The phasor-domain circuit diagram for phase-a is shown in Fig. 9-17c and the corresponding combined space vector diagram for $\overrightarrow{e_{ms}}$ and $\overrightarrow{i_{ms}}$ at $t = 0$ is shown in Fig. 9-17d. In general, at any time t,

$$\overrightarrow{e_{ms}}(t) = (j\omega L_m)\overrightarrow{i_{ms}}(t) \quad \text{where } \hat{E}_{ms} = (\omega L_m)\hat{I}_{ms} = \frac{3}{2}(\omega L_m)\hat{I}_m \tag{9-40}$$

In Eq. 9-40, substituting for $\overrightarrow{i_{ms}}(t)$ in terms of $\overrightarrow{B_{ms}}(t)$ from Eq. 9-21a and substituting for L_m from Eq. 9-36,

$$\overrightarrow{e_{ms}}(t) = j\omega(\frac{3}{2}\pi r\ell \frac{N_s}{2})\overrightarrow{B_{ms}}(t) \qquad (9\text{-}41)$$

Eq. 9-41 shows an important relationship: the induced voltages in the stator windings can be interpreted as back-emfs induced by the rotating flux-density distribution. This flux-density distribution, represented by $\overrightarrow{B_{ms}}(t)$, is rotating at a speed ω_{syn} (which equals ω in a 2-pole machine) and is "cutting" the stationary conductors of the stator phase windings. A similar expression can be derived for a multi-pole machine with $p>2$ (see homework problem 9-17).

▲ **Example 9-8**   In a 2-pole machine in a balanced sinusoidal steady state, the applied voltages are 208 V (L-L, rms) at a frequency of 60 Hz. Assume the phase-a voltage to be the reference phasor. The magnetizing inductance $L_m = 55\,mH$. Neglect the stator winding resistances and leakage inductances and assume the rotor to be electrically open-circuited. (a) Calculate and draw the $\overline{E}_{ma}$ and $\overline{I}_{ma}$ phasors. (b) Calculate and draw the space vectors $\overrightarrow{e_{ms}}$ and $\overrightarrow{i_{ms}}$ at $\omega t = 0^0$ and $\omega t = 60^0$. (c) If the peak flux density in the air gap is $1.1\,T$, draw the $\overrightarrow{B_{ms}}$ space vector in part (b) at the two instants of time.

Solution

(a) With the phase-a voltage as the reference phasor,

$$\overline{E}_{ma} = \frac{208\sqrt{2}}{\sqrt{3}} \angle 0^\circ = 169.83 \angle 0^\circ\, V$$

and

$$\overline{I}_{ma} = \frac{\overline{E}_{ma}}{j\omega L_m} \angle 0^\circ = \frac{169.83}{2\pi \times 60 \times 55 \times 10^{-3}} \angle -90^\circ = 8.19 \angle -90^\circ\, A .$$

These two phasors are drawn in Fig. 9-18a.

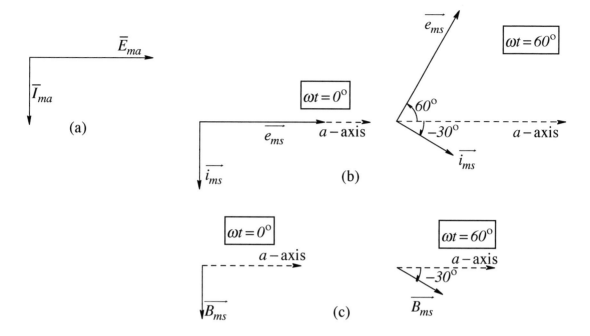

Figure 9-18 Example 9-7.

(b) At $\omega t = 0^o$, from Eq. 9-34, as shown in Fig. 9-18b,

$$\left.\overrightarrow{e_{ms}}\right|_{\omega t=o} = \frac{3}{2}\overline{E}_{ma} = \frac{3}{2}169.83\angle 0^o = 254.74\angle 0^o\, V$$

and

$$\left.\overrightarrow{i_{ms}}\right|_{\omega t=0} = \frac{3}{2}\overline{I}_{ma} = \frac{3}{2}8.19\angle -90^o = 12.28\angle -90^o\, A.$$

At $\omega t = 60^o$, both space vectors have rotated by an angle of 60 degrees in a counter-clockwise direction, as shown in Fig. 9-18b. Therefore,

$$\left.\overrightarrow{e_{ms}}\right|_{\omega t=60^o} = \left.\overrightarrow{e_{ms}}\right|_{\omega t=0}(1\angle 60^0) = 254.74\angle 60^o\, V$$

and

$$\left.\overrightarrow{i_{ms}}\right|_{\omega t=60^o} = \left.\overrightarrow{i_{ms}}\right|_{\omega t=0}(1\angle 60^0) = 12.28\angle -30^o\, A.$$

(c) In this example, at any time, the stator flux density space vector $\overrightarrow{B_{ms}}$ is oriented in the same direction as the $\overrightarrow{i_{ms}}$ space vector. Therefore, as plotted in Fig. 9-18c,

$$\overrightarrow{B_{ms}}\Big|_{\omega t=0^\circ} = 1.1\angle -90^\circ \ T \quad \text{and} \quad \overrightarrow{B_{ms}}\Big|_{\omega t=60^\circ} = 1.1\angle -30^\circ \ T. \qquad \blacktriangle$$

SUMMARY/REVIEW QUESTIONS

1. Draw the three-phase axis in the motor cross-section. Also, draw the three phasors $\overline{V_a}$, $\overline{V_b}$, and $\overline{V_c}$ in a balanced sinusoidal steady state. Why is the phase-b axis ahead of the phase-a axis by 120 degrees, but $\overline{V_b}$ lags $\overline{V_a}$ by 120 degrees?

2. Ideally, what should be the field (F, H, and B) distributions produced by each of the three stator windings? What is the direction of this field in the air gap? What direction is considered positive and what is considered negative?

3. What should the conductor-density distribution in a winding be in order to achieve the desired field distribution in the air gap? Express the conductor-density distribution $n_s(\theta)$ for phase-a.

4. How is sinusoidal distribution of conductor density in a phase winding approximated in practical machines with only a few slots available to each phase?

5. How are the three field distributions (F, H, and B) related to each other, assuming that there is no magnetic saturation in the stator and the rotor iron?

6. What is the significance of the magnetic axis of any phase winding?

7. Mathematically express the field distributions in the air gap due to i_a as a function of θ. Repeat this for i_b and i_c.

8. What do the phasors $\overline{V}$ and $\overline{I}$ denote? What are the meanings of the space vectors $\overrightarrow{B_a}(t)$ and $\overrightarrow{B_s}(t)$ at time t, assuming that the rotor circuit is electrically open-circuited?

9. What is the constraint on the sum of the stator currents?

10. What are physical interpretations of various stator winding inductances?

11. Why is the per-phase inductance L_m greater than the single-phase inductance $L_{m,1-phase}$ by a factor of 3/2?

12. What are the characteristics of space vectors which represent the field distributions $F_s(\theta)$, $H_s(\theta)$, and $B_s(\theta)$ at a given time? What notations are used for these space vectors? Which axis is used as a reference to express them mathematically in this chapter?

13. Why does a dc current through a phase winding produce a sinusoidal flux-density distribution in the air gap?

14. How are the terminal phase voltages and currents combined for representation by space vectors?

15. What is the physical interpretation of the stator current space vector $\vec{i}_s(t)$?

16. With no excitation or currents in the rotor, are all of the space vectors associated with the stator $\overrightarrow{i_{ms}}(t), \overline{F_{ms}}(t), \overline{B_{ms}}(t)$ collinear (oriented in the same direction)?

17. In ac machines, a stator space vector $\vec{v}_s(t)$ or $\vec{i}_s(t)$ consists of a unique set of phase components. What is the condition on which these components are based?

18. Express the phase voltage components in terms of the stator voltage space vector.

19. Under three-phase balanced sinusoidal condition with no rotor currents, and neglecting the stator winding resistances R_s and the leakage inductance $L_{\ell s}$ for simplification, answer the following questions: (a) What is the speed at which all of the space vectors rotate? (b) How is the peak flux density related to the magnetizing currents? Does this relationship depend on the frequency f of the excitation? If the peak flux density is at its rated value, then what about the peak value of the magnetizing currents? (c) How do the magnitudes of the applied voltages depend on the frequency of excitation, in order to keep the flux density constant (at its rated value for example)?

20. What is the relationship between space vectors and phasors under balanced sinusoidal operating conditions?

REFERENCES

1. Fitzgerald, Kingsley, and Umans, *Electric Machinery*, 5th edition, McGraw Hill, 1990.
2. G. R. Slemon, *Electric Machines and Drives,* Addison-Wesley publishing company, Inc., 1992.
3. P. K. Kovacs, *Transient Phenomena in Electrical Machines*, Elsevier, 1984.

PROBLEMS

9-1 In a three-phase, 2-pole ac machine, assume that the neutral of the wye-connected stator windings is accessible. The rotor is electrically open-circuited. The phase-*a* is applied a current $i_a(t) = 10\sin \omega t$. Calculate $\overrightarrow{B_a}$ at the following instants of ωt: 0, 90, 135, and 210 degrees. Also, plot the $B_a(\theta)$ distribution at these instants.

9-2 In the sinusoidal conductor-density distribution shown in Fig. 9-3, make use of the symmetry at θ and at $(\pi - \theta)$ to calculate the field distribution $H_a(\theta)$ in the air gap.

9-3 In ac machines, why is the stator winding for phase-*b* placed 120 degrees ahead of phase-*a* (as shown in Fig. 9-1), whereas the phasors for phase-*b* (such as $\overline{V}_b$) lag behind the corresponding phasors for phase-*a*?

9-4 In Example 9-2, derive the expression for $n_s(\theta_e)$ for a 4-pole machine. Generalize it for a multi-pole machine.

9-5 In Example 9-2, obtain the expressions for $H_a(\theta_e)$, $B_a(\theta_e)$, and $F_a(\theta_e)$.

9-6 In a 2-pole, three-phase machine with $N_s = 100$, calculate $\overrightarrow{i}_s$ and $\overrightarrow{F}_s$ at a time t if at that time the stator currents are as follows: (a) $i_a = 10\,A$, $i_b = -5\,A$, and $i_c = -5\,A$; (b) $i_a = -5\,A$, $i_b = 10\,A$, and $i_c = -5\,A$; (c) $i_a = -5\,A$, $i_b = -5\,A$, and $i_c = 10\,A$.

9-7 In a wye-connected stator, at a time t, $\overrightarrow{v}_s = 150\angle -30^o\,V$. Calculate v_a, v_b, and v_c at that time.

9-8   Show that the expression in the square brackets of Eq. 9-26 simplifies to $\frac{3}{2}\angle\omega t$.

9-9   In a 2-pole, three-phase ac machine, $\ell_g = 1.5\,mm$ and $N_s = 100$. During a balanced, sinusoidal, 60-Hz steady-state with the rotor electrically open-circuited, the peak of the magnetizing current in each phase is 10 A. Assume that at $t = 0$, the phase-a current is at its positive peak. Calculate the flux-density distribution space vector as a function of time. What is the speed of its rotation?

9-10   In Problem 9-9, what would be the speed of rotation if the machine had 6 poles?

9-11   By means of drawings similar to Example 9-7, show the rotation of the flux lines, and hence the speed, in a 4-pole machine.

9-12   In a three-phase ac machine, $\overline{V}_a = 120\sqrt{2}\angle 0^o\,V$ and $\overline{I}_{ma} = 5\sqrt{2}\angle -90^o\,A$. Calculate and draw $\overrightarrow{e_{ms}}$ and $\overrightarrow{i_{ms}}$ space vectors at $t = 0$. Assume a balanced, sinusoidal, three-phase steady-state operation at 60 Hz. Neglect the resistance and the leakage inductance of the stator phase windings.

9-13   Show that in a 2-pole machine, $L_{m,1-phase} = \frac{\pi\mu_o r\ell}{\ell_g}\left(\frac{N_s}{2}\right)^2$.

9-14   Show that $L_m = \frac{3}{2}L_{m,1-phase}$.

9-15   In a three-phase ac machine, $\overline{V}_a = 120\sqrt{2}\angle 0^o\,V$. The magnetizing inductance $L_m = 75\,mH$. Calculate and draw the three magnetizing current phasors. Assume a balanced, sinusoidal, three-phase steady-state operation at 60 Hz.

9-16   In a 2-pole, three-phase ac machine, $\ell_g = 1.5\,mm$, $\ell = 24\,cm$, $r = 6\,cm$, and $N_s = 100$. Under a balanced, sinusoidal, 60-Hz steady state, the peak of the magnetizing current in each phase is 10 A. Assume that at $t = 0$, the current in phase-a is at its positive peak. Calculate the expressions for the induced back-emfs in the three-stator phases.

9-17   Recalculate Eq. 9-41 for a multi-pole machine with $p > 2$.

9-18   Calculate L_m in a p-pole machine ($p \geq 2$).

9-19   Combine the results of Problems 9-17 and 9-18 to show that for $p \geq 2$,

$$\vec{e}_{ms}(t) = j\omega L_m \vec{i}_{ms}(t).$$

CHAPTER 10

SINUSOIDAL PERMANENT MAGNET AC (BRUSHLESS DC) DRIVES, LCI-SYNCHRONOUS MOTOR DRIVES, AND SYNCHRONOUS GENERATORS

10-1   INTRODUCTION

Having been introduced to ac machines and their analysis using space vector theory, we will now study an important class of ac drives, namely sinusoidal-waveform, permanent-magnet ac (PMAC) drives. In trade literature, they are also called "brushless dc" drives. The motors in these drives have three phase, sinusoidally-distributed ac stator windings and the rotor has dc excitation in the form of permanent magnets. We will examine these machines for servo applications, usually in small ($< 10 \ kW$) power ratings. In such drives, the stator windings of the machine are supplied by controlled currents which require a closed-loop operation, as shown in the block diagram of Fig. 10-1.

These drives are also related to the ECM drives of Chapter 7. The difference here is the sinusoidally-distributed nature of the stator windings that are supplied by sinusoidal wave-form currents. Also, the permanent magnets on the rotor are shaped to induce (in the stator windings) back-emfs that are ideally sinusoidally-varying with time. Unlike the ECM drives, PMAC drives are capable of producing a smooth torque, and thus they are used in high performance

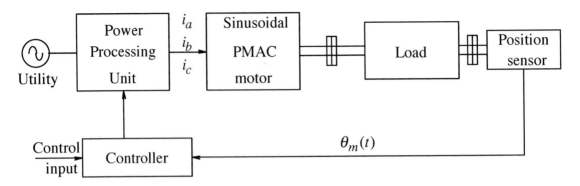

Figure 10-1 Block diagram of the closed loop operation of a PMAC drive.

applications. They do not suffer from the maintenance problems associated with brush-type dc machines. They are also used where a high efficiency and a high power density are required.

PMAC drives used in low power ratings are in principle similar to synchronous-motor drives used in very large power ratings (in excess of one megawatt) in applications such as controlling the speed of induced-draft fans and boiler feed-water pumps in the central power plants of electric utilities. Such synchronous-motor drives are briefly described in section 10-5.

The discussion of PMAC drives also lends itself to the analysis of line-connected synchronous machines, which are used in very large ratings in the central power plants of utilities to generate electricity. We will briefly analyze these synchronous generators in section 10-6.

10-2 THE BASIC STRUCTURE OF PERMANENT-MAGNET AC SYNCHRONOUS MACHINES

We will first consider 2-pole machines, like the one shown schematically in Fig. 10-2a, and then we will generalize our analysis to p-pole machines where $p > 2$. The stator contains three-phase, wye-connected, sinusoidally-distributed windings (discussed in Chapter 9), which are shown in the cross-section of Fig. 10-2a. These sinusoidally-distributed windings produce a sinusoidally-distributed mmf in the air gap.

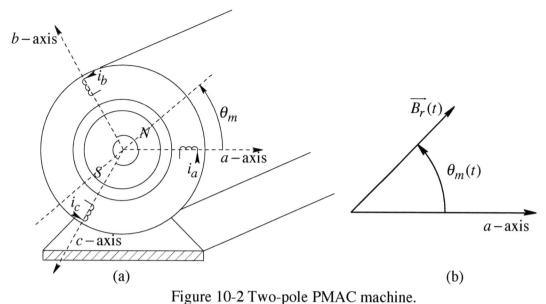

Figure 10-2 Two-pole PMAC machine.

10-3   PRINCIPLE OF OPERATION

10-3-1 Rotor-Produced Flux Density Distribution

The permanent-magnet pole pieces mounted on the rotor surface are shaped to ideally produce a sinusoidally-distributed flux density in the air gap. Without delving into detailed construction, Fig. 10-2a schematically shows a two-pole rotor. Flux lines leave the rotor at the north pole to re-enter the air gap at the south pole. The rotor-produced flux-density distribution in the air gap (due to flux lines that completely cross the two air gaps) has its positive peak $\hat{B}_r$ directed along the north pole axis. Because this flux density is sinusoidally distributed, it can be represented, as shown in Fig. 10-2b, by a space vector of length $\hat{B}_r$, and its orientation can be established by the location of the positive peak of the flux-density distribution.   As the rotor turns, the entire rotor-produced flux density distribution in the air gap rotates with it. Therefore, using the stationary stator phase-a axis as the reference, we can represent the rotor-produced flux density space vector at a time t as

$$\vec{B}_r(t) = \hat{B}_r \angle \theta_m(t) \qquad (10\text{-}1)$$

where the rotor flux-density distribution axis is at an angle $\theta_m(t)$ with respect to the a-axis. In Eq. 10-1, permanent magnets produce a constant $\hat{B}_r$, but $\theta_m(t)$ is a function of time, as the rotor turns.

10-3-2 Torque Production

We would like to compute the electromagnetic torque produced by the rotor. However, the rotor consists of permanent magnets and we have no direct way of computing this torque. Therefore, we will first calculate the torque exerted on the stator; this torque is transferred to the motor foundation. The torque exerted on the rotor is equal in magnitude to the stator torque but acts in the opposite direction.

An important characteristic of the machines under consideration is that they are supplied through the power-processing unit shown in Fig. 10-1, which controls the currents $i_a(t)$, $i_b(t)$, and $i_c(t)$ supplied to the stator at any instant of time. At any time t, the three stator currents combine to produce a stator current space vector $\vec{i}_s(t)$ which is controlled to be ahead of (or leading) the space vector $\vec{B}_r(t)$ by an angle of 90^0 in the direction of rotation, as shown in Fig. 10-3a. This produces a torque on the rotor in a counter-clockwise direction. The reason for maintaining a 90^0 angle will be justified shortly. With the a-axis as the reference axis, the stator current space vector can be expressed as

$$\vec{i}_s(t) = \hat{I}_s(t) \angle \theta_{i_s}(t) \quad \text{where} \quad \theta_{i_s}(t) = \theta_m(t) + 90^0 \quad (10\text{-}2)$$

During a steady-state operation, $\hat{I}_s$ is kept constant while $\theta_m(=\omega_m t)$ changes linearly with time.

We have seen the physical interpretation of the current space vector $\vec{i}_s(t)$ in Chapter 9. In Fig. 10-3a at a time t, the three stator phase currents combine to produce an mmf distribution in the air gap. This mmf distribution is the same as that produced in Fig. 10-3b by a single equivalent stator winding which has N_s

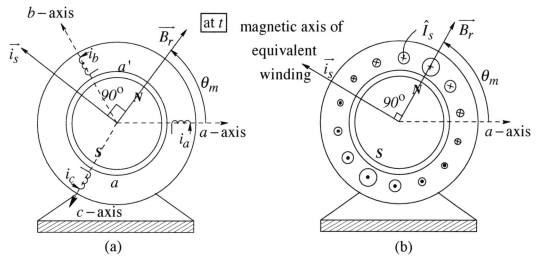

Figure 10-3 Stator current space vector and rotor field space vector in a PMAC drive.

sinusoidally-distributed turns supplied by a current $\hat{I}_s$ and which has its magnetic axis situated along the $\vec{i}_s(t)$ vector.

As seen from Fig. 10-3b, by controlling the stator current space vector $\vec{i}_s(t)$ to be 90^0 ahead of $\vec{B}_r(t)$, all of the conductors in the equivalent stator winding will experience a force acting in the same direction, which in this case is clockwise on the stator (and hence produces a counter-clockwise torque on the rotor). This justifies the choice of 90^0: it results in the maximum torque per ampere of stator current because at any other angle some conductors will experience a force in the direction opposite that on other conductors, a condition which will result in a smaller net torque.

As $\vec{B}_r(t)$ rotates with the rotor, the space vector $\vec{i}_s(t)$ is made to rotate at the same speed, maintaining a "lead" of 90^0. Thus, the torque developed in the machine of Fig. 10-3 depends only on $\hat{B}_r$ and $\hat{I}_s$, and is independent of θ_m. Therefore, to simplify our calculation of this torque in terms of the machine parameters, we will redraw Fig. 10-3b as in Fig. 10-4 by assuming $\theta_m = 0^0$. Using the expression for force ($f_{em} = B\ell i$), we can calculate the clockwise torque acting on the stator as follows: in the equivalent stator winding shown in Fig. 10-

4, at an angle ξ, the differential angle $d\xi$ contains $n_s(\xi) \cdot d\xi$ conductors. Using Eq. 9-5 and noting that the angle ξ is measured here from the location of the peak conductor density, the conductor density $n_s(\xi) = (N_s/2) \cdot \cos\xi$. Therefore,

$$\text{The number of conductors in the differential angle } d\xi = \frac{N_s}{2}\cos\xi \cdot d\xi \qquad (10\text{-}3)$$

The rotor-produced flux density at angle ξ is $\hat{B}_r \cos\xi$. Therefore, the torque $dT_{em}(\xi)$ produced by these conductors (due to the current $\hat{I}_s$ flowing through them) located at angle ξ, at a radius r, and of length ℓ is

$$dT_{em}(\xi) = r \underbrace{\hat{B}_r \cos\xi}_{flux\,density\,at\,\xi} \cdot \underbrace{\ell}_{cond.\,length} \cdot \hat{I}_s \cdot \underbrace{\frac{N_s}{2}\cos\xi \cdot d\xi}_{no.\,of\,cond.\,in\,d\xi} \qquad (10\text{-}4)$$

To account for the torque produced by all of the stator conductors, we will integrate the above expression from $\xi = -\pi/2$ to $\xi = \pi/2$, and then multiply by a factor of 2, making use of symmetry:

$$T_{em} = 2 \times \int_{\xi=-\pi/2}^{\xi=\pi/2} dT_{em}(\xi) = 2\frac{N_s}{2}r\ell\hat{B}_r\hat{I}_s \int_{-\pi/2}^{\pi/2} \cos^2\xi \cdot d\xi = (\pi\frac{N_s}{2}r\ell\hat{B}_r)\hat{I}_s \quad (10\text{-}5)$$

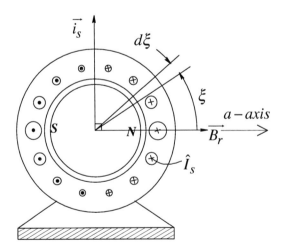

Figure 10-4 Torque calculation on the stator.

In the above equation, all quantities within the brackets, including $\hat{B}_r$ in a machine with permanent magnets, depend on the machine design parameters and are constants. As noted earlier, the electromagnetic torque produced by the rotor is equal to that in Eq. 10-5 in the opposite direction (counter-clockwise in this case). This torque in a 2-pole machine can be expressed as

$$T_{em} = k_T \hat{I}_s \quad \text{where} \quad k_T = \pi \frac{N_s}{2} r \ell \hat{B}_r \quad (p=2) \quad (10\text{-}6)$$

In the above equation, k_T is the *machine torque constant*, which has the units of *Nm/A*. Eq. 10-6 shows that by controlling the stator phase currents so that the corresponding stator current space vector is ahead (in the desired direction) of the rotor-produced flux-density space vector by 90^0, the torque developed is only proportional to $\hat{I}_s$. This torque expression is similar to that in the brush-type dc-motor drives of Chapter 7. This is the reason why such drives are called "brushless-dc" drives.

The similarities between the brush-type dc motor drives of Chapter 7 and the "brushless-dc" motor drives are shown by means of Fig. 10-5. In the brush-type dc motors, the flux ϕ_f produced by the stator and the armature flux ϕ_a produced by the armature winding remain directed orthogonal (at 90°) to each other, as shown in Fig. 10-5a. The stator flux ϕ_f is stationary, and so is ϕ_a (due to the commutator action), even though the rotor is turning. The torque produced is controlled by the armature current $i_a(t)$. In "brushless-dc" motor drives, the stator-produced flux-density $\vec{B}_{s,\vec{i}_s}(t)$ due to $\vec{i}_s(t)$ is controlled to be directed orthogonal (at 90^0 in the direction of rotation) to the rotor flux-density $\vec{B}_r(t)$, as shown in Fig. 10-5b. Both of these space vectors rotate at the speed ω_m of the rotor, maintaining the 90^0 angle between the two. The torque is controlled by the magnitude $\hat{I}_s(t)$ of the stator-current space vector.

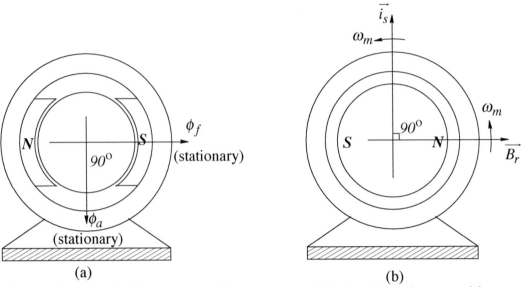

Figure 10-5 Similarities between (a) dc motor and (b) brushless dc motor drives.

At this point, we should note that PMAC drives constitute a class which we will call *self-synchronous* motor drives, where the speed of the stator-produced mmf distribution is synchronized to be equal the mechanical speed of the rotor. This feature characterizes a machine as a synchronous machine. The term "*self*" is added to distinguish these machines from the conventional synchronous machines described in section 10-6. In PMAC drives, this synchronism is established by a closed feedback loop in which the measured instantaneous position of the rotor directs the power-processing unit to locate the stator mmf distribution 90 degrees ahead of the rotor-field distribution. Therefore, there is no possibility of losing synchronism between the two, unlike in the conventional synchronous machines of section 10-6.

10-3-3 Mechanical System of PMAC Drives

The electromagnetic torque acts on the mechanical system connected to the rotor, as shown in Fig. 10-6, and the resulting speed ω_m can be obtained from the equation below:

$$\frac{d\omega_m}{dt} = \frac{T_{em} - T_L}{J_{eq}} \tag{10-7}$$

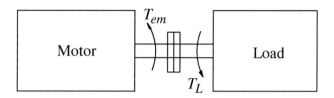

Figure 10-6 Rotor-load mechanical system.

where J_{eq} is the combined motor-load inertia and T_L is the load torque, which may include friction. The rotor position $\theta_m(t)$ is

$$\theta_m(t) = \theta_m(0) + \int_o^t \omega_m(\tau) \cdot d\tau \quad (\tau = \text{variable of integration}) \tag{10-8}$$

where $\theta_m(0)$ is the rotor position at time $t=0$.

10-3-4 Calculation of the Reference Values $i_a^*(t)$, $i_b^*(t)$, and $i_c^*(t)$ of the Stator Currents

The controller in Fig. 10-1 is responsible for controlling the torque, speed, and position of the mechanical system. It does so by calculating the instantaneous value of the desired (reference) torque $T_{em}^*(t)$ that the motor must produce. The reference torque may be generated by the cascaded controller discussed in Chapter 8. From Eq. 10-6, $\hat{I}_s^*(t)$, the reference value of the amplitude of the stator-current space vector, can be calculated as

$$\hat{I}_s^*(t) = \frac{T_{em}^*(t)}{k_T} \tag{10-9}$$

where k_T is the motor torque constant given in Eq. 10-6 (k_T is usually listed in the motor specification sheet).

The controller in Fig. 10-1 receives the instantaneous rotor position θ_m, which is measured, as shown in Fig. 10-1, by means of a mechanical sensor such as a resolver or an optical encoder (with some restrictions), as discussed in Chapter 17.

With $\theta_m(t)$ as one of the inputs and $\hat{I}_s^*(t)$ calculated from Eq. 10-9, the instantaneous reference value of the stator-current space vector becomes

$$\vec{i}_s^*(t) = \hat{I}_s^*(t) \angle \theta_{i_s}^*(t) \quad \text{where} \quad \theta_{i_s}^*(t) = \theta_m(t) + \frac{\pi}{2} \quad \text{(2-pole)} \quad (10\text{-}10)$$

Eq. 10-10 assumes a 2-pole machine and the desired rotation to be in the counter-clockwise direction. For a clockwise rotation, the angle $\theta_{i_s}^*(t)$ in Eq. 10-10 will be $\theta_m(t) - \pi/2$. In a multi-pole machine with $p > 2$, the electrical angle $\theta_{i_s}^*(t)$ will be

$$\theta_{i_s}^*(t) = \frac{p}{2}\theta_m(t) \pm \frac{\pi}{2} \qquad (p \geq 2) \qquad (10\text{-}11)$$

where $\theta_m(t)$ is the mechanical angle. From $\vec{i}_s^*(t)$ in Eq. 10-10 (with Eq. 10-11 for $\theta_{i_s}^*(t)$ in a machine with $p > 2$), the instantaneous reference values $i_a^*(t)$, $i_b^*(t)$, and $i_c^*(t)$ of the stator phase currents can be calculated using the analysis in the previous chapter (Eqs. 9-24a through 9-24c):

$$i_a^*(t) = \frac{2}{3}\text{Re}\left[\vec{i}_s^*(t)\right] = \frac{2}{3}\hat{I}_s^*(t)\cos\theta_{i_s}^*(t) \qquad (10\text{-}12\text{a})$$

$$i_b^*(t) = \frac{2}{3}\text{Re}\left[\vec{i}_s^*(t)\angle-\frac{2\pi}{3}\right] = \frac{2}{3}\hat{I}_s^*(t)\cos(\theta_{i_s}^*(t) - \frac{2\pi}{3}) \qquad (10\text{-}12\text{b})$$

and

$$i_c^*(t) = \frac{2}{3}\text{Re}\left[\vec{i}_s^*(t)\angle-\frac{4\pi}{3}\right] = \frac{2}{3}\hat{I}_s^*(t)\cos(\theta_{i_s}^*(t) - \frac{4\pi}{3}) \qquad (10\text{-}12\text{c})$$

Section 10-4, which deals with the power-processing unit and the controller, describes how the phase currents, based on the above reference values, are supplied to the motor. Eqs. 10-12a through 10-12c show that in the balanced sinusoidal steady state, the currents have the constant amplitude of $\hat{I}_s^*$; they vary sinusoidally with time as the angle $\theta_{i_s}^*(t)$ in Eq. 10-10 or Eq. 10-11 changes continuously with time at a constant speed ω_m:

$$\theta_{i_s}^*(t) = \frac{p}{2}[\theta_m(0) + \omega_m t] \pm \frac{\pi}{2} \qquad (10\text{-}13)$$

where $\theta_m(0)$ is the initial rotor angle, measured with respect to the phase-a magnetic axis.

▲ **Example 10-1**   In a three-phase, 2-pole, brushless-dc motor, the torque constant $k_T = 0.5\,Nm/A$. Calculate the phase currents if the motor is to produce a counter-clockwise holding torque of $5\,Nm$ to keep the rotor, which is at an angle of $\theta_m = 45^0$, from turning.

Solution   From Eq. 10-6, $\hat{I}_s = T_{em}/k_T = 10\,A$.   From Eq. 10-10, $\theta_{i_s} = \theta_m + 90^0 = 135^0$. Therefore, $\vec{i}_s(t) = \hat{I}_s \angle \theta_{i_s} = 10\angle 135^0\,A$, as shown in Fig. 10-7. From Eqs. 10-12a through 10-12c,

$$i_a = \frac{2}{3}\hat{I}_s \cos\theta_{i_s} = -4.71\,A,$$

$$i_b = \frac{2}{3}\hat{I}_s \cos(\theta_{i_s} - 120^0) = 6.44\,A, \text{ and}$$

$$i_c = \frac{2}{3}\hat{I}_s \cos(\theta_{i_s} - 240^0) = -1.73\,A.$$

Since the rotor is not turning, the phase currents in this example are dc.   ▲

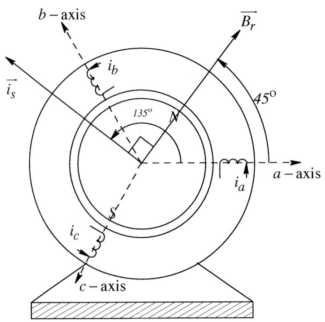

Figure 10-7 Stator current space vector for Example 10-1.

10-3-5 Induced EMFs in the Stator Windings during Balanced Sinusoidal Steady State

In the stator windings, emfs are induced due to two flux-density distributions:

1)   As the rotor rotates with an instantaneous speed of $\omega_m(t)$, so does the space vector $\overrightarrow{B_r}(t)$ shown in Fig. 10-3a. This rotating flux-density distribution "cuts" the stator windings to induce a back-emf in them.

2)   The stator phase-winding currents under a balanced sinusoidal steady state produce a rotating flux-density distribution due to the rotating $\overrightarrow{i_s}(t)$ space vector. This rotating flux-density distribution induces emfs in the stator windings, similar to those induced by the magnetizing currents in the previous chapter.

Neglecting saturation in the magnetic circuit, the emfs induced due to the two causes mentioned above can be superimposed to calculate the resultant emf in the stator windings.

In the following subsections, we will assume a 2-pole machine in a balanced sinusoidal steady state, with a rotor speed of ω_m in the counter-clockwise direction. We will also assume that at $t = 0$ the rotor is at $\theta_m = -90^0$ for ease of drawing the space vectors.

10-3-5-1 Induced EMF in the Stator Windings due to Rotating $\overrightarrow{B_r}(t)$

We can make use of the analysis in the previous chapter that led to Eq. 9-41. In the present case, the rotor flux-density vector $\overrightarrow{B_r}(t)$ is rotating at the instantaneous speed of ω_m with respect to the stator windings. Therefore, in Eq. 9-41, substituting $\overrightarrow{B_r}(t)$ for $\overrightarrow{B_{ms}}(t)$ and ω_m for ω_{syn},

$$\overrightarrow{e_{ms,\overline{B_r}}}(t) = j\omega_m \frac{3}{2}(\pi r \ell \frac{N_s}{2})\overrightarrow{B_r}(t) \qquad (10\text{-}14)$$

We can define a voltage constant k_E, equal to the torque constant k_T in Eq. 10-6 for a 2-pole machine:

$$k_E \left[\frac{V}{rad/s} \right] = k_T \left[\frac{Nm}{A} \right] = \pi\, r\, \ell \frac{N_s}{2} \hat{B}_r \qquad (10\text{-}15)$$

where $\hat{B}_r$ (the peak of the rotor-produced flux-density) is a constant in permanent-magnet synchronous motors. In terms of the voltage constant k_E, the induced voltage space vector in Eq. 10-14 can be written as

$$\overrightarrow{e_{ms,\overline{B_r}}}(t) = j\frac{3}{2}k_E\omega_m \angle \theta_m(t) = \frac{3}{2}k_E\omega_m \angle \{\theta_m(t) + 90^0\} \qquad (10\text{-}16)$$

The rotor flux-density space vector $\overrightarrow{B_r}(t)$ and the induced-emf space vector $\overrightarrow{e_{ms,\overline{B_r}}}(t)$ are drawn for time $t = 0$ in Fig. 10-8a.

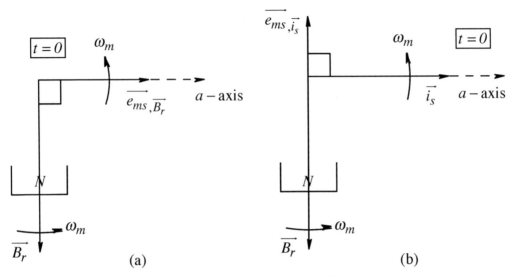

Figure 10-8 (a) Induced emf due to rotating rotor flux density space vector; (b) induced emf due to rotating stator-current space vector.

10-3-5-2   Induced EMF in the Stator Windings due to Rotating $\vec{i}_s(t)$: Armature Reaction

In addition to the flux-density distribution in the air gap created by the rotor magnets, another flux-density distribution is established by the stator phase currents. As shown in Fig. 10-8b, the stator-current space vector $\vec{i}_s(t)$ at time $t = 0$ is made to lead the rotor position by 90^0. Because we are operating under a balanced sinusoidal steady state, we can make use of the analysis in the previous chapter, where Eq. 9-40 showed the relationship between the induced-emf space vector and the stator-current space vector. Thus, in the present case, due to the rotation of $\vec{i}_s(t)$, the induced voltages in the stator phase windings can be represented as

$$\overrightarrow{e_{ms,\vec{i}_s}}(t) = j\omega_m L_m \vec{i}_s(t) \tag{10-17}$$

Space vectors $\overrightarrow{e_{ms,\vec{i}_s}}$ and $\vec{i}_s$ are shown in Fig. 10-8b at time $t = 0$.

Note that the magnetizing inductance L_m in the PMAC motor has the same meaning as in the generic ac motors discussed in Chapter 9. However, in PMAC motors, the rotor on its surface has permanent magnets (exceptions are motors with interior permanent magnets) whose permeability is effectively that of the air gap. Therefore, PMAC motors have a larger equivalent air gap, thus resulting in a smaller value of L_m (see Eq. 9-36 of the previous chapter).

10-3-5-3 Superposition of the Induced EMFs in the Stator Windings

In PMAC motors, rotating $\vec{B}_r(t)$ and $\vec{i}_s(t)$ are present simultaneously. Therefore, the emfs induced due to each one can be superimposed (assuming no magnetic saturations) to obtain the resultant emf (excluding the leakage flux of the stator windings):

$$\overrightarrow{e_{ms}}(t) = \overrightarrow{e_{ms,\overline{B}_r}}(t) + \overrightarrow{e_{ms,\vec{i}_s}}(t) \tag{10-18}$$

Substituting from Eqs. 10-16 and 10-17 into Eq. 10-18, the resultant induced emf $\overrightarrow{e_{ms}}(t)$ is

$$\overrightarrow{e_{ms}}(t) = \frac{3}{2}k_E\omega_m\angle\{\theta_m(t)+90^o\} + j\omega_m L_m \vec{i}_s(t) \tag{10-19}$$

The space vector diagram is shown in Fig. 10-9a at time $t=0$. The phase-a phasor equation corresponding to the space vector equation above can be written, noting that the phasor amplitudes are smaller than the space vector amplitudes by a factor of 3/2, but the phasor and the corresponding space vector have the same orientation:

$$\overline{E}_{ma} = \underbrace{k_E\omega_m\angle\{\theta_m(t)+90^o\}}_{\overline{E}_{ma,\overline{B}_r}} + j\omega_m L_m \overline{I}_a \tag{10-20}$$

The phasor diagram from Eq. 10-20 for phase-a is shown in Fig. 10-9b.

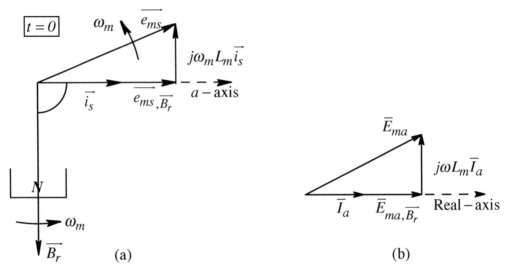

(a)   (b)

Figure 10-9 (a) Space vector diagram of induced emfs;
(b) phasor diagram for phase-a.

Per-Phase Equivalent Circuit

Corresponding to the phasor representation in Eq. 10-20 and the phasor diagram in Fig. 10-9b, a per-phase equivalent circuit for phase-a can be drawn as shown in Fig. 10-10a. The voltage $\overline{E}_{ma,\overline{B_r}}$, induced due to the rotation of the rotor field distribution $\overrightarrow{B_r}$, is represented as an induced back-emf. The second term on the right side of Eq. 10-20 is represented as a voltage drop across the magnetizing inductance L_m. To complete this per-phase equivalent circuit, the stator-winding leakage inductance $L_{\ell s}$ and the resistance R_s are added in series. The sum of the magnetizing inductance L_m and the leakage inductance $L_{\ell s}$ is called the

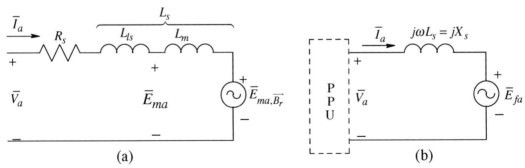

(a)   (b)

Figure 10-10 (a) Per-phase equivalent circuit; (b) simplified equivalent circuit.

synchronous inductance L_s:

$$L_s = L_{\ell s} + L_m \tag{10-21}$$

We can simplify the equivalent circuit of Fig. 10-10a by neglecting the resistance and by representing the two inductances by their sum, L_s, as done in Fig. 10-10b. To simplify the notation, the induced back-emf is called the field-induced back-emf $\overline{E}_{fa}$ in phase-a, where, from Eq. 10-20, the peak of this voltage in each phase is

$$\hat{E}_f = k_E \omega_m \tag{10-22}$$

Notice that in PMAC drives the power-processing unit is a source of controlled currents such that $\overline{I}_a$ is in phase with the field-induced back-emf $\overline{E}_{fa}$, as confirmed by the phasor diagram of Fig. 10-9b. The power-processing unit supplies this current by producing a voltage which, for phase-a in Fig. 10-10b is

$$\overline{V}_a = \overline{E}_{fa} + j\omega_m L_s \overline{I}_a \tag{10-23}$$

▲ **Example 10-2** In a 2-pole, three-phase (PMAC) brushless-dc motor drive, the torque constant k_T and the voltage constant k_E are 0.5 in *MKS* units. The synchronous inductance is *15 mH* (neglect the winding resistance). This motor is supplying a torque of *3 Nm* at a speed of *3,000* rpm in a balanced sinusoidal steady state. Calculate the per-phase voltage across the power-processing unit as it supplies controlled currents to this motor.

Solution   From Eq. 10-6,

$$\hat{I}_s = \frac{3.0}{0.5} = 6\,A\,,\text{ and } \hat{I}_a = \frac{2}{3}\hat{I}_s = 4\,A\,.$$

The speed $\omega_m = \dfrac{3000}{60}(2\pi) = 314.16\,rad\,/\,s\,.$ From Eq. 10-22,

$$\hat{E}_f = k_E \omega_m = 0.5 \times 314.16 = 157.08V \ .$$

Assuming $\theta_m(0) = -90^o$, from Eq. 10-10, $\theta_{i_s}\big|_{t=0} = 0^o$. Hence, in the per-phase equivalent circuit of Fig. 10-10b,

$$\overline{I}_a = 4.0\angle 0^o \ A \ \text{and} \ \overline{E}_{fa} = 157.08\angle 0^0 \ V \ .$$

Therefore, from Eq. 10-23, in the per-phase equivalent circuit of Fig. 10-10b,

$$\overline{V}_a = \overline{E}_{fa} + j\omega_m L_s \overline{I}_a = 157.08\angle 0^0 + j314.16 \times 15 \times 10^{-3} \times 4.0 \angle 0^0$$
$$= 157.08 + j18.85$$
$$= 158.2\angle 6.84^0 \ V.$$

▲

10-4 THE CONTROLLER AND THE POWER-PROCESSING UNIT (PPU)

As shown in the block diagram of Fig. 10-1, the task of the controller is to dictate the switching in the power-processing unit, such that the desired currents are supplied to the PMAC motors. This is further illustrated in Fig. 10-11a, where phases b and c are omitted for simplification. The reference signal T_{em}^* is generated from the outer speed and position loops discussed in Chapter 8. The rotor position θ_m is measured by the resolver (discussed in Chapter 17) connected to the shaft. Knowing the torque constant k_T allows us to calculate the reference current $\hat{I}_s^*$ to be T_{em}^*/k_T (from Eq. 10-9). Knowing $\hat{I}_s^*$ and θ_m allows the reference currents i_a^*, i_b^*, and i_c^* to be calculated at any instant of time from Eq. 10-11 and Eqs. 10-12a through 10-12c.

One of the easiest ways to ensure that the motor is supplied the desired currents is to use hysteresis control similar to that discussed in Chapter 7 for ECM drives. The measured phase current is compared with its reference value in the hysteresis

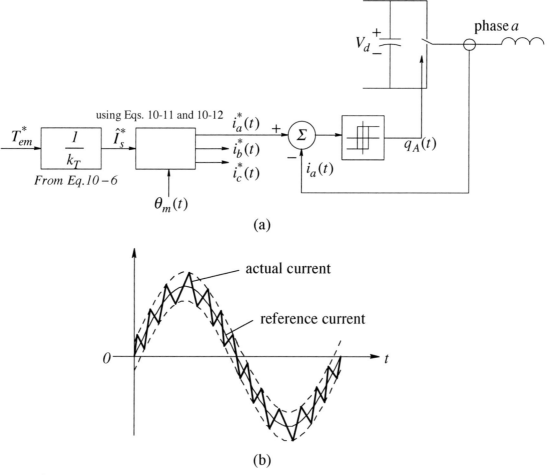

Figure 10-11 (a) Block diagram representation of hysteresis current control; (b) current waveform.

comparator, whose output determines the switch state (up or down), resulting in current as shown in Fig. 10-11b.

In spite of the simplicity of the hysteresis control, one perceived drawback of this controller is that the switching frequency changes as a function of the back-emf waveform. For this reason, constant switching frequency controllers are used. They are beyond the scope of this book, but Reference [3], listed at the end of this chapter, is an excellent source of information on them.

10-5   LOAD-COMMUTATED-INVERTER (LCI) SUPPLIED
SYNCHRONOUS MOTOR DRIVES

Applications such as induced-draft fans and boiler feed-water pumps in the central power plants of electric utilities require adjustable-speed drives in very large power ratings, often in excess of one megawatt. At these power levels, even the slightly higher efficiency of synchronous motors, compared to the induction motors which we will discuss in the next three chapters, can be substantial. Moreover, to adjust the speed of synchronous motors, it is possible to use thyristor-based power-processing units, which are less expensive at these megawatt power ratings compared to the switch-mode power-processing units discussed in Chapter 4.

The block diagram of LCI drives is shown in Fig. 10-12, where the synchronous motor has a field winding on the rotor, which is supplied by a dc current that can be adjusted, thus providing another degree of control. On the utility side, a line-commutated thyristor converter, which is described in Chapter 17 in connection with dc drives, is used. A similar converter is used on the motor side, where the commutation of currents is provided by the load, which in this case is a synchronous machine. This is also the reason for calling the motor-side converter a load-commutated inverter (LCI). A filter inductor, which makes the input to the load-commutated inverter appear as a dc current source, is used in the dc-link between the two converters. Hence, this inverter is also called a current-source inverter (in contrast to the switch-mode converters discussed in Chapter 4, where a parallel-connected capacitor appears as a dc voltage source - thus such converters are sometimes called voltage-source inverters). Further details of LCI-synchronous motor drives can be found in Reference [1].

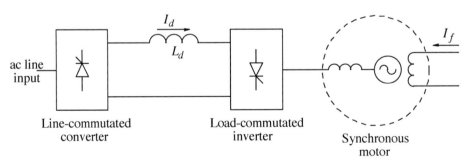

Figure 10-12 LCI-synchronous motor drive.

10-6   SYNCHRONOUS GENERATORS

Today it is rare for synchronous machines without any power electronics interface (PPU) to be used as motors, which run at a constant speed that is dictated by the frequency of the utility grid. In the past, constant-speed synchronous machines in large power ratings were used as synchronous condensers (many still exist) in utility substations to provide voltage support and stability enhancement. However, the recent trend is to use static (semiconductor-based) controllers, which can provide reactive power (leading and lagging) without the maintenance problems associated with rotating equipment. Therefore, the role of synchronous machines is mainly to generate electricity in large central power plants of electric utilities, where they are driven by turbines fueled by gas, by steam in coal-fired or nuclear plants, or propelled by water flow in hydroelectric plants.

10-6-1 The Structure of Synchronous Machines

In the above application, turbines and synchronous generators are large and massive, but their stator windings, in principle, are the same as their smaller-power counterpart. Generators driven by gas and steam turbines often rotate at high speeds and thus have a 2-pole, round-rotor structure. Hydraulic-turbine driven generators operate at very low speeds, and thus must have a large number of poles to generate a 60-Hz (or 50-Hz) frequency. This requires a salient-pole structure for the rotor, as discussed in Chapter 6. This saliency causes unequal magnetic reluctance along various paths through the rotor. Analysis of such salient-pole machines requires a sophisticated analysis, which is beyond the scope of this book. Therefore, we will assume the rotor to be perfectly round (non-salient) with a uniform air gap and thus to have a uniform reluctance in the path of flux lines.

A field winding is supplied by a dc voltage, resulting in a dc current I_f. The field-current I_f produces the rotor field in the air gap (which was established by permanent magnets in the PMAC motor discussed earlier). By controlling I_f and hence the rotor-produced field, it is possible to control the reactive power delivered by synchronous generators, as discussed in section 10-6-2-2.

10-6-2 The Operating Principles of Synchronous Machines

In steady state, the synchronous generator must rotate at the synchronous speed established by the line-fed stator windings. Therefore, in steady state, the per-phase equivalent circuit of PMAC motor drives in Fig. 10-10a or 10-10b applies to the synchronous machines as well. The important difference is that in PMAC motor drives a PPU is present, which under feedback of rotor position supplies appropriate phase currents to the motor. Of course, the PPU produces a voltage $\overline{V}_a$ shown in Fig. 10-10b, but its main purpose is to supply controlled currents to the motor.

Line-connected synchronous machines lack the control over the currents that PMAC drives have. Rather, on a per-phase basis, synchronous machines have two voltage sources, as shown in Fig. 10-13a - one belonging to the utility source and the other to the internally-induced back-emf $\overline{E}_{fa}$. Following the generator convention, the current is defined as being supplied by the synchronous generator, as shown in Fig. 10-13a. This current can be calculated as follows where $\overline{V}_a$ is chosen as the reference phasor ($\overline{V}_a = \hat{V}\angle 0^0$) and the torque angle δ associated with $\overline{E}_{fa}$ is positive in the generator mode:

$$\overline{I}_a = \frac{\overline{E}_{fa} - \overline{V}_a}{jX_s} = \frac{\hat{E}_f \sin\delta}{X_s} - j\frac{\hat{E}_f \cos\delta - \hat{V}}{X_s} \tag{10-24}$$

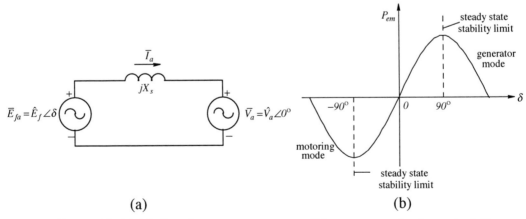

(a)   (b)

Figure 10-13 (a) Synchronous generator; (b) power-angle characteristic.

Taking the conjugate of $\overline{I}_a$ (represented by "*" as a superscript),

$$\overline{I}_a^* = \frac{\hat{E}_f \sin \delta}{X_s} + j \frac{\hat{E}_f \cos \delta - \hat{V}}{X_s} \tag{10-25}$$

The total (three-phase) power supplied by the generator, in terms of peak quantities, is

$$P_{em} = \frac{3}{2} \text{Re}(\overline{V}_a \overline{I}_a^*) = \frac{3}{2} \hat{V} \text{Re}[\frac{\hat{E}_f \sin \delta}{X_s} + j \frac{\hat{E}_f \cos \delta - \hat{V}}{X_s}]$$

or

$$P_{em} = \frac{3}{2} \frac{\hat{E}_f \hat{V} \sin \delta}{X_s} \tag{10-26}$$

If the field current is constant, $\hat{E}_f$ at the synchronous speed is also constant, and thus the power output of the generator is proportional to the sine of the torque angle δ between $\overline{E}_{fa}$ and $\overline{V}_a$. This power-angle relationship is plotted in Fig. 10-13b for both positive and negative values of δ.

10-6-2-1 Stability and Loss of Synchronism

Fig. 10-13b shows that the power supplied by the synchronous generator, as a function of δ, reaches its peak at 90^0. This is the steady-state limit, beyond which the synchronism is lost. This can be explained as follows: for values of δ below 90 degrees, to supply more power, the power input from the mechanical prime-mover is increased (for example, by letting more steam into the turbine). This momentarily speeds up the rotor, causing the torque angle δ associated with the rotor-induced voltage $\overline{E}_{fa}$ to increase. This in turn, from Eq. 10-26, increases the electrical power output, which finally settles at a new steady state with a higher value of the torque angle δ. However, beyond $\delta = 90$ degrees, increasing δ causes the output power to decline, which results in a further increase in δ (because more mechanical power is coming in while less electrical power is going out). This increase in δ causes an intolerable increase in machine currents, and the circuit breakers trip to isolate the machine from the grid, thus saving the machine from being damaged.

The above sequence of events is called the "loss of synchronism," and the stability is lost. In practice, transient stability, in which there may be a sudden change in the electrical power output, forces the maximum value of the steady-state torque angle δ to be much less than 90 degrees, typically in a range of 30 to 45 degrees. A similar explanation applies to the motoring mode with negative values of δ.

10-6-2-2 Field (Excitation) Control to Adjust Reactive Power and Power Factor

The reactive power associated with synchronous machines can be controlled in magnitude as well as in sign (leading or lagging). To discuss this, let us assume, as a base case, that a synchronous generator is supplying a constant power, and the field current I_f is adjusted such that this power is supplied at a unity power factor, as shown in the phasor diagram of Fig. 10-14a.

Over-Excitation: Now, an increase in the field current (called over-excitation) will result in a larger magnitude of $\overline{E}_{fa}$ (assuming no magnetic saturation, $\hat{E}_f$ depends linearly on the field current I_f). However, $\hat{E}_f \sin \delta$ must remain constant (from Eq. 10-26, since the power output is constant). This results in the

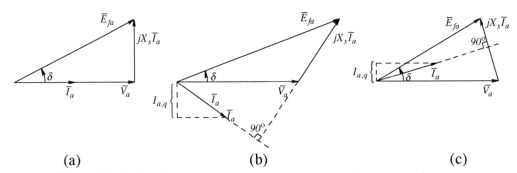

(a)   (b)   (c)

Figure 10-14 (a) Synchronous generator at (a) unity power factor; (b) over-excited; (c) under-excited.

phasor diagram of Fig. 10-14b, where the current is lagging $\overline{V}_a$. Considering the utility grid to be a load (which it is, in the generator mode of the machine), it absorbs reactive power as an inductive load does. Therefore, the synchronous generator, operating in an over-excited mode, supplies reactive power like a capacitor does. The three-phase reactive power Q can be computed from the reactive component of the current $I_{a,q}$ as

$$Q = \frac{3}{2}\hat{V}I_{a,q} \tag{10-27}$$

Under-Excitation: In contrast to over-excitation, decreasing I_f results in a smaller magnitude $\hat{E}_f$, and the corresponding phasor diagram, assuming that the power output remains constant as before, can be represented as in Fig. 10-14c. Now the current $\overline{I}_a$ leads the voltage $\overline{V}_a$, and the load (the utility grid) supplies reactive power as a capacitive load does. Thus, the generator in an under-excited mode absorbs reactive power like an inductor does.

Similar control over the reactive power can be observed by drawing phasor diagrams, if the machine is operating as a synchronous motor (see homework problem 10-10).

The reactive power of the machine can be calculated, similar to the calculations of the real power that led to Eq. 10-26. This is left as homework problem 10-11.

SUMMARY/REVIEW QUESTIONS

1. List various names associated with the PMAC drives and the reasons behind them.
2. Draw the overall block diagram of a PMAC drive. Why must they operate in a closed-loop?
3. How do sinusoidal PMAC drives differ from the ECM drives described in Chapter 7?
4. Ideally, what are the flux-density distributions produced by the rotor and the stator phase windings?

5. What does the $\overrightarrow{B}_r(t) = \hat{B}_r \angle \theta_m(t)$ space vector represent?

6. In PMAC drives, why at all times is the $\overrightarrow{i}_s(t)$ space vector placed 90 degrees ahead of the $\overrightarrow{B}_r(t)$ space vector in the intended direction of rotation?

7. Why do we need to measure the rotor position in PMAC drives?

8. What does the electromagnetic torque produced by a PMAC drive depend on?

9. How can regenerative braking be accomplished in PMAC drives?

10. Why are PMAC drives called self-synchronous? How is the frequency of the applied voltages and currents determined? Are they related to the rotational speed of the shaft?

11. In a p-pole PMAC machine, what is the angle of the $\overrightarrow{i}_s(t)$ space vector in relation to the phase-a axis, for a given θ_m?

12. What is the frequency of currents and voltages in the stator circuit needed to produce a holding torque in a PMAC drive?

13. In calculating the voltages induced in the stator windings of a PMAC motor, what are the two components that are superimposed? Describe the procedure and the expressions.

14. Does L_m in the per-phase equivalent circuit of a PMAC machine have the same expression as in Chapter 9? Describe the differences, if any.

15. Draw the per-phase equivalent circuit and describe its various elements in PMAC drives.

16. Draw the controller block diagram and describe the hysteresis control of PMAC drives.

17. What is an LCI-synchronous motor drive? Describe it briefly.

18. For what purpose are line-connected synchronous generators used?

19. Why are there problems of stability and loss of synchronism associated with line-connected synchronous machines?

20. How can the power factor associated with synchronous generators be made to be leading or lagging?

REFERENCES

1. N. Mohan, T. Undeland, and W. Robbins, *Power Electronics: Converters, Applications, and Design*, 2nd edition, 1995, John Wiley & Sons, New York, NY.
2. T. Jahns, *Variable Frequency Permanent Magnet AC Machine Drives*, Power Electronics and Variable Frequency Drives, (edited by B. K. Bose), IEEE Press, 1997.
3. Kazmierkowski and Tunia, "*Automatic Control of Converter-Fed Drives,*" Elsevier, 1994.

PROBLEMS

10-1 Calculate the torque constant, similar to that in Eq. 10-6, for a 4-pole machine, where N_s equals the total number of turns per-phase.

10-2 Prove that Eq. 10-11 is correct.

10-3 Repeat Example 10-1 for $\theta_m = -45^o$.

10-4 Repeat Example 10-1 for a 4-pole machine with the same value of k_T as in Example 10-1.

10-5 The PMAC machine of Example 10-2 is supplying a load torque $T_L = 5\,Nm$ at a speed of 5,000 *rpm*. Draw a phasor diagram showing $\overline{V}_a$ and $\overline{I}_a$, along with their calculated values.

10-6 Repeat Problem 10-5 if the machine has *p=4*, but has the same values of k_E, k_T, and L_s as before.

10-7 Repeat Problem 10-5, assuming that at time t=0, the rotor angle $\theta_m(0) = 0^o$.

10-8 The PMAC motor in Example 10-2 is driving a purely inertial load. A constant torque of *5 Nm* is developed to bring the system from rest to a speed of 5,000 rpm in 5 s. Neglect the stator resistance and the leakage inductance. Determine and plot the voltage $v_a(t)$ and the current $i_a(t)$ as functions of time during this 5-second interval.

10-9 In Problem 10-8, the drive is expected to go into a regenerative mode at $t = 5^+ s$, with a torque $T_{em} = -5 \, Nm$. Assume that the rotor position at this instant is zero: $\theta_m = 0$. Calculate the three stator currents at this instant.

10-10 Draw the phasor diagrams associated with under-excited and over-excited synchronous motors and show the power factor of operation associated with each.

10-11 Calculate the expression for the reactive power in a 3-phase synchronous machine in terms of $\hat{E}_f$, $\hat{V}$, X_s, and δ. Discuss the influence of $\hat{E}_f$.

CHAPTER 11

INDUCTION MOTORS: BALANCED, SINUSOIDAL STEADY STATE OPERATION

11-1   INTRODUCTION

Induction motors with squirrel-cage rotors are the workhorses of industry because of their low cost and rugged construction. When operated directly from line voltages (a 50- or 60-*Hz* utility input at essentially a constant voltage), induction motors operate at a nearly constant speed. However, by means of power electronic converters, it is possible to vary their speed efficiently. Induction-motor drives can be classified into two broad categories based on their applications:

1. *Adjustable-Speed Drives.* An important application of these drives is to adjust the speeds of fans, compressors, pumps, blowers, and the like in the process control industry. In a large number of applications, this capability to vary speed efficiently can lead to large savings. Adjustable-speed induction-motor drives are also used for electric traction, including hybrid vehicles.

2. *Servo Drives.* By means of sophisticated control discussed in Chapter 12, induction motors can be used as servo drives in machine tools, robotics, and so on by emulating the performance of dc-motor drives and brushless-dc motor drives.

Because the subject of induction-motor drives is extensive, we will cover it in three separate chapters. In this chapter, we will examine the behavior of induction machines supplied by balanced sinusoidal line-frequency voltages at their rated values. In Chapter 12, we will discuss energy-efficient speed control of induction motor drives for process control and traction applications. In Chapter 13, we will qualitatively examine how it is possible to use induction machines in servo applications where the dynamics of speed and motion control need to be very fast and precise.

There are many varieties of induction motors. Single-phase induction motors are used in low power ratings (fractional *kW* to a few *kW*) in applications where their speed does not have to be controlled in a continuous manner. Wound-rotor induction generators are used in large power ratings (300 *kW* and higher) for wind-electric generation. However, our focus in this chapter and in subsequent ones is on three-phase, squirrel-cage induction motors, which are commonly used in adjustable-speed applications.

11-2   THE   STRUCTURE   OF   THREE-PHASE,   SQUIRREL-CAGE INDUCTION MOTORS

The stator of an induction motor consists of three-phase windings, sinusoidally-distributed in the stator slots as discussed in Chapter 9. These three windings are displaced by 120° in space with respect to each other, as shown by their axes in Fig. 11-1a.

The rotor, consisting of a stack of insulated laminations, has electrically conducting bars of copper or aluminum inserted (molded) through it, close to the periphery in the axial direction. These bars are electrically shorted at each end of the rotor by electrically-conducting end-rings, thus producing a cage-like structure, as shown in Fig. 11-1b. Such a rotor, called a squirrel-cage rotor, has a simple construction, low-cost, and rugged nature.

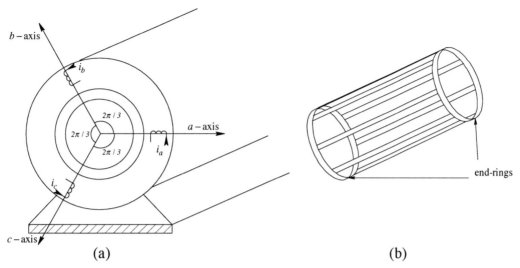

(a)   (b)

Figure 11-1 (a) Three-phase stator winding axes of an induction motor;
(b) squirrel-cage rotor.

11-3 THE PRINCIPLES OF INDUCTION MOTOR OPERATION

Our analysis will be under the line-fed conditions in which a balanced set of
sinusoidal voltages of rated amplitude and frequency are applied to the stator
windings. In the following discussion, we will assume a 2-pole structure which
can be extended to a multi-pole machine with p > 2.

Figure 11-2 shows the stator windings. Under a balanced sinusoidal steady state
condition, the motor-neutral "n" is at the same potential as the source-neutral.
Therefore, the source voltages v_a and so on appear across the respective phase
windings, as shown in Fig. 11-2a. These phase voltages are shown in the phasor
diagram of Fig. 11-2b, where

$$\overline{V}_a = \hat{V} \angle 0^o, \quad \overline{V}_b = \hat{V} \angle -120^o, \quad \text{and} \quad \overline{V}_c = \hat{V} \angle -240^o \qquad (11\text{-}1)$$

and $f(= \dfrac{\omega}{2\pi})$ is the frequency of the applied line-voltages to the motor.

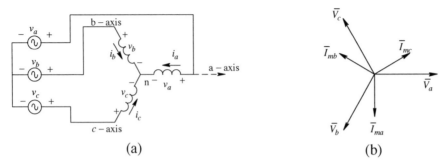

Figure 11-2 Balanced 3 phase sinusoidal voltages applied to the stator of an induction motor, rotor open-circuited.

To simplify our analysis, we will initially assume that the stator windings have a zero resistance ($R_s = 0$). Also, we will assume that $L_{\ell s} = 0$, implying that the leakage flux is zero; that is, all of the flux produced by each stator winding crosses the air gap and links with the other two stator windings and the rotor.

11-3-1 Electrically Open-Circuited Rotor

Initially, we will assume that the rotor is magnetically present but that its rotor bars are somehow open-circuited so that no current can flow. Therefore, we can use the analysis of Chapter 9, where the applied stator voltages given in Eq. 11-1 result only in the following magnetizing currents, which establish the rotating flux-density distribution in the air gap:

$$\overline{I}_{ma} = \hat{I}_m \angle -90^o, \quad \overline{I}_{mb} = \hat{I}_m \angle -210^o, \quad \text{and} \quad \overline{I}_{mc} = \hat{I}_m \angle -330^o \tag{11-2}$$

These phasors are shown in Fig. 11-2b, where, in terms of the per-phase magnetizing inductance L_m, the amplitude of the magnetizing currents is

$$\hat{I}_m = \frac{\hat{V}}{\omega L_m} \tag{11-3}$$

The space vectors at $t=0$ are shown in Fig. 11-3a, where, from Chapter 9,

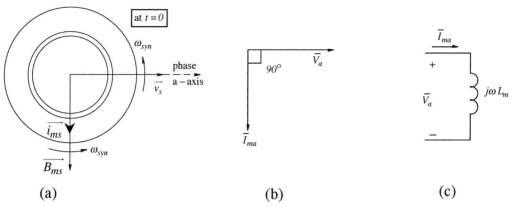

(a)   (b)   (c)

Figure 11-3 Space vector representations at time $t=0$; (b) voltage and current phasors for phase-a; (c) equivalent circuit for phase-a.

$$\vec{v}_s(t) = \frac{3}{2}\hat{V}\angle\omega t \tag{11-4}$$

$$\vec{i}_{ms}(t) = \frac{3}{2}\hat{I}_m \angle(\omega t - \frac{\pi}{2}) \tag{11-5}$$

$$\vec{B}_{ms}(t) = \frac{\mu_o N_s}{2\ell_g}\hat{I}_{ms}\angle(\omega t - \frac{\pi}{2}) \quad \text{where} \quad \hat{B}_{ms} = \frac{3}{2}\frac{\mu_o N_s}{2\ell_g}\hat{I}_m \tag{11-6}$$

and

$$\vec{v}_s(t) = \vec{e}_{ms}(t) = j\omega(\frac{3}{2}\pi r\ell\frac{N_s}{2})\vec{B}_{ms}(t) \tag{11-7}$$

These space vectors rotate at a constant synchronous speed ω_{syn}, which in a 2-pole machine is

$$\omega_{syn} = \omega \qquad (\omega_{syn} = \frac{\omega}{p/2} \text{ for a } p\text{-pole machine}) \tag{11-8}$$

▲ **Example 11-1** A 2-pole, 3-phase induction motor has the following physical dimensions: radius $r = 7\,cm$, length $\ell = 9\,cm$, and the air gap length $\ell_g = 0.5\,mm$. Calculate N_s, the number of turns per-phase, so that the peak of the flux-density distribution does not exceed $0.8T$ when the rated voltages of 208 V (line-line, rms) are applied at the 60-Hz frequency.

Solution   From Eq. 11-7, the peak of the stator voltage and the flux-density distribution space vectors are related as follows:

$$\hat{V}_s = \frac{3}{2}\pi r \ell \frac{N_s}{2} \omega \hat{B}_{ms} \quad \text{where} \quad \hat{V}_s = \frac{3}{2}\hat{V} = \frac{3}{2}\frac{208\sqrt{2}}{\sqrt{3}} = 254.75V \, .$$

Substituting given values in the above expression, $N_s = 56.9$ *turns.* Since the number of turns must be an integer, $N_s \simeq 57$ *turns* is selected.   ▲

11-3-2 The Short-Circuited Rotor

The voltages applied to the stator completely dictate the magnetizing currents (see Eqs. 11-2 and 11-3) and the flux-density distribution, which is represented in Eq. 11-6 by $\overrightarrow{B_{ms}}(t)$ and is "cutting" the stator windings. Assuming the stator winding resistances and the leakage inductances to be zero, this flux-density distribution is unaffected by the currents in the rotor circuit, as illustrated by the transformer analogy below.

Transformer Analogy

A two-winding transformer is shown in Fig. 11-4a, where two air gaps are introduced to bring the analogy closer to the case of induction machines where flux lines must cross the air gap twice. The primary winding resistance and the leakage inductance are neglected (similar to neglecting the stator winding resistances and leakage inductances). The transformer equivalent circuit is shown in Fig. 11-4b. The applied voltage $v_1(t)$ and the flux $\phi_m(t)$ linking the primary winding are related by Faraday's Law:

$$v_1 = N_1 \frac{d\phi_m}{dt} \tag{11-9}$$

11-6

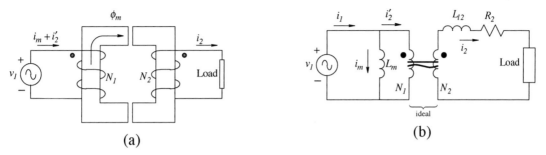

Fig 11-4 (a) Idealized two winding transformer; (b) equivalent circuit of the two winding transformer.

or, in the integral form,

$$\phi_m(t) = \frac{1}{N_1} \int v_1 \cdot dt \qquad (11\text{-}10)$$

This shows that in this transformer, the flux $\phi_m(t)$ linking the primary winding is completely determined by the time-integral of $v_1(t)$, independent of the current i_2 in the secondary winding.

This observation is confirmed by the transformer equivalent circuit of Fig. 11-4b, where the magnetizing current i_m is completely dictated by the time-integral of $v_1(t)$, independent of the currents i_2 and i_2':

$$i_m(t) = \frac{1}{L_m} \int v_1 \cdot dt \qquad (11\text{-}11)$$

In the ideal transformer portion of Fig. 11-4b, the ampere-turns produced by the load current $i_2(t)$ are "nullified" by the additional current $i_2'(t)$ drawn by the primary winding, such that

$$N_1 i_2'(t) = N_2 i_2(t) \qquad \text{or} \qquad i_2'(t) = \frac{N_2}{N_1} i_2(t) \qquad (11\text{-}12)$$

Thus, the total current drawn by the primary winding is

$$i_1(t) = i_m(t) + \underbrace{\frac{N_2}{N_1} i_2(t)}_{i_2'(t)}$$

(11-13)

Returning to our discussion of induction machines, the rotor consists of a short-circuited cage made up of rotor bars and the two end-rings. Regardless of what happens in the rotor circuit, the flux-density distribution "cutting" the stator windings must remain the same as under the assumption of an open-circuited rotor, as represented by $\overrightarrow{B_{ms}}(t)$ in Eq. 11-6.

Assume that the rotor is turning (due to the electromagnetic torque developed, as will be discussed shortly) at a speed ω_m in the same direction as the rotation of the space vectors which represent the stator voltages and the air gap flux-density distribution. For now, we will assume that $\omega_m < \omega_{syn}$. The space vectors at time $t=0$ are shown in the cross-section of Fig. 11-5a. There is a relative speed between the flux-density distribution rotating at ω_{syn} and the rotor conductors

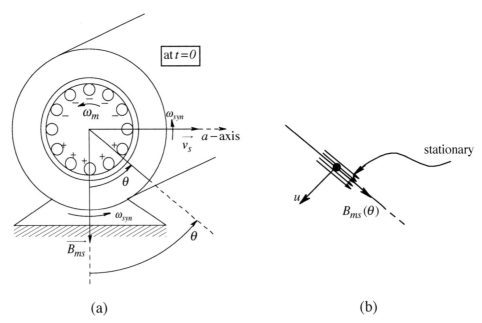

(a)   (b)

Figure 11-5 (a) Induced voltages in the rotor bar; (b) motion of the rotor bar relative to the flux density.

rotating at ω_m. This relative speed - that is, the speed at which the rotor is "slipping" with respect to the rotating flux-density distribution - is called the slip speed:

$$slip\ speed \quad \omega_{slip} = \omega_{syn} - \omega_m \qquad (11\text{-}14)$$

By Faraday's Law $(e = B\ell u)$, voltages are induced in the rotor bars due to the relative motion between the flux-density distribution and the rotor. At this time $t = 0$, the bar located at an angle θ from $\overrightarrow{B_{ms}}$ in Fig. 11-5a is "cutting" a flux density $B_{ms}(\theta)$. The flux-density distribution is moving ahead of the bar at position θ at the angular speed of ω_{slip} rad/s or at the linear speed of $u = r\omega_{slip}$, where r is the radius. To determine the voltage induced in this rotor bar, we can consider the flux-density distribution to be stationary and the bar (at the angle θ) to be moving in the opposite direction at the speed u, as shown in Fig. 11-5b. Therefore, the voltage induced in the bar can be expressed as

$$e_{bar}(\theta) = B_{ms}(\theta)\ell \underbrace{r\,\omega_{slip}}_{u} \qquad (11\text{-}15)$$

where the bar is of length ℓ and is at a radius r. The direction of the induced voltage can be established by visualizing that on a positive charge q in the bar, the force f_q equals $\mathbf{u}\times\mathbf{B}$ where u and B are vectors shown in Fig. 11-5b. This force will cause the positive charge to move towards the front-end of the bar, establishing that the front-end of the bar will have a positive potential with respect to the back-end, as shown in Fig. 11-5a.

At any time, the flux-density distribution varies as the cosine of the angle θ from its positive peak. Therefore in Eq. 11-15, $B_{ms}(\theta) = \hat{B}_{ms}\cos\theta$. Hence,

$$e_{bar}(\theta) = \ell r\,\omega_{slip}\hat{B}_{ms}\cos\theta \qquad (11\text{-}16)$$

11-3-2-1 The Assumption of Rotor Leakage $L'_{\ell r} = 0$

At this point, we will make another *extremely* important simplifying assumption, to be analyzed later in more detail. The assumption is that the rotor cage has no leakage inductance; that is, $L'_{\ell r} = 0$. This assumption implies that the rotor has no leakage flux and that all of the flux produced by the rotor-bar currents crosses the air gap and links (or "cuts") the stator windings. Another implication of this assumption is that, at any time, the current in each squirrel-cage bar, short-circuited at both ends by conducting end-rings, is inversely proportional to the bar resistance R_{bar}.

In Fig. 11-6a at *t=0,* the induced voltages are maximum in the top and the bottom rotor bars "cutting" the peak flux density. Elsewhere, induced voltages in rotor bars depend on $\cos\theta$, as given by Eq. 11-16. The polarities of the induced voltages at the near-end of the bars are indicated in Fig. 11-6a. Figure 11-6b shows the electrical equivalent circuit which corresponds to the cross-section of the rotor shown in Fig. 11-6a. The size of the voltage source represents the magnitude of the voltage induced. Because of the symmetry in this circuit, it is easy to visualize that the two end-rings (assumed to have negligible resistances themselves) are at the same potential. Therefore, the rotor bar at an angle θ from

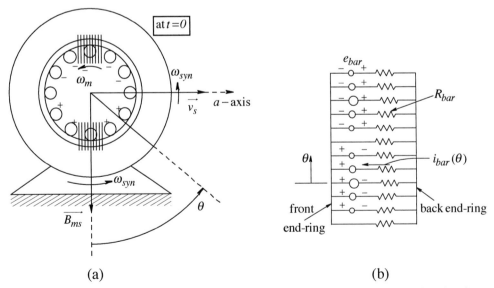

(a)   (b)

Figure 11-6 (a) Polarities of voltages induced; (b) electrical equivalent circuit of rotor.

the positive flux-density peak location has a current which is equal to the induced voltage divided by the bar resistance:

$$i_{bar}(\theta) = \frac{e_{bar}(\theta)}{R_{bar}} = \frac{\ell r \omega_{slip} \hat{B}_{ms} \cos\theta}{R_{bar}} \quad \text{(using Eq. 11-16)} \quad (11\text{-}17)$$

where each bar has a resistance R_{bar}. From Eq. 11-17, the currents are maximum in the top and the bottom bars at this time, indicated by the largest circles in Fig. 11-7a; elsewhere, the magnitude of the current depends on $\cos\theta$, where θ is the angular position of any bar as defined in Fig. 11-6a.

It is important to note that the rotor has a uniform bar density around its periphery, as shown in Fig. 11-6a. The sizes of the circles in Fig. 11-7a denote the relative current magnitudes. The sinusoidal rotor-current distribution is different than that in the stator phase winding, which has a sinusoidally-distributed conductor density but the same current flowing through each conductor. In spite of this key difference, the outcome is the same - the ampere-turns need to be sinusoidally distributed in order to produce a sinusoidal field distribution in the air gap. In the rotor with a uniform bar density, a sinusoidal ampere-turn distribution is achieved because the currents in various rotor bars are sinusoidally distributed with position at any time.

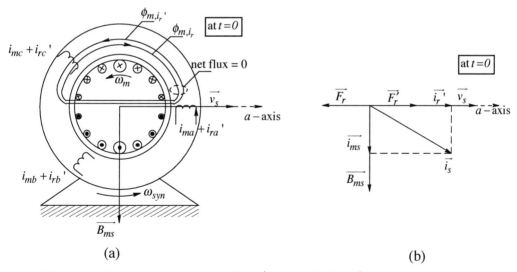

(a)   (b)

Figure 11-7 (a) Rotor-produced flux ϕ_{m,i_r} and the flux ϕ'_{m,i_r}; (b) space vector diagram with short-circuited rotor ($L'_{lr} = 0$).

The combined effect of the rotor-bar currents is to produce a sinusoidally-distributed mmf acting on the air gap. This mmf can be represented by a space vector $\overrightarrow{F_r}(t)$, as shown in Fig. 11-7b at time $t = 0$. Due to the rotor-produced mmf, the resulting flux "cutting" the stator winding is represented by ϕ_{m,i_r} in Fig. 11-7a. As argued earlier by means of the transformer analogy, the net flux-density distribution "cutting" the voltage-supplied stator windings must remain the same as in the case of the open-circuited rotor. Therefore, in order to cancel the rotor-produced flux ϕ_{m,i_r}, the stator windings must draw the additional currents i_{ra}', i_{rb}', and i_{rc}' to produce the flux represented by $\phi_{m,i_r'}$.

In the space vector diagram of Fig. 11-7b, the mmf produced by the rotor bars is represented by $\overrightarrow{F_r}$ at time $t=0$. As shown in Fig. 11-7b, the stator currents i_{ra}', i_{rb}', and i_{rc}' (which flow in addition to the magnetizing currents) must produce an mmf $\overrightarrow{F_r'}$, which is equal in amplitude but opposite in direction to $\overrightarrow{F_r}$, in order to neutralize its effect:

$$\overrightarrow{F_r'} = -\overrightarrow{F_r} \qquad (11\text{-}18)$$

The additional currents i_{ra}', i_{rb}', and i_{rc}' drawn by the stator windings to produce $\overrightarrow{F_r'}$ can be expressed by a current space vector $\overrightarrow{i_r'}$, as shown in Fig. 11-7b at $t=0$, where

$$\overrightarrow{i_r'} = \frac{\overrightarrow{F_r'}}{N_s/2} \qquad (\hat{I}_r' = \text{the amplitude of } \overrightarrow{i_r'}) \qquad (11\text{-}19)$$

The total stator current $\overrightarrow{i_s}$ is the vector sum of the two components: $\overrightarrow{i_{ms}}$, which sets up the magnetizing field, and $\overrightarrow{i_r'}$, which neutralizes the rotor-produced mmf:

$$\overrightarrow{i_s} = \overrightarrow{i_{ms}} + \overrightarrow{i_r'} \qquad (11\text{-}20)$$

These space vectors are shown in Fig. 11-7b at $t=0$. Eq. 11-17 shows that the rotor-bar currents are proportional to the flux-density peak and the slip speed. Therefore, the "nullifying" mmf peak and the peak current $\hat{I}_r'$ must also be linearly proportional to $\hat{B}_{ms}$ and ω_{slip}. This relationship can be expressed as

$$\hat{I}_r' = k_i \hat{B}_{ms} \omega_{slip} \qquad (k_i = \text{a constant}) \qquad (11\text{-}21)$$

where k_i is a constant based on the design of the machine.

During the sinusoidal steady state operating condition in Fig. 11-7b, the rotor-produced mmf distribution (represented by $\overrightarrow{F_r}$) and the compensating mmf distribution (represented by $\overrightarrow{F_r'}$) rotate at the synchronous speed ω_{syn} and each has a constant amplitude. This can be illustrated by drawing the motor cross-section and space vectors at some arbitrary time $t_1 > 0$, as shown in Fig. 11-8, where the $\overrightarrow{B_{ms}}$ space vector has rotated by an angle $\omega_{syn}t_1$ because $\overrightarrow{v_s}$ has rotated by $\omega_{syn}t_1$. Based on the voltages and currents induced in the rotor bars, $\overrightarrow{F_r}$ is still 90° behind the $\overrightarrow{B_{ms}}$ space vector, as in Fig. 11-7a and 11-7b. This implies that the

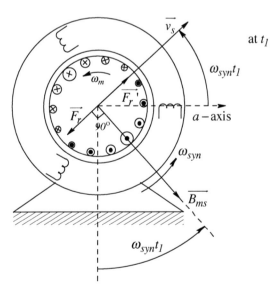

Figure 11-8 Rotor produced mmf and the compensating mmf at time $t = t_1$.

$\vec{F}_r(t)$ and $\vec{F}'_r(t)$ vectors are rotating at the same speed as $\overrightarrow{B}_{ms}(t)$ - that is, the synchronous speed ω_{syn}. At a given operating condition with constant values of ω_{slip} and $\hat{B}_{ms}$, the bar-current distribution, relative to the peak of the flux-density vector, is the same in Fig. 11-8 as in Fig. 11-7. Therefore, the amplitudes of $\vec{F}_r(t)$ and $\vec{F}'_r(t)$ remain constant as they rotate at the synchronous speed.

▲ **Example 11-2** Consider an induction machine that has 2 poles and is supplied by a rated voltage of 208 V (line-to-line, rms) at the frequency of 60 Hz. It is operating in steady state and is loaded to its rated torque. Neglect the stator leakage impedance and the rotor leakage flux. The per-phase magnetizing current is 4.0 A (rms). The current drawn per-phase is 10 A (rms) and is at an angle of 23.56 degrees (lagging). Calculate the per-phase current if the mechanical load decreases so that the slip speed is one-half that of the rated case.

Solution We will consider the phase-a voltage to be the reference phasor. Therefore,

$$\overline{V}_a = \frac{208\sqrt{2}}{\sqrt{3}} \angle 0° = 169.8\angle 0° \; V \; .$$

It is given that at the rated load, as shown in Fig. 11-9a,

$$\overline{I}_{ma} = 4.0\sqrt{2}\angle -90° \; A \text{ and } \overline{I}_a = 10.0\sqrt{2}\angle -23.56° \; A \; .$$

From the phasor diagram in Fig. 11-9a,

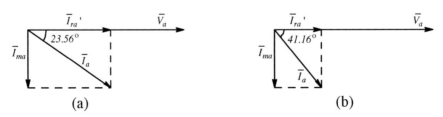

Figure 11-9 Example 11-2.

$$\overline{I}'_{ra} = 9.173\sqrt{2}\angle 0^{o}\ A\,.$$

At one-half of the slip speed, the magnetizing current is the same but the amplitudes of the rotor-bar currents, and hence of $\overline{I}'_{ra}$ are reduced by one-half:

$$\overline{I}_{ma} = 4.0\sqrt{2}\angle -90^{o}\ A\ \text{and}\ \overline{I}'_{ra} = 4.59\sqrt{2}\angle 0^{o}\ A\,.$$

Therefore,

$$\overline{I}_{a} = 6.1\sqrt{2}\angle -41.16^{o}\ A\,,\ \text{as shown in the phasor diagram of Fig. 11-9b.}\ \blacktriangle$$

Revisiting the Transformer Analogy

The transformer equivalent circuit in Fig. 11-4b illustrated so that the voltage-supplied primary winding draws a compensating current to neutralize the effect of the secondary winding current in order to ensure that the resultant flux linking the *primary winding* remains the same as under the open-circuited condition. Similarly, in an induction motor, the stator neutralizes the rotor-produced field to ensure that the resultant flux "cutting" the *stator windings* remains the same as under the rotor open-circuited condition. In induction machines, this is how the stator "keeps track" of what is happening in the rotor. However, compared to transformers, induction machine operation is more complex where the rotor-cage quantities are at the slip frequency (discussed below) and are transformed into the stator-frequency quantities "seen" from the stator.

11-3-2-2 The Slip Frequency, f_{slip}, in the Rotor Circuit

The frequency of induced voltages (and currents) in the rotor bars can be obtained by considering Fig. 11-10a. At $t=0$, the bottom-most bar labeled "p" is being "cut" by the positive peak flux density and has a positive induced voltage at the front-end. The $\overrightarrow{B_{ms}}(t)$ space vector, which is rotating with a speed of ω_{syn}, is "pulling ahead" at the slip speed ω_{slip} with respect to the rotor bar "p," which is

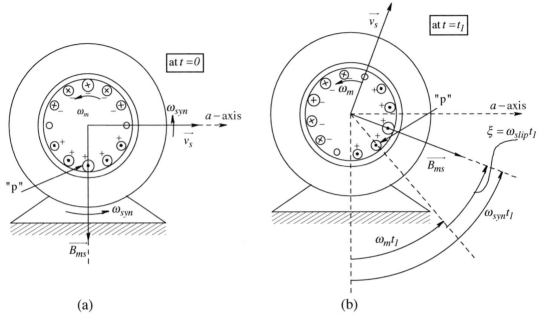

(a)   (b)

Figure 11-10 (a) Voltage induced in bar "p" at $t = 0$; (b) voltage induced in bar "p" at $t = t_1$.

rotating at ω_m. Therefore, as shown in Fig. 11-10b, at sometime $t_1 > 0$, the angle between $\overrightarrow{B_{ms}}(t)$ and the rotor bar "p" is

$$\xi = \omega_{slip}\, t_1 \tag{11-22}$$

Therefore, the first time (call it $T_{2\pi}$) when the bar "p" is again being "cut" by the positive peak flux density is when $\zeta = 2\pi$. Therefore, from Eq. 11-22,

$$T_{2\pi} = \frac{\xi(=2\pi)}{\omega_{slip}} \tag{11-23}$$

where $T_{2\pi}$ is the time-period between the two consecutive positive peaks of the induced voltage in the rotor bar "p." Therefore, the induced voltage in the rotor bar has a frequency (which we will call the slip frequency f_{slip}) which is the inverse of $T_{2\pi}$ in Eq. 11-23:

$$f_{slip} = \frac{\omega_{slip}}{2\pi} \qquad (11\text{-}24)$$

For convenience, we will define a unitless (dimensionless) quantity called slip, s, as the ratio of the slip speed to the synchronous speed:

$$s = \frac{\omega_{slip}}{\omega_{syn}} \qquad (11\text{-}25)$$

Substituting for ω_{slip} from Eq. 11-25 into Eq. 11-24 and noting that $\omega_{syn} = 2\pi f$ (in a 2-pole machine),

$$f_{slip} = s f \qquad (11\text{-}26)$$

In steady state, induction machines operate at ω_m, very close to their synchronous speed, with a slip s of generally less than 0.03 (or 3 percent). Therefore, in steady state, the frequency (f_{slip}) of voltages and currents in the rotor circuit is typically less than a few Hz.

Note that $\overrightarrow{F_r}(t)$, which is created by the slip-frequency voltages and currents in the rotor circuit, rotates at the slip speed ω_{slip}, relative to the rotor. Since the rotor itself is rotating at a speed of ω_m, the net result is that $\overrightarrow{F_r}(t)$ rotates at a total speed of ($\omega_{slip} + \omega_m$), which is equal to the synchronous speed ω_{syn}. This confirms what we had concluded earlier about the speed of $\overrightarrow{F_r}(t)$ by comparing Figs. 11-7 and 11-8.

▲ **Example 11-3** In Example 11-2, the rated speed (while the motor supplies its rated torque) is 3475 rpm. Calculate the slip speed ω_{slip}, the slip s, and the slip frequency f_{slip} of the currents and voltages in the rotor circuit.

Solution This is a 2-pole motor. Therefore, at the rated frequency of 60 *Hz*, the rated synchronous speed, from Eq. 11-8, is

$$\omega_{syn} = \omega = 2\pi \times 60 = 377 \, rad \, / \, s.$$

The rated speed is $\omega_{m,rated} = \dfrac{2\pi \times 3475}{60} = 363.9 \, rad \, / \, s.$

Therefore,

$$\omega_{slip,rated} = \omega_{syn,rated} - \omega_{m,rated} = 377.0 - 363.9 = 13.1 \, rad \, / \, s.$$

From Eq. 11-25,

$$slip \; s_{rated} = \frac{\omega_{slip,rated}}{\omega_{syn,rated}} = \frac{13.1}{377.0} = 0.0347 = 3.47\%$$

and, from Eq. 11-26,

$$f_{slip,rated} = s_{rated} f = 2.08 \, Hz. \qquad\qquad \blacktriangle$$

11-3-2-3 Electromagnetic Torque

The electromagnetic torque on the rotor is produced by the interaction of the flux-density distribution represented by $\overrightarrow{B_{ms}}(t)$ in Fig. 11-7a and the rotor-bar currents producing the mmf $\overrightarrow{F_r}(t)$. As in Chapter 10, it will be easier to calculate the torque produced on the rotor by first calculating the torque on the stator equivalent winding that produces the nullifying mmf $\overrightarrow{F_r'}(t)$. At *t=0*, this equivalent stator winding, sinusoidally distributed with N_s turns, has its axis along the $\overrightarrow{F_r'}(t)$ space vector, as shown in Fig. 11-11. The winding also has a current $\hat{I}_r'$ flowing thorough it.

Following the derivation of the electromagnetic torque in Chapter 10, from Eq. 10-5,

$$T_{em} = \pi \ r \ell \frac{N_s}{2} \hat{B}_{ms} \hat{I}_r' \qquad\qquad (11\text{-}27)$$

The above equation can be written as

$$T_{em} = k_t \hat{B}_{ms} \hat{I}_r' \quad (\text{where } k_t = \pi \ r \ell \frac{N_s}{2}) \qquad\qquad (11\text{-}28)$$

where k_t is a constant which depends on the machine design. The torque on the stator in Fig. 11-11 acts in a clockwise direction and the torque on the rotor is equal in magnitude and acts in a counter-clockwise direction.

The current peak $\hat{I}_r'$ depends linearly on the flux-density peak $\hat{B}_{ms}$ and the slip speed ω_{slip}, as expressed by Eq. 11-21 ($\hat{I}_r' = k_i \hat{B}_{ms} \omega_{slip}$). Therefore, substituting for $\hat{I}_r'$ in Eq. 11-28,

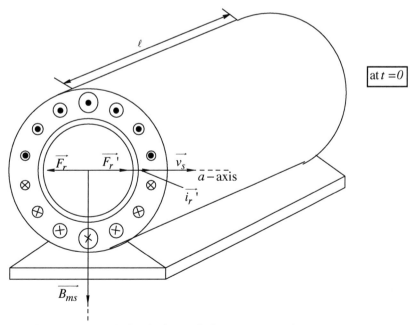

Figure 11-11 Calculation of electromagnetic torque.

$$T_{em} = k_{t\omega} \hat{B}_{ms}^2 \omega_{slip} \qquad\qquad (k_{t\omega} = k_t k_i) \qquad\qquad (11\text{-}29)$$

where $k_{t\omega}$ is a machine torque constant. If the flux-density peak is maintained at its rated value in Eq. 11-29,

$$T_{em} = k_{T\omega} \omega_{slip} \qquad\qquad (k_{T\omega} = k_{t\omega} \hat{B}_{ms}^2) \qquad\qquad (11\text{-}30)$$

where $k_{T\omega}$ is another torque constant of the machine.

Eq. 11-30 expresses the torque-speed characteristic of induction machines. For a rated set of applied voltages, which result in $\omega_{syn,rated}$ and $\hat{B}_{ms,rated}$, the torque developed by the machine increases linearly with the slip speed ω_{slip} as the rotor slows down. This torque-speed characteristic is shown in Fig. 11-12 in two different ways. At zero torque, the slip speed ω_{slip} is zero, implying that the motor rotates at the synchronous speed. This is only a theoretical operating point because the motor's internal bearing friction and windage losses would require that a finite amount of electromagnetic torque be generated to overcome them. The torque-speed characteristic beyond the rated torque is shown dotted because the assumptions of neglecting stator leakage impedance and the rotor leakage inductance begin to breakdown.

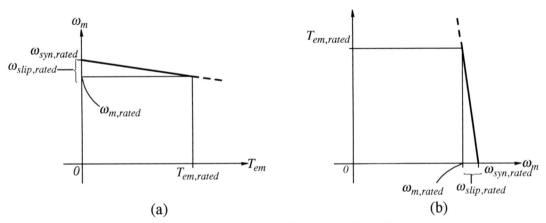

Figure 11-12 Torque speed characteristic of induction motors.

The torque-speed characteristic helps to explain the operating principle of induction machines, as illustrated in Fig. 11-13. In steady state, the operating speed ω_{m1} is dictated by the intersection of the electromagnetic torque and the mechanical-load torque T_{L1}. If the load torque is increased to T_{L2}, the induction motor slows down to ω_{m2}, increasing the slip speed ω_{slip}. This increased slip speed results in higher induced voltages and currents in the rotor bars, and hence a higher electromagnetic torque is produced to meet the increase in mechanical load torque. On a dynamic basis, the electromagnetic torque developed by the motor interacts with the shaft-coupled mechanical load, in accordance with the following mechanical-system equation:

$$\frac{d\omega_m}{dt} = \frac{T_{em} - T_L}{J_{eq}}$$

(11-31)

where J_{eq} is the combined motor-load inertia constant and T_L (generally a function of speed) is the torque of the mechanical load opposing the rotation. The acceleration torque is $(T_{em} - T_L)$.

Note that the electromagnetic torque developed by the motor equals the load toque in steady state. Often, the torque required to overcome friction and windage (including that of the motor itself) can be included lumped with the load torque.

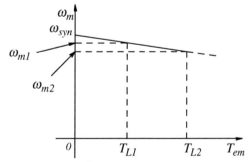

Figure 11-13 Operation of an induction motor.

▲ **Example 11-4**   In Example 11-3, the rated torque supplied by the motor is 8 *Nm*. Calculate the torque constant $k_{T\omega}$, which linearly relates the torque developed by the motor to the slip speed.

Solution

From Eq. 11-30,

$$k_{T\omega} = \frac{T_{em}}{\omega_{slip}} \cdot$$

Therefore, using the rated conditions,

$$k_{T\omega} = \frac{T_{em,rated}}{\omega_{slip,rated}} = \frac{8.0}{13.1} = 0.61 \frac{Nm}{rad \, / \, s} \cdot$$

The torque-speed characteristic is as shown in Fig. 11-12, with the slope given above. ▲

11-3-2-4 The Generator (Regenerative Braking) Mode of Operation

Induction machines can be used as generators, for example many wind-electric systems use induction generators to convert wind energy to electrical output which is fed into the utility grid. Most commonly, however, while slowing down, induction motors go into regenerative-braking mode (which, from the machine's standpoint, is the same as the generator mode), where the kinetic energy associated with the inertia of the mechanical system is converted into electrical output. In this mode of operation, the rotor speed exceeds the synchronous speed ($\omega_m > \omega_{syn}$) where both are in the same direction. Hence, $\omega_{slip} < 0$.

Under the condition of negative slip speed shown in Fig. 11-14, the voltages and currents induced in the rotor bars are of opposite polarities and directions compared to those with positive slip speed in Fig. 11-7a. Therefore, the electromagnetic torque on the rotor acts in a clockwise direction, opposing the

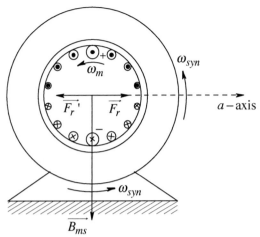

$a-\text{axis}$

Figure 11-14 Regenerative braking in induction motors.

rotation and thus slowing down the rotor. In this regenerative breaking mode, T_{em} in Eq. 11-31 has a negative value.

▲ **Example 11-5**   The induction machine of Example 11-2 is to produce the rated torque in the regenerative-braking mode. Draw the voltage and current phasors for phase-a.

Solution   With the assumption that the stator leakage impedance can be neglected, the magnetizing current is the same as in Example 11-2: $\overline{I}_{ma} = 4.0\sqrt{2}\angle -90^o \ A$. However, since we are dealing with a regenerative-braking torque,

$$\overline{I}'_{ra} = -9.173\sqrt{2}\angle 0^o \ A$$

as shown in the phasor diagram of Fig. 11-15. Hence,

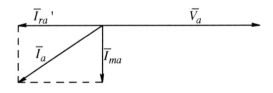

Figure 11-15 Example 11-5.

$$\bar{I}_a = 10.0\sqrt{2}\angle -156.44^\circ \ A.$$
▲

11-3-2-5 Reversing the Direction of Rotation

Reversing the sequence of applied voltages (*a-b-c* to *a-c-b*) causes the reversal of direction, as shown in Fig. 11-16.

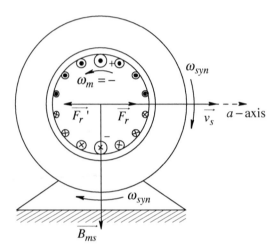

Figure 11-16 Reversing the direction of rotation in an induction motor.

11-3-2-6   Including the Rotor Leakage Inductance

Up to the rated torque, the slip speed and the slip frequency in the rotor circuit are small, and hence it is reasonable to neglect the effect of the rotor leakage inductance. However, loading the machine beyond the rated torque results in larger slip speeds and slip frequencies, and the effect of the rotor leakage inductance should be included in the analysis, as described below.

Of all the flux produced by the currents in the rotor bars, a portion (which is called the leakage flux and is responsible for the rotor leakage inductance) does not completely cross the air gap and does not "cut" the stator windings. *First considering only the stator-established flux-density distribution* $\overrightarrow{B_{ms}}(t)$ *at* $t = 0$ *as* in Fig. 11-6a, the top and the bottom bars are "cut" by the peak $\hat{B}_{ms}$ of the flux-density distribution, and due to this flux the voltages induced in them are the maximum. However (as shown in Fig. 11-17a), the bar currents lag due to the

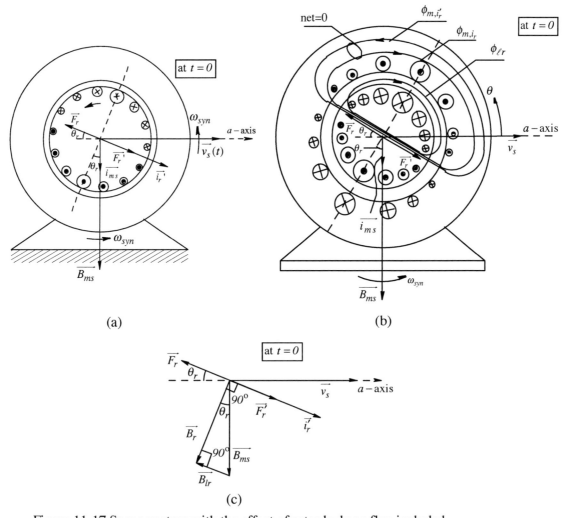

Figure 11-17 Space vectors with the effect of rotor leakage flux included.

inductive effect of the rotor leakage flux and are maximum in the bars which were "cut" by $\overrightarrow{B_{ms}}(t)$ sometime earlier. Therefore, the rotor mmf space vector $\overrightarrow{F_r}(t)$ in Fig. 11-17a lags $\overrightarrow{B_{ms}}(t)$ by an angle $\frac{\pi}{2}+\theta_r$, where θ_r is called the rotor power factor angle.

At $t=0$, the flux lines produced by the rotor currents in Fig. 11-17b can be divided into two components: ϕ_{m,i_r}, which crosses the air gap and "cuts" the stator windings, and $\phi_{\ell r}$, the rotor leakage flux, which does *not* cross the air gap to "cut" the stator windings.

The stator excited by ideal voltage sources (and assuming that R_s and L_{ls} are zero) demands that the flux-density distribution $\overrightarrow{B_{ms}}(t)$ "cutting" it be unchanged. Therefore, additional stator currents, represented by $\vec{i}_r(t)$ in Fig. 11-17a, are drawn to produce $\phi_{m,i_r'}$ in Fig. 11-17b to compensate for ϕ_{m,i_r} (but not to compensate for $\phi_{\ell r}$, whose existence the stator is unaware of), such that $\phi_{m,i_r'}$ is equal in magnitude and opposite in direction to ϕ_{m,i_r}.

The additional currents drawn from the three stator phase windings can be represented by means of the equivalent stator winding with N_s turns and carrying a current $\hat{I}_r'$, as shown in Fig. 11-17b. The resulting $\overrightarrow{F_r}$, $\overrightarrow{F_r'}$, and $\vec{i}_r'$ space vectors at $t=0$ are shown in Fig. 11-17c. The rotor bars are "cut" by the net flux-density distribution represented by $\overrightarrow{B_r}(t)$, shown in Fig. 11-17c at $t=0$, where

$$\overrightarrow{B_r}(t) = \overrightarrow{B_{ms}}(t) + \overrightarrow{B_{\ell r}}(t) \tag{11-32}$$

$\overrightarrow{B_{\ell r}}(t)$ represents in the air gap the rotor leakage flux density distribution (due to $\phi_{\ell r}$) which, for our purposes, is also assumed to be radial and sinusoidally distributed. Note that $\overrightarrow{B_r}$ is *not* created by the currents in the rotor bars; rather it is the flux-density distribution "cutting" the rotor bars.

The equivalent stator winding shown in Fig. 11-17b has a current $\hat{I}_r'$ and is "cut" by the flux-density distribution represented by $\overrightarrow{B_{ms}}$. As shown in Fig. 11-17c, the $\overrightarrow{B_{ms}}$ and $\vec{i}_r'$ space vectors are at an angle of $(\pi/2 - \theta_r)$ with respect to each other. Using a procedure similar to the one which led to the torque expression in Eq. 11-28, we can show that the torque developed depends on the sine of the angle $(\pi/2 - \theta_r)$ between $\overrightarrow{B_{ms}}$ and $\vec{i}_r'$:

$$T_{em} = k_t \hat{B}_{ms} \hat{I}_r' \sin(\frac{\pi}{2} - \theta_r) \tag{11-33}$$

In the space vector diagram of Fig. 11-17c,

$$\hat{B}_{ms} \sin(\frac{\pi}{2} - \theta_r) = \hat{B}_r \qquad (11\text{-}34)$$

Therefore, in Eq. 11-33,

$$T_{em} = k_t \hat{B}_r \hat{I}_r' \qquad (11\text{-}35)$$

The above development suggests how we can achieve vector control of induction machines. In an induction machine, $\overrightarrow{B_r}(t)$ and $\overrightarrow{i_r'}(t)$ are naturally at right angles (90 degrees) to each other. (Note in Fig. 11-17b that the rotor bars with the maximum current are those "cutting" the peak of the rotor flux-density distribution $\hat{B}_r$.) Therefore, if we can keep the rotor flux-density peak $\hat{B}_r$ constant, then

$$T_{em} = k_T \hat{I}_r' \qquad \text{where} \quad k_T = k_t \hat{B}_r \qquad (11\text{-}36)$$

The torque developed by the motor can be controlled by $\hat{I}_r'$. This allows induction-motor drives to emulate the performance of dc-motor and brushless-dc motor drives.

11-3-3 Per-Phase Steady-State Equivalent Circuit (Including Rotor Leakage)

The space vector diagram at $t=0$ is shown in Fig. 11-18a for the rated voltages applied. This results in the phasor diagram for phase-a in Fig. 11-18b. The current $\overline{I}_{ra}'$, which is lagging behind the applied voltage $\overline{V}_a$, can be represented as flowing through an inductive branch in the equivalent circuit of Fig. 11-18c, where R_{eq} and L_{eq} are yet to be determined. For the above determination, assume that the rotor is blocked and that the voltages applied to the stator create the same conditions ($\overrightarrow{B_{ms}}$ with the same $\hat{B}_{ms}$ and at the same ω_{slip} with respect to the rotor) in the rotor circuit as in Fig. 11-18. Therefore, in Fig. 11-19a with the blocked rotor, we will apply stator voltages at the slip frequency $f_{slip}(=\omega_{slip}/2\pi)$ from Eq. 11-8 and of amplitude $\dfrac{\omega_{slip}}{\omega_{syn}}\hat{V}$ from Eq. 11-7, as shown in Figs. 11-19a and 11-19b.

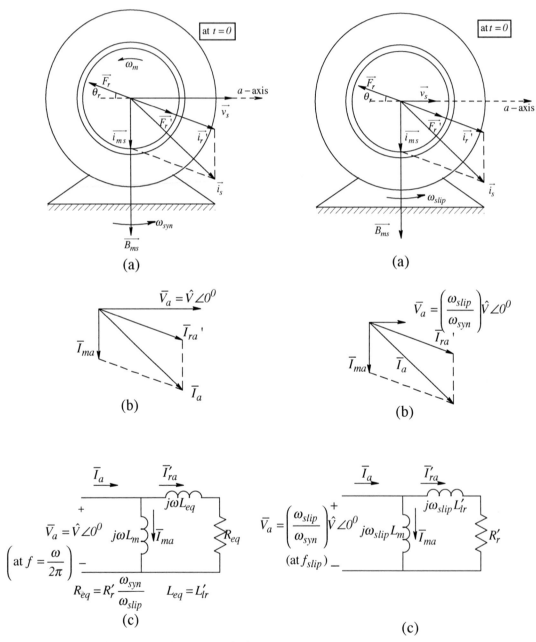

Figure 11-18 Rated voltage applied.

Figure 11-19 Blocked rotor and slip -frequency voltages applied.

The blocked-rotor bars, similar to those in the rotor turning at ω_m, are "cut" by an identical flux-density distribution (which has the same peak value $\hat{B}_{ms}$ and which rotates at the same slip speed ω_{slip} with respect to the rotor). The phasor diagram in the blocked-rotor case is shown in Fig. 11-19b and the phase equivalent circuit is shown in Fig. 11-19c. (The quantities at the stator terminals in the blocked-rotor case of Fig. 11-19 are similar to those of a transformer primary, with its secondary winding short-circuited.) The current $\overline{I}_{ra}'$ in Fig. 11-19c is at the slip frequency f_{slip} and flowing through an inductive branch which consists of R_r' and $L_{\ell r}'$ connected in series. Note that R_r' and $L_{\ell r}'$ are the equivalent rotor resistance and the equivalent rotor leakage inductance, "seen" on a per-phase basis from the stator side. The impedance of the inductive branch with $\overline{I}_{ra}'$ in this blocked-rotor case is

$$Z_{eq,blocked} = R_r' + j\omega_{slip}L_{\ell r}'$$
(11-37)

The three-phase power loss in the bar resistances of the blocked rotor is

$$P_{r,loss} = 3R_r'(I_{ra}')^2$$
(11-38)

where I_{ra}' is the rms value.

As far as the conditions "seen" by an observer sitting on the rotor are concerned, they are identical to the original case with the rotor turning at a speed ω_m but slipping at a speed ω_{slip} with respect to ω_{syn}. Therefore, in both cases, the current component $\overline{I}_{ra}'$ has the same amplitude and the same phase angle with respect to the applied voltage. Therefore, in the original case of Fig. 11-18, where the applied voltages are higher by a factor of $\dfrac{\omega_{syn}}{\omega_{slip}}$, the impedance must be higher by the same factor; that is, from Eq. 11-37,

$$\underbrace{Z_{eq}}_{at\,f} = \frac{\omega_{syn}}{\omega_{slip}} \underbrace{(R_r' + j\omega_{slip}L_{\ell r}')}_{Z_{eq\,blocked}\,at\,f_{slip}} = R_r' \frac{\omega_{syn}}{\omega_{slip}} + j\omega_{syn}L_{\ell r}' \qquad (11\text{-}39)$$

Therefore, in the equivalent circuit of Fig. 11-18c at frequency f, $R_{eq} = R_r' \dfrac{\omega_{syn}}{\omega_{slip}}$ and $L_{eq} = L_{\ell r}'$.

The per-phase equivalent circuit of Fig. 11-18c is repeated in Fig. 11-20a, where $\omega_{syn} = \omega$ for a 2-pole machine. The power loss $P_{r,loss}$ in the rotor circuit in Fig. 11-20a is the same as that given by Eq. 11-38 for the blocked-rotor case of Fig. 11-19c. Therefore, the resistance $R_r' \dfrac{\omega_{syn}}{\omega_{slip}}$ can be divided into two parts: R_r' and $R_r' \dfrac{\omega_m}{\omega_{slip}}$, as shown in Fig. 11-20b, where $P_{r,loss}$ is lost as heat in R_r' and the power dissipation in $R_r' \dfrac{\omega_m}{\omega_{slip}}$, on a three-phase basis, gets converted into mechanical power (which also equals T_{em} times ω_m):

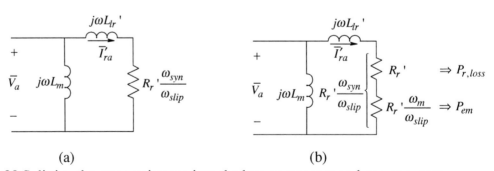

(a)   (b)

Figure 11-20 Splitting the rotor resistance into the loss component and power output component (neglecting the stator-winding leakage impedance).

$$P_{em} = 3\frac{\omega_m}{\omega_{slip}} R_r' (I_{ra}')^2 = T_{em}\omega_m \qquad (11\text{-}40)$$

Therefore,

$$T_{em} = 3R_r' \frac{(I_{ra}')^2}{\omega_{slip}} \qquad (11\text{-}41)$$

From Eqs. 11-38 and 11-41,

$$\frac{P_{r,loss}}{T_{em}} = \omega_{slip} \qquad (11\text{-}42)$$

This is an important relationship because it shows that to produce the desired torque T_{em} we should minimize the value of the slip speed in order to minimize the power loss in the rotor circuit.

▲ **Example 11-6**   Consider a 60-*Hz* induction motor with $R_r' = 0.45\,\Omega$ and $X_{\ell r}' = 0.85\,\Omega$. The rated slip speed is 4 percent. Ignore the stator leakage impedance. Compare the torque at the rated slip speed by (a) ignoring the rotor leakage inductance and (b) including the rotor leakage inductance.

Solution   To calculate T_{em} at the rated slip speed we will make use of Eq. 11-41, where I_{ra}' can be calculated from the per-phase equivalent circuit of Fig. 11-20a. Ignoring the rotor leakage inductance,

$$\left. I_{ra}'\right|_{L_{\ell r}'=0} = \frac{V_a}{R_r' \dfrac{\omega_{syn}}{\omega_{slip}}}, \text{ and from Eq. 11-41 } \left. T_{em}\right|_{L_{\ell r}'=0} = \frac{3R_r'}{\omega_{slip}} \frac{V_a^{\,2}}{\left(R_r' \dfrac{\omega_{syn}}{\omega_{slip}}\right)^2}.$$

Including the rotor leakage inductance,

$$I'_{ra} = \frac{V_a}{\sqrt{\left(R'_r \dfrac{\omega_{syn}}{\omega_{slip}}\right)^2 + \left(X'_{\ell r}\right)^2}}, \text{ and from Eq. 11-41}$$

$$T_{em} = \frac{3R'_r}{\omega_{slip}} \frac{V_a^2}{\left(R'_r \dfrac{\omega_{syn}}{\omega_{slip}}\right)^2 + \left(X'_{\ell r}\right)^2}.$$

At the rated slip speed of 4%, $\dfrac{\omega_{slip}}{\omega_{syn}} = 0.04$. Therefore, comparing the above two

expressions for torque by substituting the numerical values,

$$\frac{T_{em}\big|_{L'_{\ell r}=0}}{T_{em}} = \frac{\left(R'_r \dfrac{\omega_{syn}}{\omega_{slip}}\right)^2 + \left(X'_{\ell r}\right)^2}{\left(R'_r \dfrac{\omega_{syn}}{\omega_{slip}}\right)^2} = \frac{126.56^2 + 0.85^2}{126.56^2} \simeq 1.0. \qquad \blacktriangle$$

The above example shows that under normal operation when the motor is supplying a torque within its rated value, it does so at very small values of slip speed. Therefore, as shown in this example, we are justified in ignoring the effect of the rotor leakage inductance under normal operation. In high performance applications requiring vector control, the effect of the rotor leakage inductance can be included, as discussed in Chapter 13.

11-3-3-1 Including the Stator Winding Resistance R_s and the Leakage Inductance $L_{\ell s}$

Including the effect of the stator winding resistance R_s and the leakage inductance $L_{\ell s}$ is analogous to including the effect of primary winding impedance in the transformer equivalent circuit. In the per-phase equivalent circuit of Fig.

11-21a, the applied voltage $\bar{V}_a$ is reduced by the voltage drop across the stator-winding leakage impedance to yield $\bar{E}_{ma}$:

$$\bar{E}_{ma} = \bar{V}_a - (R_s + j\omega L_{\ell s})\bar{I}_s \qquad (11\text{-}43)$$

where $\bar{E}_{ma}$ represents the voltage induced in the stator phase-a by the rotating flux-density distribution $\overrightarrow{B_{ms}}(t)$. The phasor diagram with $\bar{E}_{ma}$ as the reference phasor is shown in Fig. 11-21b.

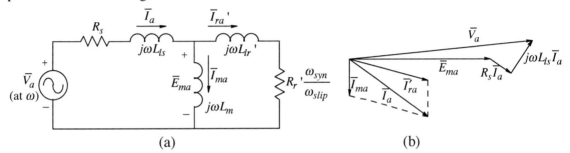

(a)   (b)

Figure 11-21 (a) Per phase, steady state equivalent circuit including the stator leakage; (b) phasor diagram.

11-4 TESTS TO OBTAIN THE PARAMETERS OF THE PER-PHASE EQUIVALENT CIRCUIT

The parameters of the per-phase equivalent circuit of Fig. 11-21a are usually not supplied by the motor manufacturers. The three tests described below can be performed to estimate these parameters.

11-4-1 DC-Resistance Test to Estimate R_s

The stator resistance R_s can best be estimated by the dc measurement of the resistance between the two phases:

$$R_s(dc) = \frac{R_{phase-phase}}{2} \qquad (11\text{-}44)$$

This dc resistance value, measured by passing a dc current through two of the phases, can be modified by a skin-effect factor [1] to help estimate its line-frequency value more closely.

11-4-2 The No-Load Test to Estimate L_m

The magnetizing inductance L_m can be calculated from the no-load test. In this test, the motor is applied its rated stator voltages in steady state and no mechanical load is connected to the rotor shaft. Therefore, the rotor turns almost at the synchronous speed with $\omega_{slip} \cong 0$. Hence, the resistance $R_r' \dfrac{\omega_{syn}}{\omega_{slip}}$ in the equivalent circuit of Fig. 11-21a becomes very large, allowing us to assume that $\overline{I}_{ra}' \cong 0$, as shown in Fig. 11-22a. The following quantities are measured: the per-phase rms voltage $V_a (= V_{LL}/\sqrt{3})$, the per-phase rms current I_a, and the three-phase power $P_{3-\phi}$ drawn by the motor. Subtracting the calculated power dissipation in R_s from the measured power, the remaining power $P_{FW,core}$ (the sum of the core losses, the stray losses, and the power to overcome friction and windage) is

$$P_{FW,core} = P_{3-\phi} - 3R_s I_a^2 \qquad (11\text{-}45)$$

With rated voltages applied to the motor, the above loss can be assumed to be a constant value which is independent of the motor loading.

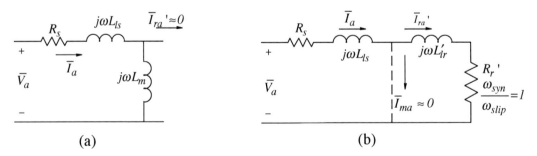

(a)   (b)

Figure 11-22 No Load Test of an induction motor; (b) blocked rotor test on an induction motor.

Assuming that $L_m \gg L_{\ell s}$, the magnetizing inductance L_m can be calculated based on the per-phase reactive power Q from the following equation:

$$Q = \sqrt{(V_a I_a)^2 - (\frac{P_{3-\phi}}{3})^2} = (\omega L_m) I_a^2 \qquad (11\text{-}46)$$

11-4-3 Blocked-Rotor Test to Estimate R_r' and the Leakage Inductances

The blocked-rotor (or locked-rotor) test is conducted to determine both R_r', the rotor resistance "seen" from the stator on a per-phase basis, and the leakage inductances in the equivalent circuit of Fig. 11-21a. Note that the rotor is blocked from turning and the stator is applied line-frequency, 3-phase voltages with a small magnitude such that the stator currents equal their rated value. With the rotor blocked, $\omega_m = 0$ and hence $\dfrac{\omega_{syn}}{\omega_{slip}} = 1$. The resulting equivalent impedance $\left(R_r' + j\omega L_{\ell r}'\right)$ in Fig. 11-22b can be assumed to be much smaller than the magnetizing reactance ($j\omega L_m$), which can be considered to be infinite. Therefore, by measuring V_a, I_a, and the three-phase power into the motor, we can calculate R_r' (having already estimated R_s previously) and $(L_{\ell s} + L_{\ell r}')$. In order to determine these two leakage inductances explicitly, we need to know their ratio, which depends on the design of the machine. As an approximation for general-purpose motors, we can assume that

$$L_{\ell s} \cong \frac{2}{3} L_{\ell r}' \qquad (11\text{-}47)$$

This allows both leakage inductances to be calculated explicitly.

11-5   INDUCTION MOTOR CHARACTERISTICS AT RATED VOLTAGES IN MAGNITUDE AND FREQUENCY

The typical torque-speed characteristic for general-purpose induction motors with name-plate (rated) values of applied voltages is shown in Fig. 11-23a, where the normalized torque (as a ratio of its rated value) is plotted as a function of the rotor speed ω_m / ω_{syn}.

With no load connected to the shaft, the torque T_{em} demanded from the motor is very low (only enough to overcome the internal bearing friction and windage) and the rotor turns at a speed very close in value to the synchronous speed ω_{syn}. Up to the rated torque, the torque developed by the motor is linear with respect to ω_{slip}, a relationship given by Eq. 11-30. Far beyond the rated condition, for which the machine is designed to operate in steady state, T_{em} no longer increases linearly with ω_{slip} for the following reasons:

1) The effect of leakage inductance in the rotor circuit at a higher frequency can no longer be ignored, and, from Eq. 11-33, the torque is less due to the declining value of $\sin(\pi/2 - \theta_r)$.

2) Large values of I'_{ra} and hence of I_a cause a significant voltage drop across

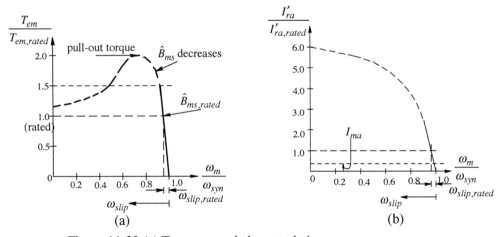

Figure 11-23 (a) Torque-speed characteristic;
(b) current-speed characteristic.

the stator winding leakage impedance $(R_s + j\omega L_{\ell s})$. This voltage drop causes E_{ma} to decrease, which in turn decreases $\hat{B}_{ms}$.

The above effects take place simultaneously, and the resulting torque characteristic for large values of ω_{slip} (which are avoided in the induction-motor drives discussed in the next chapter) is shown dotted in Fig. 11-23a. The rated value of the slip-speed ω_{slip} at which the motor develops its rated torque is typically in a range of 0.03 to 0.05 times the synchronous speed ω_{syn}.

In the torque-speed characteristic of Fig. 11-23a, the maximum torque that the motor can produce is called the pull-out (breakdown) torque. The torque when the rotor speed is zero is called the starting torque. The values of the pull-out and the starting torques, as a ratio of the rated torque, depend on the design class of the motor, as discussed in the next section.

Figure 11-23b shows the plot of the normalized rms current I'_{ra} as a function of the rotor speed. Up to the rated slip speed (up to the rated torque), I'_{ra} is linear with respect to the slip speed. This can be seen from Eq. 11-21 (with $\hat{B}_{ms} = \hat{B}_{ms,rated}$):

$$\hat{I}'_r = (k_i \hat{B}_{ms,rated})\omega_{slip} \tag{11-48}$$

Hence,

$$I'_{ra} = k_I \omega_{slip} \qquad\qquad (k_I = \frac{1}{\sqrt{2}}\frac{2}{3}k_i \hat{B}_{ms,rated}) \tag{11-49}$$

where k_I is a constant which linearly relates the slip speed to the rms current I'_{ra}. Notice that this plot is linear up to the rated slip speed, beyond which the effects of the stator and the rotor leakage inductances come into effect. At the rated operating point, the value of the rms magnetizing current I_{ma} is typically in a range of 20 to 40 percent of the per-phase stator rms current I_a. The magnetizing current I_{ma} remains relatively constant with speed, decreasing slightly at very large values of ω_{slip}. At or below the rated torque, the per-phase stator current magnitude I_a can be calculated by assuming the $\overline{I}_{ra}'$ and $\overline{I}_{ma}$ phasors to be at 90^0 with respect to each other; thus

$$I_a \cong \sqrt{I_{ra}'^2 + I_{ma}^2} \qquad \text{(below the rated torque)} \qquad (11\text{-}50)$$

While delivering a torque higher than the rated torque, $\overline{I}_{ra}'$ is much larger in magnitude than the magnetizing current $\overline{I}_{ma}$ (also considering a large phase shift between the two). This allows the stator current to be approximated as follows:

$$I_a \cong I_{ra}' \qquad \text{(above the rated torque)} \qquad (11\text{-}51)$$

Fig. 11-24 shows the typical variations of the power factor and the motor efficiency as a function of motor loading. These curves depend on the class and size of the motor and are discussed in Chapter 15, which deals with efficiency.

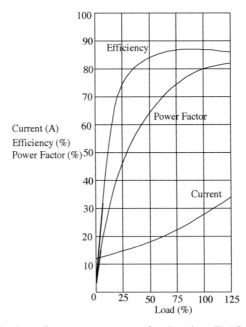

Figure 11-24 Typical performance curves for Design B 10-kW, 4-pole, three-phase induction motor.

11-6　INDUCTION MOTORS OF NEMA DESIGN A, B, C, AND D

Three-phase induction machines are classified in the American Standards (NEMA) under five design letters: A, B, C, D, and F. Each design class of motors has different torque and current specifications. Figure 11-25 illustrates typical torque-speed curves for design A, B, C and D motors; Design F motors have low pull-out and starting torques and thus are very limited in applications. As a ratio of the rated quantities, each design class specifies minimum values of pull-out and starting torques, and a maximum value of the starting current.

As noted previously, Design Class B motors are used most widely for general-purpose applications. These motors must have a minimum of a 200 percent pull-out torque.

Design A motors are similar to the general-purpose Design B motors except that they have a somewhat higher pull-out (breakdown) torque and a smaller full-load slip. Design A motors are used when unusually low values of winding losses are required - in totally enclosed motors, for example.

Design C motors are high starting-torque, low starting-current machines. They also have a somewhat lower pull-out (breakdown) torque than Design A and B machines. Design C motors are almost always designed with double-cage rotor windings to enhance the rotor-winding skin effect.

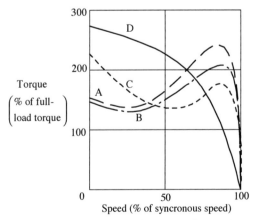

Figure 11-25 Typical torque-speed curves for NEMA Design A, B, C, D motors.

Finally, Design D motors are high starting-torque, high-slip machines. The minimum starting torque is 275 percent of the rated torque. The starting torque in these motors can be assumed to be the same as the pull-out torque.

11-7   LINE START

It should be noted that the induction-motor drives, discussed in detail in the next chapter, are operated so as to keep ω_{slip} at low values. Hence, the dotted portions of the characteristics shown in Fig. 11-23 are of no significance. However, if an induction motor is started from the line-voltage supply without an electronic power converter, it would at first draw 6 to 8 times its rated current, as shown in Fig. 11-23b, limited mainly by the leakage inductances. Fig. 11-26 shows that the available acceleration torque $T_{acc}(=T_{em}-T_L)$ causes the motor to accelerate from standstill, in accordance with Eq. 11-31. In Fig. 11-26, an arbitrary torque-speed characteristic of the load is assumed and the intersection of the motor and the load characteristics determines the steady-state point of operation.

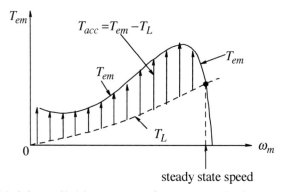

Figure 11-26 Available acceleration torque during motor start-up.

11-8   REDUCED VOLTAGE STARTING ("SOFT START") OF INDUCTION MOTORS

The circuit of Fig. 11-27a can be used to reduce the motor voltages at starting, thereby reducing the starting currents. The motor voltage and current waveforms are shown in Fig. 11-27b. In normal (low-slip) induction motors, the starting currents can be as large as 6 to 8 times the full-load current. Provided that the torque developed at reduced voltages is sufficient to overcome the load torque, the motor accelerates (the slip speed ω_{slip} decreases) and the motor currents decrease. During steady-state operation, each thyristor conducts for an entire half-cycle. Then, these thyristors can be shorted out (bypassed) by mechanical contactors, connected in parallel, to eliminate power losses in the thyristors due to a finite (1-2 *V*) conduction voltage drop across them.

11-9   ENERGY-SAVINGS IN LIGHTLY-LOADED MACHINES

The circuit of Fig. 11-27a can also be used to minimize motor core losses in very lightly-loaded machines. Induction motors are designed such that it is most efficient to apply rated voltages at the full-load condition. With line-frequency voltages, the magnitude of the stator voltage at which the power loss is minimized slightly decreases with a decreasing load. Therefore, it is possible to use the circuit of Fig. 11-27a to reduce the applied voltages at reduced loads and hence save energy. The amount of energy saved is significant (compared to extra losses in the motor due to current harmonics and in the thyristors due to a finite conduction voltage drop) only if the motor operates at very light loads for substantial periods of time. In applications where reduced voltage starting ("soft start") is required, the power switches are already implemented and only the controller for the minimum power loss needs to be added. In such cases, the concept of reducing the voltage may be economical.

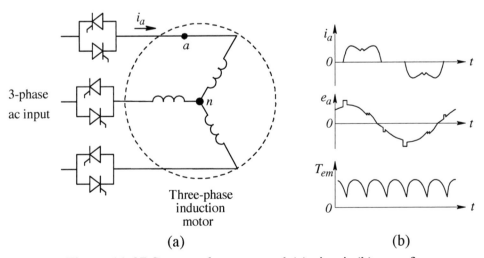

Figure 11-27 Stator voltage control (a) circuit (b) waveforms.

SUMMARY/REVIEW QUESTIONS

1. Describe the construction of squirrel-cage induction machines.

2. With the rated voltages applied, what does the magnetizing current depend on? Does this current, to a significant extent, depend on the mechanical load on the motor? How large is it in relation to the rated motor current?

3. Draw the space vector diagram at $t=0$, and the corresponding phasor diagram, assuming the rotor to be open-circuited.

4. Under a balanced, three-phase, sinusoidal steady state excitation, what is the speed of the rotating flux-density distribution called? How is this speed related to the angular frequency of the electrical excitation in a p-pole machine?

5. In our analysis, why did we initially assume the stator leakage impedance to be zero? How does the analogy to a transformer, with the primary winding leakage impedance assumed to be zero, help? Under the assumption that the stator leakage impedance is zero, is the flux-density space vector $\overrightarrow{B_{ms}}(t)$ completely independent of the motor loading?

6. What is the definition of the slip speed ω_{slip}? Does ω_{slip} depend on the number of poles? How large is the rated slip speed, compared to the rated synchronous speed?

7. Write the expressions for the voltage and the current (assuming the rotor leakage inductance to be zero) in a rotor bar located at an angle θ from the peak of the flux-density distribution represented by $\overrightarrow{B_{ms}}$.

8. The rotor bars located around the periphery of the rotor are of uniform cross-section. In spite of this, what allows us to represent the mmf produced by the rotor bar currents by a space vector $\overrightarrow{F_r}(t)$ at any time t?

9. Assuming the stator leakage impedance and the rotor inductance to be zero, draw the space vector diagram, the phasor diagram, and the per-phase equivalent circuit of a loaded induction motor.

10. In the equivalent circuit of Problem 9, what quantities does the rotor-bar current peak, represented by $\hat{I}'_{ra}$, depend on?

11. What is the frequency of voltages and currents in the rotor circuit called? How is it related to the slip speed? Does it depend on the number of poles?

12. What is definition of slip s, and how does it relate the frequency of voltages and currents in the stator circuit to that in the rotor circuit?

13. What is the speed of rotation of the mmf distribution produced by the rotor bar currents: (a) with respect to the rotor? (b) in the air gap with respect to a stationary observer?

14. Assuming $L'_{\ell r}$ to be zero, what is the expression for the torque T_{em} produced? How and why does it depend on ω_{slip} and $\hat{B}_{ms}$? Draw the torque-speed characteristic.

15. Assuming $L'_{\ell r}$ to be zero, explain how induction motors meet load-torque demand.

16. What makes an induction machine go into the regenerative-braking mode? Draw the space vectors and the corresponding phasors under the regenerative-braking condition.

17. Can an induction machine be operated as a generator that feeds into a passive load, for example a bank of three-phase resistors?

18. How is it possible to reverse the direction of rotation of an induction machine?

19. Explain the effect of including the rotor leakage flux by means of a space vector diagram.

20. How do we derive the torque expression, including the effect of $L'_{\ell r}$?

21. What is $\overrightarrow{B_r}(t)$ and how does it differ from $\overrightarrow{B_{ms}}(t)$? Is $\overrightarrow{B_r}(t)$ perpendicular to the $\overrightarrow{F_r}(t)$ space vector?

22. Including the rotor leakage flux, which rotor bars have the highest currents at any instant of time?

23. What clue do we have for the vector control of induction machines, to emulate the performance of brush-type and brush-less dc motors discussed in Chapters 7 and 10?

24. Describe how to obtain the per-phase equivalent circuit, including the effect of the rotor leakage flux.

25. What is the difference between $\overline{I'_{ra}}$ in Fig. 11-18c and in Fig. 11-19c, in terms of its frequency, magnitude, and phase angle?

26. Is the torque expression in Eq. 11-41 valid in the presence of the rotor leakage inductance and the stator leakage impedance?

27. When producing a desired torque T_{em}, what is the power loss in the rotor circuit proportional to?

28. Draw the per-phase equivalent circuit, including the stator leakage impedance.

29. Describe the tests and the procedure to obtain the parameters of the per-phase equivalent circuit.

30. In steady state, how is the mechanical torque at the shaft different than the electromechanical torque T_{em} developed by the machine?

31. Do induction machines have voltage and torque constants similar to other machines that we have studied so far? If so, write their expressions.

32. Plot the torque-speed characteristic of an induction motor for applied rated voltages. Describe various portions of this characteristic.

33. What are the various classes of induction machines? Briefly describe their differences.

34. What are the problems associated with the line-starting of induction motors? Why is the starting current so high?

35. Why is reduced-voltage starting used? Show the circuit implementation and discuss the pros and cons of using it to save energy.

REFERENCES

1. N. Mohan, T. Undeland, and W. Robbins, *Power Electronics: Converters, Applications, and Design*, 2nd edition, 1995, John Wiley & Sons, New York, NY.

2. Fitzgerald, Kingsley, and Umans, *Electric Machinery*, 5th edition, McGraw Hill, 1990.

3. G. R. Slemon, *Electric Machines and Drives*, Addison-Wesley, Inc., 1992.

PROBLEMS

11-1 Consider a three-phase, 2-pole induction machine. Neglect the stator winding resistance and the leakage inductance. The rated voltage is 208 V (line-line, rms) at 60 Hz. $L_m = 60\,mH$, and the peak flux density in the air gap is $0.85T$. Consider that the phase-a voltage reaches its positive peak at $\omega t = 0$. Assuming that the rotor circuit is somehow open-circuited, calculate and draw the following space vectors at $\omega t = 0$ and at $\omega t = 60^\circ$: $\overrightarrow{v}_s$, $\overrightarrow{i}_{ms}$, and $\overrightarrow{B}_{ms}$. Draw the phasor diagram with $\overline{V}_a$ and $\overline{I}_{ma}$. What is the relationship between $\hat{B}_{ms}$, $\hat{I}_{ms}$, and $\hat{I}_m$?

11-2 Calculate the synchronous speed in machines with a rated frequency of 60 Hz and with the following number of poles p: 2, 4, 6, 8, and 12.

11-3 The machines in Problem 11-2 produce the rated torque at a slip $s = 4$ percent, when supplied with rated voltages. Under the rated torque condition, calculate in each case the slip speed ω_{slip} in rad/s and the frequency f_{slip} (in Hz) of the currents and voltages in the rotor circuit.

11-4 In the transformer of Fig. 11-4a, each air gap has a length $\ell_g = 1.0\,mm$. The core iron can be assumed to have an infinite permeability. $N_1 = 100$ *turns* and $N_2 = 50$ *turns*. In the air gap, $\hat{B}_g = 1.1T$ and $v_1(t) = 100\sqrt{2}\cos\omega t$ at a frequency of 60 Hz. The leakage impedance of the primary winding can be neglected. With the secondary winding open-circuited, calculate and plot $i_m(t)$, $\phi_m(t)$, and the induced voltage $e_2(t)$ in the secondary winding due to $\phi_m(t)$, along with $v_1(t)$.

11-5 In Example 11-1, calculate the magnetizing inductance L_m.

11-6 In an induction machine, the torque constant $k_{T\omega}$ (in Eq. 11-30) and the rotor resistance R'_r are specified. Calculate $\hat{I}'_r$ as a function of ω_{slip}, in terms of $k_{T\omega}$ and R'_r, for torques below the rated value. Assume that the flux-density in the air gap is at its rated value. Hint: use Eq. 11-41.

11-7 An induction motor produces rated torque at a slip speed of 100 rpm. If a new machine is built with bars of a material that has twice the resistivity of the old machine (and nothing else is changed), calculate the slip speed in the new machine when it is loaded to the rated torque.

11-8 In the transformer circuit of Fig. 11-4b, the load on the secondary winding is a pure resistance R_L. Show that the emf induced in the secondary winding (due to the time-derivative of the combination of ϕ_m and the secondary-winding leakage flux) is in phase with the secondary current i_2. Note: this is analogous to the induction-motor case, where the rotor leakage flux is included and the current is maximum in the bar which is "cut" by $\hat{B}_r$, the peak of the rotor flux-density distribution (represented by $\overrightarrow{B_r}$).

11-9 In a 60-Hz, 208 V (line-line, rms), 5-kW motor, $R'_r = 0.45\Omega$ and $X'_{\ell r} = 0.83\Omega$. The rated torque is developed at the slip $s = 0.04$. Assuming that the motor is supplied with rated voltages and is delivering the rated torque, calculate the rotor power factor angle. What is $\hat{B}_r / \hat{B}_{ms}$?

11-10 In a 2-pole, 208 V (line-to-line, rms), 60-Hz, motor, $R_s = 0.5\Omega$, $R'_r = 0.45\Omega$, $X_{\ell s} = 0.6\Omega$, and $X'_{\ell r} = 0.83\Omega$. The magnetizing reactance $X_m = 28.5\Omega$. This motor is supplied by its rated voltages. The rated torque is developed at the slip $s = 0.04$. At the rated torque, calculate the rotor power loss, the input current, and the input power factor of operation.

11-11 In a 208-V (line-to-line, rms), 60-Hz, 5-kW motor, tests are carried out with the following results: $R_{phase-phase} = 1.1\,\Omega$. No-Load Test: applied voltages of 208 V (line-line, rms), $I_a = 6.5\,A$, and $P_{no-load,3-phase} = 175W$. Blocked-Rotor Test: applied voltages of 53 V (line-line, rms), $I_a = 18.2\,A$, and $P_{blocked,3-phase} = 900W$. Estimate the per-phase equivalent circuit parameters.

CHAPTER 12

INDUCTION-MOTOR DRIVES: SPEED CONTROL

12-1 INTRODUCTION

Induction-motor drives are used in the process-control industry to adjust the speeds of fans, compressors, pumps and the like. In many applications, the capability to vary speed efficiently can lead to large savings in energy. Adjustable-speed induction-motor drives are also used for electric traction, and for motion control to automate factories.

Figure 12-1 shows the block diagram of an adjustable-speed induction-motor drive. The utility input can be either single-phase or three-phase. It is converted by the power-processing unit into three-phase voltages of appropriate magnitude and frequency, based on the controller input. In most general-purpose adjustable-speed drives (ASDs), the speed is not sensed and hence the speed-sensor block and its input to the controller are shown dotted.

It is possible to adjust the induction-motor speed by controlling only the magnitude of the line-frequency voltages applied to the motor. For this purpose, a thyristor circuit, similar to that for "soft-start" in Fig. 11-27a, can be used.

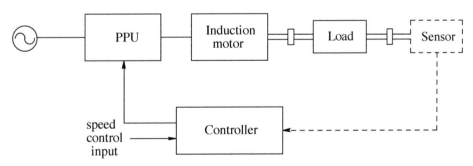

Figure 12-1 Block diagram of an induction-motor drive.

Although simple and inexpensive to implement, this method is extremely energy-*in*efficient if the speed is to be varied over a wide range. Also, there are various other methods of speed control, but they require wound-rotor induction motors. Their description can be found in references listed at the end of Chapter 11. Our focus in this chapter is on examining energy-efficient speed control of squirrel-cage induction motors over a wide range. The emphasis is on general-purpose speed control rather than precise control of position using vector control, which is discussed in Chapter 13.

12-2 CONDITIONS FOR EFFICIENT SPEED CONTROL OVER A WIDE RANGE

In the block diagram of the induction-motor drive shown in Fig. 12-1, we find that an energy-efficient system requires that both the power-processing unit and the induction motor maintain high energy efficiency over a wide range of speed and torque conditions. In Chapter 4, it was shown that the switch-mode techniques result in very high efficiencies of the power-processing units. Therefore, the focus in this section will be on achieving high efficiency of induction motors over a wide range of speed and torque.

We will begin this discussion by first considering the case in which an induction motor is applied the rated voltages (line-frequency sinusoidal voltages of the rated amplitude $\hat{V}_{rated}$ and the rated frequency f_{rated}, which are the same as the name-plate values). In Chapter 11, we derived the following expressions for a line-fed induction motor:

$$\frac{P_{r,loss}}{T_{em}} = \omega_{slip} \qquad \text{(Eq. 11-42, repeated)} \qquad (12\text{-}1)$$

and

$$T_{em} = k_{t\omega}\, \hat{B}_{ms}^2\, \omega_{slip} \qquad \text{(Eq. 11-29, repeated)} \qquad (12\text{-}2)$$

Eq. 12-1 shows that to meet the load-torque demand ($T_{em} = T_L$), the motor should be operated with as small a slip speed ω_{slip} as possible in order to minimize power loss in the rotor circuit (this also minimizes the loss in the stator resistance). Eq. 12-2 can be written as

$$\omega_{slip} = \frac{T_{em}}{k_{t\omega} \hat{B}_{ms}^2} \tag{12-3}$$

This shows that to minimize ω_{slip} at the required torque, the peak flux density $\hat{B}_{ms}$ should be kept as high as possible, the highest value being $\hat{B}_{ms,rated}$, for which the motor is designed and beyond which the iron in the motor will become saturated. (For additional discussion, please see Section 12-9.) Therefore, keeping $\hat{B}_{ms}$ constant at its rated value, the electromagnetic torque developed by the motor depends linearly on the slip speed ω_{slip}:

$$T_{em} = k_{T\omega} \omega_{slip} \qquad (k_{T\omega} = k_{t\omega} \hat{B}_{ms,rated}^2) \tag{12-4}$$

This is the similar to Eq. 11-30 of the previous chapter.

Applying rated voltages (of amplitude $\hat{V}_{rated}$ and frequency f_{rated}), the resulting torque-speed characteristic based on Eq. 12-4 is shown in Fig. 12-2a, repeated from Fig. 11-12a. The synchronous speed is $\omega_{syn,rated}$. This characteristic is a straight line based on the assumption that the flux-density peak is maintained at its rated value $\hat{B}_{ms,rated}$ throughout the torque range up to $T_{em,rated}$. As shown in Fig. 12-2a, a family of such characteristics corresponding to various frequencies $f_3 < f_2 < f_1 < f_{rated}$ can be achieved (assuming that the flux-density peak is maintained throughout at its rated value $\hat{B}_{ms,rated}$, as discussed in the next section). Focusing on the frequency f_1 corresponding to one of the characteristics in Fig. 12-2a, the synchronous speed at which the flux-density distribution in the air gap rotates is given by

$$\omega_{syn,1} = \frac{2\pi f_1}{p/2} \tag{12-5}$$

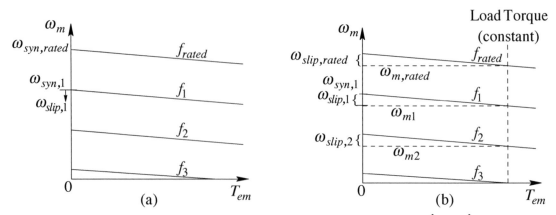

Figure 12-2 Operating characteristics with constant $\hat{B}_{ms} = \hat{B}_{ms,rated}$.

Therefore, at a rotor speed $\omega_m (< \omega_{syn,1})$, the slip speed, measured with respect to the synchronous speed $\omega_{syn,1}$, is

$$\omega_{slip,1} = \omega_{syn,1} - \omega_m \qquad (12\text{-}6)$$

Using the above $\omega_{slip,1}$ in Eq. 12-4, the torque-speed characteristic at f_1 has the same slope as at f_{rated}. This shows that the characteristics at various frequencies are parallel to each other, as shown in Fig. 12-2a. Considering a load whose torque requirement remains independent of speed, as shown by the dotted line in Fig. 12-2b, the speed can be adjusted by controlling the frequency of the applied voltages; for example, the speed is $\omega_{m,1} (= \omega_{syn,1} - \omega_{slip,1})$ at a frequency of f_1, and $\omega_{m,2} (= \omega_{syn,2} - \omega_{slip,2})$ at f_2.

▲ **Example 12-1** A three-phase, 60-*Hz*, 4-pole, 440-*V* (line-line, rms) induction-motor drive has a full-load (rated) speed of 1746 *rpm*. The rated torque is 40 *Nm*. Keeping the air gap flux-density peak constant at its rated value, (a) plot the torque-speed characteristics (the linear portion) for the following values of the frequency f : 60 *Hz*, 45 *Hz*, 30 *Hz*, and 15 *Hz*. (b) This motor is supplying a load whose torque demand increases linearly with speed, such that it equals the rated torque of the motor at the rated motor speed. Calculate the speeds of operation at the four values of frequency in part (a).

Solution

(a)   In this example, it is easier to make use of speed (denoted by the symbol "*n*") in *rpm*. At the rated frequency of 60 *Hz*, the synchronous speed in a 4-pole motor can be calculated as follows: from Eq. 12-5,

$$\omega_{syn,rated} = \frac{2\pi f_{rated}}{p/2}.$$

Therefore,

$$n_{syn,rated} = \frac{\omega_{syn,rated}}{\underbrace{2\pi}_{\text{rev. per sec.}}} \times 60 \, rpm = \frac{f_{rated}}{p/2} \times 60 \, rpm$$

$$= 1800 \, rpm.$$

Therefore,

$$n_{slip,rated} = 1800 - 1746 = 54 \, rpm.$$

The synchronous speeds corresponding to the other three frequency values are: 1350 *rpm* at 45 *Hz*, 900 *rpm* at 30 *Hz*, and 450 *rpm* at 15 *Hz*. The torque-speed characteristics are parallel, as shown in Fig. 12-3, for the four frequency values, keeping $\hat{B}_{ms} = \hat{B}_{ms,rated}$.

(b)   The torque-speed characteristic in Fig. 12-3 can be described for each frequency by the equation below, where n_{syn} is the synchronous speed corresponding to that frequency:

$$T_{em} = k_{Tn}(n_{syn} - n_m). \tag{12-7}$$

In this example, $k_{Tn} = \dfrac{40 \, Nm}{(1800-1746)\,rpm} = 0.74 \, \dfrac{Nm}{rpm}.$

The linear load torque-speed characteristic can be described as

$$T_L = c_n n_m \tag{12-8}$$

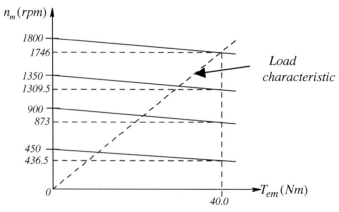

Figure 12-3 Example 12-1.

where, in this example, $c_n = \dfrac{40\,Nm}{1746\,rpm} = 0.023\,\dfrac{Nm}{rpm}$.

In steady state, the electromagnetic torque developed by the motor equals the load toque. Therefore, equating the right sides of Eqs. 12-7 and 12-8,

$$k_{Tn}(n_{syn} - n_m) = c_n\, n_m. \tag{12-9}$$

Hence,

$$n_m = \frac{k_{Tn}}{k_{Tn} + c_n} n_{syn} \tag{12-10}$$
$$= 0.97 n_{syn} \quad \text{(in this example)}.$$

Therefore, we have the following speeds and slip speeds at various values of f :

f (Hz)	n_{syn} (rpm)	n_m (rpm)	n_{slip} (rpm)
60	1800	1746	54
45	1350	1309.5	40.5
30	900	873	27
15	450	436.5	13.5

▲

12-3   APPLIED VOLTAGE AMPLITUDES TO KEEP $\hat{B}_{ms} = \hat{B}_{ms,rated}$

Maintaining $\hat{B}_{ms}$ at its rated value minimizes power loss in the rotor circuit. To maintain $\hat{B}_{ms,rated}$ at various frequencies and torque loading, the applied voltages should be of the appropriate amplitude, as discussed in this section.

The per-phase equivalent circuit of an induction motor under the balanced sinusoidal steady state is shown in Fig. 12-4a. With the rated voltages at $\hat{V}_{a,rated}$ and f_{rated} applied to the stator, loading the motor by its rated (full-load) torque $T_{em,rated}$ establishes the rated operating point. At the rated operating point, all quantities related to the motor are at their rated values: the synchronous speed $\omega_{syn,rated}$, the motor speed $\omega_{m,rated}$, the slip speed $\omega_{slip,rated}$, the flux-density peak $\hat{B}_{ms,rated}$, the internal voltage $\hat{E}_{ma,rated}$, the magnetizing current $\hat{I}_{ma,rated}$, the rotor-branch current $\hat{I}'_{ra,rated}$, and the stator current $\hat{I}_{a,rated}$.

The objective of maintaining the flux density at $\hat{B}_{ms,rated}$ implies that in the equivalent circuit of Fig. 12-4a, the magnetizing current should be maintained at $\hat{I}_{ma,rated}$:

$$\hat{I}_{ma} = \hat{I}_{ma,rated} \text{ (a constant)} \tag{12-11}$$

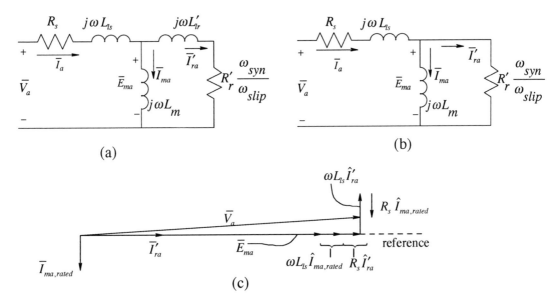

(a)

(b)

(c)

Figure 12-4 (a) Per phase equivalent circuit in balanced sinusoidal steady state; (b) equivalent circuit with the rotor leakage neglected; (c) phasor diagram during steady state operation at the rated flux density.

With this magnetizing current, the internal voltage $\bar{E}_{ma}$ in Fig. 12-4a has the following amplitude:

$$\hat{E}_{ma} = \omega L_m \hat{I}_{ma,rated} = \underbrace{2\pi L_m \hat{I}_{ma,rated}}_{\text{constant}} f \tag{12-12}$$

This shows that $\hat{E}_{ma}$ is linearly proportional to the frequency f of the applied voltages.

For torques below the rated value, the leakage inductance of the rotor can be neglected (see Example 11-6), as shown in the equivalent circuit of Fig. 12-4b. With this assumption, the rotor-branch current $\bar{I}'_{ra}$ is in phase with the internal voltage $\bar{E}_{ma}$, and its amplitude $\hat{I}'_{ra}$ depends linearly on the electromagnetic torque developed by the motor (as in Eq. 11-28) to provide the load torque. Therefore, in terms of the rated values,

$$\hat{I}'_{ra} = (\frac{T_{em}}{T_{em,rated}}) \hat{I}'_{ra,rated} \tag{12-13}$$

At some frequency and torque, the phasor diagram corresponding to the equivalent circuit in Fig. 12-4b is shown in Fig. 12-4c. If the internal emf is the reference phasor $\bar{E}_{ma} = \hat{E}_{ma} \angle 0^0$, then $\bar{I}'_{ra} = \hat{I}'_{ra} \angle 0^0$ and the applied voltage is

$$\bar{V}_a = \hat{E}_{ma} \angle 0^0 + (R_s + j2\pi f L_{\ell s}) \bar{I}_s \tag{12-14}$$

where

$$\bar{I}_s = \hat{I}'_{ra} \angle 0^0 - j\hat{I}_{ma,rated} \tag{12-15}$$

Substituting Eq. 12-15 into Eq. 12-14 and separating the real and imaginary parts,

$$\bar{V}_a = [\hat{E}_{ma} + (2\pi f L_{\ell s}) \hat{I}_{ma,rated} + R_s \hat{I}'_{ra}] + j[(2\pi f L_{\ell s}) \hat{I}'_{ra} - R_s \hat{I}_{ma,rated}] \tag{12-16}$$

These phasors are plotted in Fig. 12-4c near the rated operating condition, using reasonable parameter values. This phasor diagram shows that in determining the magnitude $\hat{V}_a$ of the applied voltage phasor $\overline{V}_a$, the perpendicular component in Eq. 12-16 can be neglected, yielding

$$\hat{V}_a \cong \hat{E}_{ma} + (2\pi f L_{\ell s})\hat{I}_{ma,rated} + R_s\hat{I}'_{ra} \tag{12-17}$$

Substituting for $\hat{E}_{ma}$ from Eq. 12-12 into Eq. 12-17 and rearranging terms,

$$\hat{V}_a = \underbrace{2\pi(L_m + L_{\ell s})\hat{I}_{ma,rated}}_{\text{constant slope}} f + R_s\hat{I}'_{ra} \quad \text{or} \quad \hat{V}_a = (slope)\ f + R_s\hat{I}'_{ra} \tag{12-18}$$

This shows that to maintain flux density at its rated value, the applied voltage amplitude $\hat{V}_a$ depends linearly on the frequency f of the applied voltages, except for the offset due to the resistance R_s of the stator windings. At a constant torque value, the relationship in Eq. 12-18 between $\hat{V}_a$ and f is a straight line, as shown in Fig. 12-5. This line has a constant slope equal to $2\pi(L_m + L_{\ell s})\hat{I}_{ma,rated}$. This slope can be obtained by using the values at the rated operating point of the motor in Eq. 12-18:

$$slope = \frac{\hat{V}_{a,rated} - R_s\hat{I}'_{ra,rated}}{f_{rated}} \tag{12-19}$$

Therefore, in terms of the slope in Eq. 12-19, the relationship in Eq. 12-18 can be expressed as

$$\hat{V}_a = (\frac{\hat{V}_{a,rated} - R_s\hat{I}'_{ra,rated}}{f_{rated}})\ f + R_s\hat{I}'_{ra} \tag{12-20}$$

At the rated torque, in Eq. 12-20, $\hat{V}_a$, $\hat{I}'_{ra}$, and f are all at their rated values. This establishes the rated point in Fig. 12-5. Continuing to provide the rated torque, as the frequency f is reduced to nearly zero at very low speeds, from Eq. 12-20,

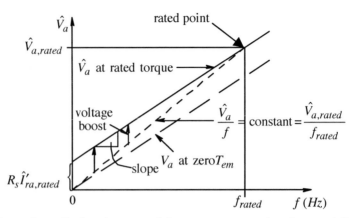

Figure 12-5 Relation of applied voltage and frequency to maintain rated flux density.

$$\hat{V}_a\Big|_{T_{em,rated},\,f\simeq 0} = R_s \hat{I}'_{ra,rated} \tag{12-21}$$

This is shown by the offset above the origin in Fig. 12-5. Between this offset point (at $f \simeq 0$) and the rated point, the voltage-frequency characteristic is linear, as shown, while the motor is loaded to deliver its rated torque. We will consider another case of no-load connected to the motor, where $\hat{I}'_{ra} \simeq 0$ in Eq. 12-20, and hence at nearly zero frequency

$$\hat{V}_a\Big|_{T_{em}=0,\,f\simeq 0} = 0 \tag{12-22}$$

This condition shifts the entire characteristic at no-load downwards compared to that at the rated torque, as shown in Fig. 12-5. An approximate V/f characteristic (independent of the torque developed by the motor) is also shown in Fig. 12-5 by the dotted line through the origin and the rated point. Compared to the approximate relationship, Fig. 12-5 shows that a "voltage boost" is required at higher torques, due to the voltage drop across the stator resistance. In percentage terms, this voltage boost is very significant at low frequencies, which correspond to operating the motor at low speeds; the percentage voltage boost that is necessary near the rated frequency (near the rated speed) is much smaller.

▲ **Example 12-2** In the motor drive of Example 12-1, the induction motor is such that while applied the rated voltages and loaded to the rated torque, it draws 10.39 A (rms) per-phase at a power factor of 0.866 (lagging). $R_s = 1.5\,\Omega$. Calculate the voltages corresponding to the four values of the frequency f to maintain $\hat{B}_{ms} = \hat{B}_{ms,rated}$.

Solution Neglecting the rotor leakage inductance, as shown in the phasor diagram of Fig. 12-6, the rated value of the rotor-branch current can be calculated as

$$\hat{I}'_{ra,rated} = 10.39\sqrt{2}(0.866) = 9.0\sqrt{2}\ A.$$

Using Eq. 12-20 and the rated values, the slope of the characteristic can be calculated as

$$slope = \frac{\hat{V}_{a,rated} - R_s \hat{I}'_{ra,rated}}{f_{rated}} = \frac{\dfrac{440\sqrt{2}}{\sqrt{3}} - 1.5\times 9.0\sqrt{2}}{60} = 5.67\,\frac{V}{Hz}.$$

In Eq. 12-20, $\hat{I}'_{ra}$ depends on the torque that the motor is supplying. Therefore, substituting for $\hat{I}'_{ra}$ from Eq. 12-13 into Eq. 12-20,

$$\hat{V}_a = (\frac{\hat{V}_{a,rated} - R_s \hat{I}'_{ra,rated}}{f_{rated}})\,f + R_s(\frac{T_{em}}{T_{em,rated}}\hat{I}'_{ra,rated}). \tag{12-23}$$

While the drive is supplying a load whose torque depends linearly on speed (and demands the rated torque at the rated speed as in Example 12-1), the torque ratio in Eq. 12-23 is

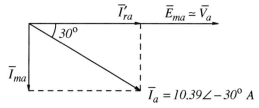

Figure 12-6 Example 12-2.

$$\frac{T_{em}}{T_{em,rated}} = \frac{n_m}{n_{m,rated}}.$$

Therefore, Eq. 12-23 can be written as

$$\hat{V}_a = (\frac{\hat{V}_{a,rated} - R_s \hat{I}'_{ra,rated}}{f_{rated}}) f + R_s (\frac{n_m}{n_{m,rated}} \hat{I}'_{ra,rated}) \qquad (12\text{-}24)$$

Substituting the four values of the frequency f and their corresponding speeds from Example 12-1, the voltages can be tabulated as below. The values obtained by using the approximate dotted characteristic plotted in Fig. 12-5 (which assumes a linear V/f relationship) are nearly identical to the values in the table below because at low values of frequency (hence, at low speeds) the torque is also reduced in this example - therefore, no voltage boost is necessary.

f	60 Hz	45 Hz	30 Hz	15 Hz
$\hat{V}_a$	359.3 V	269.5 V	179.6 V	89.8 V

▲

12-4 STARTING CONSIDERATIONS IN DRIVES

Starting currents are primarily limited by the leakage inductances of the stator and the rotor, and can be 6 to 8 times the rated current of the motor, as shown in the plot of Fig. 11-23b in Chapter 11. In the motor drives of Fig. 12-1, if large currents are drawn even for a short time, the current rating required of the power-processing unit will become unacceptably large.

At starting, the rotor speed ω_m is zero, and hence the slip speed ω_{slip} equals the synchronous speed ω_{syn}. Therefore, at start-up, we must apply voltages of a low frequency in order to keep ω_{slip} low, and hence avoid large starting currents. Figure 12-7a shows the torque-speed characteristic at a frequency $f_{start} (= f_{slip,rated})$ of the applied voltages, such that the starting torque (at $\omega_m = 0$)

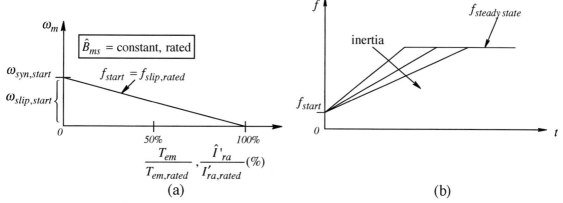

Figure 12-7 Start-up considerations in induction-motor drives.

is equal to the rated value. The same is true of the rotor-branch current. It is assumed that the applied voltage magnitudes are appropriately adjusted to maintain $\hat{B}_{ms}$ constant at its rated value.

As shown in Fig. 12-7b, as the rotor speed builds up, the frequency f of the applied voltages is increased continuously at a preset rate until the final desired speed is reached in steady state. The rate at which the frequency is increased should not let the motor current exceed a specific limit (usually 150 percent of the rated). The rate should be decreased for higher inertia loads to allow the rotor speed to catch up. Note that the voltage amplitude is adjusted, as a function of the frequency f, as discussed in the previous section, to keep $\hat{B}_{ms}$ constant at its rated value.

▲ **Example 12-3** The motor drive in Examples 12-1 and 12-2 needs to develop a starting torque of 150 percent of the rated in order to overcome the starting friction. Calculate f_{start} and $\hat{V}_{a,start}$.

Solution The rated slip of this motor is 54 *rpm*. To develop 150 percent of the rated torque, the slip speed at start-up should be $1.5 \times n_{slip,rated} = 81$ *rpm*. Note that at start-up, the synchronous speed is the same as the slip speed. Therefore, $n_{syn,start} = 81$ *rpm*. Hence, from Eq. 12-5 for this 4-pole motor,

$$f_{start} = \left(\frac{n_{syn,start}}{\underbrace{60}_{\text{rev. per second}}} \right) \frac{p}{2} = 2.7 \, Hz \, .$$

At 150 percent of the rated torque, from Eq. 12-13,

$$\hat{I}'_{ra,start} = 1.5 \times \hat{I}'_{ra,rated} = 1.5 \times 9.0\sqrt{2} \ A \, .$$

Substituting various values at start-up into Eq. 12-20,

$$\hat{V}_{a,start} = 43.9V \, . \qquad\qquad\qquad \blacktriangle$$

12-5 CAPABILITY TO OPERATE BELOW AND ABOVE THE RATED SPEED

Due to the rugged construction of the squirrel-cage rotor, induction-motor drives can be operated at speeds in the range of zero to almost twice the rated speed. The following constraints on the drive operation should be noted:

- The magnitude of applied voltages is limited to their rated value. Otherwise, the motor insulation may be stressed and the rating of the power-processing unit will have to be larger.

- The motor currents are also limited to their rated values. This is because the rotor-branch current $\hat{I}'_{ra}$ is limited to its rated value in order to limit the loss $P_{r,loss}$ in the rotor bar resistances. This loss, dissipated as heat, is difficult to remove; beyond its rated value, it will cause the motor temperature to exceed its design limit, thus shortening the motor life.

The torque-capability regions below and above the rated speed are shown in Fig. 12-8 and discussed in the following sections.

12-5-1 Rated Torque Capability Below the Rated Speed (with $\hat{B}_{ms,rated}$)

This region of operation has already been discussed in Section 12-3 where the motor is operated at the rated flux density $\hat{B}_{ms,rated}$. Therefore at any speed below the rated speed, a motor in steady state can deliver its rated torque while $\hat{I}_{ra}'$ stays equal to its rated value. This capability region is shown in Fig. 12-8 as the rated-torque capability region. At low speeds, due to poor cooling, the steady state torque capability may have to be reduced, as shown by the dotted curve.

12-5-2 Rated Power Capability Above the Rated Speed by Flux-Weakening

Speeds above the rated value are obtained by increasing the frequency f of the applied voltages above the rated frequency, thus increasing the synchronous speed at which the flux-density distribution rotates in the air gap:

$$\omega_{syn} > \omega_{syn,rated} \tag{12-25}$$

The amplitude of the applied voltages is limited to its rated value $\hat{V}_{a,rated}$, as discussed earlier. Neglecting the voltage drop across the stator winding leakage inductance and resistance, in terms of the rated values, the peak flux density $\hat{B}_{ms}$ declines below its rated value, such that it is inversely proportional to the increasing frequency f (in accordance with Eq. 11-7 of the previous chapter):

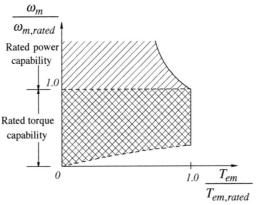

Figure 12-8 Capability above and below rated speed.

$$\hat{B}_{ms} = \hat{B}_{ms,rated} \frac{f_{rated}}{f} \qquad (f > f_{rated}) \qquad (12\text{-}26)$$

In the equivalent circuit of Fig. 12-4b, the rotor-branch current should not exceed its rated value $\hat{I}'_{ra,rated}$ in steady state; otherwise the power loss in the rotor will exceed its rated value. Neglecting the rotor leakage inductance when estimating the capability limit, the maximum three-phase power crossing the air gap, in terms of the peak quantities (the additional factor of $1/2$ is due to the peak quantities) is

$$P_{max} = \frac{3}{2}\hat{V}_{a,rated}\,\hat{I}'_{a,rated} = P_{rated} \qquad (f > f_{rated}) \qquad (12\text{-}27)$$

Therefore, this region is often referred to as the rated-power capability region. With $\hat{I}'_{ra}$ at its rated value, as the frequency f is increased to obtain higher speeds, the maximum torque that the motor can develop can be calculated by substituting the flux density given by Eq. 12-26 into Eq. 11-28 of the previous chapter:

$$T_{em}\big|_{\hat{I}'_{r,rated}} = k_t \hat{I}'_{r,rated}\hat{B}_{ms} = \underbrace{k_t \hat{I}'_{r,rated}\hat{B}_{ms,rated}}_{T_{em,rated}} \frac{f}{f_{rated}}$$
$$= T_{em,rated}\frac{f_{rated}}{f} \qquad\qquad (f > f_{rated}) \qquad (12\text{-}28)$$

This shows that the maximum torque, plotted in Fig. 12-8, is inversely proportional to the frequency.

12-6 REGENERATIVE BRAKING IN INDUCTION-MOTOR DRIVES

Similar to dc-motor and brushless-dc motor drives, the speed of induction-motor drives can be reduced by regenerative braking, which makes the induction machine operate as a generator, as discussed in section 11-3-2-4. To make the induction machine go into the generator mode, the applied voltages must be at a frequency at which the synchronous speed is less than the rotor speed, resulting in a negative slip speed:

$$\omega_{slip} = (\omega_{syn} - \omega_m) < 0 \qquad \omega_{syn} < \omega_m \qquad (12\text{-}29)$$

Maintaining the flux density at $\hat{B}_{ms,rated}$ by controlling the voltage amplitudes, the torque developed, according to Eq. 12-4, is negative (in a direction opposite that of rotation) for negative values of slip speed. Figure 12-9 shows the motor torque-speed characteristics at two frequencies, assuming a constant $\hat{B}_{ms} = \hat{B}_{ms,rated}$. These characteristics are extended into the negative torque region for the rotor speeds above the corresponding synchronous speeds. Consider that the induction machine is initially operating as a motor with a stator frequency f_0 and at the rotor speed of ω_{m_0}, which is less than ω_{syn_0}. If the stator frequency is decreased to f_1, the new synchronous speed is ω_{syn_1}. This makes the slip speed negative, and thus T_{em} becomes negative, as shown in Fig. 12-9. This negative T_{em} causes the motor speed to decrease, and some of the energy associated with the motor-load inertia is fed into the power-processing unit, which either dissipates it or supplies it back to the electric source.

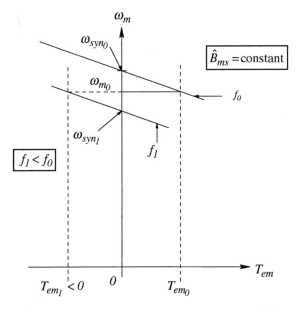

Figure 12-9 Braking in induction motor drives.

This regenerative braking is performed in a controlled manner: the stator frequency is reduced slowly (keeping $\hat{B}_{ms} = \hat{B}_{ms,rated}$) to avoid causing large currents through the power-processing unit. This procedure, if used to bring the motor to a halt, can be thought of as the opposite of the starting procedure.

12-7   SPEED CONTROL OF INDUCTION-MOTOR DRIVES

The focus of this section is to discuss speed control of induction-motor drives in general-purpose applications where very precise speed control is not necessary, and therefore, as shown in Fig. 12-10, the speed is not measured (rather it is estimated). The reference speed $\omega_{m,ref}$ is set either manually or by a slow-acting control loop of the process where the drive is used. Use of induction-motor drives in high performance servo-drive applications is discussed in the next chapter.

In addition to the reference speed, the other two inputs to the controller are the measured dc-link voltage V_d and the input current i_d of the inverter. This dc-link current represents the instantaneous three-phase currents of the motor. Some of the salient points of the control in Fig. 12-10 are described below.

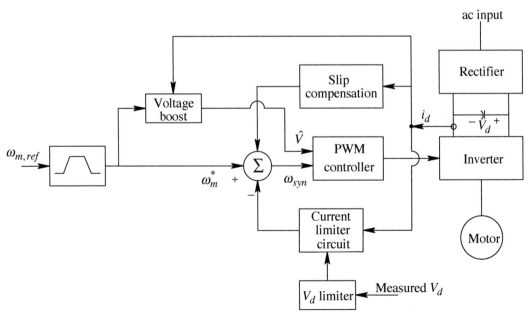

Figure 12-10 Speed control of induction motor drives.

<u>Limiting of Acceleration/Deceleration.</u> During acceleration and deceleration, it is necessary to keep the motor currents and the dc-link voltage V_d within their design limits. Therefore, in Fig. 12-10, the maximum acceleration and deceleration are usually set by the user, resulting in a dynamically-modified reference speed signal ω_m^*.

<u>Current-Limiting.</u> In the motoring mode, if ω_{syn} increases too fast compared to the motor speed, then ω_{slip} and the motor currents may exceed their limits. To limit acceleration so that the motor currents stay within their limits, i_d (representing the actual motor current) is compared with the current limit, and the error though the controller acts on the speed control circuit by reducing acceleration (i.e., by reducing ω_{syn}).

In the regenerative-braking mode, if ω_{syn} is reduced too fast, the negative slip will become too large in magnitude and will result in a large current through the motor and the inverter of the PPU. To restrict this current within the limit, i_d is compared with the current limit, and the error is fed through a controller to decrease deceleration (i.e., by increasing ω_{syn}).

During regenerative-braking, the dc-bus capacitor voltage must be kept within a maximum limit. If the rectifier of the PPU is unidirectional in power flow, a dissipation resistor is switched on, in parallel with the dc-link capacitor, to provide a dynamic braking capability. If the energy recovered from the motor is still larger than that lost through various dissipation means, the capacitor voltage could become excessive. Therefore, if the voltage limit is exceeded, the control circuit decreases deceleration (by increasing ω_{syn}).

<u>Slip Compensation.</u> In Fig. 12-10, to achieve a rotor speed equal to its reference value, the machine should be applied voltages at a frequency f, with a corresponding synchronous speed ω_{syn} such that it is the sum of ω_m^* and the slip speed:

$$\omega_{syn} = \omega_m^* + \underbrace{T_{em} / k_{T\omega}}_{\omega_{slip}} \qquad\qquad (12\text{-}30)$$

where the required slip speed, in accordance with Eq. 12-4, depends on the torque to be developed. The slip speed is calculated by the slip-compensation block of Fig. 12-10. Here, T_{em} is estimated as follows: the dc power input to the inverter is measured as a product of V_d and the average of i_d. From this, the estimated losses in the inverter of the PPU and in the stator resistance are subtracted to estimate the total power P_{ag} crossing the air gap into the rotor. We can show, by adding Eqs. 11-40 and 11-42 of the previous chapter that $T_{em} = P_{ag} / \omega_{syn}$.

<u>Voltage Boost</u>. To keep the air gap flux density $\hat{B}_{ms}$ constant at its rated value, the motor voltage must be controlled in accordance with Eq. 12-18, where $\hat{I}_{ra}'$ is linearly proportional to T_{em} estimated earlier.

12-8   PULSE-WIDTH-MODULATED POWER-PROCESSING UNIT

In the block diagram of Fig. 12-10, the inputs $\hat{V}$ and ω_{syn} generate the three control voltages that are compared with a switching-frequency triangular waveform v_{tri} of a constant amplitude. The power-processing unit of Fig. 12-11a, as described in Chapter 4, supplies the desired voltages to the stator windings. By averaging, each pole is represented by an ideal transformer in Fig. 12-11b whose turns-ratio is continuously controlled, proportional to the control voltage.

12-8-1 Harmonics in the PPU Output Voltages

The instantaneous voltage waveforms corresponding to the logic signals are shown in Fig. 12-12a. These are best discussed by means of computer simulations. The harmonic spectrum of the line-line output voltage waveform shows the presence of harmonic voltages as the sidebands of the switching frequency f_s and its multiples. The PPU output voltages, for example $v_a(t)$, can

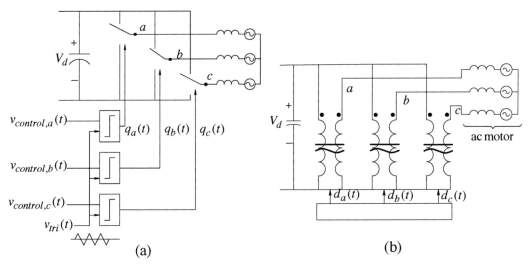

Figure 12-11 Power Processing Unit (PPU) (a) bi-positional switch representation; (b) average representation.

be decomposed into the fundamental-frequency component (designated by the subscript "1") and the ripple voltage

$$v_a(t) = v_{a1}(t) + v_{a,ripple}(t) \qquad (12\text{-}31)$$

where the ripple voltage consists of the components in the range of and higher than the switching frequency f_s, as shown in Fig. 12-12b. With the availability of higher switching-speed power devices such as modern IGBTs, the switching frequency in low and medium-power motor drives approach, and in some cases exceed, 20 kHz. The motivation for selecting a high switching frequency f_s, if the switching losses in the PPU can be kept manageable, is to reduce the ripple in the motor currents, thus reducing the electromagnetic torque ripple and the power losses in the motor resistances.

To analyze the motor's response to the applied voltages with ripple, we will make use of superposition. The motor's dominant response is determined by the fundamental-frequency voltages, which establish the synchronous speed ω_{syn} and the rotor speed ω_m. The per-phase equivalent circuit at the fundamental frequency is shown in Fig. 12-13a.

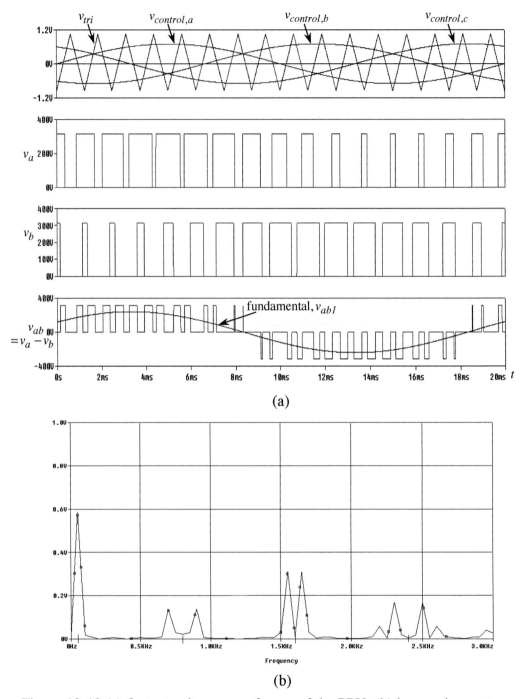

Figure 12-12 (a) Output voltage waveforms of the PPU; (b) harmonic spectrum of line-to-line voltages.

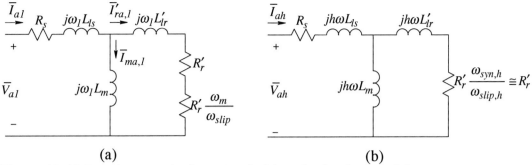

Figure 12-13 Per phase equivalent circuit (a) at the fundamental frequency; (b) at harmonic frequencies.

In the PPU output voltages, the voltage components at a harmonic frequency $f_h \gg f$ produce rotating flux distribution in the air gap at a synchronous speed $\omega_{syn,h}$ where

$$\omega_{syn,h} (= h \times \omega_{syn}) \gg \omega_{syn}, \omega_m \tag{12-32}$$

The flux-density distribution at a harmonic frequency may be rotating in the same or opposite direction as the rotor. In any case, because it is rotating at a much faster speed compared to the rotor speed ω_m, the slip speed for the harmonic frequencies is

$$\omega_{slip,h} = \omega_{syn,h} \pm \omega_m \cong \omega_{syn,h} \tag{12-33}$$

Therefore, in the per-phase equivalent circuit at harmonic frequencies,

$$R_r' \frac{\omega_{syn,h}}{\omega_{slip,h}} \cong R_r' \tag{12-34}$$

which is shown in Fig. 12-13b. At high switching frequencies, the magnetizing reactance is very large and can be neglected in the circuit of Fig. 12-13b, and the harmonic frequency current is determined primarily by the leakage reactances (which dominate over R_r'):

$$\hat{I}_{ah} \cong \frac{\hat{V}_{ah}}{X_{\ell s,h} + X'_{tr,h}} \tag{12-35}$$

The additional power loss due to the these harmonic frequency currents in the stator and the rotor resistances, on a three-phase basis, can be expressed as

$$\Delta P_{loss,R} = 3\sum_h \frac{1}{2}(R_s + R'_r)\hat{I}_{ah}^2 \tag{12-36}$$

In addition to these losses, there are additional losses in the stator and the rotor iron due to eddy currents and hysteresis at harmonic frequencies. These are further discussed in Chapter 15 dealing with efficiencies in drives.

12-8-2 Modeling the PPU-Supplied Induction Motors in Steady State

In steady state, an induction motor supplied by voltages from the power-processing unit should be modeled such that it allows the fundamental-frequency currents in Fig. 12-13a and the harmonic-frequency currents in Fig. 12-13b to be superimposed. This can be done if the per-phase equivalent is drawn as shown in Fig. 12-14a, where the voltage drop across the resistance $R'_r \dfrac{\omega_m}{\omega_{slip}}$ in Fig. 12-13a at the fundamental frequency is represented by a fundamental-frequency voltage $R'_r \dfrac{\omega_m}{\omega_{slip}} i'_{ra,1}(t)$. All three phases are shown in Fig. 12-14b.

12-9   REDUCTION OF $\hat{B}_{ms}$ AT LIGHT LOADS

In section 12-2, no attention was paid to core losses (only to the copper losses) in justifying that the machine should be operated at its rated flux density at any torque, while operating at speeds below the rated value. As illustrated by the discussion in section 11-9 of Chapter 11, it is possible to improve the overall efficiency under lightly-loaded conditions by reducing $\hat{B}_{ms}$ below its rated value.

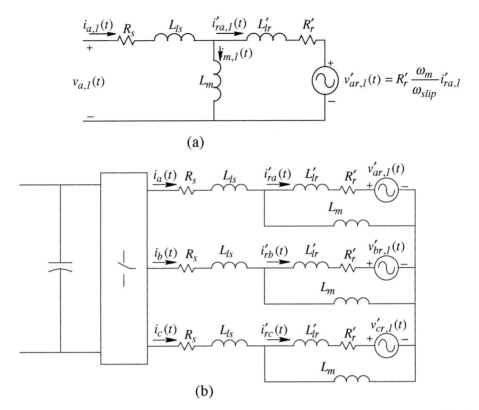

(a)

(b)

Figure 12-14 (a) Equivalent circuit for fundamental and harmonic frequencies in steady state; (b) three-phase equivalent circuit.

SUMMARY/REVIEW QUESTIONS

1. What are the applications of adjustable-speed drives?
2. Why are the thyristor-based, voltage reduction circuits for controlling induction-motor speed so inefficient?
3. In operating below the rated speed (and not considering the core losses), why is it most efficient to keep the flux-density peak in the air gap at the rated value?
4. Since an induction motor is operated at different values of frequency, hence different values of synchronous speed, how is the slip speed defined?
5. Supplying a load that demands a constant torque independent of speed, what is the slip speed at various values of the frequency f of the applied voltages?

6. To keep the flux-density peak in the air gap at the rated value, why do the voltage magnitudes, at a given frequency of operation, depend on the torque being supplied by the motor?

7. At start-up, why should small-frequency voltages be applied initially? What determines the rate at which the frequency can be ramped up?

8. At speeds below the rated value, what is the limit on the torque that can be delivered, and why?

9. At speeds above the rated value, what is the limit on the power that can be delivered, and why? What does it mean for the torque that can be delivered above the rated speed?

REFERENCES

1. N. Mohan, T. Undeland, and W. P. Robbins, *Power Electronics: Converters, Applications, and Design*, 2nd edition, 1995, John Wiley & Sons, New York, NY.

2. B. K. Bose, *Power Electronics and AC Drives*, Prentice-Hall, 1986.

3. M. Kazmierkowski, R. Krishnan and F. Blaabjerg, "Control of Power Electronics," Academic Press, 2002, 518 pages.

PROBLEMS

12-1 Repeat Example 12-1 if the load is a centrifugal load that demands a torque, proportional to the speed squared, such that it equals the rated torque of the motor at the motor rated speed.

12-2 Repeat Example 12-2 if the load is a centrifugal load that demands a torque, proportional to the speed squared, such that it equals the rated torque of the motor at the motor rated speed.

12-3 Repeat Example 12-3 if the starting torque is to be equal to the rated torque.

12-4 Consider the drive in Examples 12-1 and 12-2, operating at the rated frequency of 60 Hz and supplying the rated torque. At the rated operating speed, calculate the voltages (in frequency and amplitude) needed to produce a regenerative braking torque that equals the rated torque in magnitude.

SIMULATION PROBLEM

12-5 Using the average representation of the PWM inverter, simulate the drive in Examples 12-1 and 12-2, while operating in steady state, at a frequency of 60 Hz. The dc bus voltage is 800 V, and the stator and the rotor leakage inductances are 2.2Ω each. Estimate the rotor resistance R'_r from the data given in Examples 12-1 and 12-2.

CHAPTER 13

VECTOR CONTROL OF INDUCTION-MOTOR DRIVES: A QUALITATIVE EXAMINATION

13-1 INTRODUCTION

Applications such as robotics and factory automation require accurate control of speed and position. This can be accomplished by vector control of induction machines, which emulate the performance of dc-motor and brushless-dc motor servo drives. Compared to dc and brushless-dc motors, induction motors have a lower cost and a more rugged construction.

In any speed and position control application, torque is the fundamental variable which needs to be controlled. The ability to produce a step-change in torque on command represents total control over the drives for high performance speed and position control.

This chapter qualitatively shows how a step-change in torque is accomplished by vector control of induction-motor drives. For this purpose, the steady state analysis of induction motors discussed in Chapter 11 serves very well because, while delivering a step-change in electromagnetic torque under vector control, an induction machine instantaneously transitions from one steady state to another.

13-2   EMULATION OF DC- AND BRUSHLESS-DC DRIVE PERFORMANCE

Under vector control, induction-motor drives can emulate the performance of dc-motor and brushless-dc motor servo drives discussed in earlier chapters. These are briefly reviewed as follows.

In the dc-motor drive shown in Fig. 13-1a, the commutator and brushes ensure that the armature-current-produced mmf is at a right angle to the field flux produced by the stator. Both of these fields remain stationary. The electromagnetic torque T_{em} developed by the motor depends linearly on the armature current i_a:

$$T_{em} = k_T i_a \tag{13-1}$$

where k_T is the dc-motor torque constant. To change T_{em} as a step, the armature current i_a is changed (at least, attempted to be changed) as a step by the power-processing unit, as shown in Fig. 13-1b.

In the brushless-dc drive shown in Fig. 13-2a, the PPU keeps the stator current space vector $\vec{i}_s(t)$ 90 degrees ahead of the rotor field vector $\vec{B}_r(t)$ (produced by the permanent magnets on the rotor) in the direction of rotation. The position $\theta_m(t)$ of the rotor field is measured by means of a sensor, for example, a resolver.

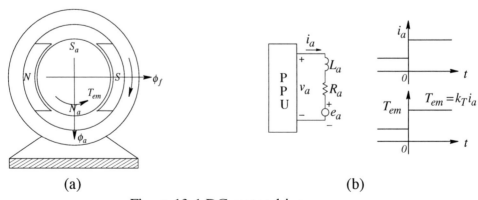

(a)   (b)

Figure 13-1 DC motor drive.

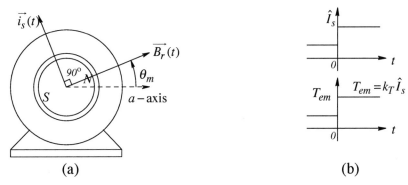

(a)   (b)

Figure 13-2 Current controlled BLDC motor drive.

The torque T_{em} depends on $\hat{I}_s$, the amplitude of the stator current space vector $\vec{i}_s(t)$:

$$T_{em} = k_T \hat{I}_s \qquad (13\text{-}2)$$

where k_T is the brushless-dc motor torque constant. To produce a step change in torque, the PPU changes the amplitude $\hat{I}_s$ in Fig. 13-2b by appropriately changing $i_a(t)$, $i_b(t)$, and $i_c(t)$, keeping $\vec{i}_s(t)$ always ahead of $\vec{B}_r(t)$ by 90^0 in the direction of rotation.

In an induction machine, the $\vec{F}_r(t)$ and $\vec{F}'_r(t)$ space vectors are naturally at 90^0 to the rotor flux-density space vector $\vec{B}_r(t)$, as shown in Fig. 13-3a. In terms of the amplitude $\hat{I}'_r$ where $\vec{i}'_r(t) = \dfrac{\vec{F}'_r(t)}{N_s/2}$, keeping $\hat{B}_r$ constant results in the following torque expression:

$$T_{em} = k_T \hat{I}'_r \qquad (13\text{-}3)$$

where k_T is the induction-motor torque constant. The previous discussion shows that induction-motor drives can emulate the performance of dc-motor and the brushless-dc motor drives. In induction machines, in this emulation (called vector control) the PPU in Fig. 13-3b controls the stator current space vector $\vec{i}_s(t)$ as

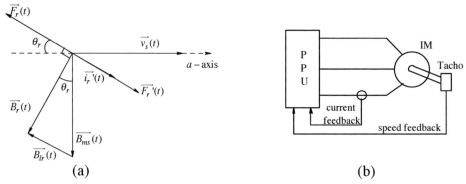

(a)   (b)

Figure 13-3 (a) Rotor flux density and mmf space vectors; (b) vector-controlled induction-motor drive.

follows: a component of $\vec{i}_s(t)$ is controlled to keep $\hat{B}_r$ constant, while the other orthogonal component of $\vec{i}_s(t)$ is controlled to produce the desired torque.

13-3   ANALOGY TO A CURRENT-EXCITED TRANSFORMER WITH A SHORTED SECONDARY

To understand vector control in induction-motor drives, an analogy of a current-excited transformer with a short-circuited secondary, as shown in Fig. 13-4, is very useful. Initially at time $t = 0^-$, both currents and the core flux are zero. The primary winding is excited by a step-current at $t = 0^+$. Changing this current as a step, in the presence of leakage fluxes, requires a voltage impulse, but as has been argued in Reference [1], the volt-seconds needed to bring about such a change are not all that large. In any case, we will assume that it is possible to produce a step-change in the primary-winding current. Our focus is on the short-circuited secondary winding; therefore, we will neglect the leakage impedance of the

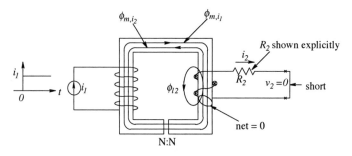

Figure 13-4 Current excited transformer with secondary short-circuited.

13-4

primary winding.

In the transformer of Fig. 13-4 at $t = 0^-$, the flux linkage $\lambda_2(0^-)$ with the secondary winding is zero, as there is no flux in the core. From the Theorem of Constant Flux Linkage, we know that the flux linkage of a short-circuited coil cannot change instantaneously. Therefore, at $t = 0^+$,

$$\lambda_2(0^+) = \lambda_2(0^-) = 0 \tag{13-4}$$

To maintain the above condition, i_2 will jump instantaneously at $t = 0^+$. As shown in Fig. 13-4 at $t = 0^+$, there are three flux components linking the secondary winding: the magnetizing flux ϕ_{m,i_1} produced by i_1, the magnetizing flux ϕ_{m,i_2} produced by i_2, and the leakage flux $\phi_{\ell 2}$ produced by i_2 which links only winding 2 but not winding 1. The condition that $\lambda_2(0^+) = 0$ requires that the net flux linking winding 2 be zero; hence, including the flux directions shown in Fig. 13-4,

$$\phi_{m,i_1}(0^+) - \phi_{m,i_2}(0^+) - \phi_{\ell 2}(0^+) = 0$$

or

$$\phi_{m,i_1}(0^+) = \phi_{m,i_2}(0^+) + \phi_{\ell 2}(0^+) \tag{13-5a}$$

Although we will not derive it, in response to a step-change in the primary-winding current, the secondary-winding current will jump as a step to the following value:

$$i_2(0^+) = \frac{L_m}{L_2} i_1(0^+) \tag{13-5b}$$

where L_m is the magnetizing inductance, as defined in the transformer equivalent circuit of Fig. 5-16, and $L_2 = L_m + L_{\ell 2}$ (assuming equal number of turns in the primary and the secondary windings). We will see later that a similar step-change in the rotor current occurs in a vector-controlled induction motor.

13-4   D- AND Q-AXIS WINDING REPRESENTATION

Before we apply the transformer analogy to induction machines, we will qualitatively look at an orthogonal set of d- and q-axis windings producing the same mmf as three stator windings (each with N_s turns, sinusoidally-distributed) with i_a, i_b, and i_c flowing through them. In Fig. 13-5a at a time t, $\vec{i}_s(t)$ and $\vec{F}_s(t)$ are produced by $i_a(t)$, $i_b(t)$, and $i_c(t)$. The resulting mmf $\vec{F}_s(t) = (N_s/2)\vec{i}_s(t)$ can be produced by the set of orthogonal windings shown in Fig. 13-5b, each sinusoidally-distributed with $\sqrt{3/2}\,N_s$ turns: one winding along the d-axis, and the other along the q-axis. The reason for using this cumbersome factor $\sqrt{3/2}$ is to yield appropriate winding inductances. Note that this d-q axis set may be at any arbitrary angle with respect to the phase-a axis. In order to keep the mmf and the flux-density distributions the same as in the actual machine with three-phase windings, the currents in these two windings would have to be i_{sd} and i_{sq} where, as shown in Fig. 13-5c, these two current components are $\sqrt{2/3}$ times the projections of the $\vec{i}_s(t)$ vector along the d-axis and q-axis:

$$i_{sd} \;=\; \sqrt{\frac{2}{3}} \text{ x the projection of } \vec{i}_s(t) \text{ vector along the } d\text{-axis} \qquad (13\text{-}6)$$

$$i_{sq} \;=\; \sqrt{\frac{2}{3}} \text{ x the projection of } \vec{i}_s(t) \text{ vector along the } q\text{-axis} \qquad (13\text{-}7)$$

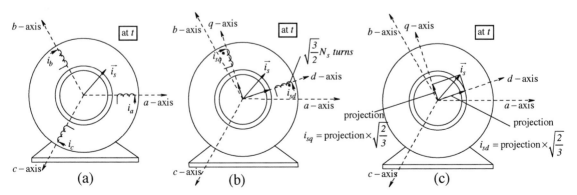

Figure 13-5 Representation by d and q-axis winding set at an arbitrary angle.

where, the reason for the factor $\sqrt{2/3}$ has to do with the choice of $\sqrt{3/2}N_s$ turns for the d- and the q- axis windings.

13-5   INITIAL FLUX BUILDUP PRIOR TO $t = 0^-$

Next, we will apply the information of the last section to vector control of induction machines. As shown in Fig. 13-6, prior to $t = 0^-$, the magnetizing currents are built up in three phases such that

$$i_a(0^-) = \hat{I}_{m,rated} \qquad \text{and} \qquad i_b(0^-) = i_c(0^-) = -\frac{1}{2}\hat{I}_{m,rated} \qquad (13\text{-}8)$$

The current buildup prior to $t = 0^-$ may occur slowly over a long period of time and represents the buildup of the flux in the induction machine up to its rated value. Therefore, these currents represent the rated magnetizing currents to bring the air gap flux density to its rated value. Note that there will be no rotor currents at $t = 0^-$ (they decay out prior to $t = 0^-$). Also, at $t = 0^-$, the stator mmf can be represented by that produced by the d-axis winding (chosen to be along the a-axis) with a current i_{sd}, where

$$i_{sd}(0^-) = \sqrt{\frac{2}{3}}\,\hat{I}_{ms,rated} = \sqrt{\frac{2}{3}}(\frac{3}{2}\hat{I}_{m,rated}) = \sqrt{\frac{3}{2}}\,\hat{I}_{m,rated} \qquad (13\text{-}9a)$$

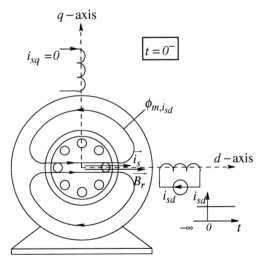

Figure 13-6 Currents and flux at $t = 0^-$.

and

$$i_{sq} = 0 \tag{13-9b}$$

Note that the i_{sd}-produced stator leakage flux does not link the rotor, and hence it is of no concern in this discussion.

At $t = 0^-$, the peak of the flux lines $\phi_{m,i_{sd}}$ linking the rotor is horizontally oriented. There is no rotor leakage flux because there are no currents flowing through the rotor bars, and hence all of the flux $\phi_{m,i_{sd}}$ produced by the stator links the rotor. Therefore, $\vec{B}_r(0^-)$, equal to $\vec{B}_{ms}(0^-)$, is horizontally oriented along the d-axis (same as the a-axis at $t = 0^-$).

13-6   STEP-CHANGE IN TORQUE AT $t = 0^+$

Next, we will see how this induction machine can produce a step-change in torque. Initially, we will assume that the rotor is blocked from turning ($\omega_m = 0$), a restriction that will soon be removed. Now at $t = 0^+$, the three stator currents are changed as a step in order to produce a step-change in the q-axis current i_{sq}, without changing i_{sd}, as shown in Fig. 13-7a. The current i_{sq} in the stator q-winding produces the flux lines $\phi_{m,i_{sq}}$ that cross the air gap and link the rotor. The leakage flux produced by i_{sq} can be safely neglected from the discussion here (because it doesn't link the shorted rotor cage), similar to neglecting the leakage flux produced by the primary winding of the transformer in the previous analogy.

Turning our attention to the rotor at $t = 0^+$, we note that the rotor is a short-circuited cage, so its flux linkage cannot change instantaneously. To oppose the flux lines produced by i_{sq}, currents are instantaneously induced in the rotor bars by the transformer action, as shown in Fig. 13-7a.

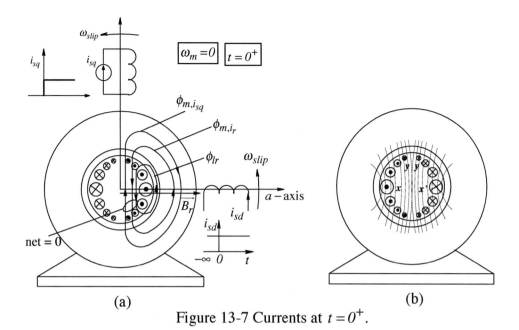

Figure 13-7 Currents at $t = 0^+$.

This current distribution in the rotor bars is sinusoidal, as justified below using Fig. 13-7b:

> To justify the sinusoidal distribution of current in the rotor bars, assume that the bars $x - x'$ constitute one short-circuited coil, and the bars $y - y'$ the other coil. The density of flux lines produced by i_{sq} is sinusoidally distributed in the air gap. The coil $x - x'$ links most of the flux lines produced by i_{sq}. But the coil $y - y'$ links far fewer flux lines. Therefore, the current in this coil will be relatively smaller than the current in $x - x'$.

These rotor currents in Fig. 13-7a produce two flux components with peak densities along the q-axis and of the direction shown:

1. The magnetizing flux ϕ_{m,i_r} that crosses the air gap and links the stator.

2. The leakage flux $\phi_{\ell r}$ that does not cross the air gap and links only the rotor.

By the Theorem of Constant Flux Linkage, at $t = 0^+$, the net flux linking the short-circuited rotor in the q-axis must remain zero. Therefore at $t = 0^+$, for the condition that $\phi_{q,net} = 0$ (taking flux directions into account):

$$\phi_{m,i_{sq}}(o^+) = \phi_{m,i_r}(o^+) + \phi_{\ell r}(o^+) \tag{13-10}$$

Since i_{sd} and the d-axis rotor flux linkage have not changed, the net flux, $\overrightarrow{B_r}$, linking the rotor remains the same at $t = 0^+$ as it was at $t = 0^-$.

The space vectors at $t = 0^+$ are shown in Fig. 13-8. No change in the net flux linking the rotor implies that $\overrightarrow{B_r}$ has not changed; its peak is still horizontal along the a-axis and of the same magnitude as before. The rotor currents produced instantaneously by the transformer action at $t = 0^+$ result in a torque $T_{em}(0^+)$. This torque will be proportional to $\hat{B}_r$ and i_{sq} (due to the rotor leakage flux, slightly less than i_{sq} by a factor of L_m / L_r where $L_r = L_m + L'_{\ell r}$ in the equivalent circuit of Fig. 11-21):

$$T_{em} \, \alpha \, \hat{B}_r, \frac{L_m}{L_r} i_{sq} \tag{13-11}$$

If no action is taken beyond $t = 0^+$, the rotor currents will decay and so will the force on the rotor bars. This current decay would be like in a transformer with a short-circuited secondary and with the primary excited with a step of current source. In the case of the transformer, decay of i_2 could be prevented by injecting a voltage equal to $R_2 i_2(0^+)$ beyond $t = 0^+$, as shown in Fig. 13-9 as a step voltage, to overcome the voltage drop across R_2.

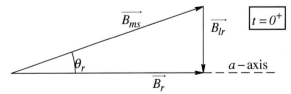

Figure 13-8 Flux densities at $t = 0^+$.

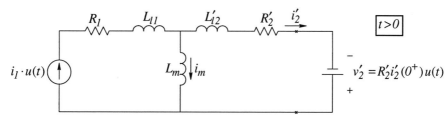

Figure 13-9 Voltage needed to prevent the decay of secondary current.

In the case of an induction machine, beyond $t = 0^+$, as shown in Fig. 13-10, we will equivalently rotate both the d-axis and the q-axis stator windings at an appropriate slip speed ω_{slip} in order to maintain $\vec{B}_r(t)$ completely along the d-axis with a constant amplitude of $\hat{B}_r$, and to maintain the same rotor-bar current distribution along the q-axis. This corresponds to the beginning of a new steady state. Therefore, the steady state analysis of Chapter 11 applies.

As the d-axis and the q-axis windings rotate at the appropriate value of ω_{slip} (notice that the rotor is still blocked from turning in Fig. 13-10), there is no net rotor flux linkage along the q-axis. The flux linkage along the d-axis remains constant with a flux density $\hat{B}_r$ "cutting" the rotor bars and inducing the bar

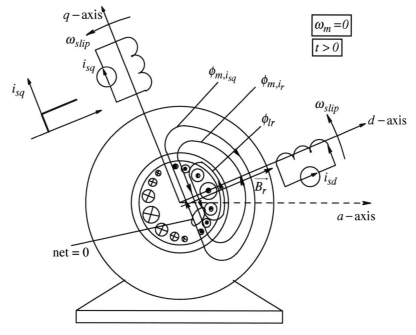

Figure 13-10 Current and fluxes at some time $t > 0$, with the rotor blocked.

voltages to cancel the iR_{bar} voltage drops. Therefore, the entire distribution rotates with time, as shown in Fig. 13-10 at any arbitrary time $t > 0$. For the relative distribution and hence the torque produced to remain the same as at $t = 0^+$, the two windings must rotate at the exact ω_{slip}, which depends linearly on both the rotor resistance R_r' and i_{sq} (slightly less by the factor L_m / L_r due to the rotor leakage flux), and inversely on $\hat{B}_r$

$$\omega_{slip} \ \alpha \ \frac{R_r', \ (L_m / L_r) i_{sq}}{\hat{B}_r} \qquad\qquad (13\text{-}12)$$

Now we can remove the restriction of $\omega_m = 0$. If we need to produce a step change in torque while the rotor is turning at some speed ω_m, then the d-axis and the q-axis windings should be equivalently rotated at the appropriate slip speed ω_{slip} relative to the rotor speed ω_m, that is, at the synchronous speed $\omega_{syn} = \omega_m + \omega_{slip}$ as shown in Fig. 13-11.

13-6-1 Similarity Between Voltage-Fed and Vector-Controlled Induction Machines in Steady State

In steady state, the voltages, the currents, and the fluxes associated with the induction machine are the same, regardless of if the machine is supplied by a three-phase voltage source, as discussed in Chapters 11, or supplied with controlled currents, as discussed in this chapter. This can be observed by drawing the relevant space vectors in Fig. 13-12, neglecting the stator leakage impedance. The applied voltage space vector $\vec{v}_s$ in the voltage-fed machine results in $\vec{i}_{ms}$ to establish $\vec{B}_{ms}$. In contrast, in the vector-controlled machine, i_{sd} is kept constant (below the rated speed) to maintain $\hat{B}_r$ at its rated value, which, including the effect of the rotor-leakage flux, establishes $\vec{B}_{ms}$ and hence $\vec{v}_s$.

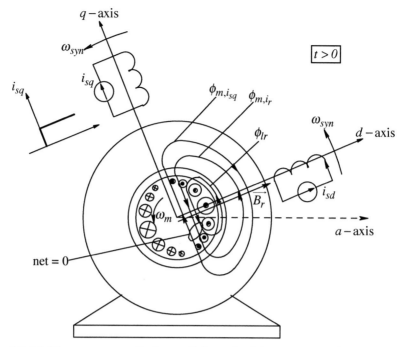

Figure 13-11 Vector controlled conditioned with rotor speed ω_m.

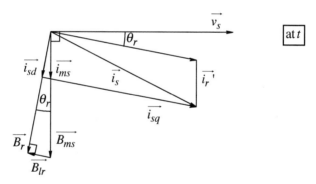

Figure 13-12 Space vectors at any time in steady state.

13-7   TORQUE, SPEED, AND POSITION CONTROL

In vector control of induction-motor drives, the stator phase currents $i_a(t)$, $i_b(t)$, and $i_c(t)$ are controlled in such a manner that $i_{sq}(t)$ delivers the desired electromagnetic torque while $i_{sd}(t)$ maintains the peak rotor-flux density at its rated value. The reference values $i_{sq}^*(t)$ and $i_{sd}^*(t)$ are generated by the torque, speed, and position control loops, as discussed below.

13-7-1 The Reference Current $i_{sq}^*(t)$

The reference value $i_{sq}^*(t)$ depends on the desired torque which can be calculated by cascade control discussed in Chapter 8. In the cascade control illustrated in Fig. 13-13, the position loop is the outermost loop and the torque loop is the innermost loop. The loop bandwidths increase from the outermost to the innermost loop. The error between the reference (desired) position, $\theta_m^*(t)$, and the measured position $\theta_m(t)$ is amplified by a proportional (P) amplifier to generate the speed reference signal $\omega_m^*(t)$. The error between the reference speed $\omega_m^*(t)$ and the measured speed $\omega_m(t)$ is amplified by a proportional-integral (PI) amplifier to generate the torque reference $T_{em}^*(t)$. Finally, the error between $T_{em}^*(t)$ and the calculated torque $T_{em}(t)$ is amplified by another PI amplifier to generate the reference value $i_{sq}^*(t)$.

13-7-2 The Reference Current $i_{sd}^*(t)$

For measured speed values below the rated speed of the motor, the rotor flux-density peak $\hat{B}_r$ is maintained at its rated value as shown by the speed versus flux-density block in Fig. 13-13. Above the rated speed, the flux density is reduced in the flux-weakening mode, as discussed in Chapter 12. The error

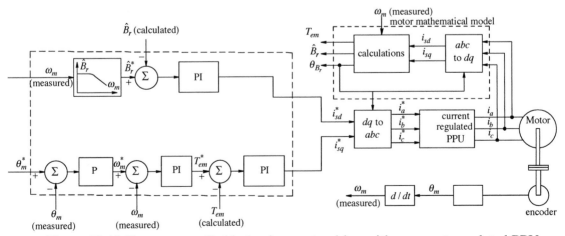

Figure 13-13 Vector controlled induction motor drive with a current-regulated PPU.

between $\hat{B}_r^*$ and the calculated flux-density peak $\hat{B}_r$ is amplified by a PI amplifier to generate the reference value $i_{sd}^*(t)$.

13-7-3 The Transformation and Inverse-Transformation of Stator Currents

Fig. 13-13 shows the angle $\theta_{B_r}(t)$ of the d-axis, with respect to the stationary a-axis, to which the rotor flux-density space vector $\vec{B}_r(t)$ is aligned at $t = 0^-$. This angle is computed by the vector-controlled motor model, which is described in the next section. Using the d-axis angle $\theta_{B_r}(t)$, the reference current signals $i_{sd}^*(t)$ and $i_{sq}^*(t)$ are transformed into the stator current reference signals $i_a^*(t)$, $i_b^*(t)$, and $i_c^*(t)$, as shown by the transform block ($dq - to - abc$) in Fig. 13-13. The current-regulated power-processing unit uses these reference signals to supply the desired currents to the motor (details of how it can be accomplished are left out [2]). The stator currents are measured and the d-axis angle $\theta_{B_r}(t)$ is used to inverse-transform them into the signals $i_{sd}(t)$ and $i_{sq}(t)$, as shown by the inverse-transform block in Fig. 13-13.

13-7-4 The Motor Model for Vector Control

The motor model in Fig. 13-13 has the following measured inputs: the three stator phase currents $i_a(t)$, $i_b(t)$, and $i_c(t)$, and the measured rotor speed $\omega_m(t)$. The motor model also needs accurate estimation of the rotor parameters L_m, $L_{\ell r}'$, and R_r'. The following parameters are calculated in the motor model for internal use and also as outputs: the angle $\theta_{B_r}(t)$, with respect to the stationary phase-a axis, to which the d-axis is aligned, the peak of the rotor flux density $\hat{B}_r(t)$, and the electromagnetic torque $T_{em}(t)$. In the motor model, $\hat{B}_r(t)$ is computed by considering the dynamics along the d-axis, which is valid in the flux-weakening mode as well, where $\hat{B}_r(t)$ is decreased to allow operation at higher than rated speed. The electromagnetic torque $T_{em}(t)$ is computed based on the mathematical expression derived based on Eq. 13-11. The angle $\theta_{B_r}(t)$ is computed by first calculating the slip speed $\omega_{slip}(t)$ based on Eq. 13-12. This slip speed is added to the measured rotor speed to yield the instantaneous synchronous speed of the d- and the q-axes:

$$\omega_{syn}(t) = \omega_m(t) + \omega_{slip}(t) \tag{13-13}$$

With $\theta_{B_r} = 0$ at starting, by initially aligning the rotor flux-density space vector along the a-axis, integrating the instantaneous synchronous speed results in the d-axis angle as follows:

$$\theta_{B_r}(t) = 0 + \int_0^t \omega_{syn}(\tau) \cdot d\tau \tag{13-14}$$

where τ is a variable of integration. Based on physical principles, the mathematical expressions are clearly and concisely developed in References [2] and [3] but are considered beyond the scope of this introductory textbook.

13-8 SENSOR-LESS DRIVES

In the vector-control principle described in this chapter, it is essential that currents supplied to the motor be measured and compared with their reference values. Measurement of these currents does not pose a problem because they are supplied by the power-processing unit, and thus can be measured where the PPU is located, even if the motor is far away, supplied by long cables. However, the necessity of the above vector-control procedure, that the motor speed ω_m be measured, can sometimes be objectionable.

In vector control of induction machines, it is adequate to use incremental speed sensors, such as optical encoders. Speed sensors are mechanical devices, which present additional cost, need space, can cause mechanical resonances, and decrease the system reliability due to their own delicate nature and the extra wires associated with the sensor to the controller for the power-processing unit. In many position control applications, it is necessary to measure position; hence the speed information can be derived from the position sensors at no cost. However, in other applications it will be highly desirable to do without speed sensors. This has been a topic of intense research of late.

Many techniques for estimating the rotor speed in vector control are discussed in the literature. Other techniques, without using the vector-control principle described earlier, deliver the ability to change the electromagnetic torque developed by the induction motor as a step. One such technique used in some commercially available drives is called direct-torque control (DTC), which is described in References [4] and [5]. In drives without speed sensors, it becomes challenging to control torque accurately at low speeds. There is no doubt that research will continue to improve the performance of sensor-less drives at low speeds.

SUMMARY/REVIEW QUESTIONS

1. How is torque controlled in brush-type dc drives and brushless-dc drives?
2. In a sentence, describe the vector-control of induction-motor drives that emulates the performance of dc drives. Why is it more challenging?
3. What does the Theorem of Constant Flux Linkage state?
4. In words, what does the analogy of a transformer with the short-circuited secondary, and excited by a step-current conclude?
5. What is the reason for introducing the d-axis and the q-axis windings?
6. Without the details, state the reason for choosing $\sqrt{3/2}N_s$ as the number for turns in the d-axis and the q-axis windings.
7. How are i_{sd} and i_{sq} obtained from the $\vec{i}_s$ space vector?
8. At the end of the initial flux build-up process at $t = 0^-$, are there any currents in the rotor bar?
9. How are the currents induced in the rotor bars at $t = 0^+$?
10. What needs to be done to maintain the torque produced at $t = 0^+$?
11. Why does the slip speed at which the d-axis and the q-axis windings need to be rotated, to maintain the torque produced beyond $t = 0^+$, depend on various quantities as given in Eq. 13-12?
12. Describe the similarity between voltage-fed induction machines and vector-controlled induction machines.

13. Describe the control block diagram of vector control.

14. Describe DTC and its objectives.

REFERENCES

1. A. Hughes, J. Corda and D. Andrade, "Vector Control of Cage Induction Motors: A Physical Insight," IEE-Proc. – Power Appl., Vol. 143, No. 1, Jan. 1996, pp. 59-68.
2. N. Mohan, "A Three-Hour Tutorial on Understanding Basics of Adjustable-Speed and Vector-Controlled Induction and Synchronous Motor Drives," at the IEEE Applied Power Electronics Annual Conference in Anaheim, CA on February 15, 1998.
3. N. Mohan, M. Riaz and A. K. Jain, "Explanation of De-tuning in Vector Controlled Induction-Motor Drives Simplified by Physical-Based Analysis and PSpice Modeling," Proceedings of the 1999 EPE, Lausanne, Switzerland.
4. M. Depenbrock, "Direct Self Control (DSC) of Inverter-Fed Induction Machines," IEEE Transactions on Power Electronics, Vol. 3, 1988, pp. 420-429.
5. I. Takahashi and Y. Ohmori, "High Performance Direct Torque Control of an Induction Motor," IEEE/IAS Annual Meeting, 1987, pp. 163-169.
6. N. Mohan, Advanced Electric Drives: Analysis, Control and Modeling using Simulink, MNPERE, 2001, pp. 180.

PROBLEMS

13-1 In a 2-pole induction machine, establishing the rated air gap flux density requires that $\hat{I}_m = 4\,A$. To build up to this rated flux, calculate the three-phase currents at $t = 0^-$.

13-2 In the machine of Problem 13-1, the desired step-torque at $t = 0^+$ requires a step change in $i_{sq} = 10\,A$. Calculate the phase currents at $t = 0^+$ which result in the desired step change in q-axis current while maintaining the rated flux density in the air gap.

13-3 In the machine of Problems 13-1 and 13-2, the slip speed at which the equivalent d-axis and the q-axis windings need to be rotated is

$\omega_{slip} = 11.31 \, rad/s$.   Assuming that the rotor is blocked from turning, calculate the phase currents at $t = 8 \, ms$.

13-4 Repeat Problem 13-3, if the rotor is turning and the speed essentially can be assumed constant at $1100 \, rpm$.

CHAPTER 14

RELUCTANCE DRIVES: STEPPER-MOTOR AND SWITCHED-RELUCTANCE DRIVES

14-1   INTRODUCTION

Reluctance machines operate on principles that are different than those associated with all of the machines discussed so far. Reluctance drives can be broadly classified into three categories: stepper-motor drives, switched-reluctance drives, and synchronous-reluctance-motor drives. Only the stepper-motor and the switched-reluctance-motor drives are discussed in this chapter.

Stepper-motor drives are widely used for position control in many applications, for example computer peripherals, textile mills, integrated-circuit fabrication processes, and robotics. A stepper-motor drive can be considered as a digital electromechanical device, where each electrical pulse input results in a movement of the rotor by a discrete angle called the step-angle of the motor, as shown in Fig. 14-1. Therefore, for the desired change in position, the corresponding number of electrical pulses is applied to the motor, without the need for any position feedback.

Switched-reluctance-motor drives are operated with controlled currents, using feedback. They are being considered for a large number of applications discussed later in this chapter.

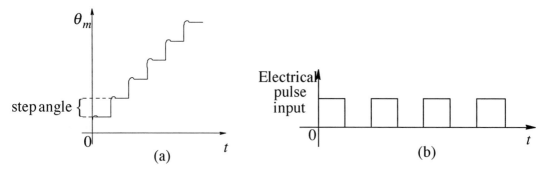

Fig 14-1 Position change in stepper motor

14-2   THE OPERATING PRINCIPLE OF RELUCTANCE MOTORS

Reluctance motors operate by generating reluctance torque. This requires that the reluctance in the magnetic-flux path be different along the various axes. Consider the cross-section of a primitive machine shown in Fig. 14-2a in which the rotor has no electrical excitation and the stator has a coil excited by a current $i(t)$. In the following analysis, we will neglect the losses in the electrical and the mechanical systems, but these losses can also be accounted for. In the machine of Fig. 14-2a, the stator current would produce a torque on the rotor in the counter-clockwise direction, due to fringing fluxes, in order to align the rotor with the stator pole. This torque can be estimated by the principle of energy conservation; this principle states that

Electrical Energy Input = Increase in Stored Energy + Mechanical Output (14-1)

Assuming that magnetic saturation is avoided, the stator coil has an inductance $L(\theta)$ which depends on the rotor position θ. Thus, the flux-linkage λ of the coil can be expressed as

$$\lambda = L(\theta)i \tag{14-2}$$

The flux-linkage λ depends on the coil inductance as well as the coil current. At any time, the voltage e across the stator coil, from Faraday's Law, is

14-2

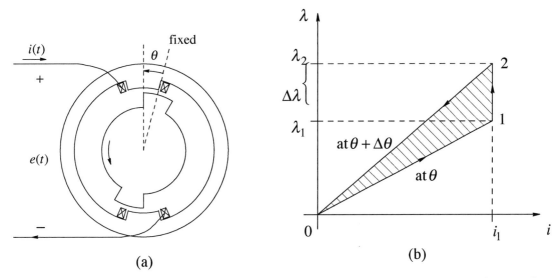

Figure 14-2 (a) Cross-section of a primitive machine; (b) $\lambda - i$ trajectory during motion.

$$e = \frac{d\lambda}{dt} \tag{14-3}$$

The polarity of the induced voltage is indicated in Fig. 14-2a. Based on Eqs. 14-2 and 14-3, the voltage in the coil may be induced due to the time-rate of change of the current and/or the coil inductance. Using Eq. 14-3, the energy supplied by the electrical source from a time t_1 (with a flux linkage of λ_1) to time t_2 (with a flux linkage of λ_2) is

$$W_{el} = \int_{t_1}^{t_2} e \cdot i \cdot dt = \int_{t_1}^{t_2} \frac{d\lambda}{dt} \cdot i \cdot dt = \int_{\lambda_1}^{\lambda_2} i \cdot d\lambda \tag{14-4}$$

In order to calculate the torque developed by this motor, we will consider the counter-clockwise movement of the rotor in Fig. 14-2a by a differential angle $d\theta$ in the following steps shown in Fig. 14-2b:

- Keeping θ constant, the current is increased from zero to a value i_1. The current follows the trajectory from 0 to 1 in the $\lambda - i$ plane in Fig. 14-2b. Using Eq. 14-4, we find that the energy supplied by the electrical source is obtained by integrating with respect to λ in Fig. 14-2b; thus the energy supplied equals $Area(0-1-\lambda_1)$

$$W_{el}(0 \to 1) = Area(0-1-\lambda_1) = \frac{1}{2}\lambda_1 i_1 \tag{14-5}$$

This is energy that gets stored in the magnetic field of the coil, since there is no mechanical output.

- Keeping the current constant at i_1, the rotor angle is allowed to be increased by a differential angle, from θ to $(\theta + \Delta\theta)$ in the counter-clockwise direction. This follows the trajectory from *1* to *2* in the $\lambda - i$ plane of Fig. 14-2b. The change in flux linkage of the coil is due to the increased inductance. From Eq. 14-2,

$$\Delta\lambda = i_1 \Delta L \tag{14-6}$$

Using Eq. 14-4 and integrating with respect to λ, we find that the energy supplied by the electrical source during this transition in Fig. 14-2b is

$$W_{el}(1 \to 2) = Area(\lambda_1 - 1 - 2 - \lambda_2) = i_1(\lambda_2 - \lambda_1) \tag{14-7}$$

- Keeping the rotor angle constant at $(\theta + \Delta\theta)$, the current is decreased from i_1 to zero. This follows the trajectory from *2* to *0* in the $\lambda - i$ plane in Fig. 14-2b. Using Eq. 14-4, we see that the energy is now supplied to the electrical source. Therefore, in Fig. 14-2b,

$$W_{el}(2 \to 0) = -Area(2-0-\lambda_2) = -\frac{1}{2}\lambda_2 i_1 \tag{14-8}$$

During these three transitions, the coil current started with a zero value and ended at zero. Therefore, the increase in the energy storage term in Eq. 14-1 is zero. The net energy supplied by the electric source is

$$\begin{aligned} W_{el,net} &= Area(0-1-\lambda_1) + Area(\lambda_1 - 1 - 2 - \lambda_2) - Area(2-0-\lambda_2) \\ &= Area(0-1-2) \end{aligned} \tag{14-9}$$

$Area(0-1-2)$ is shown hatched in Fig. 14-2b. This triangle has a base of $\Delta\lambda$ and a height of i_1. Thus we can find its area:

$$W_{el,net} = Area(0-1-2) = \frac{1}{2}i_1(\Delta\lambda) \tag{14-10}$$

Using Eq. 14-6 and Eq. 14-10,

$$W_{el,net} = \frac{1}{2}i_1(\Delta\lambda) = \frac{1}{2}i_1(i_1 \cdot \Delta L) = \frac{1}{2}i_1^2 \Delta L \tag{14-11}$$

Since there is no change in the energy stored, the electrical energy has been converted into mechanical work by the rotor, which is rotated by a differential angle $\Delta\theta$ due to the developed torque T_{em}. Therefore,

$$T_{em}\Delta\theta = \frac{1}{2}i_1^2 \Delta L \qquad \text{or} \qquad T_{em} = \frac{1}{2}i_1^2 \frac{\Delta L}{\Delta\theta} \tag{14-12}$$

Assuming a differential angle,

$$T_{em} = \frac{1}{2}i_1^2 \frac{dL}{d\theta} \tag{14-13}$$

This shows that the electromagnetic torque in such a reluctance motor depends on the current squared. Therefore, the counter-clockwise torque in the structure of Fig. 14-2a is independent of the direction of the current. This torque, called the reluctance torque, forms the basis of operation for stepper motors and switched-reluctance motors.

14-3   STEPPER-MOTOR DRIVES

Stepper motors come in a large variety of constructions, with three basic categories: variable-reluctance motors, permanent-magnet motors, and hybrid motors. Each of these is briefly discussed.

14-3-1 Variable-Reluctance Stepper Motors

Variable-reluctance stepper motors have double saliency; that is, both the stator and the rotor have different magnetic reluctances along various radial axes. The stator and the rotor also have a different number of poles. An example is shown in Fig. 14-3, in which the stator has six poles and the rotor has four poles. Each phase winding in this three-phase machine is placed on the two diametrically opposite poles.

Exciting phase-a with a current i_a results in a torque that acts in a direction to minimize the magnetic reluctance to the flux produced by i_a. With no load connected to the rotor, this torque will cause the rotor to align at $\theta = 0^0$, as shown in Fig. 14-3a. This is the no-load equilibrium position. If the mechanical load causes a small deviation in θ, the motor will develop an opposing torque in accordance with Eq. 14-13.

To turn the rotor in a clockwise direction, i_a is reduced to zero and phase-b is excited by i_b, resulting in the no-load equilibrium position shown in Fig. 14-3b. The point z on the rotor moves by the step-angle of the motor. The next two transitions with i_c and back to i_a are shown in Figs. 14-3c and 14-3d. Following the movement of point z, we see that the rotor has moved by one rotor-pole-pitch for three changes in excitation ($i_a \rightarrow i_b$, $i_b \rightarrow i_c$, and $i_c \rightarrow i_a$). The rotor-pole-pitch equals $(360^0 / N_r)$, where N_r equals the number of rotor poles. Therefore, in a q-phase motor, the step-angle of rotation for each change in excitation will be

$$\text{step-angle} = \frac{360^0}{q N_r} \qquad (14\text{-}14)$$

In the motor of Fig. 14-3 with $N_r = 4$ and $q = 3$, the step-angle equals 30^0. The direction of rotation can be made counter-clockwise by excitation in the sequence a-c-b-a.

14-6

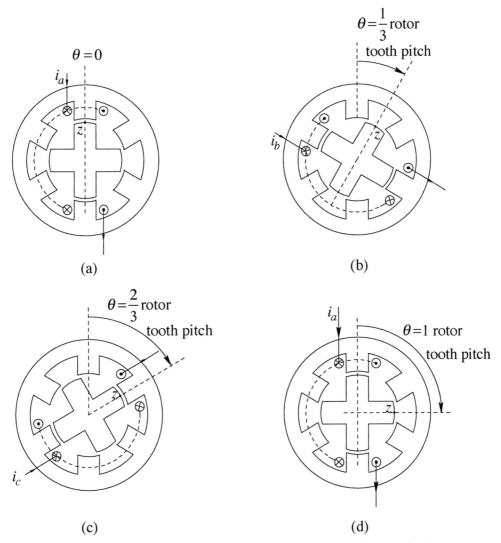

Figure 14-3 Variable reluctance motor; excitation sequence *a-b-c-a* (a) phase-*a* excited; (b) phase-*b* excited; (c) phase-*c* excited; (d) phase *a* excited.

14-3-2 Permanent-Magnet Stepper-Motors

In permanent-magnet stepper-motors, permanent magnets are placed on the rotor, as in the example shown in Fig. 14-4. The stator has two phase windings. Each winding is placed on four poles, the same as the number of poles on the rotor. Each phase winding produces the same number of poles as the rotor. The phase currents are controlled to be positive or negative. With a positive current i_a^+, the resulting stator poles and the no-load equilibrium position of the rotor are as shown in Fig. 14-4a. Reducing the current in phase-a to zero, a positive current i_b^+ in phase-b results in a clockwise rotation (following the point z on the rotor)

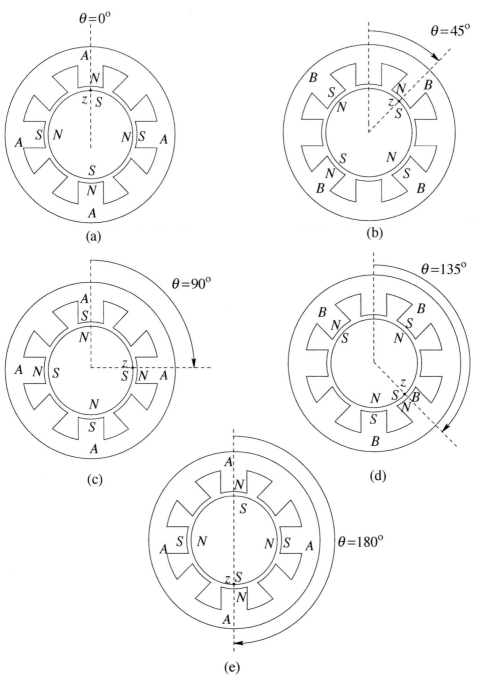

Figure 14-4 Two-phase permanent-magnet step motor; excitation sequence i_a+, i_b+, i_a-, i_b-, i_a+
(a) i_a+ ; (b) i_b+ ; (c) i_a-; (d) i_b-; (e) i_a+.

shown in Fig. 14-4b. To rotate further, the current in phase-b is reduced to zero and a negative current i_a^- causes the rotor to be in the position shown in Fig. 14-4c. Figure 14-4 illustrates that an excitation sequence $(i_a^+ \rightarrow i_b^+, \ i_b^+ \rightarrow i_a^-, \ i_a^- \rightarrow i_b^-, \ i_b^- \rightarrow i_a^+)$ produces a clockwise rotation. Each change in excitation causes rotation by one-half of the rotor-pole-pitch, which yields a step-angle of 45^0 in this example.

14-3-3 Hybrid Stepper-Motors

Hybrid stepper-motors utilize the principles of both the variable-reluctance and the permanent-magnet stepper-motors. An axial cross-section is shown in Fig. 14-5. The rotor consists of permanent magnets with a north and a south pole at the two opposite ends. In addition, each side of the rotor is fitted with an end cap with N_r teeth; N_r is equal to 10 in this figure. The flux produced by the permanent magnets is shown in Fig. 14-5. All of the end-cap teeth on the left act like south poles, while all of the end-cap teeth on the right act like north poles.

The left and the right cross-sections, perpendicular to the shaft, along $L-L'$ and $R-R'$, are shown in Fig. 14-6. The two rotor end caps are intentionally displaced with respect to each other by one-half of the rotor-tooth-pitch. The

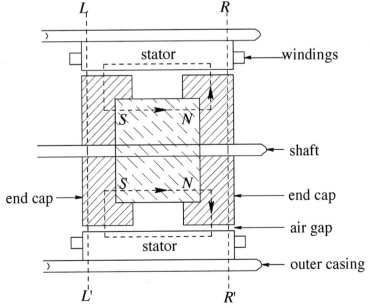

Figure 14-5 Axial view of a hybrid stepper motor.

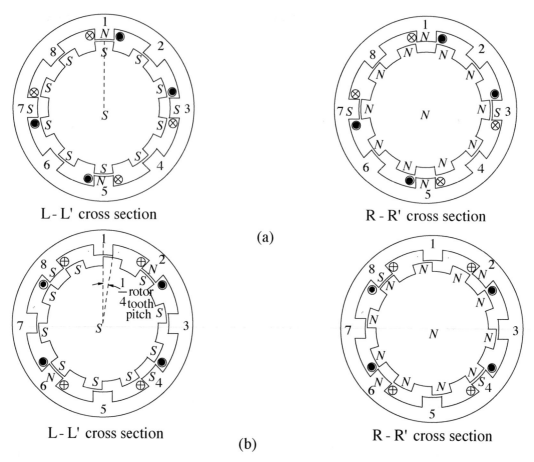

L - L' cross section   R - R' cross section

(a)

L - L' cross section   R - R' cross section

(b)

Figure 14-6 Hybrid step-motor excitation (a) phase-a is excited with i_a+; (b) phase-b is excited with i_b+ .

stator in this figure consists of 8 poles in which the slots run parallel to the shaft axis.

The stator consists of two phases; each phase winding is placed on 4 alternate poles, as shown in Fig. 14-6.

Excitation of phase-a by a positive current i_a^+ results in north and south poles, as shown in both cross-sections in Fig. 14-6a. In the no-load equilibrium position shown in Fig. 14-6a, on both sides, the opposite stator and rotor poles align while the similar poles are as far apart as possible. For a clockwise rotation, the current in phase-a is brought to zero and phase-b is excited by a positive current i_b^+, as shown in Fig. 14-6b. Again, on both sides, the opposite stator and rotor poles align while the similar poles are as far apart as possible. This change of excitation ($i_a^+ \rightarrow i_b^+$) results in clockwise rotation by one-fourth of the rotor-tooth-pitch. Therefore, in a two-phase motor,

$$\text{step-angle} = \frac{360^0 / N_r}{4} \tag{14-15}$$

which, in this example with $N_r = 10$, equals 9^0.

14-3-4 Equivalent-Circuit Representation of a Stepper-Motor

Similar to other machines discussed previously, stepper-motors can be represented by an equivalent circuit on a per-phase basis. Such an equivalent circuit for phase-a is shown in Fig. 14-7 and consists of a back-emf, a winding resistance R_s, and a winding inductance L_s. The magnitude of the induced emf depends on the speed of rotation, and the polarity of the induced emf is such that it absorbs power in the motoring mode.

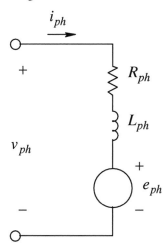

Figure 14-7 Per-phase equivalent circuit of a step-motor.

14-3-5 Half-Stepping and Micro-Stepping

It is possible to get smaller angular movement for each transition in the stator currents. For example, consider the variable-reluctance motor for which the no-load equilibrium positions with i_a and i_b were shown in Figs. 14-3a and 14-3b, respectively. Exciting phases *a* and *b* simultaneously causes the rotor to be in the position shown in Fig. 14-8, which is one-half of a step-angle away from the position in Fig. 14-3a with i_a. Therefore, if "half-stepping" in the clockwise direction is required in the motor of Fig. 14-3, the excitation sequence will be as follows:

$$i_a \rightarrow (i_a, i_b) \rightarrow i_b \rightarrow (i_b, i_c) \rightarrow i_c \rightarrow (i_c, i_a) \rightarrow i_a \qquad (14\text{-}16)$$

By precisely controlling the phase currents, it is possible to achieve micro-step angles. For example, there are hybrid-stepper motors in which a step-angle can be divided into 125 micro-steps. This results in 25,000 micro-steps/revolution in a two-phase hybrid motor with a step-angle of 1.8°.

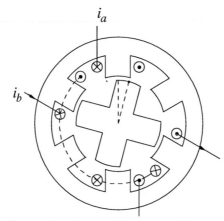

Figure 14-8 Half-stepping by exciting two phases.

14-3-6 Power-Processing Units for Stepper-Motors

In variable-reluctance drives, the phase currents need not reverse direction. A unidirectional-current converter for such motors is shown in Fig. 14-9a. Turning both switches on simultaneously causes the phase current to build up quickly, as shown in Fig. 14-9b. Once the current builds up to the desired level, it is maintained at that level by pulse-width-modulating one of the switches (for example T_1) while keeping the other switch on. By turning both switches off, the current is forced to flow into the dc-side source through the two diodes, thus decaying quickly.

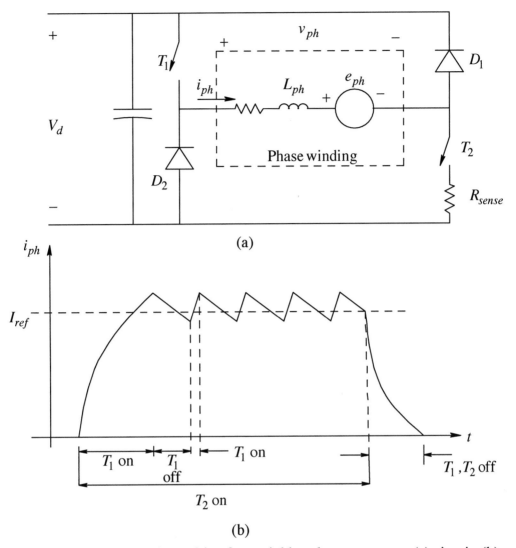

Figure 14-9 Unipolar voltage drive for variable-reluctance motor (a) circuit; (b) current waveform.

Bi-directional currents are needed in permanent-magnet and hybrid stepper-motors. Supplying these currents requires a converter such as that shown in Fig. 14-10. This converter is very similar to those used in dc-motor drives and was discussed in Chapter 7.

14-4 SWITCHED-RELUCTANCE MOTOR DRIVES

Switched-reluctance motors are essentially variable-reluctance stepper-motors that are operated in a closed-loop manner with controlled currents. In these

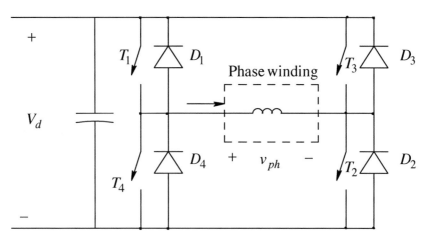

Figure 14-10 Bipolar voltage drive.

drives, the appropriate phases are energized or de-energized based on the rotor position. These drives can potentially compete with other servo and adjustable-speed drives in a variety of applications.

Consider the cross-section shown in Fig. 14-11. This motor is similar to the variable-reluctance stepper motor of Fig. 14-3. At $t = 0$, the rotor is at an angle of $\theta = -\pi/6$ and the inductance of the phase-a winding is small due to a large air gap in the path of the flux lines. In order to move the rotor in Fig. 14-11a counter-clockwise, the current i_a is built up quickly while the inductance is still small. As the rotor moves counter-clockwise, the phase-a inductance increases due to the stator and the rotor poles moving towards alignment, as shown in Fig. 14-11b at $\theta = 0$. This increases the flux-linkage, causing the magnetic structure to go into a significant degree of saturation. Once at $\theta = 0$, phase-a is de-energized. The $\lambda - i$ trajectories for $\theta = -\pi/6$ and $\theta = 0$ are shown in Fig. 14-11c. There are, of course, trajectories at the intermediate values of θ. The shaded area between the two trajectories in Fig. 14-11c represents the energy that is converted into mechanical work. A sequence of excitations similar to that in the variable-reluctance drive of Fig. 14-3 follows.

In order for switched-reluctance motors to be able to compete with other drives, they must be designed to go into magnetic saturation. A unidirectional-current converter such as that in Fig. 14-9a can be used to power these motors.

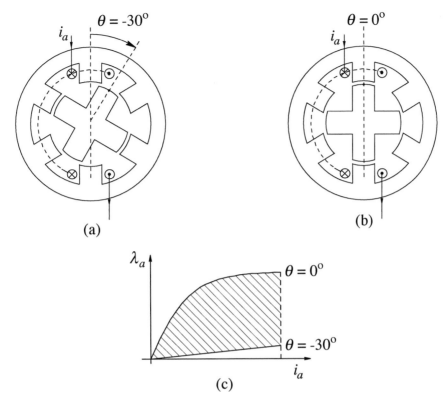

Figure 14-11 (a) rotor at $\theta = -30°$; (b) rotor at $\theta = 0°$; (c) $\lambda - i$ trajectory.

There are many applications in which switched-reluctance drives may find their rightful place - from washing machines to automobiles to airplanes. Some of the strengths of switched-reluctance drives are their rugged and inexpensive rotor construction and their simple and reliable power electronics converter. On the negative side, these machines, due to their double saliency, produce large amounts of noise and vibrations.

SUMMARY/REVIEW QUESTIONS

1. What are the three broad categories of reluctance drives?
2. How is the principle on which reluctance drives operate different than that seen earlier with other drives?
3. Write down the reluctance torque expression. What does the direction of torque depend on?
4. Describe the operating principle of a variable-reluctance stepper-motor.
5. Describe the operating principle of a permanent-magnet stepper-motor.

6. Describe the operating principle of a hybrid stepper-motor.
7. What is the equivalent-circuit representation of a stepper-motor?
8. How is half-stepping and micro-stepping achieved in stepper-motors?
9. What is the nature of power-processing units in stepper-motor drives?
10. Describe the operating principles of switched-reluctance drives.
11. What are the application areas of switched-reluctance drives?

REFERENCES

1. Takashi Kenjo, *Stepping Motors and Their Microprocessor Control,* Oxford Science Publications, Claredon Press, Oxford, 1985.
2. P.P. Acarnley, *Stepping Motors: A guide to Modern Theory and Practice,* IEE Control Engineering Series 19, Revised 2nd Ed. 1984.
3. G. R. Slemon, *Electrical Machines for Drives*, Chapter 2, *Power Electronics and Variable Frequency Drives*, edited by B. K. Bose, IEEE Press, 1997.

PROBLEMS

14-1 Determine the phase excitation sequence, and draw the rotor positions, in a variable-reluctance step drive for a counter-clockwise rotation.

14-2 Repeat Problem 14-1 for a permanent-magnet stepper-motor drive.

14-3 Repeat Problem 14-1 for a hybrid stepper-motor drive.

14-4 Describe the half-step operation in a permanent-magnet stepper-motor drive.

14-5 Describe the half-step operation in a hybrid stepper-motor drive.

CHAPTER 15

ENERGY EFFICIENCY OF ELECTRIC DRIVES AND INVERTER-MOTOR INTERACTIONS

15-1 INTRODUCTION

Electric drives have enormous potential for improving energy efficiency in motor-driven systems. A market assessment of industrial electric-motor systems in the United States, available in January, 1999, contains some startling, call-for-action statistics:

- Industrial motor systems consume 25 percent of the nation's electricity, making them the largest single electrical end-use.
- Potential yearly energy savings using mature, proven and cost-effective technologies could equal the annual electricity use in the entire state of New York.

To achieve these energy savings would require a variety of means, but chief among them are the replacement of standard-efficiency motors by premium-efficiency motors and the use of electric drives to improve system efficiencies.

The objective of this chapter is to briefly discuss the energy efficiencies of electric motors and electric drives over a range of loads and speeds. Since induction machines are the "workhorses" of industry, the discussion is limited to induction motors and induction-motor drives. The economics of investing in energy-efficient means are discussed. The interactions between induction motors and PWM inverters are briefly described as well.

The bulk of the material in this chapter is based on References [1] and [2]. A survey of the recent status and future trends is provided in [3]. Readers are urged to look at Reference [4], an excellent source of information on the potential of achieving higher energy efficiencies using permanent-magnet machines.

15-2 THE DEFINITION OF ENERGY EFFICIENCY IN ELECTRIC DRIVES

As we briefly discussed in Chapter 6, the efficiency of an electric drive η_{drive} at an operating condition is the product of the corresponding motor efficiency η_{motor} and the PPU efficiency η_{PPU} :

$$\eta_{drive} = \eta_{motor} \times \eta_{PPU} \tag{15-1}$$

In Eq. 15-1, note that η_{motor} is the efficiency of a PPU-supplied motor. The output voltages of a power-processing unit consist of switching frequency harmonics, which usually lower the motor efficiency by one to two percentage points compared to the efficiency of the same motor when supplied by a purely sinusoidal source.

In the following section, we will look at the loss mechanisms and the energy efficiencies of induction motors and power-processing units.

15-3 THE ENERGY EFFICIENCY OF INDUCTION MOTORS WITH SINUSOIDAL EXCITATION

Initially, we will look at various loss mechanisms and energy efficiencies of motors with sinusoidal excitation, while later we will discuss the effects of switching-frequency harmonics of the PPU on motor losses.

15-3-1 Motor Losses

Motor power losses can be divided into four categories: core losses, winding losses, friction and windage losses, and stray-load losses. We will now briefly examine each of these.

15-3-1-1 Magnetic Core Losses

Magnetic losses are caused by hysteresis and eddy-currents in the magnetic core of the stator and the rotor. The losses depend on the frequency and the peak flux-density. Eddy-current losses can be reduced by thinner gauge steel laminations, between 0.014 and 0.025 inches thick, but at the expense of a higher assembly cost. Hyteresis losses cannot be reduced by thinner laminations but can be reduced by utilizing materials such as silicon steels with improved core-loss characteristics. For sinusodal excitation at the rated slip, the loss in the rotor core is very small because the frequency of the flux variation in the rotor core is at the slip frequency and is very small. The magnetic core losses typically comprise 20 to 25 percent of the total motor losses at the rated voltage and frequency.

15-3-1-2 Winding Power Losses

These losses occur due to the ohmic (i^2R) heating of the stator winding and the rotor bars. The stator-winding loss is due to the sum of the magnetizing current and the torque-component of the stator current. This loss can be reduced by using larger cross-section conductors in the stator winding and by reducing the magnetizing current component. In the rotor, reducing the bar resistances causes the motor to run closer to the synchronous speed, thus reducing the losses in the rotor bars. At full-load, the losses in the rotor bars are comparable to those in the stator winding, but drop to almost zero at no-load (although they do not do so in the presence of the switching-frequency harmonics of the PPU). At full-load, the combined stator and the rotor (i^2R) losses typically comprise 55 to 60 percent of the total motor losses.

15-3-1-3   Friction and Windage Losses

Losses in the bearings are caused by friction; windage losses are caused by the cooling fan and the rotor assembly. These losses are relatively fixed and can be reduced only indirectly by reducing the ventilation needed, which in turn is done by lowering other losses. These losses typically contribute 5 to 10 percent of the total motor losses.

15-3-1-4   Stray-Load Losses

This is a catch-all category for the losses which cannot be accounted for in any of the other three categories. These losses are load-dependent and vary as the square of the output torque. They typically contribute 10 to 15 percent of the total motor losses.

15-3-2   Dependence of Motor Losses and Efficiency on the Motor Load (With the Speed Essentially Constant)

A typical loss versus load curve is shown in Fig. 15-1a. It shows that the core loss and the friction and windage losses are essentially independent of the load, whereas the stray-load losses and the winding losses vary as the square of the load.

A typical efficiency versus load plot is shown in Fig. 15-1b. At a nominal voltage and frequency, most motors reach their maximum efficiency near the rated load. The efficiency remains nearly constant down to a 50 percent load and then falls rapidly down to zero below that level.

15-3-3   Dependence of Motor Losses and Efficiency on Motor Speed (With the Torque Essentially Constant)

If an induction machine is operated from a variable-frequency sinusoidal source, the motor losses for constant-torque operation (assuming a constant air-gap flux) will vary as follows:

- Core losses are reduced at lower speeds because of the reduced frequencies.

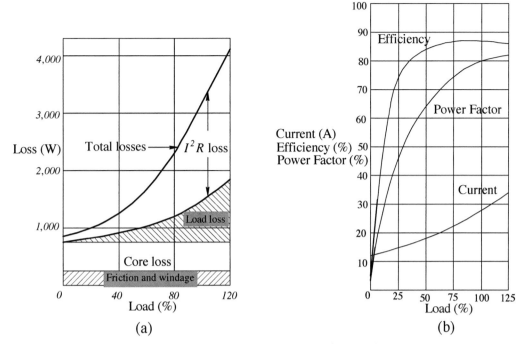

Figure 15-1 (a) Typical loss vs. load characteristics for Design B, 50 hp 4 pole 3-phase induction motor; (b) typical performance curves for Design B 10 Hp, 4 pole three-phase induction motor.

- Stator-winding losses remain approximately unchanged because constant torque requires a constant current.
- Rotor-bar losses remain approximately unchanged because constant torque requires constant bar currents at a constant slip speed.
- Friction and windage losses are reduced at lower speeds.
- Stray-load losses are reduced at lower speeds.

We can see that the total losses drop as the frequency is reduced. Depending on whether the losses drop faster or slower than the output, the efficiency of the machine can increase or decrease with speed. The published literature in 40-400 horsepower machines indicates that for a constant torque, their efficiency is nearly constant down to 20 percent speed and exhibits a rapid drop toward zero below this speed level. With pump-loads requiring torque proportional to speed squared, the motor efficiency drops gradually to about 50 percent of speed and drops rapidly below that speed.

Premium-Efficiency Motors

With the advent of the Energy Policy Act of 1992, several manufactures have developed premium-efficiency motors. In these motors, the motor losses are reduced to typically 50 percent of those in the standard NEMA design B motors. This reduction in losses is accomplished by using thinner, higher quality laminations, reducing the flux-density levels by increasing the core cross-section, using larger conductors in the stator windings and in the rotor cage, and carefully choosing the air gap dimensions and lamination design to reduce stray-load losses. Because of the reduced value of the rotor resistance, these high-efficiency machines have lower full-load slip speeds. Fig. 15-2 shows a comparison between the nominal efficiencies of standard-efficiency motors and premium-efficiency motors as a function of their power ratings. The typical increase in efficiency is 2 percentage points.

Typically, the power factor of operation associated with premium-efficiency motors is similar to that of motors of standard design; the power factor of premium-efficiency motors is slightly higher than that of standard motors at smaller power ratings and slightly lower at larger power ratings.

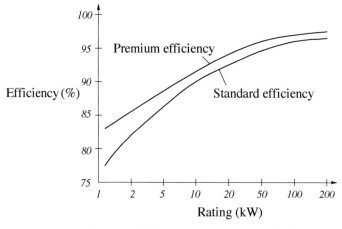

Figure 15-2 Comparison of efficiencies.

15-4   THE EFFECTS OF SWITCHING-FREQUENCY HARMONICS ON MOTOR LOSSES

All motor-loss components, except friction and windage, are increased as a result of the inverter-produced harmonics associated with the power-processing unit. For typical inverter waveforms, the total increase in losses is in the range of 10 to 20 percent and results in a decrease in energy efficiency of 1 to 2 percentage points at full load. Due to harmonics, increases in the various loss components are as follows:

- The core losses are slightly increased because of the slightly higher peak flux density caused by the superimposed harmonics. This increase is often negligibly small compared to other losses arising due to inverter harmonics.
- The stator-winding loss is increased due to the sum of the $(i^2 R)$ losses associated with the additional harmonic currents. At the harmonic frequencies, the stator resistance may be larger in bigger machines due to the skin effect. The increase in stator-winding loss is usually significant but it is not the largest harmonic loss.
- The rotor-cage loss is increased due to the sum of $(i^2 R)$ losses associated with the additional harmonic currents. In large machines at harmonic frequencies, the deep-bar effect (similar to the skin effect) can greatly increase the rotor resistance and cause large rotor $(i^2 R)$ losses. These losses are often the largest loss attributable to harmonics.
- The stray-load losses are significantly increased by the presence of harmonic currents. These losses are the least understood, requiring considerable research activity.

In all cases, the harmonic losses are nearly independent of the load, because the harmonic slip is essentially unaffected by slight speed changes (in contrast to the fundamental slip).

In pulse-width-modulated inverters, the harmonic components of the output voltage depend on the modulation strategy. Further, the harmonic currents are limited by the machine-leakage inductances. Therefore, inverters with improved pulse-width-modulation strategies and machines with higher leakage inductances help to reduce these harmonic losses.

15-4-1 Motor De-Rating Due to Inverter Harmonic Losses

The increase in losses caused by inverter harmonics requires some de-rating of the motor in order to avoid overheating. It is often recommended that this "harmonic de-rating" be 10 percent of name-plate rating. Recently, many manufacturers have introduced inverter-grade motors which need not be de-rated.

15-5 THE ENERGY EFFICIENCIES OF POWER-PROCESSING UNITS

The block diagram of a typical power-processing unit is shown in Fig. 15-3. It consists of a diode-rectifier bridge to rectify line-frequency ac into dc and a switch-mode inverter to synthesize input dc into three-phase ac of adjustable magnitude and frequency. Approximately 1 to 2 percent of the power is lost as conduction losses in the diode-rectifier bridge. The conduction and switching losses in the inverter total approximately 3 to 4 percent of the total power.

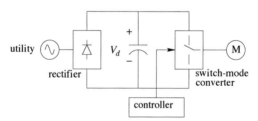

Figure 15-3 Block diagram of PPUs.

Therefore, typical power loss in the PPU is in the range of 4 to 6 percent, resulting in the full-load PPU energy efficiency η_{PPU} in the range of 94 to 96 percent.

15-6 ENERGY EFFICIENCIES OF ELECTRIC DRIVES

Very little data is available to show the trend of the efficiencies of electric drives. A recent paper, however, shows that at full speed and full torque, the drive efficiency from a variety of manufacturers varies in the range of 74 to 80 percent for a 3-hp drive and in the range 86 to 89 percent for a 20-hp drive. At half-torque and half-speed (at one-fourth power), these efficiencies drop to 53 to 72 percent for a 3-hp drive and to 82 to 88 percent for a 20-hp drive. However, it is possible to modify the drive PPU so as to keep the energy efficiency high at light loads by slightly reducing the amplitude of the fundamental-frequency voltage.

15-7 THE ECONOMICS OF ENERGY SAVINGS BY PREMIUM-EFFICIENCY ELECTRIC MOTORS AND ELECTRIC DRIVES

In constant-speed applications, energy efficiency can be improved by replacing standard-design motors with premium-efficiency motors. In systems with dampers and throttling valves, and in compressors with on/off cycling, the use of adjustable-speed drives can result in dramatic savings in energy and thus savings in the cost of electricity. These savings accrue at the expense of the higher initial investment of replacing a standard motor, either with a slightly more expensive but more efficient-motor, or with an adjustable-speed electric drive. Therefore, a user must consider the economics of initial investment - the payback period, at which the initial investment will have paid for itself, and the subsequent savings are "money-in-the-bank."

15-7-1 The Present Worth of Savings and the Payback Period

The energy savings E_{save} take place every year over the period that the system is in operation. The present worth of these energy savings depends on many factors, such as the present cost of electricity, the rate of increase of the electricity cost, and the rate of investment of the money that could have been invested elsewhere. Inflation is another factor. Based on these factors, the present worth of the savings over the lifetime of the system can be obtained and compared to the additional initial investment. For a detailed discussion of this, Reference [5] is an excellent source. However, we can get an approximate idea of the payback period of the additional initial investment, if we ignore all of the previously mentioned factors and simply divide the additional initial investment by the yearly operational savings. This is illustrated by the following example.

▲ **Example 15-1**   Calculate the payback period for investing in a premium-efficiency motor that costs $300 more than the standard motor, given the following parameters: the load demands a power of 25 kW, the efficiency of the standard motor is 89 percent, the efficiency of the premium-efficiency motor is 92 percent, the cost of electricity is 0.10 $/kWh$, and the annual operating time of the motor is 4500 hours.

Solution

(a) The power drawn by the standard motor would be

$$P_{in} = \frac{P_0}{\eta_{motor}} = \frac{25.0}{0.89} = 28.09\,kW.$$

Therefore, the annual cost of electricity would be

$$\text{Annual Electricity Cost} = 28.09 \times 4500 \times 0.1 = \$12,640.$$

(b) The power drawn by the premium-efficiency motor would be

$$P_{in} = \frac{P_0}{\eta_{motor}} = \frac{25.0}{0.92} = 27.17\,kW.$$

Therefore, the annual cost of electricity would be

$$\text{Annual Electricity Cost} = 27.17 \times 4500 \times 0.1 = \$12,226.$$

Thus, the annual savings in the operating cost = 12,640 - 12,226 = $414. Therefore, the initial investment of $300 would be paid back in

$$\frac{300}{414} \times 12 \approx 9 \text{ months}. \qquad\qquad ▲$$

An excellent source for comparing the efficiencies and the list prices of a very large number of motors, including those from most common manufacturers, is Reference [6].

15-8   THE DELETERIOUS EFFECTS OF THE PWM-INVERTER VOLTAGE WAVEFORM ON MOTOR LIFE

In supplying motors with PWM inverters, there are certain factors that users must be aware of. The additional harmonic losses due to the pulsating waveforms have already been discussed. If the motor is not specifically designed to operate with PWM inverters, it may be necessary to de-rate it (by a factor of 0.9) in order to accommodate addition harmonic losses without exceeding the motor's normal operating temperature.

The PWM-inverter output, particularly due to the ever-increasing switching speeds of IGBTs (which are good for keeping switching losses low in inverters), results in pulsating voltage waveforms with a very high dv/dt. These rapid changes in the output voltage have several deleterious effects: they stress the motor-winding insulation, they cause the flow of currents through the bearing (which can result in pitting), and they cause voltage doubling at the motor terminal due to the long cables between the inverter and the motor. One practical but limited solution is to attempt to slow down the switching of IGBTs at the expense of higher switching losses within the inverter. The other solution, which requires additional expense, is to add a small filter between the inverter and the motor.

SUMMARY/REVIEW QUESTIONS

1. What is the definition of energy efficiency of electric drives?
2. What are the various mechanisms of losses in motors, assuming a sinusoidal excitation?
3. How do the losses and the efficiency depend on motor speed, assuming a constant torque loading?
4. What are premium-efficiency motors? How much more efficient are they, compared to standard motors?
5. What are the effects of switching-frequency harmonics on the motor? How much should the motor be de-rated?
6. What is the typical range associated with the energy efficiency of power-processing units and of overall drives?

7. Discuss the economics and the payback period of using premium-efficiency motors.

8. Describe the various deleterious effects of PWM-inverter output voltage waveforms. Describe the techniques for mitigating these effects.

REFERENCES

1. N. Mohan, *Techniques for Energy Conservation in AC Motor-Driven Systems*, EPRI Final Report EM-2037, Project 1201-13, September 1981.

2. N. Mohan and J. Ramsey, *A Comparative Study of Adjustable-Speed Drives for Heat Pumps*, EPRI Final Report EM-4704, Project 2033-4, August 1986.

3. P. Thogersen and F. Blaabjerg, "Adjustable-Speed Drives in the Next Decade: The Next Steps in Industry and Academia," Proceedings of the PCIM Conference, Nuremberg, Germany, June 6-8, 2000.

4. G. R. Slemons, *Electrical Machines for Drives*, in *Power Electronics and Variable Frequency Drives*, (edited by B. K. Bose), IEEE Press, 1997.

5. J. C. Andreas, *Energy-Efficient Electric Motors: Selection and Application*, Marcel Dekker, New York, 1982.

6. MotorMaster+3.0 software, downloadable from www.motor.doe.gov.

PROBLEMS

15-1   Repeat Example 15-1 if the motor runs fully loaded for one-half of each day and is shut off for the other half.

CHAPTER 16

POWERING ELECTRIC DRIVES: POWER QUALITY ISSUES

16-1 INTRODUCTION

Electric drives, except in a few applications such as electric and electric-hybrid vehicles, get their power from the utility source, as shown by the block diagram in Fig. 16-1. Unless remedial action is taken, this power is drawn by means of highly distorted currents, which have a deleterious effect on the power quality of the utility source. On the other hand, power system disturbances in the utility source can disrupt electric drive operation. Both of these issues are examined in this chapter.

16-2 DISTORTION AND POWER FACTOR

To quantify distortion in the current drawn by electric drives, it is necessary to define certain indices. As a base case, consider the linear $R-L$ load shown in Fig. 16-2a which is supplied by a sinusoidal source in steady state. The voltage and current phasors are shown in Fig. 16-2b, where ϕ is the angle by which the current lags the voltage. Using rms values for the voltage and current magnitudes, the average power supplied by the source is

$$P = V_s I_s \cos\phi \qquad (16\text{-}1)$$

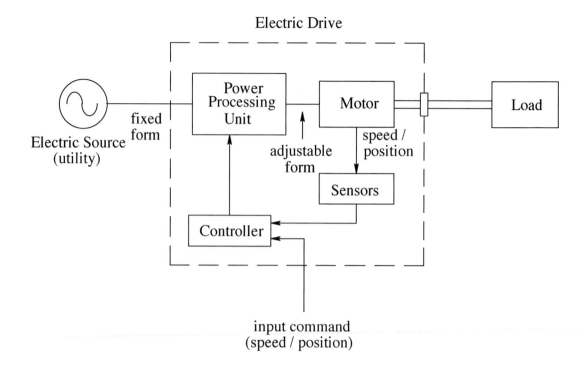

Electric Drive

Figure 16-1 Block diagram of an electric drive.

The power factor (*PF*) at which power is drawn is defined as the ratio of the real average power *P* to the product of the rms voltage and the rms current:

$$PF = \frac{P}{V_s I_s} = \cos\phi \qquad \text{(using Eq. 16-1)} \tag{16-2}$$

For a given voltage, from Eq. 16-2, the rms current drawn is

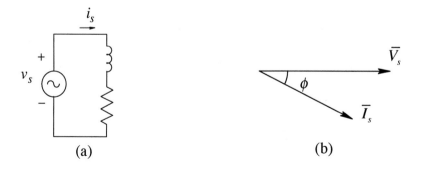

Figure 16-2 Voltage and current phasors in a simple *R-L* circuit.

$$I_s = \frac{P}{V_s(PF)} \tag{16-3}$$

This shows that the power factor PF and the current I_s are inversely proportional. The current flows through the utility distribution lines, transformers, and so on, causing losses in their resistances. This is the reason why utilities prefer unity power factor loads that draw power at the minimum value of the rms current.

16-2-1 RMS Value of Distorted Current and the Total Harmonic Distortion (*THD*)

The sinusoidal current drawn by the linear load in Fig. 16-2 has zero distortion. However, electric drives draw currents with a distorted waveform such as that shown by $i_s(t)$ in Fig. 16-3a. The utility voltage $v_s(t)$ is assumed to be sinusoidal. The following analysis is general, applying to the utility supply that is either single-phase or three-phase, in which case the analysis is on a per-phase basis.

The repetitive waveform of the current $i_s(t)$ in Fig. 16-3a can be expressed in terms of its Fourier components:

$$i_s(t) = i_{s1}(t) + \underbrace{\sum_{h=2}^{\infty} i_{sh}(t)}_{i_{distortion}(t)} \tag{16-4}$$

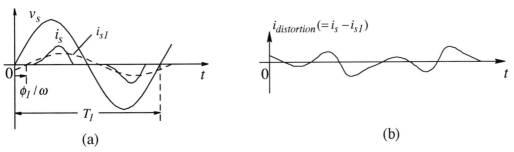

(a)   (b)

Figure 16-3 Current drawn by an electric drive (a) phase current and its fundamental component; (b) distortion component.

where the dc component is assumed to be zero and $i_{s1}(t)$ is the fundamental (line-frequency) component, shown dotted in Fig. 16-3a. Some of the harmonic frequencies in Eq. 16-4 may be absent. From Eq. 16-4, the distortion component in the current is the difference between $i_s(t)$ and its fundamental-frequency component:

$$i_{distortion}(t) = i_s(t) - i_{s1}(t) = \sum_{h=2}^{\infty} i_{sh}(t) \qquad (16\text{-}5)$$

The distortion component is plotted in Fig. 16-3b. In a waveform repeating with the line-frequency f_1 and the time-period $T_1 (= 1/f_1)$, the components in the expression of Eq. 16-5 are at the multiple h of the fundamental frequency; for example, the 3rd harmonic $(h = 3)$ is at the $180 - Hz$ frequency in a $60 - Hz$ system.

In the following derivation, we will use this basic concept: in a repetitive waveform, the integral of the products of the two harmonic components (including the fundamental) at unequal frequencies, over the repetition time-period, equals zero:

$$\int_{T_1} f_{h_1}(t) \cdot g_{h_2}(t) \cdot dt = 0 \qquad h_1 \ne h_2 \qquad (16\text{-}6)$$

To obtain the rms value of $i_s(t)$ in Fig. 16-3a, we will apply the basic definition of rms:

$$I_s = \sqrt{\frac{1}{T_1} \int_{T_1} i_s^2(t) \cdot dt} \qquad (16\text{-}7)$$

where, from Eq. 16-4,

$$i_s^2 = (i_{s1} + \sum_{h=2}^{\infty} i_{sh})^2 = i_{s1}^2 + \sum_{h=2}^{\infty} i_{sh}^2 + \text{products of cross-frequency terms} \qquad (16\text{-}8)$$

Substituting Eq. 16-8 into Eq. 16-7 and recognizing that each integral of the cross-frequency product terms equals zero (in accordance with Eq. 16-6),

$$I_s = \sqrt{\underbrace{\frac{1}{T_1}\int_{T_1} i_{s1}^2(t) \cdot dt}_{I_{s1}^2} + \underbrace{\sum_{h=2}^{\infty} \frac{1}{T_1}\int_{T_1} i_{sh}^2(t) \cdot dt}_{I_{distortion}^2}}$$ (16-9)

Therefore,

$$I_s = \sqrt{I_{s1}^2 + I_{distortion}^2}$$ (16-10)

where the rms values of the fundamental-frequency component and the distortion component are as follows:

$$I_{s1} = \sqrt{\frac{1}{T_1}\int_{T_1} i_{s1}^2(t) \cdot dt}$$ (16-11)

and

$$I_{distortion} = \sqrt{\sum_{h=2}^{\infty} \underbrace{\left(\frac{1}{T_1}\int_{T_1} i_{sh}^2(t) \cdot dt\right)}_{I_{sh}^2}} = \sqrt{\sum_{h=2}^{\infty} I_{sh}^2} \quad \text{(using Eq. 16-6)}$$ (16-12)

Eq. 16-12 shows that the rms value of the distortion component in Fig. 16-3b can be obtained from the rms values of individual harmonic components.

Based on the rms values of the fundamental and the distortion components in the current $i_s(t)$, a distortion index called the Total Harmonic Distortion (*THD*) is defined in percentage. This index can be expressed in several ways based on the previous equations:

$$\% THD = 100 \times \frac{I_{distortion}}{I_{s1}}$$

$$= 100 \times \frac{\sqrt{I_s^2 - I_{s1}^2}}{I_{s1}} \qquad (16\text{-}13)$$

$$= 100 \times \frac{\sqrt{\sum_{h=2}^{\infty} I_{sh}^2}}{I_{s1}}$$

▲ **Example 16-1** A current i_s of square waveform is shown in Fig. 16-4a. Calculate and plot its fundamental frequency component and its distortion component. What is the %*THD* associated with this waveform?

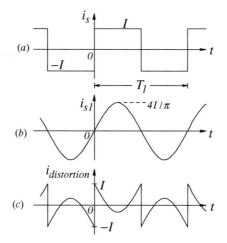

Figure 16-4 Example 16-1.

Solution   From Fourier analysis, $i_s(t)$ can be expressed as

$$i_s = \frac{4}{\pi} I (\sin \omega_1 t + \frac{1}{3}\sin 3\omega_1 t + \frac{1}{5}\sin 5\omega_1 t + \frac{1}{7}\sin 7\omega_1 t + ...).$$

The fundamental frequency component and the distortion component are plotted in Figs. 16-4b and 16-4c. From the above Fourier series, the rms value of the fundamental-frequency component is

$$I_{s1} = \frac{1}{\sqrt{2}}(\frac{4}{\pi}I) = 0.9I.$$

Since the rms value I_s of the square waveform is equal to I, the rms value of the distortion component can be calculated from Eq. 16-10 as

$$I_{distortion} = \sqrt{I_s^2 - I_{s1}^2} = \sqrt{I^2 - (0.9I)^2} = 0.436I .$$

Therefore, using the definition of THD,

$$\% THD = 100 \times \frac{I_{distortion}}{I_{s1}} = 100 \times \frac{0.436I}{0.9I} = 48.4\% . \qquad \blacktriangle$$

16-2-2 The Displacement Power Factor (DPF) and Power Factor (PF)

Next, we will consider the power factor at which the power is drawn by the load with a distorted current waveform such as that shown in Fig. 16-3a. As before, it is reasonable to assume that the utility-supplied line-frequency voltage $v_s(t)$ is sinusoidal, with an rms value of V_s and a frequency $f_1 (= \dfrac{\omega_1}{2\pi})$. Based on Eq. 16-6, which states that the product of the cross-frequency terms has a zero average, the average power P drawn by the load in Fig. 16-3a is due only to the fundamental-frequency component of the current:

$$P = \frac{1}{T_1} \int_{T_1} v_s(t) \cdot i_s(t) \cdot dt = \frac{1}{T_1} \int_{T_1} v_s(t) \cdot i_{s1}(t) \cdot dt \qquad (16\text{-}14)$$

Therefore, in contrast to Eq. 16-1 for a linear load, in a load which draws distorted current,

$$P = V_s I_{s1} \cos \phi_1 \qquad (16\text{-}15)$$

where ϕ_1 is the angle by which the fundamental-frequency current component $i_{s1}(t)$ lags behind the voltage, as shown in Fig. 16-3a. At this point, another term called the Displacement Power Factor (DPF) needs to be introduced, where

$$DPF = \cos\phi_1 \qquad (16\text{-}16)$$

Therefore, using the DPF in Eq. 16-15,

$$P = V_s I_{s1}(DPF) \qquad (16\text{-}17)$$

In the presence of distortion in the current, the meaning and therefore the definition of the power factor, at which the real average power P is drawn, remains the same as in Eq. 16-2, that is, the ratio of the real power to the product of the rms voltage and the rms current:

$$PF = \frac{P}{V_s I_s} \qquad (16\text{-}18)$$

Substituting Eq. 16-17 for P into Eq. 16-18,

$$PF = \frac{I_{s1}}{I_s}(DPF) \qquad (16\text{-}19)$$

In linear loads which draw sinusoidal currents, the current-ratio (I_{s1}/I_s) in Eq. 16-19 is unity, hence $PF = DPF$. Eq. 16-19 shows the following: the higher the distortion in the current waveform, the lower the power factor compared to the DPF. Using Eq. 16-13, the ratio (I_{s1}/I_s) in Eq. 16-19 can be expressed in terms of the Total Harmonic Distortion as

$$\frac{I_{s1}}{I_s} = \frac{1}{\sqrt{1+THD^2}} \qquad (16\text{-}20)$$

Therefore, in Eq. 16-19,

$$PF = \frac{1}{\sqrt{1+THD^2}} \cdot DPF \qquad (16\text{-}21)$$

The effect of *THD* on the power factor is shown in Fig. 16-5 by plotting, (*PF / DPF*) versus *THD*. It shows that even if the displacement power factor is unity, a total harmonic distortion of 100 percent (which is possible in drives unless corrective measures are taken) can reduce the power factor to approximately 0.7 (or $\dfrac{1}{\sqrt{2}} = 0.707$ to be exact), which is unacceptably low.

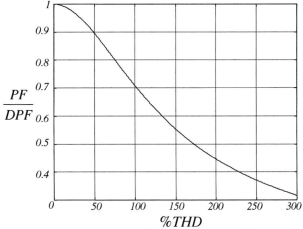

Figure 16-5 Relation between *PF/DPF* and *THD*.

16-2-3 Deleterious Effects of Harmonic Distortion and a Poor Power Factor

There are several deleterious effects of high distortion in the current waveform and the poor power factor that results as a consequence. These are as follows:

- Power loss in utility equipment such as distribution and transmission lines, transformers, and generators increases, possibly to the point of overloading them.

- Harmonic currents can overload the shunt capacitors used by utilities for voltage support and may cause resonance conditions between the capacitive reactance of these capacitors and the inductive reactance of the distribution and transmission lines.

- The utility voltage waveform will also get distorted, adversely affecting other linear loads, if a significant portion of the load supplied by the utility draws power by means of distorted currents.

16-2-3-1 HARMONIC GUIDELINES

In order to prevent degradation in power quality, recommended guidelines (in the form of the IEEE-519) have been suggested by the IEEE (Institute of Electrical and Electronics Engineers). These guidelines place the responsibilities of maintaining power quality on the consumers and the utilities as follows: 1) on the power consumers, such as the users of electric drives, to limit the distortion in the current drawn, and 2) on the utilities to ensure that the voltage supply is sinusoidal with less than a specified amount of distortion.

The limits on current distortion placed by the IEEE-519 are shown in Table 16-1, where the limits on harmonic currents, as a ratio of the fundamental component, are specified for various harmonic frequencies. Also, the limits on the *THD* are specified. These limits are selected to prevent distortion in the voltage waveform of the utility supply. Therefore, the limits on distortion in Table 16-1 depend on the "stiffness" of the utility supply, which is shown in Fig. 16-6a by a voltage source $\overline{V}_s$ in series with an internal impedance Z_s. An ideal voltage supply has zero internal impedance. In contrast, the voltage supply at the end of a long distribution line, for example, will have a large internal impedance.

Table 16-1 Harmonic current distortion (I_h/I_1)

I_{SC}/I_1	Odd Harmonic Order h (in %)					Total Harmonic Distortion(%)
	$h < 11$	$11 \le h < 17$	$17 \le h < 23$	$23 \le h < 35$	$35 \le h$	
< 20	4.0	2.0	1.5	0.6	0.3	5.0
$20 - 50$	7.0	3.5	2.5	1.0	0.5	8.0
$50 - 100$	10.0	4.5	4.0	1.5	0.7	12.0
$100 - 1000$	12.0	5.5	5.0	2.0	1.0	15.0
> 1000	15.0	7.0	6.0	2.5	1.4	20.0

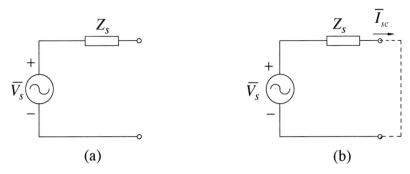

Figure 16-6 (a) Utility supply; (b) short circuit current.

To define the "stiffness" of the supply, the short-circuit current I_{sc} is calculated by hypothetically placing a short-circuit at the supply terminals, as shown in Fig. 16-6b. The stiffness of the supply must be calculated in relation to the load current. Therefore, the stiffness is defined by a ratio called the Short-Circuit-Ratio *(SCR)*:

$$\text{Short-Circuit-Ratio } SCR = \frac{I_{sc}}{I_{s1}} \qquad (16\text{-}22)$$

where I_{s1} is the fundamental-frequency component of the load current. Table 16-1 shows that a smaller short-circuit ratio corresponds to lower limits on the allowed distortion in the current drawn. For the short-circuit-ratio of less than 20, the total harmonic distortion in the current must be less than 5 percent. A drive that meets this limit would also meet the limits of more stiff supplies.

It should be noted that the IEEE-519 does not propose harmonic guidelines for individual pieces of equipment but rather for the aggregate of loads (such as in an industrial plant) seen from the service entrance, which is also the point-of-common-coupling (PCC) with other customers. However, the IEEE-519 is frequently interpreted as the harmonic guidelines for specifying individual pieces of equipment such as motor drives. There are other harmonic standards, such as the IEC-1000, which apply to individual pieces of equipment.

16-3   CLASSIFYING THE "FRONT-END" OF ELECTRIC DRIVES

Interaction between the utility supply and electric drives depends on the "front-ends" (within the power-processing units), which convert line-frequency ac into dc. These front-ends can be broadly classified as follows:

- Diode-bridge rectifiers (shown in Fig. 16-7a) in which power flows only in one direction.

- Switch-mode converters (shown in Fig. 16-7b) in which the power flow can reverse and the line currents are sinusoidal at the unity power factor.

- Thyristor converters (shown in Fig. 16-7c for dc drives) in which the power flow can be made bi-directional.

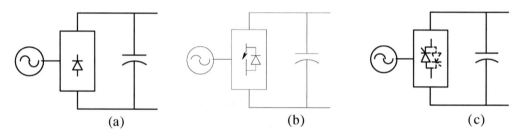

(a)   (b)   (c)

Figure 16-7 Front-ends of electric drives.

All of these front-ends can be designed to interface with single-phase or three-phase utility systems. For a detailed description of all of the above, please see Reference [1]. In the following discussion, a brief description of basic operating principles is supplemented by analysis of results obtained through computer simulations.

16-4   DIODE-RECTIFIER BRIDGE "FRONT-ENDS"

Most general-purpose drives use diode-bridge rectifiers, like the one shown in Fig. 16-7a, even though they draw currents with highly distorted waveforms and the power through them can flow only in one direction. Diode rectifiers rectify line-frequency ac into dc across the dc-bus capacitor, without any control over the dc-bus voltage. For analyzing the interaction between the utility and the drive, the switch-mode converter and the motor load can be represented by an equivalent resistance R_{eq} across the dc-bus capacitor, as shown in Fig. 16-8. In our theoretical discussion, it is adequate to assume the diodes to be ideal.

In the following subsections, we will consider single-phase as well as three-phase diode rectifiers operating in steady state, where waveforms repeat from one line-frequency cycle $T_1(=1/f_1)$ to the next.

16-4-1 The Single-Phase Diode-Rectifier Bridge

At power levels below a few kW, for example in residential applications, drives are supplied by a single-phase utility source. A commonly-used full-bridge rectifier circuit is shown in Fig. 16-8, in which L_s is the sum of the inductance internal to the utility supply and an external inductance, which may be intentionally added in series. Losses on the ac side can be represented by the series resistance R_s.

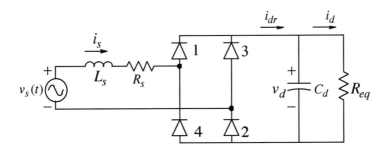

Figure 16-8 Full bridge diode rectifier.

As shown in Fig. 16-9, at the beginning of the positive half-cycle of the input voltage v_s, the capacitor is already charged to a dc voltage v_d. So long as v_d exceeds the input voltage magnitude, all diodes get reverse biased and the input current is zero. Power to the equivalent resistance R_{eq} is supplied by the energy stored in the capacitor up to time t_1. Beyond t_1, the input current $i_s(=i_{dr})$ builds up, flowing through the diodes D_1 and D_2. Beyond t_2, the input voltage becomes smaller than the capacitor voltage and the input current begins to decline, falling to zero at t_3. Beyond t_3, until one-half cycle later than t_1, the

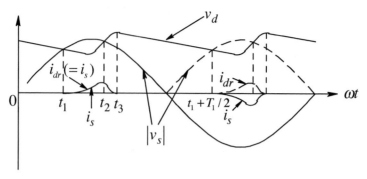

Figure 16-9 Current and voltage waveforms for the full bridge diode rectifier.

input current remains zero and the power to R_{eq} is supplied by the energy stored in the capacitor.

At $(t_1 + \dfrac{T_1}{2})$ during the negative half-cycle of the input voltage, the input current flows through the diodes D_3 and D_4. The rectifier dc-side current i_{dr} continues to flow in the same direction as during the positive half-cycle; however, the input current $i_s = -i_{dr}$, as shown in Fig. 16-9.

The fact that i_{dr} flows in the same direction during both the positive and the negative half-cycles represents the rectification process. In Fig. 16-8 in steady state, all waveforms repeat from one cycle to the next. Therefore, the average value of the capacitor current over a line-frequency cycle must be zero so that the dc-bus voltage is in steady state. As a consequence, the average current through the equivalent load-resistance R_{eq} equals the average of the rectifier dc-side current; that is, $I_d = I_{dr}$.

16-4-1-1 The Effects of the L_s and the C_d on the Waveforms and the *THD*

As Fig. 16-9 shows, power is drawn from the utility supply by means of a pulse of current every half-cycle. The larger the "base" of this pulse during which the current flows, the lower its peak value and the lower the total harmonic distortion. This pulse-widening can be accomplished by increasing the ac-side inductance L_s, as shown in Fig. 16-10a, by carrying out a parametric analysis using a

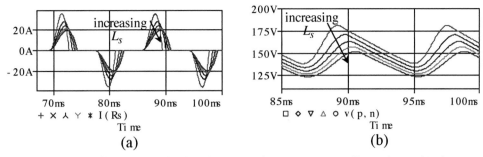

Figure 16-10 Effect of variation in L_S (a) input current distortion; (b) the output voltage.

computer program such as PSpice™ (see Reference [2]). For the same power transfer, waveforms are shown for five values of L_s. Increasing L_s decreases the *THD*; however, it also decreases the average dc-output voltage, as shown in Fig. 16-10b.

Another parameter under the designer's control is the value of the dc-bus capacitor C_d. At its minimum, it should be able to carry the ripple current (in i_{dr} and in the current drawn by the switch-mode converters discussed in Chapter 4) and keep the peak-to-peak ripple in the dc-bus voltage to some acceptable value, for example less than 5 percent of the dc-bus average value. Assuming that these constraints are met, the effect of C_d is shown by means of parametric analysis in Figs. 16-11a and 16-11b, which show that the lower the value of C_d, the lower the *THD* and the higher the ripple in the dc-bus voltage, respectively.

In practice, it is almost impossible to meet the harmonic limits specified by the IEEE-519 by using the above techniques. Rather, the remedial techniques that will be described in section 16-5 are needed to meet the harmonic specifications.

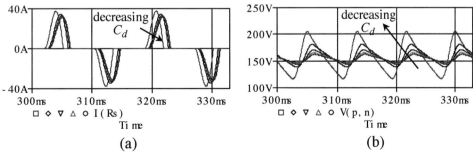

Figure 16-11 Variation in C_d (a) input current; (b) output voltage.

16-4-2 Three-Phase Diode-Rectifier Bridge

It is preferable to use a three-phase utility source, except at a fractional kilowatt, if such a supply is available. A commonly-used full-bridge rectifier circuit is shown in Fig. 16-12a.

To understand the circuit operation, the rectifier circuit can be drawn as in Fig. 16-12b. The circuit consists of a top group and a bottom group of diodes. Initially, the effects of L_s and C_d can be ignored. At least one diode from each group must conduct for the input current to flow. In the top group, all diodes have their cathodes connected together. Therefore, the diode connected to the most positive voltage will conduct; the other two will be reverse biased. In the bottom group, all diodes have their anodes connected together. Therefore, the diode connected to the most negative voltage will conduct; the other two will be reverse biased.

Ignoring the effects of L_s and C_d and assuming that a resistance is connected

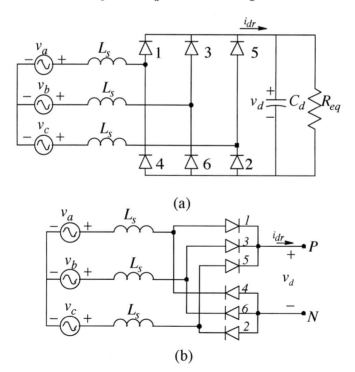

Figure 16-12 (a) Three-phase diode bridge rectifier; (b) circuit redrawn.

across the dc-side between points P and N, the waveforms can be represented as shown in Fig. 16-13. In Fig. 16-13a, the waveforms (identified by the dark portions of the curves) show that each diode, based on the principle described above, conducts for 120^0. The diodes are numbered so that they begin conducting sequentially: 1, 2, 3, and so on.

The waveforms for the voltages v_P and v_N, with respect to the source-neutral, consist of 120^0-segments of the phase voltages, as shown in Fig. 16-13a. The waveform of the dc-side voltage $v_d(=v_P-v_N)$ is shown in Fig. 16-13b. It consists of 60^0-segments of the line-line voltages supplied by the utility. Under the assumption that a resistance R_{eq} is connected across the dc side between points P and N, the dc-side current i_{dr} will have a waveform identical to that of v_d, shown in Fig. 16-13b. However, for ease of drawing, we will assume that a large filter inductor is present on the dc side (between the rectifier and R_{eq}) so that i_{dr} is a pure dc current. With this assumption, the line currents on the ac-side are as shown in Fig. 16-13c. For example, the phase-a current flows for 120^0 during each half-cycle; it flows through diode D_1 during the positive half-cycle and through diode D_4 during the negative half-cycle.

The average value of the dc-side voltage can be obtained by considering only a 60^0-segment in the 6-pulse (per line-frequency cycle) waveform shown in Fig.

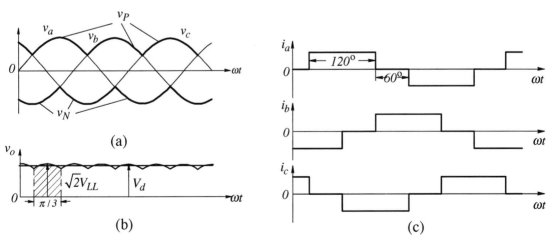

Figure 16-13 Voltage and current waveforms in a three phase diode bridge rectifier (without C_d).

16-13b. Let us consider the instant of the peak in the 60^0-segment to be the time-origin, with the peak equal to $\sqrt{2}$ times the rms value V_{LL} of the line-line voltage. The average value V_d can be obtained by calculating the integral from $\omega t = -\pi/6$ to $\omega t = \pi/6$ (the area shown by the hatched area in Fig. 16-13b) and then dividing by the interval $\pi/3$:

$$V_d = \frac{1}{\pi/3} \int_{-\pi/6}^{\pi/6} \sqrt{2} V_{LL} \cos \omega t \cdot d(\omega t) = \frac{3\sqrt{2}}{\pi} V_{LL} = 1.35 V_{LL} \qquad (16\text{-}23)$$

This average value is plotted as a straight line in Fig. 16-13b.

In the three-phase rectifier of Fig. 16-12a with the dc-bus capacitor filter, the input current waveforms obtained by computer simulations are shown in Fig. 16-14. Fig. 16-14a shows that the input current waveform within each half-cycle consists of two distinct pulses when L_s is small. For example, in the i_a waveform during the positive half-cycle, the first pulse corresponds to the flow of dc-side current through the diode pair (D_1, D_6) and then through the diode pair (D_1, D_2). At larger values of L_s, within each half-cycle, the input current between the two pulses does not go to zero, as shown in Fig. 16-14b.

The effects of L_s and C_d on the waveforms can be determined by parametric analysis, similar to the case of single-phase rectifiers. The *THDs* in the current

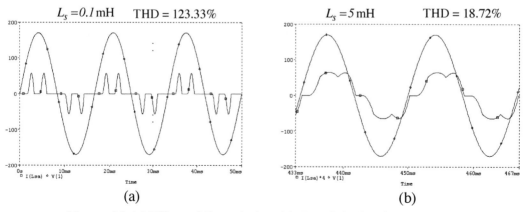

Figure 16-14 Effect of L_s variation (a) $L_s = 0.1\,\text{mH}$; (b) $L_s = 5$ mH.

waveforms of Fig. 16-14 are indicated. The ac-side inductance L_s is required to provide a line-frequency reactance $X_{L_s}(=2\pi f_1 L_s)$ that is greater than 2 percent of the base impedance Z_{base}, which is defined as follows:

$$\text{Base Impedance } Z_{base} = 3\frac{V_s^2}{P_{drive}} \qquad (16\text{-}24)$$

where P_{drive} is the three-phase power rating of the drive and V_s is the rms value of the phase voltage. Therefore, the minimum ac-side inductance should be such that

$$X_{L_s} \geq (0.02 \times Z_{base}) \qquad (16\text{-}25)$$

16-4-3 Comparison of Single-Phase and Three-Phase Rectifiers

Examination of single-phase and three-phase rectifier waveforms, shown in Fig. 16-9 and Fig. 16-14 respectively, shows the differences in their characteristics. Three-phase rectification is a six-pulse rectification process, whereas single-phase rectification is a two-pulse process. Therefore, three-phase rectifiers are superior in terms of minimizing distortion in line currents and ripple across the dc-bus voltage. Consequently, as stated earlier, three-phase rectifiers should be used if a three-phase supply is available. However, three-phase rectifiers, just like single-phase rectifiers, are also unable to meet the harmonic limits specified within the IEEE-519 unless remedial actions such as those described in section 16-5 are taken.

16-5   POWER-FACTOR-CORRECTED (PFC) INTERFACE

Technical solutions to the problem of distortion in input current have been known for a long time. However, only recently has concern about the deleterious effects of harmonics led to the formulation of guidelines and standards, which in turn has focused attention on ways of limiting current distortion.

In the following section, power-factor-corrected (PFC) interface, as they are often called, are briefly examined for single-phase and three-phase rectification. It is assumed that the power needs to flow only in one direction - thus the interface with bi-directional power flow capability are too expensive (front-ends with bi-directional power flow capability are discussed in section 16-6).

It should be noted that another way to meet harmonic guidelines is to use active filters, which synthesize out-of-phase harmonic currents. These currents are injected into the utility system, thus "neutralizing" the drive-produced harmonic currents. So far, there are very few commercial installations of active filters, but these filters represent an economically viable way of mitigating harmonics produced by a group of drives and other nonlinear loads.

16-5-1 SINGLE-PHASE *PFC*s

The operating principle of a commonly-used single-phase *PFC* is shown in Fig. 16-15a where, between the utility supply and the dc-bus capacitor, a step-up (boost) dc-dc converter is introduced. This boost converter consists of a semiconductor switch such an IGBT, a diode, and a small inductor L_d. By pulse-width-modulating the on and off intervals of the switch at a constant switching frequency, the current i_L through the inductor L_d is shaped to be of the full-

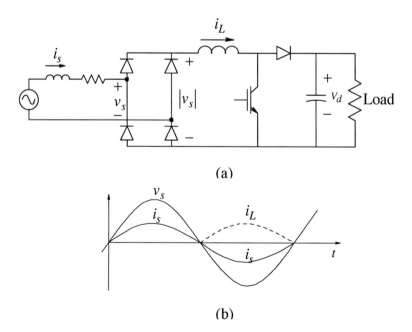

Figure 16-15 Single phase power factor correction (a) circuit; (b) waveforms.

wave-rectified waveform, similar to $\left|v_s(t)\right|$, as shown in Fig. 16-15b. Removing the high switching-frequency ripple with a small filter, the input current i_s is sinusoidal and in phase with the supply voltage, as shown in Fig. 16-15b. Because of the boost converter, it is essential that the dc-bus voltage be greater than the peak of the supply voltage:

$$V_d > \hat{V}_s \qquad (16\text{-}26)$$

A simple feedback circuit controls the input current to be sinusoidal with an amplitude such that the dc-bus voltage is regulated to be of a desired value, so long as this value is greater than $\hat{V}_s$. A detailed description of this *PFC* can be found in Reference [1]. The process of designing this *PFC* feedback control is described in Reference [3].

16-5-2 THREE-PHASE *PFC*s

Just like single-phase *PFC*s, where the topology of Fig. 16-15a dominates, three-phase *PFC*s in drives can benefit from the three-switch topology shown in Fig. 16-16, which is described in Reference [4]. This is a boost topology; hence

$$V_d > \hat{V}_{LL} \qquad (16\text{-}27)$$

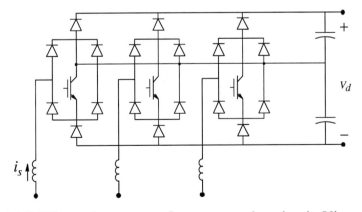

Figure 16-16 Three phase power factor correction circuit: Vienna Rectifier.

Means to Avoid Transient Inrush Currents at Starting

In drives with rectifier front-ends, it may be necessary to take steps to avoid a large inrush of current at the instant the drive is connected to the utility source. In such drives, the dc-bus capacitor is very large and initially has no voltage across it. Therefore, at the instant the switch in Fig. 16-17a is closed to connect the drive to the utility source, a large current flows through the diode-bridge rectifier, charging the dc-bus capacitor.

This transient current inrush is highly undesirable; fortunately, several means of avoiding it are available. These include using a front-end that consists of thyristors discussed later in this chapter or using a series semiconductor switch as shown in Fig. 16-17b. At the instant of starting, the resistance across the switch lets the dc-bus capacitor get charged without a large inrush current, and subsequently the semiconductor switch is turned on to bypass the resistance.

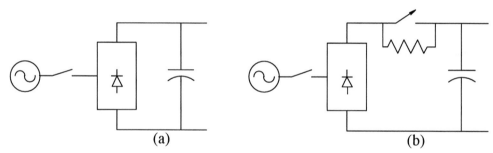

(a)   (b)

Figure 16-17 Means to avoid inrush current.

16-6   FRONT-ENDS WITH BI-DIRECTIONAL POWER FLOW

In stop-and-go applications such as elevators, it is cost-effective to feed the energy recovered by regenerative braking of the drive back into the utility supply. In such applications, the utility supply is generally three-phase, and therefore we will only consider three-phase front-ends.

Fig. 16-18a shows the circuit in which the front-end of the utility is similar to the dc-to-ac switch-mode inverter used in induction-motor drives. In Chapter 12 we saw that the power flow through a switch-mode inverter can reverse and such a converter can be modeled on an average basis by representing each pole by an ideal transformer, as shown in Fig. 16-18b. In a similar manner, the front-end switch-mode converter can be represented on an average basis by ideal transformers, as shown in Fig. 16-18b.

The per-phase representation of the overall system at the fundamental frequency (hence, the subscript "1") is shown in Fig. 16-18c, where "o" is the hypothetical midpoint of the capacitor dc bus. The front-end converter is controlled so as to

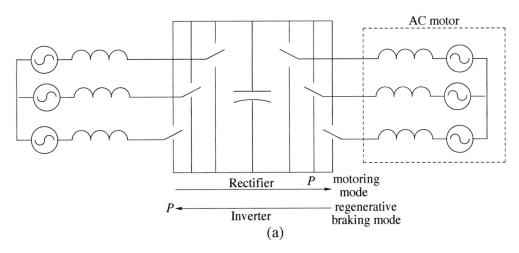

(a)

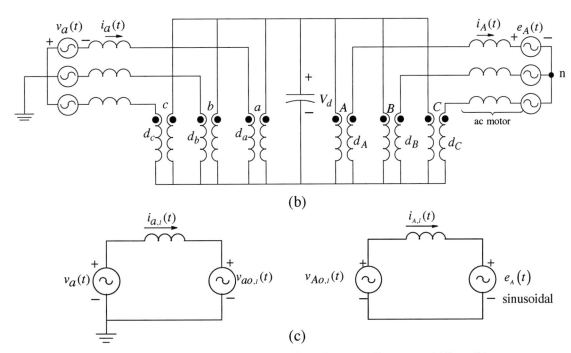

(b)

(c)

Figure 16-18 (a) Front-end with bi-directional power flow capability; (b) average model; (c) per-phase equivalent circuits.

draw sinusoidal currents at a unity power factor to maintain the dc-bus voltage at a predetermined value, as described in Reference [1].

In the normal motoring mode of the drive, the front-end converter operates in its rectifier mode and the converter at the motor-end operates in its inverter mode. These modes of operation are interchanged during the regenerative braking of the drive and the power is fed into the utility system. The line currents can be kept sinusoidal with a very low *THD*, within the limits imposed by the IEEE-519.

In these drives, steps similar to those described in section 16-5-3 may be necessary to avoid large transient inrush currents at starting.

16-7 PHASE-CONTROLLED THYRISTOR CONVERTERS FOR DC-MOTOR DRIVES

In high performance dc-motor drives, as discussed in Chapter 7, power-processing units use switch-mode converters to supply adjustable dc voltage and current to the dc motor, and the front-end consists of the diode-bridge rectifier discussed earlier. However, in dc drives where performance in terms of torque ripple and speed of response is not critical, using phase-controlled thyristor converters, which are shown by the block diagram of Fig. 16-7c, can be more economical. In this section, we will examine the operating principles of thyristor converters and their impact on the power quality of the utility system.

16-7-1 Thyristors (SCRs)

Thyristors are 4-layer (n-p-n-p) devices, sometimes referred to by their trade name of Silicon Controlled Rectifiers (SCRs). The operation of thyristors is illustrated by means of the simple circuit in Fig. 16-19a. At $\omega t = 0$, the positive-half-cycle of the input voltage begins, beyond which a positive voltage appears across the thyristor (anode A is positive with respect to cathode K). With a positive-polarity voltage across the thyristor, the start of its conduction can be controlled by means of the delay $\omega t = \alpha$ (called phase control) at which a positive pulse of current is applied to the thyristor gate terminal. This delay angle α, at which the gate current pulse is applied, is defined with respect to $\omega t = 0$ (which is referred to as the instant of natural conduction).

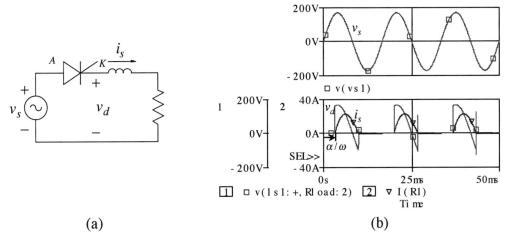

Figure 16-19 (a) Thyristor controlled half bridge rectifier; (b) waveforms associated with it.

Once the thyristor begins to conduct, it latches on and the gate current can be removed. Once in the conducting state, a thyristor behaves like a diode with a very small voltage drop of the order of 1 to 2 volts across it (we will idealize it to be zero). The current through the thyristor cannot be interrupted by means of its gate terminal. The waveforms in Fig. 16-19b show that the current becomes zero sometime in the negative half-cycle of the input voltage. The current cannot reverse and remains zero, thus allowing the gate terminal to regain control. In the next cycle of the input voltage, the current conduction again depends on the instant during the positive half-cycle at which the gate pulse is applied. By controlling the delay angle, we can control the average voltage across the resistance. This principle can be extended to the practical circuits discussed here.

16-7-2 Single-Phase, Phase-Controlled Thyristor Converters

To ensure that the dc (average) component of the current drawn from the utility source is zero, the full-bridge phase-controlled converter shown in Fig. 16-20 is used. To help us understand the operating principle, this circuit is simplified as shown in Fig. 16-21a, where the ac-side inductance L_s is ignored and the dc motor is represented as drawing a constant current I_d. The waveforms are shown in Fig. 16-21b. Thyristors (1 and 2) and thyristors (3 and 4) are treated as pairs. The thyristor pairs are supplied gate pulses which are delayed from their respective instants of natural conduction by an angle α. In the positive-half

16-25

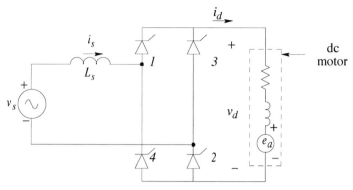

Figure 16-20 Full-bridge phase-controlled converter.

cycle of the input voltage, as soon as thyristors 1 and 2 are gated at $\omega t = \alpha$ they immediately begin to conduct. Therefore, in Fig. 16-21b,

$$v_d(t) = v_s(t) \quad \text{and} \quad i_s(t) = I_d \quad \alpha < \omega t \le \alpha + \frac{\pi}{2} \tag{16-28}$$

These relationships hold true until $\alpha + \dfrac{\pi}{2}$ in the negative half-cycle of the input voltage, when thyristors 3 and 4 are gated. At this instant, negative input voltage applies a forward-polarity voltage across thyristors 3 and 4, which, upon gating, immediately takeover current from thyristors 1 and 2 (immediately because of the assumption of zero L_s). With thyristors 3 and 4 conducting,

$$v_d(t) = -v_s(t) \quad \text{and} \quad i_s(t) = -I_d \qquad \alpha + \frac{\pi}{2} < \omega t \le \alpha + \pi \tag{16-29}$$

This holds true for one half-cycle, until the next cycle begins with the gating of thyristors 1 and 2.

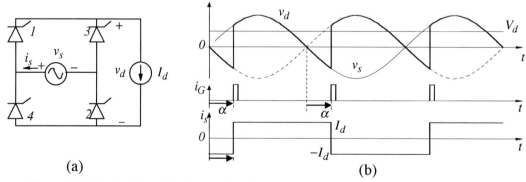

(a) (b)

Figure16-21 (a) Simplified circuit diagram of the converter; (b) waveforms.

16-26

Thyristors 1 and 2 continue conducting for an interval α, even after the input voltage has become negative. Similarly, thyristors 3 and 4 continue conducting even after the input voltage has become positive. Increasing the delay angle α would reduce the average dc-side voltage V_d while simultaneously shifting the input current $i_s(t)$ waveform farther away with respect to the input voltage waveform.

The average value V_d of the voltage across the motor terminal can be obtained by averaging the $v_d(t)$ waveform over one half-cycle during $\alpha < \omega t \le \alpha + \dfrac{\pi}{2}$:

$$V_d = \frac{1}{\pi} \int_{\alpha}^{\alpha+\frac{\pi}{2}} \sqrt{2} V_s \sin \omega t \cdot d(\omega t) = \frac{2\sqrt{2}}{\pi} V_s \cos \alpha = 0.9 V_s \cos \alpha \qquad (16\text{-}30)$$

where V_s is the rms value of the input voltage.

The plot in Fig. 16-22a shows that for the delay angle α in a range of 0^0 to 90^0, V_d has a positive value and the converter operates as a rectifier, with the power flowing into the dc motor. This corresponds to the first-quadrant operation of the dc machine, motoring in the forward direction, shown in Fig. 16-22b and discussed in Chapter 7.

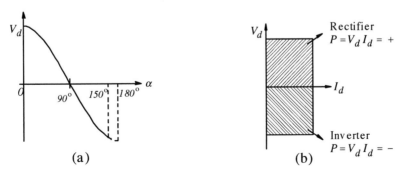

Figure 16-22 (a) Variation of V_d with delay angle α; (b) operating quadrants of the converter.

For values of α greater than 90^0, V_d has a negative value and the converter operates as an inverter, with the power flowing out of the dc motor. This corresponds to the fourth-quadrant operation of the dc machine, regenerative braking in the reverse direction of rotation, as discussed in Chapter 7. In practice, the upper limit on α is somewhat below 180^0 to avoid a phenomenon known as commutation failure.

On the ac-side, the fundamental-frequency component $i_{s1}(t)$ of the input current is shown in Fig. 16-23a which has an rms value I_{s1}, where

$$I_{s1} = 0.9I_d \tag{16-31}$$

Fig. 16-23b shows the phasors, where $\bar{I}_{s1}$ lags behind $\bar{V}_s$ by an angle $\phi_1 = \alpha$. Therefore, the power input from the ac-side is

$$P = V_s I_{s1} \cos\alpha \tag{16-32}$$

which, assuming that there is no power loss in the thyristor converter, equals the power to the dc machine. Using Eqs. 16-30 and 16-31,

$$P = V_s \underbrace{I_{s1}}_{(=0.9I_d)} \cos\alpha = \underbrace{0.9V_s \cos\alpha}_{(=V_d)} I_d = V_d I_d \tag{16-33}$$

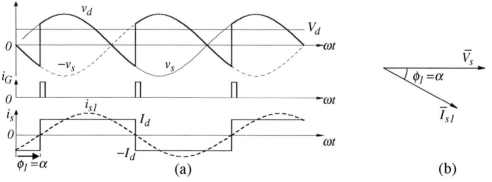

Figure 16-23(a) AC side waveforms; (b) current and voltage phasors.

16-7-3 The Effect of L_s on Current Commutation

Previously, our assumption was that the ac-side inductance L_s was zero. In practice, this inductance is usually required to be at least 5 percent of the base impedance (the base impedance is defined in a similar fashion as in Eqs. 16-24 and 16-25). In the presence of this inductance, the input current takes a finite amount of time to reverse its direction, as the current "commutates" from one thyristor pair to the next.

From basic principles, we know that changing the current through the inductor L_s in the circuit of Fig. 16-24a requires a finite amount of volt-seconds. The dc-side is still represented by a dc current I_d. The waveforms are shown in Fig. 16-24b, where thyristors 3 and 4 are conducting prior to $\omega t = \alpha$, and $i_s = -I_d$. At $\omega t = \alpha$, thyristors 1 and 2 are gated on and immediately begin to conduct. However, the current through them doesn't jump instantaneously as in the case of $L_s = 0$ where i_s instantaneously changed to $i_s = +I_d$. With a finite L_s, during a short interval called the commutation interval u, all thyristors conduct, causing the voltage across L_s to be equal to v_s. The volt-radians needed to change the inductor current from $(-I_d)$ to $(+I_d)$ can be calculated by integrating the inductor voltage $v_L (= L_s \dfrac{d}{dt} i_s)$ from α to $(\alpha + u)$, as follows:

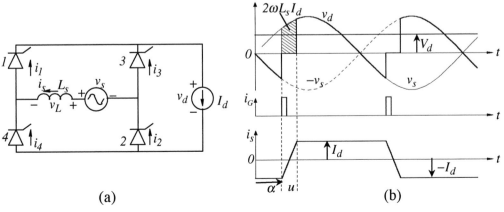

(a)   (b)

Figure 16-24 (a) Thyristor converter along with source inductance; (b) waveforms.

$$\int_{\alpha}^{\alpha+u} v_L \, d(\omega t) = \omega L_s \int_{-I_d}^{I_d} di_s = 2\omega L_s I_d \qquad (16\text{-}34)$$

Therefore, the above volt-radians are "lost" every half-cycle from the integral of the dc-side voltage waveform, as shown by the shaded area in Fig. 16-24b. This corresponds to a "lossless" voltage drop of

$$\Delta V_d = \frac{2}{\pi} \omega L_s I_d \qquad (16\text{-}35)$$

This voltage is lost from the dc-side average voltage in the presence of L_s. Therefore, the average voltage is smaller than that in Eq. 16-30:

$$V_d = 0.9 V_s \cos\alpha - \frac{2}{\pi} \omega L_s I_d \qquad (16\text{-}36)$$

16-7-4 Three-Phase, Phase-Controlled Thyristor Converters

DC drives with a three-phase utility input are generally used at higher power ratings. Three-phase converters use six thyristors, as shown in Fig. 16-25a. A simplified converter is shown in Fig. 16-25b, where the thyristors are divided into a top group and a bottom group, similar to the three-phase diode rectifiers. These converters are systematically analyzed in Reference [1]. In the continuous-current conduction mode, the average voltage V_d in three-phase converters can be derived to be

$$V_d = 1.35 V_{LL} \cos\alpha - \frac{3}{\pi} \omega L_s I_d \qquad (16\text{-}37)$$

where V_{LL} is the rms value of the line-line voltages, and the delay angle α for each thyristor is measured from the respective instant of natural conduction. Further details can be found in Reference [1].

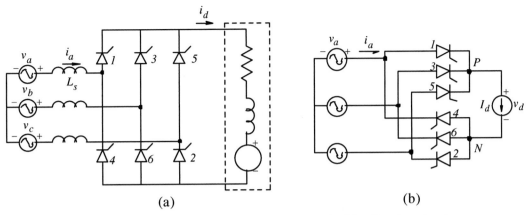

Figure 16-25 (a) Three phase thyristor converter (b) idealized and redrawn.

16-7-5 Thyristor Converters for Four-Quadrant Operation

The following discussion applies to both single-phase and three-phase inputs. Two thyristor converters connected in anti-parallel, as shown in Fig. 16-26a, can deliver the 4-quadrant operation shown in Fig. 16-26b. While discussing a single-phase thyristor converter, we observed that converter 1 operates in the rectifier mode while the dc-machine operates as a motor in the forward direction; it operates in the inverter mode during regenerative braking of the dc machine, while rotating in the reverse direction. Similarly, converter 2 operates in the rectifier mode while the dc-machine operates as a motor in the reverse direction; it operates in the inverter mode during regenerative braking of the dc machine, while rotating in the forward direction.

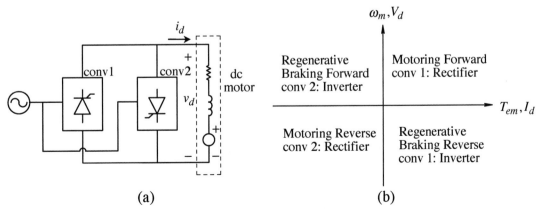

Figure 16-26 (a) Four quadrant thyristor converter; (b) DC motor drive operation in four quadrants.

16-7-6 The Power Quality Impact of Thyristor Converters

Both single-phase and three-phase thyristor converters draw power by means of non-sinusoidal currents with total harmonic distortion above the limits specified by the IEEE-519. These converters suffer from the additional serious drawbacks described below.

16-7-6-1 Poor Displacement Power Factor (*DPF*) at Low Speeds

As discussed in Chapter 7, dc motors operating at low speeds have a low induced back-emf E_a. Therefore, the required terminal voltage V_d is also low. This is accomplished by increasing the delay angle α towards the 90^0 value. The input current waveform, with respect to the phase voltage waveform, shifts by the delay angle; hence both the displacement power factor and the power factor become extremely poor at low speeds in thyristorized dc drives with single-phase and three-phase inputs.

16-7-6-2 The Notching of Input Voltage Waveforms

The ac-side inductance consists of the internal inductance L_{s1} of the utility supply and an external inductance L_{s2} added in series:

$$L_s = L_{s1} + L_{s2} \tag{16-38}$$

This is shown in Fig. 16-27a. Other loads may be connected at the point-of-common-coupling (PCC), as shown.

As was discussed in detail for thyristor converters with single-phase inputs, during current commutation, all thyristors conduct, causing a short-circuit on the input line through the ac-side inductance. This results in undesirable notches, as shown in Fig. 16-27b, in the waveform of the voltage across other loads, potentially causing them to malfunction. Similar voltage notching can be observed in 3-phase converters.

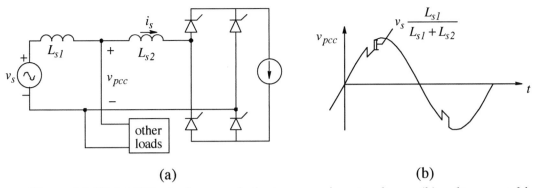

Figure 16-27 (a) Effect of source inductance on input voltage; (b) voltage notching at the point of common coupling.

16-8 THE EFFECTS OF POWER SYSTEM DISTURBANCES ON ELECTRIC DRIVES

Power electronics has matured to the extent that the mean time between failure (MTBF) of drives is several tens of thousands of hours. However, interruption in drive operation is much more frequent due to power system disturbances in the form of power outages and reduction (sag) in the utility voltages.

Electric drives should be designed to tolerate some disturbances without being effected. The "tolerance" limits developed by the Computer Business Equipment Manufacturers Association (CBEMA) are shown in the CBEMA curve in Fig. 16-28. The CBEMA curve has been adopted by some drive manufacturers in designing the drives. It shows that a drive should be able to tolerate a complete power outage for 20 *ms*, followed by a voltage sag of 30 percent for 0.5 *s*, 20 percent for 10 *s*, and 10 percent in steady state. Similarly, it specifies the upper limits on the input voltage that should be tolerated.

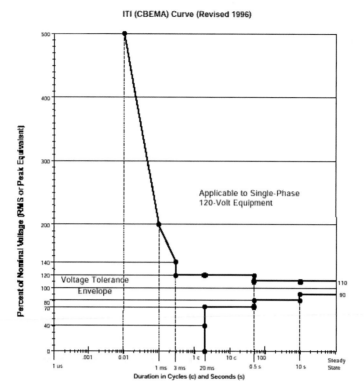

Figure 16-28 The CBEMA curve.

16-8-1 Power Outages, Voltage "Sags," and Ride-Through Capability

In applications where it is critical that drive operation not be interrupted, uninterruptible power supplies (UPS) consisting of energy storage means such as batteries are used as a backup power source during prolonged power outage.

Using UPS is an expensive solution, reserved only for very critical applications. Since a voltage "sag" for a few cycles is far more likely to occur than a complete and prolonged power outage, it is possible to devise cheaper solutions (compared to UPS) for tolerating voltage disturbances outside the CBEMA curve. One such solution is the Dynamic Voltage Restorer (DVR) shown in Fig. 16-29 in a per-phase block-diagram form. In a DVR, a voltage is injected in series with the utility supply to make up for the voltage "sag." The series voltage is then synthesized by means of a power electronics converter, to which the power is supplied by the energy stored in the capacitor.

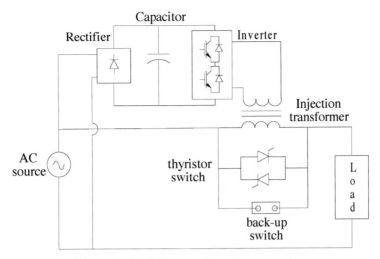

Figure 16-29 Dynamic voltage restorer.

In most drive applications, using a UPS or a DVR is economically unfeasible. In such cases, the capability to ride-through power outages or voltage sags outside the CBEMA limits can be built into the drive's power-processing unit (PPU). One suggested control modification to the PPU is to make the machine go into the regenerative-braking mode during the power disturbance, thus supplying the kinetic energy associated with the motor-load inertia to hold up the dc-bus voltage. Ultra-capacitors are also being considered for the dc bus. Other techniques for ride-through are discussed in Reference [5]

16-8-2 Nuisance Tripping Due to Over-Voltages Caused by Capacitor Switching

The switching in of capacitors in the distribution system of a utility can cause transient over-voltages at the input of the drives and thus across the dc-bus capacitor. These issues need to be resolved in collaboration with the friendly utility.

SUMMARY/REVIEW QUESTIONS

1. How is the power factor (*PF*) defined with linear loads?
2. How does the definition of power factor change with loads which draw distorted currents?

3. What is meant by the distortion component of the current?
4. How is the Total Harmonic Distortion (*THD*) defined?
5. What is the Displacement Power Factor (*DPF*)? What is it equal to in linear loads which draw sinusoidal waveform currents?
6. What is the power factor equal to in terms of the displacement power factor?
7. What are the deleterious effects of a high *THD* and a poor power factor?
8. What are the various harmonic guidelines? Briefly describe the IEEE-519 and the rationale behind it.
9. What is the most common type of "front-end" used to interface drives with single-phase and three-phase utility systems?
10. Briefly describe the operation of single-phase diode-rectifier bridges with a large capacitor at the dc output. Why is the current drawn by these highly distorted? What is the impact of the values of L_s and C_d on the input current waveform?
11. Repeat Question 10 for a three-phase diode-rectifier bridge.
12. How do single-phase and three-phase rectifier bridges compare in terms of performance? At higher power levels, if there is a choice available, why is one much more favorable than the other?
13. Describe the operating principle of the single-phase power-factor-corrected (*PFC*) circuit, where the power flow is unidirectional.
14. What is a good solution for a three-phase *PFC* in systems where the power is not fed back into the utility grid?
15. In the case of a bi-directional power flow, assuming a three-phase utility input, draw the complete topology of the power-processing unit. How can we analyze it in steady state on a per-phase basis?
16. For which type of motor drives are thyristor converters still used?
17. Describe phase control and its effect on the simplest possible thyristor circuit.
18. Describe the operation of a single-phase, full-bridge thyristor converter. How is the average value of the output voltage controlled?
19. Describe current commutation and the effect of L_s on the operation of a single-phase, full-bridge thyristor converter.
20. How is it possible to achieve four-quadrant operation using thyristor converters? Describe the role of each converter, based on the quadrant in which the "front-end" is operating.

21. What are the two worst power quality impacts of thyristor converter "front-ends"?

22. Briefly describe the impact of utility disturbances on the proper operation of drives. Also, briefly describe various mitigation measures that can be applied.

REFERENCES

1. N. Mohan, T. Undeland, and W. P. Robbins, *Power Electronics: Converters, Applications, and Design*, 2nd edition, 1995, John Wiley & Sons, New York, NY.

2. N. Mohan, Power Electronics: *Computer Simulation, Analysis and Education using PSpice*™, a complete simulation package available from www.mnpere.com.

3. N. Mohan, *Power Electronics Design Video Course*, available on 4-1/2 hours of videotapes from www.mnpere.com.

4. J. Kolar and F. Zach, "A Novel Three-Phase Three-Switch Three-Level PWM Rectifier," Proceedings of the 28th Power Conversion Conference, Nuremberg, Germany, June 28-30, pp. 125-138 (1994). Since then, Professor Kolar has written several articles on this topic in general, and on this topology in particular.

5. A. von Jouanne, P. Enjeti, and B. Banerjee, "Ride-Through Alternatives for ASDs," in three parts, PowerPulseCD by Darnell Group, www.darnell.com.

PROBLEMS

16-1 Repeat Example 16-1 if the current waveform is a rectangular pulse, as shown in Fig. 16-13c.

SIMULATION PROBLEMS

Model a single-phase diode bridge rectifier shown in Fig. 16-8 with the following nominal values: V_s (rms) = 120V at 60 Hz, L_s = 1 mH, R_s = 1 mΩ, C_d = 1,000 μF, and R_{eq} = 20 Ω. Answer the following questions:

16-2 From the results of the Fourier analysis contained in the output file of the simulation, calculate the input power factor and the displacement power factor.

16-3 Plot i_s, i_{s1}, i_{s3} and i_{s5}. Superimpose the distortion current component $i_{distortion}$ on this plot.

16-4 Calculate I_{cap} (the rms current though the filter capacitor) as a ratio of the average load current I_d.

16-5 Vary L_s to investigate its influence on the input displacement power factor, the input power factor, %THD, and the peak-peak ripple in the dc voltage v_d.

16-6 Vary the filter capacitor C_d to investigate its influence on the percentage ripple in v_d, input displacement power factor and %THD. Plot the percentage ΔV_d (peak-to-peak)/V_d (average) as a function of C_d.

16-7 Vary the load power to investigate its influence on the average dc voltage.

16-8 Obtain the v_s, i_s and v_d waveforms during the start-up transient when the filter capacitor is initially not charged. Obtain the peak inrush current as a ratio of the peak current in steady state. Vary the switching instant by simply varying the phase angle of the source voltage v_s.

16-9 For the following design specifications, calculate the capacitance of the filter capacitor: $V_s = 120\ V$ (nominal) +/- 10% at 60 Hz, $P_{max} = 1\ kW$, $L_s = 1\ mH$, and maximum ΔV_d (peak-peak) < 10 V.

Model the three-phase diode-bridge rectifier shown in Fig. 16-12a, with the following nominal values: V_{LL} (rms) = 208 V at 60 Hz, $L_s = 0.1\ mH$, $C_d = 500\ \mu F$, and $R_{eq} = 16.5\ \Omega$. Answer the following questions:

16-10 By means of Fourier analysis of i_a, calculate its harmonic components as a ratio of I_{a1}.

16-11 Calculate I_a, I_{a1}, I_{dis}, %THD in the input current, the input displacement power factor, and the input power factor. How do your results compare with the 1-phase diode-bridge rectifier, whose modeling was performed earlier?

16-12 Calculate I_{cap} (the rms current through the filter capacitor) as a ratio of the average load current I_{load}. How do your results compare with those for the 1-phase diode-bridge rectifier, whose modeling was performed earlier?

16-13 Investigate the influence of L_d on the input displacement power factor, the input power factor, and the average dc voltage V_d. Suggested range of L_d: 0.1 *mH* to 10 *mH.*

16-14 Investigate the influence of C_d on the percent ripple in v_d. Plot the percentage ΔV_d (peak-to-peak)/V_d (average) as a function of C_d. Suggested range of C_d: 100 μF to 2,000 μF.

16-15 Investigate the influence of C_d on the input displacement power factor and the input power factor. Suggested range of C_d: 100 μF to 2,000 μF.

16-16 Plot the average dc voltage as a function of load. Suggested range of R_{eq}: 8 to 50 Ω.

Model the single-phase thyristor converter shown in Fig. 16-20, where the ac-side inductance is the sum of the internal source inductance L_{s1} = 0.2 *mH* and an externally added inductance L_{s2} =1.0 *mH.* The dc-side consists of a series connection of L_d = 20 *mH* and R_{eq} = 20 Ω. V_s (rms) = 120 *V* at 60 *Hz.* The delay angle α = 45^0. Answer the following questions:

16-17 From the plots, obtain the commutation interval *u* and the dc-side current at the start of the commutation.

16-18 By means of Fourier analysis of i_s, calculate its harmonic components as a ratio of I_{s1}.

16-19 Calculate I_s, %*THD* in the input current, the input displacement power factor, and the input power factor.

16-20 At the point of common coupling, obtain the following from the voltage v_{PCC} waveform: (a) line-notch depth, (b) line-notch area, and (c) voltage %THD.

Model the three-phase thyristor converter shown in Fig. 16-25a, where the ac-side inductance is the sum of the internal source inductance $L_{s1} = 0.2$ mH, and an externally added inductance $L_{s2} = 1.0$ mH. The dc-side consists of a series connection of $L_d = 16$ mH, and $R_{eq} = 8$ Ω. V_{LL} (rms) $= 208$ V at 60 Hz. The delay angle $\alpha = 45^0$. Answer the following questions:

16-21 By means of Fourier analysis of i_s, calculate its harmonic components as a ratio of I_{s1}.

16-22 Calculate I_s, %THD in the input current, the input displacement power factor, and the input power factor.

16-23 At the point of common coupling, obtain the following from the voltage v_{pcc} waveform: (a) line-notch depth, (b) line-notch area, and (c) voltage %THD.

CHAPTER 17

ANCILLARY ISSUES IN DRIVES: SENSORS, ASICs, AND MICRO-CONTROLLERS

17-1 INTRODUCTION

This chapter briefly describes various subsystems that are essential in a drive system, but which have not been discussed. This chapter is by no means complete; rather, it is intended be a "roadmap" to a wealth of information found in manufacturers' websites regarding product specifications and application notes on sensors, application-specific ICs (ASICs), and micro-controllers. A very small fraction of these websites is listed at the end of this chapter.

17-2 SENSORS

Sensors are an essential part of any feedback control system because they provide both control and protection. In connection with drive systems, we will look at current, speed, and position sensors.

17-2-1 Current Sensors

Current sensors are available from various manufacturers. Most current sensors utilize the Hall-Effect principle and produce an isolated voltage output (isolated from the circuit in which the current is measured) which is proportional to the current. These current sensors can measure currents from dc to a large bandwidth, extending into several tens of *kHz*. They are described in some detail in Reference [1]; the product information can be found on websites [2] and [3].

17-2-2 Speed and Position Sensors

Sensors are needed to measure speed and position in the feedback controllers of drives. In modern drive systems, these sensors either utilize the Hall-Effect principle, the optical principle, or the magnetic principle.

17-2-2-1   Position Sensors for Commutation in ECM Drives

These are low-resolution sensors. As discussed in Chapter 7, Electronically-Commutated Motor (ECM) drives require that, every 60 degrees of rotation, the current be switched to the two appropriate windings in the three-phase motor. Commonly, a magnetic rotor and three Hall-Effect sensors are used to detect each 60-degree zone that the rotor is in. Alternatively, a toothed disk (coupled to the motor shaft) can be made to rotate, interrupting the light emitted by LEDs and resulting in a digital signal that indicates the direction of the rotation.

17-2-2-2   Incremental Encoders

Incremental encoders are the most commonly used sensors for measuring position and speed. They often operate on the optical principle, but magnetic incremental encoders are also available.

The schematic of an optical, incremental encoder is shown in Fig. 17-1. In such an encoder, a lens collimates the light from an LED, which passes through a coded wheel (which is slotted and fastened to the rotor shaft) and a stationary aperture plate. It is then detected by a light-receiver. As the coded wheel rotates, square pulses shaped by the light-receiver circuit are produced. Each pulse represents an incremental rotation by a specified amount. By counting these pulses, it is possible to determine the change in position. Also, by counting the number of pulses produced per second, and by knowing the number of pulses (or lines) per revolution associated with the sensor, it is possible to calculate the rotor speed.

Another series of pulses is generated at a 90-degree phase-shift with respect to the first channel. These two channels allow the direction of rotation to be

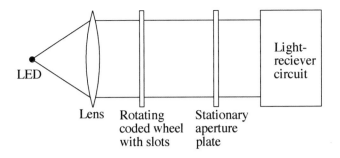

Figure 17-1 Optical incremental encoder.

determined. The third series of pulses is called the marker pulse, and occurs once every cycle of rotation. It establishes the "home position," beyond which the incremental encoder produces information about the absolute position.

The rotating coded wheel usually consists only of a glass disc, and therefore adds very little inertia. These encoders are commonly available from a few hundred to a few thousand lines per revolution, though higher resolutions extending to 100,000 lines per revolution can be achieved by utilizing lasers. Information regarding incremental encoders can be found on websites [3], [4], and [5].

17-2-2-3 Absolute Position Encoders and Resolvers

In the PMAC drives discussed in Chapter 10, the absolute position of the rotor is needed. This can be provided by the optical principle using a rotating disk, featuring multiple tracks of patterns and multiple LEDs and receivers. The digital output from these multiple receivers is combined to form a distinct "word" for each position of the shaft. Information about these absolute encoders can be found on websites [4] and [5].

Another way of detecting the absolute position is by using resolvers. These are sophisticated magnetic devices in which the rotor, as shown schematically in Fig. 17-2, is coupled to the motor shaft and is supplied (either through slip-rings or by a rotating transformer) by a sinusoidal voltage at a high frequency f_r, usually in the range of one to five *kHz*. The stator consists of two sinusoidally-distributed windings which are spatially 90-degrees out-of-phase with respect to each other. As the rotor turns, the outputs of the stator windings are amplitude-modulated

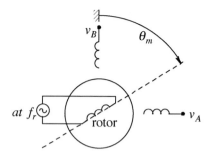

Figure 17-2 Resolver for position sensing.

sine waves, which are modulated proportional to the sine and the cosine, respectively of the rotor angle θ_m as follows:

$$v_A = A\sin(2\pi f_r t) \cdot \sin\theta_m \qquad (17\text{-}1)$$

and

$$v_B = A\sin(2\pi f_r t) \cdot \cos\theta_m \qquad (17\text{-}2)$$

where A is a constant amplitude.

This information from the electro-mechanical portion of the resolver is processed in a resolver-to-digital converter IC. If α is an estimate of the rotor position (with the objective of forcing α to become equal to the actual value θ_m), the input voltages v_A and v_B to the converter IC are multiplied by the cosine and the sine of the estimated angle:

$$v_A \cos\alpha = A\sin(2\pi f_r t) \cdot \sin\theta_m \cdot \cos\alpha \qquad (17\text{-}3)$$

and

$$v_B \sin\alpha = A\sin(2\pi f_r t) \cdot \cos\theta_m \cdot \sin\alpha \qquad (17\text{-}4)$$

Subtracting Eq. 17-4 from Eq. 17-3 results in the error:

$$\begin{aligned} error &= A\sin(2\pi f_r t) \cdot (\sin\theta_m \cos\alpha - \cos\theta_m \sin\alpha) \\ &= A\sin(2\pi f_r t) \cdot \sin(\theta_m - \alpha) \end{aligned} \qquad (17\text{-}5)$$

The error in Eq. 17-5 is proportional to $\sin(\theta_m - \alpha)$, which is used to modify the estimate α, until the error goes to zero and the estimate is equal to the actual angle - that is, $\alpha = \theta_m$. In addition to giving absolute position information, resolvers also deliver speed information. Resolvers are available in a wide range of resolutions; further information can be found on website [6].

17-3 APPLICATION-SPECIFIC ICs (ASICs)

Over the years, several application-specific ICs have become available to control the switch-mode converters for dc-, ECM, PMAC, induction- and stepper-motor drives. The advantage of ASICs is that they contain many functions, such as protection. The drawback of ASICs, however, can be their lack of flexibility. Information about these ICs can be found on website [3]. An ASIC for induction-motor control is described in Reference [1].

17-4 MICRO-CONTROLLERS AND FPGAs

Most modern drives are digitally controlled. Micro-controllers, specially designed to make motion control easy, are available from a variety of sources, such as [7], [8], and [9]. It is possible to parcel some of their logic functions to hardware outside of the micro-controller, thus speeding up the computation cycle time. This hardware function can be performed in Field-Programmable Gate Arrays (FPGAs) [10], which can be programmed in a higher-level language [11].

17-5 RAPID-PROTOTYPING TOOLS

Rapid-prototyping tools have been developed for testing digital control designs quickly. One such system, available from [12], allows the controller to be designed in a commonly used control software SIMULINK®, available from [13]. Once this controller is designed, the code is simply generated and loaded into the micro-controller for real-time control, thus allowing the control algorithm to be tested rapidly. After the control design is finalized, it can be implemented into a micro-controller by traditional means. Such rapid-prototyping tools also provide an excellent means for developing micro-controller-based, software re-configurable hardware laboratories for educational purposes.

SUMMARY/REVIEW QUESTIONS

1. What types of sensors are generally needed?
2. What are ASICs?
3. What are micro-controllers and FPGAs?
4. What are the advantages of rapid-prototyping tools?

REFERENCES

1. N. Mohan, T. Undeland, and W. P. Robbins, *Power Electronics: Converters, Applications, and Design*, 2nd edition, 1995, John Wiley & Sons, New York, NY.
2. WWW.LEM.COM
3. WWW.AGILENT.COM
4. WWW.RENCO.COM
5. WWW.DANCON.COM
6. WWW.LITTON-PS.COM
7. WWW.TI.COM
8. WWW.MOTOROLA.COM
9. WWW.ANALOGDEVICES.COM
10. WWW.XILINX.COM
11. WWW.ORCAD.COM
12. WWW.DSPACE.DE
13. WWW.MATHWORKS.COM

INDEX

AC Machines, 9-1
    Balanced Sinusoidal Steady-State
        Excitation, 9-22
    Induced Voltages in Stator Windings,
        9-29
    Multi-Pole Machines, 9-4
    Radial Field Distributions in the Air
        Gap, 9-5
    Rotating Stator MMF Space Vector,
        9-23
    Sinusoidally-Distributed Stator
        Windings, 9-2
    Stator Windings, 9-10
ASICs, 17-1, 17-5
DC-Motor Drives, 7-1
    Armature Reaction, 7-11
    Back-EMF, 7-13
    Commutating Windings, 7-12
    Commutation, 7-6
    Commutator Action, 7-9
    Commutator, 7-3
    Compensating Windings, 7-12
    DC-Machine Equivalent Circuit, 7-13
    Electronically-Commutated Motor
        Drives, 7-1
    Flux Weakening in Wound-Field
        Machines, 7-19
    Four-Quadrant Operation, 7-18
    Motor Torque Constant, 7-10
    Motor Voltage Constant, 7-11
    Operating Modes in DC-Motor
        Drives, 7-15
    Operating Principles of DC Machines,
        7-4
    Power-Processing Units in DC Drives,
        7-20
    Regenerative-Braking, 7-16
    Reverse Direction, 7-18
    Structure of DC Machines, 7-3

Electric Drive Systems, 1-1
    Air Conditioners, 1-7
    Applications, 1-5
    Blowers, 1-7
    Electric Drive, 1-3
    Electric Transportation, 1-10
    Electric Vehicles, 1-10
    Electric-Motor Drive, 1-3
    Energy Conservation, 1-6
    Fans, 1-7
    Growth, 1-4
    Heat Pumps, 1-7
    Hybrid-Electric Vehicles, 1-1, 1-10
    Introduction, 1-1
    Power-Processing Unit, 1-3
    Pumps, 1-7
    Wind Energy, 1-9
    World Market, 1-4
Electrical Circuits, 3-1
    Apparent Power, 3-9
    Per-Phase Analysis, 3-13
    Phasor Representation, 3-2
    Power Factor, 3-6, 3-10
    Power, 3-6
    Reactive Power, 3-6
    Three-Phase Circuits, 3-11
**Electromechanical Energy Conversion,
    6-1**
    Basic Principles of Operation, 6-6
    Electromagnetic Force, 6-6
    Energy Conversion, 6-11
    Induced EMF, 6-8
    Machine Ratings, 6-14
    Magnetic Field, 6-3
    Magnetic Shielding of Conductors in
        Slots, 6-9
    Power Losses and Energy Efficiency,
        6-13
    Regenerative Braking, 6-12

Safe Operating Area (SOA), 6-14
Structure, 6-1
Electronically-Commutated
  (Trapezoidal Waveform Brush-
  Less DC) Motor Drives, 7-1, 7-21
ECM, 7-21
Electromagnetic Torque, 7-25
Induced EMF, 7-24
Torque Ripple, 7-27
Trapezoidal Waveform Brush-Less
  DC Motor Drives, 7-1, 7-21
Energy Efficiency, 15-1
Definition of Energy Efficiency in
  Electric Drives, 15-2
Deleterious Effects of the PWM-
  Inverter Voltage Waveform on
  Motor Life, 15-11
Dependence of Motor Losses and
  Efficiency on Motor Speed,
  15-4
Dependence of Motor Losses and
  Efficiency on the Motor Load,
  15-4
Economics of Energy Savings by
  Premium-Efficiency Electric
  Motors and Electric Drives,
  15-9
Effects of Switching-Frequency
  Harmonics on Motor Losses,
  15-7
Efficiency of a PPU-Supplied Motor,
  15-2
Efficiency of an Electric Drive, 15-2
Energy Efficiencies of Power-
  Processing Units, 15-8
Energy Efficiencies of Electric Drives,
  15-8
Energy Efficiency of Induction
  Motors with Sinusoidal
  Excitation, 15-2

Friction and Windage Losses, 15-4
Inverter-Motor Interactions, 15-1
Magnetic Core Losses, 15-3
Motor De-Rating Due to Inverter
  Harmonic Losses, 15-8
Motor Efficiency, 15-2
Motor Losses, 15-3
Payback Period, 15-9
Permanent-Magnet Machines, 15-2
Premium-Efficiency Motors, 15-6
Present Worth of Savings, 15-9
Stray-Load Losses, 15-4
Winding Power Losses, 15-3
Feedback Controllers, 8-1
Anti-Windup (Non-Windup)
  Integration, 8-20
Average Representation of the Power-
  Processing Unit (PPU)   8-7
Bandwidth, 8-4
Cascade Control Structure, 8-5
Closed-Loop Bandwidth, 8-4
Closed-Loop Transfer Function, 8-2
Control Objectives, 8-2
Controller Design, 8-10
Crossover Frequency, 8-3
Current Control Loop, 8-12
Designing the Feedback Controller,
  8-6
Feed-Forward, 8-18
Limits, 8-19
Modeling of the DC Machine and the
  Mechanical Load, 8-8
Open-Loop Transfer Function, 8-2
Phase Margin (PM), 8-3
PI Controllers, 8-10
Position Control Loop, 8-17
Small-Signal Analysis, 8-6
Speed Control Loop, 8-15
Torque (Current) Control Loop, 8-12
Unity Feedback, 8-2

FPGAs, 17-5
Induction Motors, 11-1
Assumption of Zero Rotor Leakage, 11-10
Balanced, Sinusoidal Steady State Operation, 11-1
Blocked-Rotor Test, 11-35
DC-Resistance Test, 11-33
Electrically Open-Circuited Rotor, 11-4
Electromagnetic Torque, 11-18
Energy-Savings in Lightly-Loaded Machines, 11-41
Generator (Regenerative Braking) Mode of Operation, 11-22
Induction Motor Characteristics at Rated Voltages, 11-36
Line Start, 11-40
NEMA Design A, B, C, and D, 11-39
No-Load Test, 11-34
Per-Phase Steady-State Equivalent Circuit, 11-27
Principles of Induction Motor Operation, 11-3
Reduced Voltage Starting ("Soft Start") of Induction Motors, 11-40
Regenerative Braking, 11-22
Reversing the Direction of Rotation, 11-24
Rotor Leakage Inductance, 11-24
Short-Circuited Rotor, 11-6
Slip Frequency, 11-15
Slip Speed, 11-9
Stator Winding Resistance and the Leakage Inductance, 11-32
Structure of Three-Phase, Squirrel-Cage Induction Motors, 11-2

Tests to Obtain the Parameters of the Per-Phase Equivalent Circuit, 11-33
Torque Constant, 11-19
Transformer Analogy, 11-6
Magnetic Circuits, 5-1
Ampere's Law, 5-2
Core Losses, 5-24
Eddy Currents, 5-24
Faraday's Law, 5-14
Ferromagnetic Materials, 5-4
Flux , 5-3
Flux Density, 5-3
Flux Linkage, 5-7
Hysteresis Loops, 5-4
Ideal Transformer, 5-22, 5-23
Induced Voltage, 5-14
Inductances, 5-11
Leakage, 5-17
Lenz's Law, 5-15
Magnetic Energy Storage in Inductors, 5-12
Magnetic Field, 5-1
Magnetic Structures with Air Gaps, 5-8
Magnetizing Inductances, 5-17
Mutual Inductances, 5-20
Nd-Fe-B Magnets, 5-29
Open-Circuit Test on Transformers, 5-25
Permanent Magnets, 5-29
Permeability, 5-3
Relative Permeability, 5-5
Reluctance, 5-6
Short-Circuit Test on Transformers, 5-26
Transformer Equivalent Circuit, 5-24
Transformer Model Parameters, 5-25
Transformers, 5-20

Mechanical Systems, 2-1
    Centrifugal Loads, 2-22
    Constant-Power Loads, 2-24
    Constant-Torque Loads, 2-23
    Conversion between Linear and
        Rotary Motion, 2-18
    Coupling Mechanisms, 2-17
    Damping Coefficient, 2-15
    Electrical Analogy, 2-15
    Four-Quadrant Operation, 2-24
    Friction, 2-12
    Gears, 2-20
    Kinetic Energy, 2-4, 2-12
    Linear Motion, 2-2
    Moment-of-Inertia, 2-7
    Newton's Law of Motion, 2-2, 2-6
    Optimum Gear Ratio, 2-21
    Rotating Systems, 2-4
    Spring Constant, 2-15
    Squared-Power Loads, 2-23
    Torque, 2-4
    Torsional Resonances, 2-15
    Types of Loads, 2-22
Power Electronics, 4-1
    Average Representation of the Pole by
        an Ideal Transformer, 4-10
    Average Representation of the Pole,
        4-6
    Boost Mode of Operation, 4-13
    Buck Mode of Operation, 4-12
    Building Block, 4-5
    Controllable Switches, 4-23
    Converter Pole as a Two-Quadrant
        Converter, 4-11
    Converters for DC-Motor Drives,
        4-17
    Converters for Three-Phase AC-Motor
        Drives, 4-19
    Cost of MOSFETs and IGBTs, 4-26
    Current Rating, 4-22

    Implementation of Bi-Positional
        Switches, 4-15
    Insulated Gate Bipolar Transistors
        (IGBTs), 4-24
    MOSFETs, 4-23
    On-State Voltage, 4-24
    Pole, 4-5
    Power Diodes, 4-23
    Power Processing Units, 4-1
    Power Semiconductor Devices, 4-22
    Pulse Width Modulation (PWM), 4-4
    Rectifier, 4-2
    Smart-Power Modules, 4-25
    Switching Speeds, 4-23
    Switch-Mode Converters, 4-3
    Voltage Rating of Devices, 4-22
Power Quality Issues, 16-1
    Classifying the "Front-End" of
        Electric Drives, 16-12
    Comparison of Single-Phase and
        Three-Phase Rectifiers, 16-19
    Diode-Rectifier Bridge "Front-Ends",
        16-12
    Displacement Power Factor (DPF),
        16-7
    Distorted Current, 16-3
    Effects of Power System Disturbances
        on Electric Drives, 16-34
    Front-Ends with Bi-Directional Power
        Flow, 16-22
    Harmonic Guidelines, 16-10
    Means to Avoid Transient Inrush
        Currents at Starting, 16-22
    Nuisance Tripping Due to Over-
        Voltages Caused by Capacitor
        Switching, 16-35
    Power Factor (PF), 16-1, 16-7
    Power Outages, 16-35
    Power Quality Impact of Thyristor
        Converters, 16-32

Power-Factor-Corrected (*PFC*)
  Interface, 16-19
Ride-Through Capability, 16-35
Single-Phase Diode-Rectifier Bridge,
  16-13
Single-Phase *PFC*s, 16-20
Three-Phase Diode-Rectifier Bridge,
  16-16
Three-Phase *PFC*s, 16-21
Total Harmonic Distortion, 16-3
Voltage "Sags", 16-34
Rapid-Prototyping Tools, 17-5
Reluctance Drives, 14-1
  Equivalent-Circuit Representation of a
    Stepper-Motor, 14-11
  Half-Stepping and Micro-Stepping,
    14-11
  Hybrid Stepper-Motors, 14-9
  Operating Principle of Reluctance
    Motors, 14-2
  Permanent-Magnet Stepper-Motors,
    14-7
  Power-Processing Units for Stepper-
    Motors, 14-12
  Principle of Energy Conservation,
    14-2
  Step-Angle, 14-6
  Stepper-Motor Drives, 14-1
  Switched-Reluctance Drives, 14-1
  Switched-Reluctance Motor Drives,
    14-13
  Synchronous-Reluctance-Motor
    Drives, 14-1
  Variable-Reluctance Stepper Motors,
    14-6
Sensors, 17-1
  Absolute Position Encoders, 17-3
  Current Sensors, 17-1
  Incremental Encoders, 17-2
  Micro-Controllers, 17-1, 17-5

Position Sensors for Commutation in
  ECM Drives, 17-2
Position Sensors, 17-2
Resolvers, 17-3
Speed Sensors, 17-2
Space Vectors, 9-1, 9-12
  Balanced Sinusoidal Steady-State
    Excitation, 9-22
  Currents and Voltages, 9-17
  Induced Voltages in Stator Windings,
    9-29
  Phase Components of Space Vectors,
    9-20
  Relationship between Space Vectors
    and Phasors, 9-27
  Rotating Stator MMF Space Vector in
    Multi-Pole Machines, 9-26
  Rotating Stator MMF Space Vector,
    9-23
  Stator Current Space Vector, 9-17
**Speed Control of Induction Machines,
  12-1**
  Applied Voltage Amplitudes, 12-6
  Capability to Operate Below and
    Above the Rated Speed, 12-14
  Conditions for Efficient Speed
    Control, 12-2
  Current-Limiting, 12-19
  Harmonics in the PPU Output
    Voltages, 12-20
  Light Loads Operation, 12-24
  Limiting of Acceleration/Deceleration,
    12-19
  Modeling the PPU-Supplied Induction
    Motors in Steady State, 12-24
  Pulse-Width-Modulated Power-
    Processing Unit, 12-20
  Rated Power Capability, 12-15
  Rated Torque Capability Below the
    Rated Speed, 12-16

Regenerative Braking in Induction-
Motor Drives, 12-16
Slip Compensation, 12-19
Speed Control of Induction-Motor
Drives, 12-18
Speed Control, 12-1
Starting Considerations in Drives,
12-12
Voltage Boost, 12-10
Synchronous Machines, 10-1
Brushless DC Drives, 10-1
Calculation of the Reference Values of
the Stator Currents, 10-8
Controller, 10-18
Field (Excitation) Control to Adjust
Reactive Power and Power
Factor, 10-24
Induced EMFs in the Stator Windings,
10-12 to 10-16
LCI-Synchronous Motor Drives, 10-1
Load-Commutated-Inverter (LCI),
10-20
Machine Torque Constant, 10-7
Mechanical System of PMAC Drives,
10-8
Operating Principles of Synchronous
Machines, 10-22
Over-Excitation, 10-24
Per-Phase Equivalent Circuit, 10-16
PMAC Drives, 10-1
Power-Processing Unit (PPU), 10-18
Principle of Operation, 10-3
Rotor-Produced Flux Density
Distribution, 10-3
Sinusoidal Permanent Magnet AC
Drives, 10-1
Stability and Loss of Synchronism,
10-23
Structure of Permanent-Magnet AC
Synchronous Machines, 10-2

Structure of Synchronous Machines,
10-21
Synchronous Generators, 10-1, 10-21
Synchronous Motor Drives, 10-20
Torque Production, 10-4
Under-Excitation, 10-25
Thyristor Converters, 16-1
Current Commutation, 16-29
Notching of Input Voltage
Waveforms, 16-32
Phase-Controlled Thyristor Converters
for DC-Motor Drives, 16-24
Poor Displacement Power Factor
(*DPF*) at Low Speeds, 16-32
Power Quality Impact of Thyristor
Converters, 16-32
Single-Phase, Phase-Controlled
Thyristor Converters, 16-25
Three-Phase, Phase-Controlled
Thyristor Converters, 16-30
Thyristor Converters for Four-
Quadrant Operation, 16-31
Thyristors (SCRs), 16-24
**Vector Control of Induction-Motor
Drives, 13-1**
Analogy to a Current-Excited
Transformer with a Shorted
Secondary, 13-4
D- and *Q*-Axis Winding
Representation, 13-6
Emulation of DC- and Brushless-DC
Drive Performance, 13-1
Initial Flux Buildup, 13-7
Motor Model for Vector Control,
13-15
Position Control, 13-13
Sensor-Less Drives, 13-16
Similarity between Voltage-Fed and
Vector-Controlled Induction,
13-12